YEAR-ROUND GARDEN

ADRIAN BLOOM

YEAR-ROUND GARDEN

· COLOUR IN YOUR GARDEN ·
· FROM JANUARY TO DECEMBER ·

ADRIAN BLOOM

TIMBER PRESS
Portland, Oregon

To my wife Rosemary, who has shared the thirty years of the development of Foggy Bottom with me, and has given much else besides, for which I thank her.

ACKNOWLEDGEMENTS
No book of this nature is the author's alone. I would like to thank those who have contributed to the book at HarperCollins and, in particular, Ruth Prentice for her sterling design work; also Richard Bonson for his true-to-life interpretations of my plant associations. Expert advice was given on specific plants by John Bond, MVO, VMH, former Keeper of the Gardens, Savill Gardens, Windsor Great Park, and John Elsley in the United States provided assistance with the hardiness zoning in the directories. I would also like to thank my father, Alan Bloom, for his original groundwork on the alpine and perennial plant directories in *Blooms of Bressingham Garden Plants*. Thanks too to George and Angela Edens, Steve and Maggie Putt, and Roy and Judy Johnson, who, although they received a "free" garden, were kind enough to put up with continual visits and photographic sessions. "Head gardener" Michel Boutet should be thanked for his dedication and effort over the years in keeping Foggy Bottom in good order. Lastly, special thanks to my wife Rosemary, who has not only helped and supported Michel and myself in the garden but also helped with the book in many ways.

First published in this edition in 1998 by HarperCollins*Publishers*, London

Originally published as *Winter Garden Glory* (1993) and *Summer Garden Glory* (1996)

Published in North America by
Timber Press, Inc.
The Haseltine Building
133 S.W. Second Avenue, Suite 450
Portland, Oregon 97204, U.S.A.

A CIP catalog record for this book is available from the Library of Congress

ISBN 0-88192-457-1

Art editor: Ruth Prentice
Photographs: Adrian Bloom
Colour illustrations: Richard Bonson

Set in Garamond
Colour origination in Great Britain by Saxon
and in Singapore by Colourscan
Printed and bound in Italy

CONTENTS

PREFACE

Gardening is exciting and never more so than when trying out new plants or plantings, watching them develop and at times adding, taking away or tinkering with ingredients. This book shows, in photographs and words, the changing seasons from autumn through winter to late summer in my garden at Foggy Bottom in Norfolk, England, and suggests plants and ideas for giving a changing display in gardens of any size or on any patio. It shows how year-round colour can be achieved on even the most modest plot. There are plant association ideas and extensive lists of plants that I have found to be successful over the years and can therefore recommend. While these lists cannot be totally comprehensive, my selection of good-value plants will, I hope, be applicable to a wide range of conditions and climates, with some to suit every gardener.

What is it that most of us want from a garden? That's almost like asking how long is a piece of string! Is it a place to relax, a place for children to play, a place to enjoy gardening and to be creative, or is its purpose merely to set off the home? From the smallest window box, trough or container to a garden of several acres, the common denominator is plants. Where you live, in terms of the size of your garden, its aspect and climate, will determine what you can grow and in which seasons you can have colour and interest from your plants. Of course, some

AUTUMN. RHUS TYPHINA 'Dissecta' makes a striking feature against a background of conifers as its leaves turn from green to yellow, orange and bronze, its spent brown flower heads still attractive in winter (above)

WINTER. AN ARRAY OF perennials, ornamental grasses, shrubs, trees and conifers are harmonized by frost on a sunny late-December day. The hoarfrost will cling to the foliage and stems until gradually dispersed by the warmth of the sun (right)

SPRING. DAFFODILS, WINTER-FLOWERING heathers and the dwarf shrub Prunus incisa *'Kojo-no-mai' (on the right) add colour among the conifers on an early spring day as a shower approaches from the south-west over Foggy Bottom* (above)

SUMMER. COLOUR IS DISPLAYED in July by foliage and flower from low-growing perennials to taller trees and conifers. Gleditsia triacanthos *'Sunburst' is centre stage,* Picea pungens *behind,* Buddleja davidii *'Pink Delight' on the left, with* Coreopsis, Delphinium, Leucanthemum *and* Artemisia *providing contrast in the foreground* (right)

tropical or sub-tropical climates, where the seasons and temperatures hardly vary, can support a range of plants which have all-season interest. In more temperate climates in both the northern and southern hemispheres we are lucky enough to have considerable seasonal diversity. It is in these areas with distinct seasons that the greatest opportunities exist for us to create year-round, but ever-changing interest in the garden with a vast selection of plants to choose from. In a way, this book is not only a chronicle of more than thirty years' experience in developing a six-acre garden from scratch but also a distillation of knowledge gained from our garden at Foggy Bottom as well as from other gardens, large and small, all over the world.

Most people tend to plan their gardens for spring and summer colour, largely ignoring the autumn and winter period when the days are shorter and it is often not so pleasant to go outside. Understandably, if snow is expected every winter, it might seem futile to plant for winter colour. But in fact vast areas of the temperate zones have limited snowfall, others almost none at all, and an enormous variety of plants can be used to provide changing colour and interest from autumn through to spring – arguably at a time of year when it is most needed and appreciated.

My own garden at Foggy Bottom, with its original emphasis on dwarf conifers and heathers, has always provided colour and interest in the winter months, as well as during the other seasons. Over the years, however, as my knowledge and interest in plants developed, so did the garden, with the emphasis gradually changing from conifers and heathers to include trees, shrubs, perennials and grasses, all complementing each other to provide an even richer tapestry of year-round colour.

Undoubtedly, if you start with a basic flat meadow, as I did, or a vacant plot on a new housing estate and plant conifers, trees and shrubs, it does not take many years to change the appearance of the garden – and before you know it, the area becomes congested, with some plants fighting for space. Areas that were once sunny are now shady, roots fight for moisture, and as a result you are faced with new challenges to keep the garden full of interest all year round – and the plants happy too. Partly by accident and partly by design, I believe that Foggy Bottom has presented me with the challenges and experiences of not only beginner gardeners but also those whose gardens are or have become more mature. The conifers, other evergreens and trees now provide a necessary structure to the flat meadow, giving a vertical background against and under which other plants can offer a changing seasonal pattern. Most average-sized gardens, too, need some vertical structure against which the more ephemeral perennials, bulbs and grasses can add colour and form at appropriate seasons in the year.

At Foggy Bottom my aim has been to fill any gaps in seasonal interest with plants that assimilate naturally with flower or foliage attributes to achieve truly year-round colour and appeal – a quest that continues to this day. In the smaller garden the challenge is both easier and more difficult. One has to use a more economical palette and be more selective about what plants are available to fit given dimensions. They must therefore be chosen to give longer periods of interest while also allowing space for those plants, such as snowdrops perhaps, that we need to surprise us each year.

There is no doubt that it is quite a challenge to achieve year-round colour and interest in a garden or on a patio, but it is one that is both immensely satisfying and very enjoyable. I hope that the advice and ideas in this book, covering all four seasons and based on many years of experience in developing my garden at Foggy Bottom, will enable you to create and enjoy your own year-round garden from January to December.

Adrian Bloom
November 1997

ABOUT FOGGY BOTTOM

At the age of 26, I was given the somewhat unique opportunity of creating a garden from an open meadow. Designing and developing Foggy Bottom for over thirty years has been a fascinating and absorbing experience during which many mistakes have been made, but much has been learnt about the art of gardening and the diversity and habits of garden plants.

The experience of collecting, trying out (and in many cases losing or discarding) over 5000 different species and varieties of plants has been enormously rewarding. But probably even more satisfying has been the opportunity to create a garden that has year-round interest and to watch it grow, develop and change over the years.

Perhaps by briefly running through the history of the garden's development, some useful tips and ideas will suggest themselves to readers.

Back in 1966, when our ranch-style house was being built, the thought of turning a meadow into a huge garden had not occurred to me. In fact, my wife Rosemary and I started with about a quarter of an acre surrounding the house. Fortunately, the soil was mostly good heavy loam with a pH of 5.5, ideally acid enough to grow summer-flowering heathers, rhododendrons and other ericaceous plants.

As I was already very involved with conifers and heathers, having started to develop production of both groups of plants for the family nursery business, it seemed logical to plant a mainly dwarf conifer and heather garden. The plan was to create a patchwork of colour using large groups of heaths and heathers, interspersed with an ever-widening selection of dwarf conifers that I was collecting both in Britain and from many other countries.

> "I first came across the name Foggy Bottom when working in the United States in 1959, and it rather caught my imagination. Located in Virginia, it is the site of many of the State Department offices. Apart from probably a lot of hot air, no doubt it gets foggy there, just as our garden does, when mist creeps up over it on cold nights."

My experience with these, however, was still limited, even though three years earlier I had pestered my father, Alan Bloom, into letting me create a small conifer and heather garden adjoining his five-acre Dell garden. So, I plunged in.

THE EARLY YEARS

Undoubtedly, most people become interested in gardening when they acquire their first garden, whether it is large or small. And so it was with me. Although the nursery business was then growing quickly, I found time in the evenings and at weekends (often working after nightfall with the headlights of the car switched on) to thoroughly prepare the beds and borders surrounding the house, constructing some semblance of undulation on what was a fairly flat piece of ground. I dug in a lot of soft sand which we had brought up from the lower meadows where the earth was more alluvial. With each plant I mixed in handfuls of peat to improve the aeration and moisture-retaining capacity of the soil. Finally, I mulched the small plants with peat or composted bark which, apart from visual appeal, also helped to retain valuable moisture in dry summer months and prevent annual weeds from germinating.

It took me nearly five years to create this first stage in the garden's development, taking on one bed at a time. But, it was surprising how quickly the plants that had been put in first started to grow. Being sheltered around the house, the plants grew well – almost too well! I soon began to wonder if these dwarf conifers I was learning about at first-hand really were quite as dwarf as the books and catalogues suggested. In many cases, they certainly were not.

Just six years after I had started, the garden was full, with no space left for any more plants. Coincidentally, at this time the conifer and heather department of *Blooms of Bressingham*, as the nursery was now called, was beginning to take off, and I desperately needed more room to trial and experiment with these plants. This was the argument that I used with my father and my brother Rob, who shared the joint managing director's responsibilities with me, as together we looked over the barbed wire fence to the five-acre meadow below my garden. To my delight both agreed that I should gradually take in the rest of the meadow. In 1974, the fence came down.

A NEW CHALLENGE

From a relatively small garden, designed around the house with a few undulations and limited views, I was now looking at the possibilities of much broader vistas. And with a flat open meadow to contend with, some forward vision was necessary. The strategy was to take in the meadow in manageable 1½-2-acre chunks, allowing the cattle to continue grazing until I was able to find the time to plant each newly prepared area.

Although the extended garden was to be primarily structured with conifers, I wanted to use a variety of deciduous trees and shrubs as well. Broad, winding pathways of grass would offer vistas and provide opportunities for creating distant focal points as well as interesting views round every corner. That, at least, was the theory.

First, I put out canes to mark the new borders, then I sprayed the grass inside the canes with a herbicide ready for soil preparation. At that time the nursery possessed a rather innovative, Dutch, machine spade digger, the revolving "spades" of which dug rather than ploughed the meadow. It was an imperfect job for a garden, but it certainly took a lot of the hard work out of the early preparation stage. The physical digging had still to be done, and I was fortunate at times to have help from the nursery to complement my own efforts.

With an open, very windswept field and little or no natural shade or shelter for most of the garden, many of the more tender conifers, shrubs and trees suffered, particularly after some severe winters. Foggy Bottom is a frost pocket. The lower part of the garden acts as a drain to cold air and is often a full degree centigrade lower in temperature than near the house, and two or three degrees lower than the slightly higher and well-sheltered Dell garden nearby.

In the first few years of the extended, unsheltered garden many Japanese maples, some magnolias and plants like eucalyptus and phormiums died. Even some of the hardy winter-flowering heathers were stunted as they tried to make new shoots after flowering.

Most gardens develop a microclimate of their own, and within each garden there are smaller microclimates. Those in Foggy Bottom were to change as the trees and conifers grew to provide shelter and shade to east- and west-facing beds. The soil, too, differs from place to

THE ORIGINAL GARDEN surrounding the house at Foggy Bottom in the summer of 1972, five years after the first planting. Soon afterwards, the fence between it and the five acres of meadow in front came down (left)

MANY NEW BEDS had been cut out by 1975 and prepared for planting. A few lonely conifers, planted in an open and windswept garden, were the first residents. Heaps of sand stand ready to be dug in to add undulation and to improve drainage (left)

THE SAME BEDS as above early on a late autumn morning, twenty years later and seen from a point a little closer to the house. The house is almost hidden from view and the original conifers have grown, packed around by heathers that were planted at about the same time (left)

place, with some low, poorly drained areas, and others which, being on a slight rise, dry out quickly. The soil in the lowest part of the garden, which was once part of a lake or valley bottom, is more alluvial than elsewhere and its pH rises to 7. Getting to know what to put where started to give the plants a better chance of success.

I did not want to create just a conifer and heather garden, but in the early years using mostly these plants did give me the opportunity to learn more about the large numbers of both that by the late 1970s I was collecting from all over the world. The garden was also an ideal vehicle for showing conifers and heathers in a garden setting, much as my father's Dell garden was used to show how to grow perennials successfully.

Foggy Bottom was first opened to the public after it was featured in a television programme in 1977. Several thousand visitors turned up to what was still a very undeveloped garden. Thus began an annual "open weekend" over the first Saturday and Sunday in September, but at least each year considerable growth and change could be seen by the regular visitors. Now the garden is open regularly from early spring to autumn.

A New Feature

A very large, flat garden, needs a special feature, and an informally shaped pond seemed appropriate for Foggy Bottom. The ideal spot was down at the lowest part of the garden, and in 1977 a bulldozer scooped out a large depression, putting the soil between the pond to be and the old woodland beyond. This raised area was destined to be the woodland part of the garden.

Unfortunately, although the area where the pond was sited often flooded in the winter, it would never hold water

SPRING MAGIC in the winter bed from forsythia, ribes and daffodils (above)

THE POND MIRRORS fading rushes and distant conifers, adding to the atmosphere (opposite)

during the spring, summer and autumn. Two unsuccessful years later, we turned to the local aquatic expert who fitted a butyl liner to the contoured shape.

The pond added a new dimension to the garden: it was a feature to walk down to and around; it offered shifting reflections; it provided a habitat for fish and other aquatic wildlife; and in cold winters it became a skating rink.

Time for Reappraisal

With the help of two full-time gardeners, I reached the woodland planting at the bottom in 1980, but the garden was by no means finished!

It was planted primarily with conifers and heathers as well as a lot of ground cover plants. The latter consisted mostly of large groups of prostrate junipers, shrubs such as *Potentilla fruticosa* varieties, *Euonymus fortunei* and so on, but with a wide range within these. Other types of shrubs and some perennials added yet more variety.

Many of those plants that had been planted in the sun were now in shade as trees and conifers had grown, and many of the earliest beds around the house were becoming overcrowded. It was time to have another look at each completed section of the garden and consider change and improvement.

Like most keen gardeners who become avid collectors of plants, I wanted to broaden my knowledge. I felt Foggy Bottom offered an ideal opportunity to experiment with plants other than the conifers and heathers which hitherto had absorbed me on both personal and business levels. So the garden continued to be a trial garden not only for conifers but for a great many of the different shrubs and perennials I was by then introducing to Britain from Europe and further afield. I tried phormiums from New Zealand, weigelas from Holland and Canada, potentillas from everywhere, hostas and hemerocallis (day lilies) from the U.S.A., and many interesting and worthwhile plants from Japan and other countries.

Not all of these widely differing plants succeeded, but many have added immeasurably to my knowledge, even though, of course, the knowledge and experience of any individual plant in my garden alone is hardly exhaustive. A young plant killed in its first year by a severe winter, for instance, might have survived if it had experienced two or three milder winters giving it a chance

to become fully established before being subjected to extremely cold weather. Now that there is more shelter and shade in the garden, many of the plants that have been tried and lost will be given another chance.

The opportunity for change should never be ignored – the challenge to create a more satisfying, diverse type of garden requires thought but gives a lot of pleasure, too, particularly when you feel something has worked well. Although we all like to see the instant garden effect, in truth I think it is much more fun to gradually build a scene, looking for the right plant, the right colour, shape or texture to create a satisfying or memorable plant association.

Redesigning parts of Foggy Bottom began in the early 1980s, and has contin-ued ever since. Overgrown plants have been thinned out and, depending upon the soil and aspect, different features have been incorporated. Existing beds have been altered and extended and new ones have been created.

Although the whole garden has year-round interest, the border that we have dubbed "the winter bed" in particular has given a lot of pleasure, both in long view and close up. It was created in a way that one should approach most gardens, by structuring with trees, shrubs and conifers of year-round appeal, then filling in with lower-growing plants, shrubs, perennials and, lastly, adding many species of bulb, each with its own particular season of interest.

Now that the garden is getting quite mature, a lot of thought has to go into not only what new plants to put in but which old plants must come out. For example, woody plants increase their dimensions in all directions as they grow, and so, even in a large garden, thinning out after some years have passed is likely to be essential. When creating a garden the ideal is to plant your choice plants wide enough apart, filling in between them with more dis-posable types. Then, when the time comes to thin, you can keep the best specimens. But, like many other things in life, such plans seldom seem to work out perfectly!

However, the "Leylandii bed", as I call it, did work out. In 1967, I had planted several 90cm/3ft high × *Cupresso-cyparis leylandii* about 10m/30ft from the house to create a shelter from strong westerly winds. Twenty years later they were 15m/45ft high even though the tops had been cut out in 1978. Knowing that eventually they would have to come down, in 1980 I planted some slow-growing but choicer conifers behind, which were hidden from view from the house. Nearly ten years later we decided it was time to remove the Leylandii, thereby revealing a more attractive and less threatening background and making room in the foreground for a range of more interesting plants. One stump was left behind and is now covered with ivy. Despite there being no Leylandii left, the bed is still known as the Leylandii bed!

In developing Foggy Bottom I have closely observed many plants. Some I would never part with, others occasionally depart, without my blessing, and yet others must be discarded. Yes, even in a six-acre garden there is not room for plants that do not perform or have little to recommend them – there are too many others waiting in the wings for their turn to show what they can do!

THE FUTURE

For the present the garden has matured and the thinking behind the broad, grass pathways is only now becoming clear. As plants grow upwards they cut out more light, and had there been only narrow pathways at Foggy Bottom, the garden would soon have become one large woodland – and probably rather dark and dingy in winter.

While it is pleasing to get many kind comments from visitors, there is still much to be done because a garden must change to survive. Plenty of gardens planted over the last fifty years which have been subsequently neglected and are now completely overgrown bear witness to this reality.

GRASSES, HERE WITH PERENNIALS, seen two summers after replanting the bed shown opposite, will guarantee interest in winter as well (above)

I want Foggy Bottom to grow old gracefully. To do this, it will need to be constantly reassessed for new opportunities, such as creating plant associations and vistas that previously had not been envisaged or possible. Larger conifers and trees will need pruning, older, established perennials will need rejuvenating, shrubs and smaller conifers might need moving to new locations.

The garden is a place of peace and tranquillity (except when we are open to the public!) and gardening is a relaxing and enjoyable pastime. Unfortunately, business and writing commitments take up a lot of my time, preventing me at present from fulfilling the ideas and plans I have in mind. Right now, for instance, I can hardly wait to create a

stream running from near the house to the pond. Hopefully, the time will come soon. It is fascinating, meanwhile, to look ahead to the next thirty years of change at Foggy Bottom.

The photographs that follow in this book are somewhat more eloquent than my words, but by progressing through the seasons at Foggy Bottom from autumn to early spring and then through to late summer, they illustrate how a garden can offer interest the year round and be full of colour and fragrance, too.

The "Quiet" Seasons

INTRODUCTION

Most gardeners, I suspect, look upon the onset of autumn with a mixture of relief and depression. Relief that the rush to keep on top of the chores of grass cutting and weeding will soon be over, and depression, perhaps, that the fresh colours of spring and the warmth of summer are so far away. For those living in northern latitudes, especially, the certain knowledge that they must endure long months of shortened days and deteriorating weather bringing rain, wind, frost and perhaps snow, is even more depressing. The temptation to close the door on the garden is very strong.

But surely this is just the time of year when we most need interest and colour in the garden. When anything is scarce, it always seems to be more appreciated than when it is readily available. And so it seems with nature. When walking in the countryside during winter, for instance, you notice the silhouettes of trees, the bright bark of silver birch, the red berries of hawthorn. If snowdrops, lovely as they are, flowered in summer, they would create less of a stir than they do in late winter, when they appear suddenly along with winter aconites. And yet strangely, in the average small garden you see so little of these delightful harbingers of spring.

There is in everyone, I think, a latent interest in and need to respond to nature and plants, particularly in winter. This was confirmed for me when, during a BBC *Gardener's World* visit to my garden at Foggy Bottom in January 1991, Stefan Buczacki and I looked at some colourful plants. Some of these, which included the hardy *Cyclamen coum* and *Cornus sanguinea* 'Winter Flame', were so striking that over 6000 visitors arrived the next weekend that the garden was open to the public. The power of television is quite amazing, but so is the lift that plants, in all their beauty and drama, can give.

There are so many things that plants can do for a garden in winter. They bring nature to your doorstep – foliage, flowers and fragrance – to be enjoyed, and even taken indoors. Trees with colourful barks, shrubs with brightly coloured stems, evergreens with flowers and fruit, deciduous shrubs with fragrant blossom, conifers providing shelter, foliage and form, perennials, late autumn and early spring-flowering bulbs, and ornamental grasses adding texture and movement.

For many people in northern latitudes winter seems to extend from the end of one summer to the beginning of the next! In the first half of this book I have 'extended' winter to cover autumn and early spring. Fortunately, there is an amazing range of plants that can be used to create interest and give enjoyment throughout these long, dull seasons in the many areas that are largely frost and snow free. Even where

I live in East Anglia, supposedly one of the coldest areas of England, we can go through the whole of January without a single frost. So why not make plans to brighten up winter days with plants that we can see and enjoy?

I am always trying to open people up to the magic of the numerous plants that can brighten our dreary winters. Whether or not you are a keen gardener, whether you have a small or large garden, a patio or even just a balcony or window box, there are lots of ways of bringing life and colour to an otherwise drab prospect.

My own interest in gardens for winter appreciation began a long time ago when I joined the family nursery business back in 1962. By then my father, Alan Bloom, had already created one of the finest hardy perennial gardens in the world – the Dell garden at Bressingham in Norfolk, England – and

LATE IN AUTUMN, a shaft of afternoon sunlight strikes a potted Juniperus × media *'Gold Sovereign' and the ripe fruits of a trained* Pyracantha *'Orange Glow' (above)*

EARLY ON A WINTER'S MORNING, sun gradually disperses mist and frost at Foggy Bottom, revealing a garden packed with colour and interest (left)

naturally I wanted to contribute a group of plants about which he knew relatively little. Conifers and heathers seemed to fit the bill, particularly the dwarf and slow-growing types. Ten years later the nursery was growing over 100,000 dwarf conifers a year. Also by then I had expanded my own garden, started in 1967 on a quarter of an acre, to nearly six acres with a collection of over 200 different varieties.

Interest in dwarf conifers and heathers, which were appreciated for their year-round appeal and easy maintenance, was spreading rapidly. In order to widen the appeal I wanted to show people what could be achieved in an average-sized, suburban garden using such plants, but as clearly my own garden was far too big the nursery agreed to 'give away' a front garden as a real example and incentive. Located in an accessible part of the neighbourhood, it proved to be a great success (pages 70-73). By the early 1980s, there were nearly one million conifers growing in the nursery, and nearly 1000 varieties at Foggy Bottom.

Although my garden began to develop and change as the years rolled by, as do all gardens, conifers remained the mainstay, providing structure and form to what was once a nearly flat meadow. The garden certainly had year-round colour because I had also planted many other types of trees and shrubs to provide a more varied aspect. I have always had a keen interest in all other hardy plants, and in recent years I have tried to assimilate a wider variety of types, adding ornamental grasses, perennials and bulbs, to create pleasing plant associations – always with the theme of year-round interest in mind.

To put some of these developing ideas into practice on a smaller scale, I persuaded the nursery to 'give away' two more front gardens, each planted rather dramatically in a single day. The first was planted in the middle of autumn, not only to create a garden with winter interest but also to demonstrate the advantages of planting before the onset of the coldest season (pages 74-77). The second garden, next door to the first and by contrast planted in late spring, was designed to be drought-resistant and to give a completely different style of interest during winter months (pages 78-81).

The greatest challenge and the greatest reward in gardening is in creating pleasing plant associations which together make more impact than do the individual plants, and this is no less so when planning effects for winter months. Drawing on my experience with all the gardens mentioned above, the following chapters discuss the best plants for introducing winter interest and show how to use them in all sizes of garden. They are not so much about gardening in winter – although that can certainly be enjoyable – as about enjoying the winter garden.

Autumn

For most gardeners the period from the middle of spring to the middle of summer is like life in the fast lane – a frenzy of activity as we prepare and plant, trim hedges, cut grass, water and weed, and generally try to keep up with events in the garden. It is a wonderful period, too, when perennials and bulbs break from the bare earth and trees and plants burst into blossom and growth, transforming themselves from a few shoots into verdant or colourful foliage and flowers that seemingly appear overnight. If our hearing were more acute, the sound of all this activity might be thunderous. And if we were to add the sound of birds singing, we could indeed imagine spring and early summer as the noisy season in the garden.

From mid-summer we begin to see the results of our endeavours and we can enjoy the peak of summer colour for annuals and many perennials, but still we must cut grass, trim, water and watch for drought, pests and diseases. It is a restless season but nevertheless a period when we can generally feel able to relax and even take time off for a well-earned holiday.

So, is that it? Is that the end of the main gardening season? The time when we can sit back and marvel at how long-lasting this or that plant is in flower this year, or how much a plant has grown. Once we have returned from holiday and the children are back at school, are we not likely to say: "The garden will have to wait until next year." Are we not, at this point, inclined to rest on our laurels and enjoy the last fine days of late summer and early autumn, watching the leaves turn and drop and looking forward to long cosy evenings in front of the fire and the television?

Perhaps, then, if we think of those months of activity as noisy, it may be

appropriate to call the long months of autumn, winter and early spring the quiet season for gardens and gardening. But while we all need a rest at this time of year, are we not missing something in the way of enjoyment and pleasure that the quiet season can give us by dismissing it so easily?

In my opinion, the period from early autumn to early spring is unfairly neglected by most gardeners, and when you think that, especially in the cooler temperate zones, these seasons comprise about half of the year, surely it is worth giving them more attention? Is this not just the time of year when we need *more* colour and interest in the garden than at any other? And, it is possible. There are hundreds of plants that you can include in your garden to lift your spirits at this time. In fact, so much is going on, that you will be amazed to discover just how much there is to see and enjoy.

One should plan to fill autumn, winter and early spring months with as much colour and variety as possible. The smaller the garden the more important that selection is. The crucial thing is to select plants that can be expected to give a good account of themselves in the particular conditions they are destined for and to be as versatile as possible.

The weather rules what we can grow in our gardens, and what we might grow well one year but perhaps not so well the next. Stipulating when a season ends

BY EARLY NOVEMBER some of the best autumn colour has gone, but the fast-falling leaves of Prunus *'Accolade' in the foreground and the silver birch beyond begin to reveal the colour to come in winter, with bark, evergreens, conifers, shrubs and ornamental grasses continuing to give months of interest* (left)

SHRUBS AND CLIMBERS FOR AUTUMN

Of the many deciduous shrubs and climbers that I have found to be particularly reliable for providing good autumn colours, the following is but a selection. More information about these plants can be found in the directory section starting on page 90.

Acer palmatum 'Senkaki'. Golden autumn leaves, coral red winter stems.

A. p. 'Osakazuki'. Consistent, brilliant crimson autumn colour.

Aronia arbutifolia 'Erecta'. Rich red in autumn.

Berberis x *carminea*. Several selections offer coral fruits and pink and red autumn leaves.

B. thunbergii. Several of these have good autumn colour. 'Dart's Red Lady' is recommended.

B. x *media* 'Red Jewel'. Its glossy leaves acquire bronze and crimson shades in autumn.

Cornus alba 'Sibirica'. Bright red autumn leaves and red winter stems.

C. a. 'Kesselringii'. Crimson-purple leaves revealing black stems when they drop.

Cornus sanguinea 'Winter Flame'. Yellow, orange and gold autumn leaves with russet and orange-red stems.

Euonymus alatus 'Compactus'. Brilliant crimson autumn foliage in hotter climates, but duller in cooler ones.

E. europaeus 'Red Cascade'. Reddish purple leaves and scarlet fruits.

Aronia arbutifolia 'Erecta'

Hydrangea quercifolia 'Snow Queen'

Fothergilla gardenii. Spectacular yellow, orange and crimson leaves. Acid soil.

F. major. Spectacular yellow, orange and crimson leaves. Acid soil.

Hamamelis × *intermedia* 'Feuerzauber' (syn. 'Magic Fire'). Brilliant crimson autumn leaves, bronze-red winter flowers.

Hydrangea quercifolia. Bronze and purple autumn leaves.

Nandina domestica. Semi-evergreen with purple, red, pink and yellow shades.

Oxydendrum arboreum. Crimson leaves in autumn. Acid lover.

Parthenocissus henryana. Pink or bright red in autumn.

P. tricuspidata. Fiery crimson in autumn.

Prunus. Many to choose from. *P. incisa* 'Kojo-no-mai' has bronze to crimson colour in autumn.

Rhododendron, deciduous azaleas. Many turn yellow, crimson or red. Acid soil.

Rhus glabra 'Laciniata'. Orange and red.

R. typhina 'Dissecta'. Orange and red in autumn.

Spiraea betulifolia var. *aemeliana*. Good orange-red leaves in autumn.

S. prunifolia 'Plena'. Crimson autumn leaves.

Vaccinium corymbosum. Crimson-tinted leaves. Acid soil.

and when the next begins, however, is a somewhat inexact science. Each year the seasons roll into each other, often over several weeks depending upon location and climate, a little earlier or a little later than the previous year. And, as we know only too well, the climate can change from year to year, too.

Autumn begins at about the last time we can expect summery weather, which at Foggy Bottom is usually about the end of September. But the end of summer is not the end of colour and interest in our garden, nor need it be in any garden, no matter what its size.

AUTUMN FOLIAGE

In some parts of the world, especially in areas of the U.S.A. and Canada, autumn leaf colour can be breathtaking. In Britain, where it can be magnificent, it also can be disappointingly fleeting. There is, however, a wide choice of deciduous shrubs and trees, some more reliable than others, that give good autumn foliage colour. The North American sweet gums are a good example. Buy and plant a seedling of *Liquidambar styraciflua*, a native of eastern U.S.A., in Britain and you take a chance as to whether its leaves will colour when it matures. There is such a tree at Foggy Bottom, now nearly 10m/30ft high, growing in moist soil which it prefers and part shade, but in autumn its leaves make a poor attempt at being anything other than a dull green or purple. But *L.s.* 'Worplesdon', a splendid form which was selected in Surrey, England, for its brilliant crimson autumn leaves, is almost certain to colour each year. It is a clone or selection and so must be propagated by cuttings or grafting, making it a little more expensive than an ordinary seedling would be but worth every extra penny.

Whether you plant for autumn leaf colour alone is a matter of choice. With a larger garden you have more space for more variety. But if a tree or a shrub has another desirable attribute in addition to autumn colour this must be a bonus and have considerable bearing on your selection. Most of the silver birch family, for instance, have good, if brief, autumn leaf colour, but they also have the great advantage of silvery white, cream or pinkish bark. Nearly all the witch hazels (hamamelis) flower profusely in winter, but some are disappointing in their autumn leaf colour. While *Hamamelis × intermedia* 'Diane' does have attractive reddish purple autumn leaves, the most spectacular for autumn leaf colour in my experience is *H. × i.* 'Feuerzauber' (translated as 'Magic Fire').

The fothergillas, acid-loving relations of the witch hazels, have both pretty and

BRILLIANT AUTUMN FOLIAGE, distinguishes Fothergilla gardenii (above)

STUNNINGLY COLOURED LEAVES and deep crimson-red, late winter flowers are features of Hamamelis × intermedia *'Diane'* (below)

fragrant bottlebrush flowers in spring and wonderful foliage colours in autumn. Although *Fothergilla gardenii* 'Blue Mist', a recent introduction, goes one better by offering metallic blue leaves in summer, regrettably it does not have good autumn colour – a difficult choice if you have room for one only!

Evergreens, of course, retain their colour all year round, and are so much more desirable if they are prettily coloured like the dependable *Euonymus fortunei* 'Emerald 'n' Gold' and 'Emerald Gaiety'. Ivies, too, are there all year long and are often beautifully variegated.

Much smaller plants can have attractive foliage at this time of year, too. The marbled, silvery green leaves which accompany the autumn flowers of the hardy *Cyclamen hederifolium*, for instance, are delightful and last throughout winter. Some of the pulmonarias, such as *Pulmonaria saccharata* 'Leopard', which has hairy, spotted leaves, and *P. saccharata* 'Argentea', the bright, silver form, contrast beautifully when sited close to plants sporting brightly coloured autumn foliage or flowers.

BERRIES AND FRUITS

When shrubs shed their leaves, it is the time for colourful berries and fruits to come into their own – at least for as long as the birds leave them on the branches. All too soon we learn that the adjective "persistent" refers to those berries that, for some reason, the birds either do not like or like least and so leave until last. Judging by the speed

A YELLOW AND BLUE combination of Rudbekia deamii *and* Aster × frikartii *forms an early autumn association against the pond and a stand of* Miscanthus sinensis *'Purpureus'. As the pond is contained by a butyl liner, the soil is not as moist as one might think* (left)

BIRDS AND BERRIES

A great many trees and shrubs fruit regularly in late summer and autumn, adding another dimension of interest to the garden, which in some plants may last well into winter months. Birds, of course, take advantage of this bounty and can strip off berries in very little time, but there appears to be a pecking order for preference and some plants manage to keep their fruit through winter. Which fruits survive seems to vary according to location and, no doubt, type of bird and density of population (bird and human). In my experience the birds start on the sorbus, particularly the coloured rather than the white fruits. Then they work their way through the cotoneasters and hollies almost simultaneously, although the fruits of certain species or cultivars survive better than others. Finally, they attack the pyracanthas. But there is no real rule of thumb and I have found that the lower-growing plants, mostly cotoneasters and vaccineums seem to last well, too. The trick is to grow a selection of species and cultivars, according to the size of your garden, from low-growing shrubs to trees, in the

Rosa rugosa *in late autumn*

knowledge that not only are you going to derive enjoyment through the autumn, but that the birds are going to profit, too. You will be making a significant contribution to wildlife in your area!

with which some of the berries in my garden disappear – almost overnight – it seems the term should apply to the birds rather than to the berries!

Viburnum, malus, crataegus, holly, pyracantha, cotoneaster, vaccinium (blueberry) and many other berry-bearing shrubs give us pleasure for weeks, sometimes months, so perhaps we should not resent sharing them with the birds as winter weather approaches.

FLOWERS FOR AUTUMN

Autumn colour does not depend only upon the changing foliage of trees and shrubs or the brightness of berries. The autumn-flowering plants give splashes of concentrated colour that foliage on its own cannot provide. Prime among these must be groups like the asters and dendranthemas, both members of the daisy family (the latter a recent and unfortunate name change from the better known chrysanthemums, but one which we will have to get used to). In these two enormous families alone there is a bewildering choice. The asters vary in colour and type, from plants growing less than 30cm/12in to over 2m/6ft, and add immeasurably to the autumn garden. Their small but abundant, daisy-like flowers can be white to pink, red and purple and there are yellow ones, too. The dendranthemas mostly originated in the Far East but have been greatly interbred in Europe and the U.S.A. as flowers for cutting, pot plants and garden plants. Single flowers, doubles and pompom types are all available

ORANGE BERRIES OF PYRACANTHA 'Orange Glow' and pretty blue flowers of the shrubby, sun-loving Ceratostigma willmottianum *achieve a cheerful autumn association on a sun-facing wall* (left)

to gardeners in almost all the colours of the rainbow. Many of the older varieties are too tall for today's gardens, but brilliant colour can be found that will provide cheerful autumn colours until severe frosts herald winter.

Among the perennials there are plenty of other stalwarts to choose from. The late-flowering, South African native kniphofia (red hot poker), for instance, adds colour and exotic brilliance. Schizostylis (Kaffir lily), which originated from the same part of the world, makes spreading clumps of spiky, iris-like foliage. Its flowering stems resemble miniature gladioli and come into flower when most perennials have finished. With a succession of delicate flowers in white, pink or red, they are excellent in the garden and for cutting.

Anemone japonica (syn. *A. × hybrida*), the Japanese anemone, has a totally different appeal. Its flat, open, single or double, rose to pink and white flowers with yellow stamens are resplendent on narrow stalks above leafy foliage. These are graceful plants ideal for mixing with other perennials or shrubs in sunny or partly shaded spots of the garden that are not too dry. The delightful *Liriope muscari* is a useful clump-forming, glossy evergreen which produces spikes which carry dense clusters of violet flowers in autumn.

If you have an acid soil, autumn-flowering gentians make an unsurpassable show. I am referring primarily to the carpet-forming *Gentiana sino-ornata* types, the blue trumpets of which create sheets of colour in moist, acid soils, although there are also selections of paler hues and even whites now available. Sedums, both alpine and larger perennial types, add not only succulent foliage of various hues, but heads of colourful, pink and red flowers that are a

THE BRILLIANT BLUE of Gentiana sino-ornata *is hard to improve on for autumn colour. This acid-loving plant appreciates some moisture and full sun or part shade* (above)

SPECTACULAR FLOWERS from late summer into autumn are provided by Anemone × hybrida *'Alba'. Here they light up a shady corner. This plant does well on lime soils* (left)

WITH MUCH FLOWER *still to come and plenty of fresh, green foliage in late autumn, this* Hebe *'Great Orme', a slightly tender shrub, looks far from ready to accept winter* (top right)

PROVIDING A WELCOME DISPLAY *in autumn, exotic, pink blooms of* Nerine bowdenii *burst open on naked stems* (below right)

A HAPPY ASSOCIATION *of autumn-flowering perennials is achieved by* Dendranthema *(formerly* Chrysanthemum*)* rubella *'Apricot' and the taller* Astilbe chinensis (below)

drug for butterflies and some bees. The flat heads of *S. spectabile* and *S. telephium* have winter interest, too. Nerines have spherical, wavy-petalled, pink to red, occasionally white, flowers which may appear before or after the leaves. The list goes on and you will find many more mentioned on pages 123-32.

Compared with perennials there are relatively few late-flowering shrubs but there is still abundant choice, of which the following are but a few. The deciduous caryopteris has clusters of small but plentiful blue flowers in late summer and early autumn. The hebes, all evergreen, include many species and cultivars whose spikes of white, pink, purple or blue often flower well into autumn. Even some of the lavandulas, mostly those with the species *L. latifolia* in them, continue to flower well into autumn and have a strong scent of camphor. Both 'Vera' and 'Fragrant Memories', with tall spikes and lavender-blue flowers can be relied on. .

There are many other shrubs which bridge the gap between the summer- and winter-flowering types. Among these long-flowering, value-for-money shrubs are buddlejas, fuchsias, many hydrangeas, hibiscus and potentillas, not forgetting autumn-flowering heathers like *Erica vagans* (Cornish heath) and *E. cinerea* (bell heather) or, indeed, many roses. Among the latter are not only bush roses (hybrid teas and floribundas) but shrub roses, which include the ground cover types and climbers. Good husbandry (pinching or removing dead flowers, for instance) will prolong flowering, and a great many roses can be a feature until late frosts.

Shrubs that flower into autumn meet up with some which, like the mahonia hybrids 'Charity' and 'Winter Sun' with lovely racemes of yellow flowers and the

BEES APPRECIATE the nectar of Caryopteris × clandonensis *'Heavenly Blue' well into autumn. Of some elegance, this sun-loving shrub is commonly called blue spiraea* (above)

THE COLOURFUL Potentilla fruticosa *'Red Robin', seen here in early autumn* (left)

FORM AND TEXTURE become more important as autumn runs its course. Here, silvery grey leaves of Artemesia stelleriana *set off the broad, flat heads of* Sedum 'Autumn Joy' *as they turn from bright pink to bronze. Sword-like foliage of crocosmia (top right) is outlasted by the evergreen leaves of* Yucca filamentosa 'Variegata' *(top left). Still in flower, as it has been for three months, is* Gaura lindheimeri *(left)*

evergreen *Viburnum tinus* and the deciduous *V.* × *bodnantense* 'Dawn', start in early autumn and continue into winter in favourable locations.

Many of the plants now available are exotic in relation to the British or European natives, but as I much prefer a "natural" look in the garden, whatever country plants originate from, overbred plants like most dahlias and many of the "chrysanths" which have been developed specifically for increased flower size and large number of petals would not find a place at Foggy Bottom. Nor would I include some of the brighter of the winter-flowering pansies, which I think do not look natural at all in the garden. There are more than enough plants for me to choose from to create a restful and natural-looking environment through the quiet season without having to resort to more splashy colour. I hasten to add, however, that the many people who do like the larger, brighter blooms have every right to use them as they think fit.

IN AN EYECATCHING early autumn combination, a five-year-old, fresh green Chamaecyparis lawsoniana *'Pygmy' nestles between a bright yellow* Erica carnea *'Aurea' and a* Calluna vulgaris *'Roma' which has just finished flowering. The dwarf conifer will soon turn a deeper green and the erica will become golden-bronze and be smothered in pink flowers (right)*

LOBED LEAVES of the bulb Arisaema candidissimum, *has spectacular flowers in summer, and changes colour in autumn (above left)*

SILKY, SILVERY SEED heads of Clematis tangutica *make this a valuable long-interest plant (above right)*

SUNLIGHT FILTERS through an unkempt hedge of English yew (opposite)

WINTER

At Foggy Bottom, we know that when the westerly winds increase in strength and bring rain, interspersed with a few sharp frosts, we are on the verge of winter. The leaves start to tumble, the last to go being the oaks. The days get rapidly shorter and there are fewer fine ones to enjoy. Only the keenest gardeners are out at this blustery time, busying themselves with sweeping up the last of the leaves, making use of some as a protective mulch (oak leaves are particularly good for this) for the more tender plants and keeping them in place with a small branch or two. By now, the heavier soils may be too wet to work on, but planting and preparation can still continue on good days. Frost on well-dug garden soil does more good than anything garden tools can do to break down clay and heavy loam.

ONSET OF WINTER

Given the shorter days and inclement weather, it is hardly surprising that most people are not anxious to garden at this time of year. But, if winter features have already been planted there is much to look forward to and enjoy, either during forays outdoors on good days or from indoors on bad days. Even something as simple as a window box planted with a cheering array of colourful winter foliage and winter-flowering plants, or a terracotta container planted with a good

AN EARLY SNOWFALL TRANSFORMS a large group of pampas grass (Cortaderia selloana) into a fairytale scene. In a sheltered position, the 3m/10ft stems, plumes and foliage all retain their grace in winter and show up well against a backdrop of dark pines. Buy named varieties, as, with the exception of C.s.'Pumila', all those grown from seed are generally inferior (right)

Frost has a magical effect on the garden, altering the appearance of foliage, stems and fruits, especially when the sun shines. Often, the transformation is fleeting, lasting only until the warmth of the sun or wind destroys it. The photographs on these pages capture a few of those icy images. Lacy fronds of the hardy fern Polystichum setiferum *'Herrenhausen' are turned from green to silver (top right). Purple autumn leaves of* Rosa virginiana *are rimmed with hoarfrost (top far right). A spider's filament along with the needles and cones of* Abies procera *'Glauca', the noble fir, are delicately encased in ice (centre right). Crimson leaves of the oak leaf hydrangea,* H. quercifolia *'Snow Queen', appear as if dusted with sugar (centre far right). Mossy* Saxifraga *'Pixie' briefly takes on an ice-crystal camouflage (bottom right). A frosty edging emphasizes the frilled fronds of* Dryopteris borreri *'Pinderi' (bottom far right)*

TINGED PURPLE *in winter, leaves of* Mahonia aquifolium *'Smaragd', a form of the Oregon grape, are outlined with frost* (top far left). *Studded with bright red berries, the thorny, leafless stems of* Berberis thunbergii *'Atropurpurea Nana', a dwarf Barberry, are encased in glinting ice* (top left). *The leaves of a miniature, sun-loving, carpet-forming alpine* Sedum spathulifolium *'Purpureum' have been crystallized by a winter frost* (centre far left). *Silky strands of the seed heads of* Clematis tangutica *are thickened and whitened by frost* (centre left). *Papery petals of* Hydrangea paniculata *'Pink Diamond' are edged with ice crystals; the sterile flowers were white in summer before turning pink in early autumn and then fading to a parchment brown* (bottom far left). *Glossy leaves of the evergreen, dwarf shrub* Leucothoë *'Scarletta', purple in autumn and winter, are enhanced by a sparkling frost* (bottom left)

selection of differently shaded evergreens can be sufficient to brighten an aspect, however small. Ideas for these are given on pages 68 and 83.

The harshness of winter can come early or late and can affect different parts of the country at different times – some parts missing snow and frost almost completely. A wider range of plants can be grown outdoors in the warmer locations but when such areas do get severe frost it can be devastating. Urban areas, too, protected by the warmth of buildings, traffic, perhaps even people, often keep temperatures a degree or two warmer than the surrounding countryside.

Defining the hardiness of plants is an inexact science. With the much greater extremes of weather in the U.S.A., the gardening fraternity there relies on a set of "hardiness zones" to indicate how much cold (and heat) each garden plant will bear. Keen gardeners already know that this is only a guide and that given more shelter and some winter protection many plants can thrive in much colder zones or areas than is indicated in the United States Department of Agriculture zone map. A European zone map exists which shows most of Britain in zone 8, except for the coastal strip from Dorset, westwards and north to the tip of Scotland influenced by the Gulf Stream, which is zone 9. When you consider that zone 8 in the U.S.A. covers South Carolina, Georgia and Alabama, you will agree that this map needs a heat tolerance figure, too, to give the full picture. In the same way that less hardy plants will succumb to winter frosts, others which are native to cooler climates can struggle to survive prolonged spells of heat and humidity. So, although hardiness zones are used in the directory sections of this book (please

OVERWINTERING FROST-TENDER PLANTS

Keen gardeners everywhere will want to try in their gardens plants which may not always come through frosty winters. A good example of such frost-tender plants is Cosmos atrosanguineus *which has velvety, chocolate-scented, deep purple-red flowers (sounds nice doesn't it?). Planted in spring, it will flower for months until well into the autumn. At this time of the year you are faced with three choices: dig it up once the foliage has died down and dry it off in a frost-proof shed or room like a dahlia; leave it where it is and mulch it with leaves, bracken or straw to a depth of 6-10cm/2-3in until early spring; or leave it alone and let it take its chance. I did the latter last year and my plants withstood -10°C for several nights, and still grew away in the spring.*

But I was testing for hardiness in my garden and so had an incentive for taking the risk. Depending on where you live, some of the mostly perennial plants mentioned in this book that you might consider protecting for the winter are: agapanthus, cautleya, Commelina coelestis, *some crocosmias, some kniphofias,* Melianthus major, *nerine, penstemon hybrids, phormium, Salvia ambigens (and many other tender species not mentioned), schizostylis and zauscheneria. At the time of writing, recent mild winters have allowed most of the above plants to come through the winter without protection in my garden. Site and soil will make a considerable difference even in colder localities. Hardiness advice is given for each group in the directory section that starts on page 90, but a basic rule might be to protect as for the cosmos above in the first winter at least.*

Cosmos atrosanguineus *(top) contrasts strikingly with* Commelina coelestis (below)

note that both cold and heat tolerance are indicated), do not take them as gospel! A key giving the temperature range for each zone appears on page 220.

The weather at the onset of winter can be pretty dull and depressing, but sometimes it can surprise us with magnificent sunny and frosty days. The magic of a brilliant hoarfrost on trees, shrubs and grasses makes one marvel at the beauty and simplicity of nature.

At Foggy Bottom, the winter sun comes up from well to the southeast and moves through a low trajectory. We could (but never seem to) sit in our lounge and watch the sparkle of frost disappear as the morning sun moves across the sky, striking the eastern side of stems and warming them. As the sun gradually moves round, the changing direction of the rays of light dramatically alters the appearance of many plants, none more so than the ornamental grasses. Shafts of sunlight flash and dazzle through the moving plumes of miscanthus and *Cortaderia selloana* 'Pumila' (pampas grass), the sun too low and too bright to be looked at directly. Dark evergreens absorb the sunlight, glossy leaves reflect it, the colours of the golden conifers and of the dogwood stems – especially *Cornus alba* 'Sibirica' and the magnificent *C. sanguinea* 'Winter Flame' – are intensified by it. On frosty days, as the sun begins its descent to the southwest, its strength declines rapidly and this seems to be the signal for the slowly swirling, ghostly mist and fog to draw in. Darkness soon falls, and another

HERE TRANSFORMED BY FROSTY weather in mid-winter, the beige stems of the ornamental grass Miscanthus sinensis *'Morning Light' create an interesting hummock shape and remain attractive until early spring* (left)

POTTED PLANTS BRING interest to a stepped patio in early winter. Three ornamental grasses, Carex comans *'Bronze Form' (front left),* Hakonechloa macra *'Alboaurea' (back) and* Imperata cylindrica *'Rubra' (front right) surround a* Bergenia *'Bressingham Ruby', the leaves of which turn ruby-purple in winter. The yellow-leaved* Choisya ternata *'Sundance' is susceptible to frost but can be placed in a conservatory, greenhouse or porch when at risk* (right)

A BLANKET OF SNOW heightens the bright colours of bare stems and their backdrop of conifers. The Foggy Bottom cat uses Betula costata *as a convenient resting place* (below right)

wonderful day is all too quickly gone. There is no other word to describe such a day but magical.

When snow comes, it transforms the garden, giving it an entirely new perspective. It may bury many of the lower-growing plants, but it can be quite dramatic to see some of the coloured-stemmed willows and dogwoods poking above the snow. Snow acts as a blanket of protection against frost, depending how deep it is of course, but it can also cause damage in the garden, especially to conifers and, to some extent, we have to be prepared for it. Heavy, wet snow can weigh down or even break branches and should be dealt with before it causes much damage.

Winter is certainly the time when we can appreciate the merits of the many different types of evergreens, which include conifers, many shrubs and a few trees. To my mind a garden needs a mixture of deciduous and evergreen plants. Evergreens can provide stability, structure, form and considerable colour in winter, as well as shelter from winter winds, whilst deciduous plants above

HUGGING A SUN-FACING WALL, a heavily berried Pyracantha *'Orange Glow' sets off a collection of containerized conifers, mostly junipers, that will provide interest through winter. From left to right, these are:* Juniperus × media *'Gold Sovereign'*, Juniperus communis *'Green Carpet'*, Chamaecyparis obtusa *'Nana Gracilis'*, Juniperus horizontalis *'Glauca'*, Juniperus × media *'Sulphur Spray'*, Thuja orientalis *'Aurea Nana'. Most of these are 4-5 years old or more* (below)

ground offer a more evident change, reflecting the seasons with their succession of spring shoots, summer maturity, autumn ripeness and winter silhouette. One should remember the role that herbaceous plants and bulbs have to play in completing the seasonal picture. If you have a small garden it is well worth reflecting on these points for the selection you make.

The middle of winter is when evergreens, barks and stems really come into their own, although there is still some coloured foliage around. By the shortest day of the year, the birds have finally got to the *Pyracantha* 'Orange Glow' growing by our front door, the blackbird cheekily darting in for a quick, wary look in case our cat is anywhere around, then off it flies with another orange lifesaver in its beak. In frosty weather, the pyracantha is stripped of its berries by the New Year.

WINTER FLOWERS

But there are flowers at this time, and how precious they are. I am sure many would agree with the plantswoman, Margery Fish, who in 1958 wrote: "we get as much pleasure from one tiny bloom on a winter's day as we do from a gardenful of roses in summer."

Almost wherever you live, winter flowers can enliven the dullest day. Of

course, if you are snowbound and frozen all winter the options are limited, but for many cooler temperate climates winter can offer a varied choice. Perennials have much to offer. *Helleborus niger* (Christmas rose) is seldom in flower for the holiday itself, but the pure white blossoms arrive a few weeks later and continue until spring. *H. corsicus, H. foetidus* and *H. orientalis* each give weeks of flower colour from mid-winter to early spring. *Iris unguicularis*, which may already have borne a few fragrant, blue flowers in autumn, continues in succession through the winter. The golden-yellow flowers of *Adonis amurensis* are out in mid- or late winter along with the early bulbs, the delightfully simple snowdrops and golden winter aconites (*Eranthis hyemalis*), considered true harbingers of spring, but often premature. Many other bulbs soon start to appear.

There are plenty of winter-flowering shrubs to choose from as well, a few of which are mentioned here. *Hamamelis × intermedia* 'Jelena' is the first of the witch hazels to flower, its coppery-orange, strap-like petals a delight in the middle of winter. It is soon followed by others bearing fragrant, red, yellow or orange blossom. Mature examples of *Chimonanthus praecox* (wintersweet) bear unusual waxy, fragrant, purple-centred flowers in late winter. With golden-yellow flowers lasting from early winter to well into spring, few shrubs can surpass the inestimable winter jasmine (*Jasminum × nudiflorum*). Evergreen and bushy, *Viburnum tinus* and its cultivars are covered in blooms from autumn through to spring. Look out for the more compact 'Eve Price' whose pink buds open into heads of slightly fragrant, white flowers. Deciduous *V. × bodnantense* 'Dawn' is taller and has successive blooms which last throughout

SUN OR SHADE, the red-stemmed form of Helleborus foetidus *'Wester Flisk' gives a show throughout the winter months. Seedlings may vary in their colouring* (above)

OFTEN FLOWERING all winter, the witch hazel Hamamelis × intermedia *'Jelena', one of the earliest to bloom, shows up best against a dark background* (left)

NOT QUITE ORANGE perhaps but resembling shredded citrus peel extending from crimson centres, petals of Hamamelis × intermedia *'Orange Beauty, drip with moisture as the sun strikes after an overnight frost. This cultivar is one of many witch hazels which offer flower and fragrance through the midwinter months (left)*

winter unless severe frosts spoil the fragrant pink buds and flowers. The bright yellow racemes of some of the evergreen, spiky-leaved mahonia hybrids such as 'Charity' and 'Winter Sun' start flowering in autumn and continue until late winter unless caught by heavy frosts, and are soon followed by the fragrant flowers of *M. japonica.*

There are many more flowering shrubs, particularly if you include catkins as flowers. Among these must be the often spectacular, evergreen *Garrya elliptica*, which has sombre, olive-green leaves, an eventually dense habit and produces a delightful show of catkins in mid-winter. The best selection is 'James Roof' whose grey-green tassels elongate from late autumn onwards, many reaching 30cm/1ft. *Corylus avellana* 'Contorta', a member of the hazel family, has light yellow catkins in addition to its interesting corkscrew stems. Where space permits, some of the alders are worth including, particularly those which have more than one desirable

attribute. Both *Alnus incana* 'Aurea' and *A. glutinosa* 'Aurea' have golden leaves in spring. The former produces pink to crimson catkins which turn yellow as they open and the latter has lovely, long yellow catkins in late winter. The catkins of some of the willows come later on in the season.

Some winter-flowering heathers are also in flower at this time, although the full flush of *Erica carnea*, *E.* × *darleyensis* and *E. erigena* is usually yet to come in early spring. For those who can grow them – almost any garden with reasonable soil and a sunny situation in Britain – they are a must for winter colour.

Colourful evergreens

Among evergreen shrubs there is considerable diversity that can be used to brighten up winter days. I have already mentioned the humble, common but invaluable *Euonymus fortunei* cultivars 'Emerald 'n' Gold' and 'Emerald Gaiety', the former perhaps having the edge as its gold and green variegations take

THESE NEW CATKINS of Garrya elliptica *'James Roof' will elongate to 30cm/1ft by late winter, to provide a spectacular display* (above)

WINTER-FLOWERING heathers, with Erica carnea *'Pink Spangles' in the foreground, dominate a colourful, twenty-year-old planting. Blue, green and gold conifers provide contrast in form and colour* (right)

FOR FOLIAGE, FLOWER and fragrance some of the mahonias take some beating. Here, Mahonia × media *'Underway' seems happy in a semi-shady, reasonably sheltered position, its prickly leaves forming an evergreen canopy above which contrasting clusters of fragrant, yellow flowers, which emerged in autumn, bring cheer into winter* (opposite)

TWO EVERGREEN SHRUBS successfully combine green and yellow. Still laden with rounded, yellow berries in early winter, this Ilex aquifolium *'Fructu Luteo' has so far escaped the attention of hungry birds which seem to strip red fruits first. Depending upon season and location, however, the yellow fruits are bound to follow, leaving the holly's glossy, green leaves for continued colour (above)*

SPLASHES OF GOLD AND GREEN are the trademark of Elaeagnus pungens *'Maculata', which gives bright colour right through winter whether sited in sun or shade (right)*

on pretty, pink tinges in the severest of winters. These shrubs are useful as ground cover, can be allowed to scramble among other shrubs, and are able to climb walls and trees! There are many other varieties, all of which have small leaves and are very hardy. Less hardy, but of a more bushy, upright habit and with larger leaves are several attractive selections of the Japanese euonymus, some with green, some with gold and some with variegated leaves.

Golden variegated leaves are also found in several elaeagnus cultivars of *E. pungens* or *E.* × *ebbingei*, larger but adaptable evergreen shrubs. Most widely used, but not to be despised for that, is *E. pungens* 'Maculata' which has leathery, silver-backed leaves with a central splash of gold. Some defoliation may occur in severe winters, but these are good, useful evergreens which will tolerate shade.

The hollies, a large family of mostly dwarf and tall, evergreen shrubs and trees, can be placed in a similar category. There is ample choice, from *Ilex crenata* 'Golden Gem', which rarely exceeds 60cm/2ft even after many years and whose small, golden leaves are at their brightest in winter, to many selections of *Ilex aquifolium* (English holly) with silver- and gold-edged leaves and growing into small trees exceeding 10m/30ft. For the best berries a male form is needed near the female fruiting forms.

Both the large-leaved *Hedera colchica* (Persian ivy) and the smaller-leaved *H. helix* (common ivy) have selections with variegated leaves to provide winter colour for walls, fences, up trees and trunks or as ground cover. All are very well adapted for shade.

The spotted laurels, which are usually represented by *Aucuba japonica*, seem to arouse either favour or intense dislike.

They are mostly eventually large-growing shrubs with leathery, green, variegated or spotted leaves which can make quite a splash, as can the fruits of some. Much used by the Victorians, they are a little difficult to accommodate in a natural-looking garden.

Other evergreen shrubs for winter colour include fatsias, hebes, even the semi-evergreen (or evergreen, depending on climate) privets or ligustrum, osmanthus and pittosporums in addition to the rhododendrons and cherry laurels (*Prunus laurocerasus*).

There are two groups of interesting foliage plants from Australasia which can be useful in suitable gardens – both require milder climates to survive winters in cooler temperate zones. The spiky, sword-like foliage in colours ranging from cream to yellow, pink, maroon and purple of the phormiums (New Zealand flax) make them ideal for gravel gardens. (Of similar appeal are the variegated yuccas.) Most gardeners need to be aware of the vigour of eucalyptus, a group of fast-growing evergreens with mostly blue or bluish green foliage and attractive bark. Many of the species are much hardier than they were once thought to be, but they can be "stooled" – cut back to the ground every two or three years if they become too tall.

CONIFERS

There are many people who consider that conifers are pretty much the same the year round. Well all I can say is (and I constantly do) that such people do not know much about conifers! Many gardeners are not even aware that there are deciduous conifers. Some, admittedly, are very dull in winter and need additional colour from other plants to make them stand out, but mixed with other trees and shrubs, their wide range of shades can create a wonderful backdrop to other plantings.

There are other conifers which respond dramatically to shorter days and lower temperatures by changing colour – from green to gold – just when such a colour is most needed. Such valuable conifers mostly belong to the pine family, and our only native, the Scots pine (*Pinus sylvestris*), has produced some variations or clones which do just this. As winter deepens, so the needles of *P. s.* 'Aurea' brighten, particularly if the tree is in a sunny, exposed position, eventually turning a light yellow. Such a tree can act as a shelter in the summer and a beacon in winter. It can be pruned to keep it more dwarf, the best time to do this is whilst it is still small and just as the new "candles" or growth begins in late spring. There are slower-growing forms such as *P. s.* 'Gold Coin' which are of a deeper golden-yellow, but these will eventually get large so the same pruning suggestions apply. *Pinus mugo* 'Winter Gold', the Swiss mountain pine, is another of my favourites and will remain dwarfer, the green needles of summer changing to a clear golden-yellow for winter. The similar *P. m.* 'Ophir' is also delightful.

Many of the conifers that have gold or blue foliage are stunning in the winter sun. Others change from green or yellow to a distinctly bronze or even purplish tone as the days shorten and the weather gets colder. The carpeting, juniper-like *Microbiota decussata* whose bright green, lacy foliage turns bronze-

A STUNNING LINE-UP of conifers provides diversity of form and bright colour. From left to right they are Picea pungens *'Thomsen' (blue spruce), the dwarfer* Chamaecyparis obtusa *'Graciosa',* Pinus sylvestris *'Aurea' (golden Scots pine) and* Pinus leucodermis *(below)*

AN OVERNIGHT FROST gives this planting at Foggy Bottom a rather ghostly effect. The ice tones down the colours of the conifers and heathers but highlights the drooping stems of Stipa tenuissima *(centre), an ornamental grass of some distinction. Grasses add both seasonal change and movement to static plantings of conifers and heathers* (right)

A SHAFT OF EARLY morning sun begins the melting process on a frosted Pinus parviflora *'Glauca'* (opposite)

purple and the feathery-foliaged *Cryptomeria japonica* 'Elegans' which changes to a similar colour are two excellent examples. For the greatest effect they should be planted next to more brightly coloured plants such as golden or yellow-foliaged conifers or shrubs, or a silver-stemmed willow like *Salix irrorata* to highlight the contrast. I have an attractive grouping with *Microbiota decussata, Erica cinerea* 'Rock Pool' which has golden, almost bronze winter foliage, and *E. carnea* 'Myretoun Ruby' whose deep ruby-red flowers act as a catalyst against the gold and purple-bronze.

TWISTING BRANCHES

Choice there certainly is among evergreen shrubs and trees that give us colourful foliage through winter, but by a freak of nature, the branch configuration and habit of some deciduous plants have given them shapes and forms that create a picturesque and mature look when they have shed their leaves. These will provide an unusual winter feature in any size of garden, whether planted in the ground or in a container.

Most conifers retain their foliage all year but there are many that are deciduous. The larches, taxodium, pseudolarix and the ginkgo are the main types, although the latter, commonly known as the fossil tree, is not considered by many as a conifer. All of them have good autumn colour and attractive new shoots in spring. In winter the bare branches of the larches and *Taxodium*

distichum (swamp cypress) and its forms make an appealing shape against winter skies, especially when their twigs are adorned with a rimy frost or when drenched in dew, as they often are.

I am particularly struck with *Larix kaempferi* 'Diana', a cultivar of the Japanese larch. In spring it has delightful, paintbrush-like, bright green shoots which become needles in summer, turning to gold in autumn before they drop off to reveal a silhouette of snake-like branches. The way winter light shines through the curling, contorted branches and stems is indescribably sensuous. A grafted plant of relatively slow growth, this beautiful tree can be grown as a container or patio plant for many years, or as a plant top-grafted onto a stem to make an interesting shape with year-round appeal.

WONDERFULLY TWISTED BRANCHES of Salix × sepulcralis *'Erythroflexuosa' come into their own in winter, revealing orange to gold lower stems and crimson, pigtailed branchlets, an inspiring sight. This plant is trimmed to the ground annually in late spring* (above)

Attractive contortions and silhouettes are found in many other plants, too. Treated correctly these also can be useful in the small garden. Pruning opens up branches, rendering them less congested, improves the winter silhouette and keeps them dwarf.

Corylus avellana 'Contorta' (corkscrew hazel, but also known as Harry Lauder's walking stick) is much more interesting during its leafless winter months than in summer. Through winter its contorted, twisted, greyish branches resemble a sculpture which as

spring approaches becomes covered with pendent, pale yellow catkins. Suckers at the base of this shrub must be removed each year.

Another of my favourites is *Salix × sepulcralis* 'Erythroflexuosa', a willow recently introduced from Argentina. In summer it is nothing much to look at but, if pruned to the ground in late spring, it will produce vigorous 2m/6ft or more shoots and twigs which twist and turn as though they were trying to escape from the name which the botanists have seen fit to give it! But when the burnished stems of maroon, gold and yellow glisten in the winter sun, what was a background shrub in summer becomes a star in winter. Prune this shrub to the ground each spring to keep it dwarf.

A shrub that epitomizes year-round value for all sizes of garden has to be *Prunus incisa* 'Kojo-no-mai', a slow-growing form of the Fuji cherry apparently found on the slopes of Mount Fuji in Japan. Translated, the name means 'Dance of the Butterflies' which is wonderfully descriptive of the myriads of small, white flowers produced in early spring. The branches of this remarkable shrub are twisted and angled to create a tangled mass of fascinating complexity in its winter nakedness. In addition it has attractive small, serrated, green leaves which usually, but according to situation, turn shades of bronze, purple and red in autumn. Attractive all year round and able to grow in a container, 'Kojo-no-mai' can earn a place even in the smallest garden. It is to my mind the best value for money.

COLOURED BARK AND STEMS

In addition to interestingly shaped branches and twigs, some trees and shrubs have yet another fine attribute

laid bare when stripped of their leaves – bark. The main stems of many trees such as the silver birches are visible throughout the year but the upper stems and branches remain hidden until the last leaves have fallen.

If you have room for a silver birch (depending on the species eventually it may require a width of 3-6m/10-20ft), which one should it be? Our own native *Betula pendula* (lady of the woods) or a more exotic selection, such as the creamy-barked *B. costata*, *B. utilis* and its forms such as 'Jermyns' all with white bark, or the slower-growing *B. jacquemontii*? There are several different species and selections at Foggy Bottom which create a spectacle in winter from both near to and far away.

Some of the maples have ornamental bark. *Acer griseum*, for example, slow though it is to develop its peeling, orange-brown bark, is well worth the wait. Some, such as *A. rufinerve*,

PRICKLY WITH ICE NEEDLES, the contorted branches of Larix × kaempferi *'Diana' are emphasized by a severe frost in early winter* (top far left)

FRESHLY FALLEN SNOW coats the snaking branches of Corylus avellana *'Contorta', the corkscrew hazel, dangling just-opened catkins in late winter* (top left)

GLOSSY, MAHOGANY-RED BARK of Prunus serrula *gleams in early winter sunshine* (bottom far left)

THE PEELING SKIN of Betula nigra *'Heritage', an improved selection of the sometimes dingy river birch, reveals delicate shrimp colouring. It may take four or five years before young plants mature to this stage* (bottom left)

BRIGHTLY COLOURED STEMS

Many shrubs are useful in the winter garden for the startlingly bright colours of their stems. These colours can usually be intensified by hard pruning each spring. The time for pruning is just as the new growth begins to show in mid-spring. Prune hard with secateurs to 10cm/4in above the ground, or in the case of Salix alba *varieties back to a stump (pollarding). Although this treatment guarantees abundant new shoots with the brightest colour, it will be at the expense of flowering in that year. The choice is yours! Some shrubs which benefit from this treatment are mentioned here.*

Dogwoods – red, yellow, orange and green stems

Cornus alba
Cornus sanguinea
Cornus stolonifera and their cultivars

Willows – orange-red and orange-yellow stems

Salix alba 'Britzensis'
Salix alba 'Vitellina'
Salix irrorata
Salix × sepulcralis 'Erythroflexuosa' (syn. *S. Erythroflexuosa*)

Brambles – white stems

Rubus biflorus
Rubus cockburnianus
Rubus thibetanus

YELLOW-GREEN STEMS *of* Cornus stolonifera *'Flaviramea' (top right)*

THE STEMS OF Salix irrorata *(foreground) and, from left to right,* Cornus alba *'Sibirica',* Pinus mugo *'Wintergold' and* Cornus sanguinea *'Winter Flame' (right)*

RED-TIPPED, *green-yellow twigs of* Cornus stolonifera *'Kelsey's Dwarf' lead the eye to red-stemmed* Cornus alba *'Sibirica' (opposite)*

A. davidii, A. capillipes and *A. hersii* have stems that are striped green and silvery white. Most spectacular of all, if you can find one, is *A. pensylvanicum* 'Erythrocladum'. It is a slow grower and not always an easy doer, but winter shoots are coral pink and they stand out against any background. I am, of course, being very selective here, as there are many other worthy trees and shrubs with colourful winter stems and bark.

GRASSES

Ornamental grasses are becoming recognized as plants that have potential for giving great pleasure in winter and are now more appreciated by gardeners than ever before. This is largely due to the introduction of a great many new species and varieties, mostly from Germany and the U.S.A., where grasses have been used more widely in gardens and to greater effect than anywhere else. The low-growing, hummocky carex from New Zealand make their mark, too, being particularly adaptable to the smaller garden.

A few years ago, I brought back from Germany a group of *Miscanthus sinensis* cultivars bred by nurseryman and plantsman Ernst Pagels. I was impressed by seeing them in full flower at the height of summer during a visit to his nursery. At that time all the varieties available in Britain either flowered very late in autumn or not at all because British summers were too cool. This remarkable group offers British gardeners a whole new perspective. Their elegant plumes last right through winter, providing a ceaseless interaction of light and movement. They are totally hardy, and dwarf forms are available for use in the smaller garden.

It is gratifying to see the increasing appreciation that more and more gardeners have for ornamental grasses. Even so, it is mostly for their summer effect in association with more colourful perennials, and many gardeners have yet to explore the increased interest and value that grasses offer from autumn until early spring – even if most of the foliage above ground is dead. There are "evergreen" grasses such as the hummocky festucas and carex which provide colour contrasts to plantings of shrubs, conifers or heathers, and there are the deciduous types such as cortaderia, stripa, miscanthus and pennisetum, whose foliage and flowers give movement and light to plantings throughout winter. I have found them particularly effective when planted imaginatively among more static groups of heathers.

For giant plumes choose *Cortaderia selloana,* one of the pampas grasses, all of which have spikes topped by silvery white plumes in early autumn which last through most of the winter, even if the foliage turns brown. That said, the taller species or varieties such as 'Sunningdale Silver' will blow over or snap in high winds, so go for the more compact *C. s.* 'Pumila' which can have as many as 30-50 plumes on established clumps.

Miscanthus ranges in size from the 90cm/3ft *Miscanthus sinensis* 'Yaku Dwarf' to the 3m/10ft *M. sacchariflorus,* which is useful as a windbreak but seldom flowers in cooler, temperate climates. In between these extremes are forms like 'Little Fountain' ('Kleine Fontane') with pendulous, silver plumes which turn white, and 'Malepartus' with crimson-maroon summer flowers which turn silver then white as autumn becomes winter. The straight, brown stems of *Calamagrostis* × *acutiflora* 'Karl Foerster' or 'Overdam', the latter with pretty green, white and, in spring, striped leaves, add a lighter touch.

Stipa calamagrostis has arching stalks carrying rich brown autumn plumes that are still attractive in winter. One of my favourites is *Stipa tenuissima* which grows to only 45cm/18in, its green, grassy spring and summer foliage producing delicate, feathery heads which blow about in the wind. These fade to beige in autumn, but the whole plant remains attractive throughout the winter. What matter if it seeds itself around since the seedlings seem natural in the most unlikely places.

The deschampsias, too, are worthwhile, particularly the one that goes by the name 'Golden Dew' ('Goldtau'). Its fine, fluffy heads attract dew in autumn and winter, which gives a quite magical effect if it freezes. I can never praise enough the virtues of a dwarf "deciduous" Japanese grass with the difficult

SHARPLY POINTED LEAVES of Yucca filamentosa *'Variegata' balance the flat heads of* Sedum *'Autumn Joy' and varieties of* Miscanthus sinensis, *an ornamental grass* (above)

ARCHING FRONDS of the ornamental grass Stipa tenuissima *fill the space between conifers in a bed overshadowed by a leaning* Pinus parviflora *'Glauca' which has been pruned to accentuate its character* (opposite)

name of *Hakonechloa macra* 'Alboaurea'. Its narrow, wavy leaves are golden yellow and green in summer. Whilst it is undoubtedly a beautiful plant in the garden, its true beauty is revealed when it is used as a container plant on a patio. In autumn its colour gradually fades to gold or russet hues through to beige, but the "dead" leaves and stems remain to give pleasure through winter.

Lastly, I would like to mention two plants which fulfil the roles of grasses, although neither of them is one. The dwarf, rush-like *Acorus gramineus* 'Ogon' makes a bright hummock of arching, golden leaves throughout winter and contrasts well with *Ophiopogon planiscapus* 'Nigrescens' which is somewhat similar but creeping in habit with startling, black leaves. These two are valuable enough on their own, but in combination with each other or with different plants they can create a year-round feature in any garden.

FRAGRANCE

Among the treasures on offer for the winter garden, fragrance is arguably one of the most valuable. Deliciously scented plants can be dotted around the garden, filling it with pleasant smells to enjoy when you venture out on fine days. Position plants where you know that you are likely to walk regularly in winter – on the way to your shed, greenhouse or garage and certainly by the front and back doors. The waft of the heady scent from the tiny, white flowers of the humble *Sarcococca humilis* can be like nectar on a winter or spring day.

Not only do those plants that are scented last for a long period through the winter outdoors, but many hold on well when cut for indoors. The exception to this are the mahonias which, fragrant as they are in the garden, unfortunately drop their yellow petals quickly once brought inside. But *Lonicera fragrantissima,* a winter honeysuckle, the bewitching witch hazels (hamamelis), chimonanthus (wintersweet), sarcococca (sweet box, although it is not a box) and *Viburnum* × *bodnantense* all keep quite well, depending on how much heat there is in the room, gently releasing fragrance into the air.

SPRING

Hardly have we settled down to enjoy the pure delights of the cold season, than winter hovers on the verge of spring. In some parts of Britain, we can go through the middle few weeks of winter without a single frost, but we often pay for that oversight of nature, since seldom do we escape frosts entirely before the arrival of spring. Mild weather early on often gives a false message to the plants which consider that spring is just around the corner, if it has not already arrived. Snowdrops and aconites pop out, even the tightly rounded, purplish brown winter buds of the Japanese hardy perennial *Adonis amurensis* start pushing through the ground. Once they have raised their heads they are inclined to go the whole way to open their buttercup-like flowers, which are followed by ferny foliage. This handsome plant is a good example of how climate affects plants, appearing in January, February, March or even April depending upon the mildness or severity of the winter. So is it a winter-flowering plant? You see the difficulty we have when trying to categorize plants. They will not be put into firm boxes, they will not always conform to what experts say about them, but surely this is what makes plants and gardening such a challenge. There is always something different happening or about to happen. Nature likes to keep us guessing, and generally does a pretty good job of it.

A FEELING OF CHEER emanates from massed, early spring blooms at Foggy Bottom. Narcissus 'Mrs R. O. Backhouse' carpets the ground. To their left, two modern representatives of popular flowering shrubs, Forsythia 'Weekend' and Ribes sanguineum 'Red Pimpernel', front the developing leaves of Acer platanoides 'Princeton Gold', a useful spring foliage plant (right)

BENEATH THE CEDAR whose needles scatter the ground, the Cyclamen coum, *aconites, snowdrops and crocus, harbingers of spring, make a pretty display* (top)

A DENSELY PLANTED corner in early spring with fading flowers of Erica carnea *'Springwood White' surrounding a mauve-flowered* Pulmonaria longifolia *'Roy Davidson' and a purple-leaved* Bergenia *'Wintermärchen'. At the back, the blue-foliaged* Abies procera *'Glauca Prostrata',* Erica carnea *'Vivellii' and* Narcissus *'Jack Snipe' make an arresting combination* (left)

SPRING FLOWERS

Even if we do not know exactly when spring is going to begin, we do know that the days are getting longer, and that inevitably the quiet season will have a limited span from now on. As the days become longer, lighter and brighter, buds start to swell, catkins lengthen, and, on milder days, bees buzz around the winter-flowering heathers.

Although at Foggy Bottom, many of the *Erica × darleyensis* types have been in flower for a couple of months already, and some of the *Erica carnea* cultivars have been showing colour since before Christmas, most start to open fully as late winter slips into early spring and only then begin to make their mark.

In my opinion, the winter-flowering heathers offer so much that they are indispensable. They are impressive in large drifts, interesting as individual plants and fascinating at close quarters. Their massed flowers, in pink, white, purple, maroon and red, last for months. Invaluable to bees as an early source of nectar, useful as weed smotherers, generally trouble-free and long-lived, what more could a gardener want from a plant?

The winter-flowering types are lime tolerant, the summer-flowering types are not, but, in the gardens that can grow them, they can offer bright golden, yellow, pink, russet or crimson winter foliage, with the dead flower heads of *Erica cinerea* (bell heather) and *Erica vagans* (Cornish heath) being particularly attractive. Winter-flowering heathers seldom require any pruning, except perhaps to tidy them up, but summer-flowering types are best pruned in spring, just as new growth begins. Remember that summer-flowering heathers require an acid soil.

There is so much else to look forward to at this time as the pace of life in the garden begins to quicken. The fewer the plants in bloom, the more they are appreciated. Each tree, shrub, perennial, alpine or bulb is eagerly watched as it prepares to do its stuff. One of my own favourites is *Cyclamen coum*. Its pretty flowers open tentatively in winter, testing the weather then, as winter turns into early spring, they gradually break into full flower one or two months later. The small flowers are bright crimson and stand out against the heart-shaped, dark green leaves. There are also forms with pink or white flowers and many that have silver or silver and green patterned leaves. Hardy cyclamens are much more readily available as young, pot-grown plants these days and they are considerably easier to establish than dried corms. Place them in a sunny or sheltered spot where they are unlikely to get disturbed or trampled, and they will reward you with years of pleasure.

By the time the cyclamen flowers have emerged, other bulbs are beginning to show themselves – *Iris danfordiae, I. histrioïdes*, various narcissi, scillas, crocuses and others. In my garden, the first two alpine plants to bloom are the creeping *Saxifraga oppositifolia* 'Florissa', with minute, bright pink flowers, and *Saxifraga juniperifolia*, its bright yellow flowers resplendent above green mats. Also among the first harbingers of spring are such plants as pulmonarias, helleborus, euphorbias, dentarias, epimediums, primulas, violas and forms of *Ranunculus ficaria*.

Late frosts

Camellias, early rhododendrons, stachyurus, magnolias and wisterias are but a few of the spring flowers which can be totally lost to spring frosts. When

FROST DAMAGE

As spring weather prompts more plants into early bloom, so there is an increasing danger from damaging frosts. No garden is perfect, and for all the benefits of site and situation at Foggy Bottom, one distinct disadvantage is that it lies in a frost pocket. Exposed, hilly sites have their problems, too, but valley bottoms, particularly if water exists at the floor, are notorious for collecting frost which literally drains down from surrounding slopes. This means that overnight spring frosts settle on plants, but if the frost is not severe it may do little damage unless the morning sun strikes shoots, buds or flowers before the temperature rises above freezing. The sun striking frozen soft plant tissue can maim and kill – and, in fact, can do far more damage than much more severe frosts in the fully dormant season. To minimize the effects of serious frost damage, it makes good sense, obviously, to avoid planting frost-susceptible plants on easterly facing beds or walls – go west facing or even north for shade-lovers where sun will not reach until later in the day.

all new developing buds and shoots are caught by a hard frost in late spring it can kill a plant outright, too. Then, not only some of those mentioned, but Japanese maples, stewartias – even hamamelis – can be lost, as I know only too well from my experience over the years at Foggy Bottom. In May 1991, I measured fourteen successive nights of frost in the garden, which did considerable damage.

Fortunately, the trees and conifers at Foggy Bottom have grown to a stature where they offer shade and shelter, so I am able to find microclimates that are protected as much as possible from the dangers of frost.

PURE YELLOW FLOWERS of Epimedium pinnatum colchicum, *one of the best evergreen types, are caught by a shaft of spring light. Epimediums are often underrated spring-flowering plants, partly because they often hide their delicate blooms among masses of evergreen foliage* (top)

PULMONARIAS, THE LUNGWORTS, are among the most hardy and versatile of the late-winter and spring-flowering perennials. Pulmonaria 'Highdown', also known as 'Lewis Palmer', flowers for over two months as winter turns into spring then follows with good-looking, spotted foliage (above)

Mottled foliage and creamy flowers of Erythronium californicum, *a woodland plant which grows quite well in the open, show up well against surrounding* Muscari armeniacum *in early spring* (top)

A small group of Helleborus orientalis *have a background of* Magnolia stellata *enhancing their flowers which have been blooming for several weeks. Cut away their leaves in midwinter, if they are unsightly* (above)

The vivid, deep pink flowers of the hardy, glossy-leaved Cyclamen coum *are a welcome sight in late winter and early spring. Here, a fine example is on excellent terms with a goldneedled* Pinus sylvestris *'Gold Coin'* (left)

Trees and shrubs are not the only plants that can have flowers and foliage ruined if frost comes at the wrong time in spring. Some early developing perennials can have their living cells destroyed by frost, making them look like lifeless compost. The flowers and foliage of some bergenias and the tender new leaves of hostas are just two examples of susceptible plants, but, fortunately, they are likely to shoot up again once the danger has passed.

Given the right selection of plants, all gardens can be given a new lease of life if the perspective of autumn, winter and spring colour and interest is studied with greater attention. Foggy Bottom is an example of a garden that has consciously developed the quiet season theme. Many of the beds, groupings and plant associations in it could be used in other gardens. I have always enjoyed the challenge of creating plant associations

IN EARLY SPRING, Ribes sanguineum *'White Icicle' makes a pleasant change from the more common red or pink flowering currants* (above left)

PINK, DOUBLE BLOOMS of Camellia *'Donation' are out by early spring in a sheltered position.* Euonymus fortunei *'Emerald 'n' Gold' provides foreground contrast* (above)

which can be adapted to smaller gardens, and in those that are featured in the next chapter I have been able to suggest ideas on what can be done on a small scale.

Of course, there are a lot of recipes available to meet individual tastes. Designing a garden is much like decorating a room – selecting and moving the furniture around to fit. The same can be done in a garden. But, to my mind, garden designs these days so often seem to concentrate more on the design principle, whether it be shape, form or colour scheming, than on the plants themselves. Hard landscaping, although necessary in a living environment for patios or terraces, is in danger of becoming an end in itself, with the plants looked upon as merely ingredients of secondary value to help create a certain effect. My belief is that you can have no better materials than plants themselves to use in a garden to create year-round effect, beauty, life and pleasure. Such designing, of course, calls for constant change and adaption as plants grow, and as such a garden becomes a living, breathing entity, a life unto itself. Learning about plants leads to a desire to widen knowledge, which in turn leads to yet more changes, and, hopefully, to more self fulfilment and a better quality of life connected to nature.

These are some thoughts as I write on a late winter evening, before the sun's warmth releases the energy of plants to produce an unstoppable burst of growth which will herald the onset of the noisy season once again. We need these quiet times to take stock, to prepare and to plan. Whether planting in spring, summer or autumn I hope this book makes you think about bringing more colour and pleasure to your garden and your life in the quieter time of the year.

A CALENDAR FOR FRAGRANCE

Anything that can introduce colour and fragrance into our lives is doubly valuable. So why not plan to have fragrant plants near your front or back door, along the path to the street, garage, washing line, shed or greenhouse. The evergreen foliage and delightfully smelling winter flowers of the sarcococcas *(Christmas or sweet box) make them ideal for this job. Their fragrance can knock you out at several metres distance and they will grow happily in shady spots. Mahonias, viburnums, chimonanthus, hamamelis and loniceras are other large-growing, winter-fragrant shrubs to plant.*

AUTUMN

Perennials and bulbs
Cosmos atrosanguineus
Cyclamen hederifolium
Cyclamen purpurascens
Iris unguicularis

Shrubs
Abelia
Akebia quinata
Clerodendrum
Elaeagnus × ebbingei
Elaeagnus pungens
Heptacodium jasminoïdes
Jasminum officinale
Mahonia × media
Pittosporum tenuifolium
Roses (some)
Viburnum × bodnantense
Viburnum farreri
Viburnum tinus (some)

WINTER

Perennials and bulbs
Galanthus 'S. Arnott'
Iris reticulata
Iris unguicularis
Leucojum vernum

Shrubs
Chimonanthus
Cornus mas
Erica arborea
Erica erigena
Hamamelis (most)
Lonicera fragantissima
Lonicera × purpusii
Mahonia japonica
Mahonia × media
Prunus mume
Rhododendron moupinense
Sarcococca
Viburnum × bodnantense
Viburnum farreri
Viburnum tinus (some)

EARLY SPRING

Perennials and bulbs
Iris foetidissima
Iris reticulata
Narcissus (some)
Muscari (some)
Viola odorata

Shrubs
Abeliophyllum distichum
Choisya ternata
Clematis armandii
Cornus mas
Corylopsis (some)
Daphnes (some)
Mahonia aquifolium
Mahonia japonica
Osmanthus × burkwoodii
Osmanthus delavayi
Pieris (some)
Rhododendron *(some)*
Ribes odoratum
Skimmia × confusa
Skimmia japonica
Viburnum × bodnantense
Viburnum × burkwoodii
and hybrids
Viburnum farreri
Viburnum tinus (some)

USEFUL FOR COVERING sheltered walls or pergolas, the strong-growing evergreen Clematis armandii *usually flowers in mid-spring (left)*

WINTER
COLOUR

WINTER COLOUR IN THE SMALLER GARDEN

oggy Bottom is much larger than the average-sized garden, of course, yet there are a great many wonderful gardens that make our six acres look relatively small in comparison. However large a garden is, it has its own individual style which results from a unique combination of ideas and designs. Naturally, the larger the garden is, the more opportunity there is to experiment. And large gardens that are open to the public can be used by ordinary gardeners as sources of inspiration, full of ideas to be taken away, adapted and tried out in smaller situations.

Being a keen gardener and plantsman as well as nurseryman, I have been only too well aware of the comments that many gardeners might make as they walk around my own "large" garden, the most obvious perhaps being: "well of course, anyone can create a good garden in six acres." So I have tried to show in practical terms how to create interest and colour the year round in more modestly sized gardens.

To put some of these ideas into practice, over the years I have adopted three typical, suburban front gardens near to my home and, with the help of some of our nursery and garden staff, I have completely replanted them, subsequently recording their growth and development at regular intervals.

Naturally, these three situations cannot possibly represent all the different types of smaller gardens in the country. To do that would require at least twenty gardens, covering categories such as town gardens, shade and dry shade gardens, gardens on slopes, seaside, chalk and limestone gardens and many more, all with their own peculiarities as to shape and restrictions. But these three gardens (shown on pages 70-73, 74-77, 78-81) do, none the less, represent a great many plots and will, I hope, provide inspiration and plenty of practical ideas for those readers seeking to introduce year-round beauty and colour on their own doorsteps.

In addition to the planting plans for these three gardens, this chapter also contains a selection of planting associations (pages 82-89). These are designed for specific situations and will be useful for creating isolated areas of winter interest within an already established garden. Small sections taken from the planting plans for the three new gardens already mentioned would also serve this purpose.

THE PERSONAL TOUCH

No matter what its size, every garden generally reflects a different approach, a different aspect according to its age, history and surrounding topography, and, of course, an individuality derived from the imagination, skill and objectives of its designer and/or owners. The common denominator of all gardens is the interaction of plants and people.

While a garden can express the individuality of the person or people who own and tend it, not everyone has the time, inclination, or, perhaps, knowledge or confidence to achieve something enduringly interesting on their own. To help in just such situations was the prime motivation for adopting the three front gardens that are described later. Even though I was doing the initial work and supplying the plants, the three families concerned all had their own likes and dislikes about their gardens, their favourite plants or associations, and they are free to develop some of their ideas further in their back gardens if they wish.

By the same token, anyone can create their own plant associations, using their own artistic flair, whether in a garden, patio, window box or simply in a container or two. Each of the gardens and planting associations featured in this chapter gives ideas from which readers can start to influence their own gardens by introducing aspects to turn them into something that will be a pleasure to see and watch the whole year through. Thus each of us can become an aspiring artist in our own garden!

ADDING WINTER INTEREST TO AN ESTABLISHED GARDEN

If your garden is already well established it will probably contain some plants that fit the category of "quiet season" plant. You can build on these by adding appropriate bulbs, perennials or shrubs to existing beds or borders. Alternatively, you could extend one of these to give more space for developing winter-interest plantings. This book contains plenty of ideas for creating more autumn, winter and early spring interest, including walls, fences, containers or window boxes in addition to beds or borders.

For those with larger gardens, the ideas for creating new beds or plant associations illustrated later in this book may be limited in scope. If this is the case, you may wish to make an even larger, bolder winter interest feature. Take time to select plants carefully according to their rates of growth and suitability to your soil conditions. A larger garden allows you scope to select more vigorous and larger-growing plants if you wish. You can use the information contained in this book as a basis for planning your own feature according to the size of your garden and your own interests in particular types of plant.

THE PRINCIPAL PLAYERS

Plants are wonderful material for artistic use. They flow and ebb with the seasons, becoming a living, expanding canvas, unlike the dry, inanimate, one-dimensional material of the painter's work. Not that I wish to denigrate this form of art, for it captures a moment, an impression, but the artist once finished with his or her painting has it under control, finished. Not so the gardener, who has a much more difficult task looking after all the diverse, living plants in his care at the same time as orchestrating an artistic creation that changes with the seasons.

Such is the range of shapes, forms and colours of garden plants that I have always maintained that one needs little else with which to create a garden, although I am not against the odd humanizing feature or two! Nor am I too much against those who wish to colour scheme their garden, but this does not always lead to the best results, and in the smaller garden it can limit the selection of plant material.

The smaller the garden the more important the selection of plants, partic-

STARTLING SCARLET TWIGS of Cornus alba *'Sibirica', contrasting brightly with green grass and a darker background of conifers, give a winter-long show at Foggy Bottom (below)*

ularly if you want colour all the year. Whilst the bold architectural look might be dramatic, it will call for relatively few, but large specimens – certainly not generally suitable for the smaller garden. My own preference, which I have used in the three gardens shown on the following pages, is for a wide range of plants. With careful planting and subsequent management this makes possible an ever-changing scene of sustained interest throughout the year and a reasonably easily maintained garden. As one plant goes past its peak it will always be followed by another at its best, and another just about to come into flower.

Gardening is about observation and learning how plants grow and how to make them grow better. Part of the fun is comparing your plants' performances with what the books say about them! It is always good to have at least one reliable reference book to pore over – even better to have two – although it can be somewhat confusing if they give conflicting advice! But whilst you can learn from books, you can never learn better than from your own experience.

TIME VERSUS COST

Something I had to face with both my own garden and the three adopted small ones was the time factor, that is, how long are people prepared to wait for results. I suspect that along with wanting a garden that looks attractive for most of the year without much looking after, most people also wish for an instant, semi-mature garden where one does not already exist. But as anyone who spends any time at all browsing around garden centres will know, the larger plants and specimens which can help to achieve this cost money.

When talking about specimen plants we can certainly use the time-honoured

phrase "time costs money" in a literal sense. But, if money is not too much of a problem, the choice is the customer's. A dwarf or slow-growing conifer, something like *Picea glauca albertiana* 'Conica' which has a narrow, cone-like habit, is a good example. A two-or three-year old plant will be 20-30cm/8-12in tall at the most. It may take at least ten years to reach 90-120cm/3-4ft and will need to be sold in quite a large container. Needless to say, a ten-year old specimen of the *Picea*, even if it is smaller than a two-or three-year old × *Cupressocyparis leylandii* (which once established grows 90cm/3ft per year!), will cost considerably more to buy. You are buying a bigger plant, of course, but what you are really paying for is seven years of growing and caring time at the nursery which enables you to install an instant, established effect in the garden. The decision is yours to make.

Conversely, and hopefully not to confuse, while purchasing fast-growing plants might save a lot of money, in the small garden this strategy can lead to problems early on as these plants will soon become unmanageable without constant, severe pruning.

On the whole, I think that most people would consider a wait of three years before seeing some positive results when developing a new garden – with plants

FOR YEAR-ROUND APPEAL in a limited space, few deciduous plants can claim as many pleasing attributes as Prunus incisa *'Kojo-no-mai', seen here with its naked, twisted branches encased in ice on a frosty mid-winter morning. Pink buds will soon swell to open at the beginning of spring as a mass of white flowers which will fade to pink as serrated, fresh green leaves emerge. In autumn the foliage turns bronze and crimson. This specimen, at 1.5m/5ft, is about ten years old (opposite)*

beginning to meet together and associations starting to work – as reasonable.

Depending upon the style of garden or the type of plants installed, after three years is usually the time when the faster-growing plants will need to start being pruned. This is the beginning of the "management" phase. Some plants will have succeeded only too well, and may either have to be pruned or even moved to another part of the garden. Others will have spread or become overgrown, some will not have done well and may want trying somewhere else.

THE FRONT GARDEN

Although the front garden is not used for recreation, it is passed or crossed by the average house-dweller at least twice a day, every day, totalling a conservative minimum of 700 times a year – and the figure is likely to be much higher. And that is just for one member of the family!

In view of its frequent use, and the fact that it is constantly on show to neighbours and passers-by as well as from the house itself, it has always amazed me that people do not do more with their front plot. With all the possibilities and opportunities it holds for enjoyment and pleasure, the front garden is arguably a more important area than the back garden.

There are large front gardens, small ones and even minuscule ones, some have even been covered with concrete and turned into car parking areas. For many people they can be a bit of a nuisance, perhaps consisting of a patch of lawn which has to be cut once or twice each week during spring, summer and autumn. Or they might be ugly, unimaginatively planted with an uninspired selection of a few shrubs, conifers, roses, bulbs or annuals in formal borders.

CHOOSING PLANTS FOR THE SMALL GARDEN

1. Think about what you would like your garden to look like and how it can be achieved.

2. Look at books to get ideas and be prepared to ask for advice from your local garden centre or nursery, or consult a garden designer.

3. Find out about the habits and requirements of the plants you choose, especially their rates of growth and eventual size.

4. Consider the garden's aspect and its soil. If necessary get a soil test taken. Seek advice from a reputable local garden centre or expert who will advise as to what will grow successfully in your locality.

5. Select plants that are in scale with each other – this applies particularly to smaller plants such as dwarf conifers, shrubs and alpines.

But it does not have to be like this. It is so easy to turn this "nuisance" into an asset by planting it up to create a living garden, a tapestry of colour and interest for year-round enjoyment. Even a front yard that has been paved over can be enlivened with pots and containers carefully planted to spice up drab winter days, or have planting holes gouged through the hard surface. And do not be put off by thinking that to create a small paradise on your front doorstep is all labour, for it can be done in easy stages.

So there is nothing to stop you creating a garden with colour and interest that you can enjoy every day of the year.

GOLD AND RUSSET for autumn but otherwise with dark green leaves, Acer palmatum *'Mikawa' is just one of the slow-growing Japanese maples that have good winter shape and are ideal for growing in containers. This magnificent example is about eight years old* (above)

Terraces, patios, balconies or window boxes, whether located in sun or shade, can all be planted to give a full six months of interest during the autumn, winter and spring – a period often neglected by books on the subject of patio or container plants. So anyone with little garden, or even none at all, need not be denied the pleasure of an attractive winter display to be enjoyed through the quiet season. Whether you have room for one or many containers, large or small, there are plants to suit, the most valuable being those that will give year-round interest. These could be conifers or evergreen shrubs but for something different some ornamental grasses, perennials or deciduous shrubs or trees could be used. I have used all at Foggy Bottom.

Containers planted with individual plants can be moved around, if you have the space, to form containerized plant associations. Alternatively you can create interesting planting associations from whatever plants take your fancy at the garden centre.

Plants in containers must have suitable composts, with plants such as camellias, rhododendrons or pieris requiring acid soil. Most make do with a general container compost supplied by your local garden centre. Containerized plants require regular watering, especially in the summer to sustain growth, and feeding, either by using a slow-release fertilizer or a regular liquid feed. You can choose containers to suit your taste and pocket, but remember that glazed or ceramic ones retain moisture better than terracotta ones and so require less watering. Recently there have been some very good plastic imitation terracotta pots on the market and these will require a different watering regime. Good drainage is essential in winter, and the plastic pots require far less watering in summer.

In countries where severe frost is a regular feature, container plants are often wrapped in hessian or even plunged into the ground. This is the ultimate way to protect pots from cracking and roots from freezing, but for most Zone 8-9 hardiness areas (page 92), which includes the British Isles, this is probably extreme. A good idea for wetter areas is to lift the containers on blocks of wood or special terracotta "legs" to allow free drainage in winter.

The ideal time to plant up containers and window boxes for a winter display is in early autumn, planting any acid-loving specimens in ericaceous compost. Such a plant grouping can look good all year if it is fed, watered and trimmed regularly. But if you want to change your plants in spring, ready for a summer show, you can leave the plants in their pots and place these in the larger container in the autumn instead of planting them out. Simply remove these plants, in their pots, in the spring and place them elsewhere. Keep them watered, fed and trimmed through the summer, potting on into a larger pot if required, ready to be reinstalled in the container the following autumn.

If you do have a garden where you can plant your winter window box plants in spring, plan for the space to plant them before purchasing your selection in autumn. Plants such as some dwarf conifers, the evergreen euonymus, skimmias, heathers, *Viburnum tinus*, even colourfully stemmed dogwoods can all be used to good effect in window boxes and other containers in autumn, winter or early spring before planting out in the garden. It is a way of bringing the garden closer to your house during the quiet months.

SOME PLANTS FOR AUTUMN, WINTER AND SPRING WINDOW BOXES AND TUBS

SOME OF THE PLANTS put in the window box at Foggy Bottom are ultimately destined for the garden, but in their first winter they will make more impact close to the window (far left)

AN INSPIRED USE for this evergreen sedge makes the most of long threads which gradually sweep downwards (left)

In recent years, we in Britain have been catching on to the idea of using a wider range of plants for pots and containers for patio or terrace gardening as well as for window boxes. But by and large, these are for late spring, summer and early autumn use. So what about winter, when a cheery planting of foliage and flowering plants can brighten any aspect? With a window box winter garden you can bring nature closer to you and this is where variety is the key. Dwarf shrubs, perennials and bulbs can all play a part depending on the size and aspect of your window boxes. If you plan to plant some shrubs in your garden in spring that are suitable for window boxes, too, why not order them early and put them in your window box, still in their pots, over winter? Dwarf conifers can be selected from garden centres in mid-autumn, as can winter-flowering heathers, the best value perhaps being in Erica × darleyensis *types which flower from late autumn until late spring. Mix in a few yellow and gold* Calluna vulgaris *to brighten things up. Dwarf shrubs with good winter foliage colour have to*
include Euonymus fortunei *'Emerald 'n' Gold' and 'Emerald Gaiety'*, and perhaps Hebe *'Red Edge' which is red-tipped in winter. Skimmias are good for their evergreen foliage and their flowers and fruits. Larger-growing shrubs like* Elaeagnus pungens *'Maculata', variegated holly or aucuba will provide splashes of colour, and one of the dogwoods –* Cornus alba *or* C. sanguinea *cultivars – will give colourful stem colour. You also can create a miniature garden. Why not use perennials like* Iris unguicularis, Bergenia *'Bressingham Ruby',* Ophiopogon planiscapus *'Nigrescens',* Helleborus niger *or* Acorus gramineus *'Ogon' to give a combination of scented flowers, ruby red leaves, black foliage, classic white flowers and bright golden leaves. If you mix winter- and early spring-flowering bulbs in with some of the above, you should have a joyous winter! When making room for summer colour, some of the plants can be removed to a sheltered spot and fed and watered for one or two years, others can be planted in the garden, but even if there is no space for some, what price months of pleasure?*

YEAR-ROUND COLOUR AND LOW MAINTENANCE
THE EDENS' CONIFER, HEATHER AND SHRUB GARDEN

'I let it be known through the local newspapers that our nursery would give away a "free garden"....Sifting through the applications, I finally selected a garden that had been established for eight years. It belonged to George and Angela Edens and became known as (you have guessed it) the Garden of Edens!'

Visitors to Foggy Bottom often said how much they admired the combination of conifers and heathers, but that "obviously these plants were suitable only for the large garden". This prompted me to prove that dwarf conifers and heathers could be used together successfully, perhaps with a few appropriate dwarf shrubs, to create an attractive, low-maintenance, trouble-free garden in a limited space.

The Edens were quite happy for me and my helpers to dig up their small, unprepossessing front garden of shrubs and none-too-healthy roses around a rather tired looking lawn. The soil, which had been imported some years before, was a mixture of clay and sandy loam. Luckily we were able to add many bags of peat and compost to improve aeration and add some acidity to the soil. Because most plants are grown in peat or organic compost, it was helpful to add a generous handful in with each plant when it was put in. Finally, the soil's surface was covered with a heavy mulch of coarse-grade composted bark to help retain moisture during dry weather and keep down weeds.

Once established, the new garden took the Edens less than half an hour a week to maintain – with the exception of the lawn – and an eye had to be kept open for potential pests or disease.

A WORD ABOUT WEEDS AND MULCHING

Weeding is therapeutic to some, a real bore to others, but it has to be done if you are to stay in control of your garden, rather than the other way round. But anything you can do to minimize the spread of weeds in the first place is always worthwhile. You must give yourself a fair chance by first eliminating perennial weeds, but annual, seeding weeds are easier to control by mulching. Planting ground covers or whatever selection of plants is desired takes up space that would otherwise be colonized by weeds but if the space between the plants is covered by a mulch it will have many benefits. A mulch refers to a covering of material over the surface of the soil. It will generally be considered as organic material such as composted bark or leaf mould and should be put on to a depth of 2.5-5cm/1-2in. Mulching helps considerably to conserve water loss, benefiting both gardener and plants. Where weeds do grow, weeding "little and often" is the catch phrase to bear in mind, and if you can get to the young weeds well before they seed, you will save yourself a lot of time and frustration later. Easier said than done, as we know all too well at Foggy Bottom.

THE LOW-MAINTENANCE GARDEN looks good in spring, just a few months after being planted in autumn (opposite top)

NINE YEARS LATER, the same garden has filled out and is looking mature (opposite below)

A GROUP OF VERY DWARF conifers six years after planting (left top)

CONSISTING MOSTLY OF DWARF conifers and heathers, the garden, seen here in spring six years after planting, is relatively easy to maintain, requiring occasional pruning (left)

DESIGN FOR YEAR-ROUND COLOUR

THE EDENS' LOW-MAINTENANCE GARDEN is made up of conifers, heathers and dwarf shrubs. It shows how easily an average-sized, square or rectangular-shaped, suburban front garden can be transformed into an informal garden, allowing the plants to form a tapestry of colour, the structure being provided by upright conifers. Some non-flowering and carpeting alpines have been included to add variety. The number of these could be increased and bulbs could be added as well to give yet more colour at certain times of the year. Even though the garden is quite small (20x10m/60x30ft), a number of vistas and focal points have been possible, making it look much larger while imparting a feeling of intimacy to anyone strolling into the central area. Summer- and winter-flowering heathers, planted in groups of three to five of the same type, make use of different foliage and flower colours to create a pleasing patchwork effect. The conifers are integral to this patchwork scheme, their various shapes, forms and colours perfectly complementing the ground-covering heathers, which in turn set off the conifers. The plants are not difficult to grow. They tolerate most soils and should not require the addition of fertilizers unless the soil is impoverished. Remember, though, that summer-flowering heathers dislike lime. They can be substituted by dwarf shrubs or more winter-flowering heathers, many of which have coloured foliage.

BED A

1 *Abies balsamea* 'Hudsonia'
2 *Juniperus squamata* 'Pygmaea'
3 *Thuja plicata* 'Rogersii'
4 *Chamaecyparis lawsoniana* 'Pygmaea Argentea'
5 *Picea mariana* 'Nana'
6 *Chamaecyparis pisifera* 'Nana Aureovariegata'
7 *Chamaecyparis obtusa* 'Nana'
8 *Picea abies* 'Little Gem'
9 *Juniperus squamata* 'Blue Star'
10 *Thuja occidentalis* 'Danica'
11 *Chamaecyparis pisifera* 'Nana'
12 *Chamaecyparis obtusa* 'Nana Lutea'
13 *Cryptomeria japonica* 'Vilmoriniana'
14 *Juniperus communis* 'Compressa'
15 *Chamaecyparis lawsoniana* 'Minima Aurea'
16 *Chamaecyparis obtusa* 'Kosteri'
17 *Chamaecyparis obtusa mariesii*
18 *Thuja orientalis* 'Aurea Nana'
19 *Chamaecyparis lawsoniana* 'Minima Glauca'

BED B section A

1 *Juniperus × media* 'Gold Sovereign'
2 *Erica carnea* 'Pink Spangles'
3 *Arabis ferdinand-coburgii* 'Variegata'
4 *Thuja occidentalis* 'Rheingold'
5 *Erica cinerea* 'C.D. Eason'
6 *Juniperus horizontalis* 'Hughes'
7 *Erica × darleyensis* 'Darley Dale'
8 *Picea glauca* 'Albertiana Conica'
9 *Calluna vulgaris* 'Robert Chapman'
10 *Calluna vulgaris* 'Silver Queen'
11 *Calluna vulgaris* 'Darkness'
12 *Chamaecyparis lawsoniana* 'Ellwood's Gold'
13 *Dianthus* 'Garland'
14 *Ajuga reptans* 'Purpurea'
15 *Chamaecyparis pisifera* 'Boulevard'
16 *Juniperus squamata* 'Holger'

BED B section B

17 *Erica erigena* 'W.T. Rackliff'
18 *Acaena buchananii*
19 *Chamaecyparis pisifera* 'Plumosa Aurea Nana'
20 *Euonymus fortunei* 'Emerald Gaiety'
21 *Chamaecyparis pisifera* 'Filifera Nana'
22 *Erica carnea* 'King George'
23 *Thuja orientalis* 'Aurea Nana'
24 *Juniperus horizontalis* 'Glauca'
25 *Erica cinerea* 'Pink Ice'

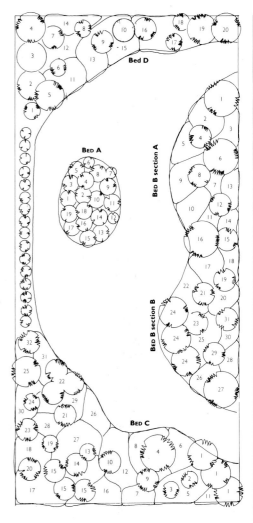

26 *Calluna vulgaris* 'Golden Carpet'
27 *Juniperus conferta* 'Blue Pacific'
28 *Sempervivum* 'Othello'
29 *Juniperus chinensis* 'Pyramidalis'
30 *Phlox subulata* 'Daniel's Cushion'
31 *Thuja occidentalis* 'Holmstrup'

BED C

1 *Juniperus sabina* 'Tamariscifolia'
2 *Thuja orientalis* 'Conspicua'
3 *Thuja occidentalis* 'Smaragd'
4 *Taxus baccata* 'Repens Aurea'
5 *Hebe pinguifolia* 'Pagei'
6 *Erica vagans* 'Mrs D.F. Maxwell'

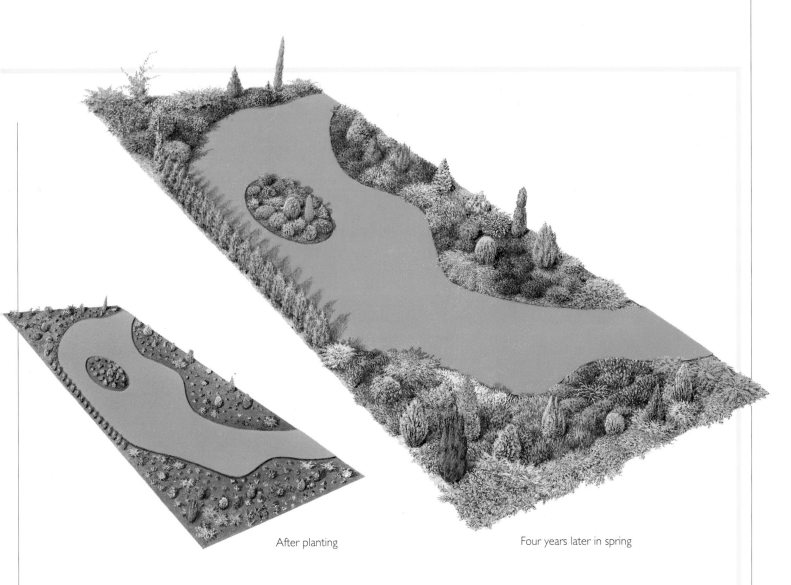

After planting

Four years later in spring

7 *Hedera helix* 'Chicago'
8 *Erica carnea* 'Myretoun Ruby'
9 *Chamaecyparis lawsoniana* 'Golden Pot'
10 *Chamaecyparis lawsoniana* 'Chilworth Silver'
11 *Hedera helix* 'Silver Queen'
12 *Erica carnea* 'Foxhollow'
13 *Chamaecyparis obtusa* 'Nana Gracilis'
14 *Thuja occidentalis* 'Sunkist'
15 *Juniperus horizontalis* 'Plumosa Youngstown'
16 *Potentilla fruticosa* 'Red Ace'
17 *Euonymus fortunei* 'Emerald 'n' Gold'
18 *Berberis thunbergii* 'Atropurpurea Nana'
19 *Juniperus scopulorum* 'Wichita Blue'
20 *Chamaecyparis lawsoniana* 'Little Spire'
21 *Chamaecyparis pisifera* 'Filifera Aurea'
22 *Juniperus squamata* 'Blue Carpet'
23 *Chamaecyparis lawsoniana* 'Moonshine'

24 *Cryptomeria japonica* 'Lobbii Nana'
25 *Taxus baccata* 'Semperaurea'
26 *Erica carnea* 'Springwood White'
27 *Erica × darleyensis* 'Furzey' (syn. 'Cherry Stevens')
28 *Calluna vulgaris* 'H.E. Beale'
29 *Erica vagans* 'Lyonesse'
30 *Erica × darleyensis* 'Arthur Johnson'
31 *Erica carnea* 'Vivellii'
32 *Juniperus × media* 'Sulphur Spray'

Bed D
1 *Taxus baccata* 'Standishii'
2 *Taxus baccata* 'Repandens'
3 *Elaeagnus pungens* 'Maculata'
4 *Juniperus × media* 'Old Gold'
5 *Tsuga canadensis* 'Jeddeloh'
6 *Chamaecyparis pisifera* 'Squarrosa Sulphurea'

7 *Juniperus scopulorum* 'Blue Heaven'
8 *Chamaecyparis pisifera* 'Filifera Aureovariegata'
9 *Juniperus squamata* 'Blue Swede'
10 *Choisya ternata* 'Sundance'
11 *Erica cinerea* 'Purple Beauty'
12 *Erica × darleyensis* 'Silberschmelze'
13 *Erica × darleyensis* 'Jack H. Brummage'
14 *Hedera helix* 'Silver Queen'
15 *Erica carnea* 'Myretoun Ruby'
16 *Thuja occidentalis* 'Smaragd'
17 *Thuja plicata* 'Stoneham Gold'
18 *Juniperus scopulorum* 'Skyrocket'
19 *Juniperus procumbens* 'Nana'
20 *Juniperus × media* 'Sulphur Spray'
21 *Erica carnea* 'Springwood Pink'
22 Hedge: *Thuja occidentalis* 'Smaragd'

MIXED PLANTING FOR YEAR-ROUND COLOUR
THE PUTTS' WINTER INTEREST GARDEN

'I had had my eye on the small front garden belonging to No. 2 Copeman Road for some time prior to my knocking on the front door late one dark October evening. It seemed the ideal size and it was in the perfect location for me to watch its progress, once, if I were allowed to, I had planted it for year-round interest – especially for colour in autumn and winter.'

My scheme for the Putts' garden, a very small plot, was to provide year-round interest using a wide range of plants. Maggie Putt was probably no different from many gardeners in cooler climates in not wanting too many large trees or shrubs in the front garden because they would block out too much light from the house.

The original garden was mainly laid down to grass, with a small central border containing a few conifers and heathers, and another narrow border just in front of the window. When we started digging, I left a small strip of grass in the centre of the plot, curving away from the front step. This feature divided the small area into two separate entities, immediately giving it a lot more interest. A pH test of the light, slightly sandy soil showed it to be neutral, so it probably would not suit most acid-loving subjects. I was to find out later, that it was also rather prone to drying out. We dug it over and prepared it by mixing in some planting compost.

We finished the two small beds with contrasting types of decorative mulch or surfacing. The larger, mixed bed received a 5-8cm/2-3in layer of composted bark that would help retain moisture in dry weather. The alpine, scree bed, appropriately enough, was finished with a 2.5-5cm/1-2in layer of fine shingle.

ONE YEAR AFTER planting, the bed in the foreground contains conifers interplanted with spring-flowering bulbs and alpines. The bed beyond is replete with flowers, fruits, stems and evergreen foliage (left)

THREE YEARS ON, the tiny garden is transformed and full of interest in autumn (below)

WINTER MAGIC goes right up to the front window on a frosty, mid-winter morning (opposite)

DESIGN FOR YEAR-ROUND INTEREST WITH WINTER HIGHLIGHTS

THE MIXED PLANTING for this 6x6m/20x20ft garden consists of over seventy species and varieties of hardy plants. The fairly dense planting allows the inclusion of a wide variety of carefully selected plants to ensure continuous colour, shape and interesting plant associations throughout the year. It manages without annuals, roses and trees for which there was just not enough space.

The smaller bed has been turned into a little scree garden, planted up with a selection of dwarf conifers, shrubs, alpines and dwarf bulbs, all more or less in proportion with one another. The larger bed, which nudges up against the similarly sized front garden next door, is crammed with a wide selection of mixed dwarf conifers, low-growing perennials, dwarf shrubs, a few larger shrubs and bulbs.

The few larger shrubs in the selection can all tolerate the fairly severe annual spring pruning that will be required to keep them in proportion with the limited size of the planting area. Few people, perhaps, would risk planting three dogwoods close together in such a restricted area, but they are included here for their year-round virtuosity. One has variegated summer leaves, the others green ones, but in winter they show stems of deep red, scarlet or orange-red. To ensure the best stem colour as well as to control their size, they must be pruned each late spring to within a few centimetres of the ground. Cultivated in this way, they seldom grow to more than 1.2m/4ft in a year. The other shrubs and the conifers will first need pruning in two or three years' time.

BED A

1 Picea pungens 'Globosa'
2. Chamaecyparis lawsoniana 'Pygmaea Argentea'
3. Juniperus × media 'Gold Sovereign'
4. Chamaecyparis obtusa 'Nana Gracilis'
5. Chamaecyparis thyoides 'Rubicon'
6. Chamaecyparis pisifera 'Nana'
7. Abies balsamea 'Hudsonia'
8. Juniperus communis 'Compressa'
9. Juniperus communis 'Green Carpet'
10. Chamaecyparis lawsoniana 'Minima Aurea'
11. Berberis thunbergii 'Bagatelle'
12. Hebe ochracea 'James Stirling'
13. Geranium sanguineum 'Alan Bloom'
14. Sempervivum arachnoideum 'Laggeri'
15. Campanula garganica 'Dickson's Gold'
16. Ajuga reptans 'Braunherz'
17. Raoulia australis
18. Campanula carpatica 'Bressingham White'
19. Sedum spathulifolium 'Capo Blanco'
20. Thymus 'Anderson's Gold'
21. Campanula turbinata 'Wheatley Violet'
22. Sisyrinchium 'May Snow'
23. Saxifraga oppositifolia
24. Saxifraga 'Winifred Bevington'
25. Geranium cinereum 'Laurence Flatman'
26. Thymus doerfleri 'Bressingham Pink'
27. Arabis ferdinandi-coburgii 'Variegata'
28. Armeria juniperifolia 'Bevan's Variety'
29. Viola 'Rebecca'

BED B

1 Viburnum tinus 'Eve Price'
2 Mahonia aquifolium 'Smaragd'
3 Viburnum davidii
4 Skimmia × confusa 'Kew Green'
5 Camellia 'Donation'
6 Hosta 'Ground Master'
7 Caryopteris × clandonensis 'Heavenly Blue'
8 Dicentra 'Snowflakes'
9 Pulmonaria saccharata 'Highdown'
10 Euonymus fortunei 'Emerald 'n' Gold'
11 Helleborus orientalis
12 Santolina incana
13 Thuja occidentalis 'Smaragd'
14 Juniperis squamata 'Blue Star'
15 Thymus 'Anderson's Gold'
16 Lamium galeobdolon 'Hermann's Pride'
17 Erica carnea 'Myretoun Ruby'

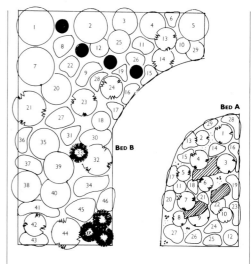

18 Hebe 'Emerald Green'
19 Lamium maculatum 'White Nancy'
20 Berberis thunbergii 'Dart's Red Lady'
21 Juniperus × media 'Sulphur Spray'
22 Bergenia 'Bressingham White'
23 Thuja occidentalis 'Rheingold'
24 Juniperus horizontalis 'Grey Pearl'
25 Spiraea japonica 'Golden Princess'
26 Primula 'Sue Jervis'
27 Iris pallida 'Argentea'
28 Fragaria 'Pink Panda'
29 Hebe 'Quicksilver'
30 Ophiopogon planiscapus 'Nigrescens'
31 Viola 'Clementina'
32 Microbiota decussata
33 Festuca glauca 'Blue Glow'
34 Coreopsis verticillata 'Golden Gain'
35 Cornus alba 'Sibirica Variegata'
36 Helleborus foetidus
37 Euonymus fortunei 'Sunspot'
38 Cornus alba 'Sibirica'
39 Cornus sanguinea 'Winter Flame'
40 Lavandula 'Hidcote Blue'
41 Bergenia 'Bressingham Ruby'
42 Thuja occidentalis 'Sunkist'
43 Erica carnea 'Pink Spangles'
44 Abies procera 'Glauca Prostrata'
45 Euphorbia myrsinites
46 Erica carnea 'Springwood White'
47 Acorus gramineus 'Ogon'

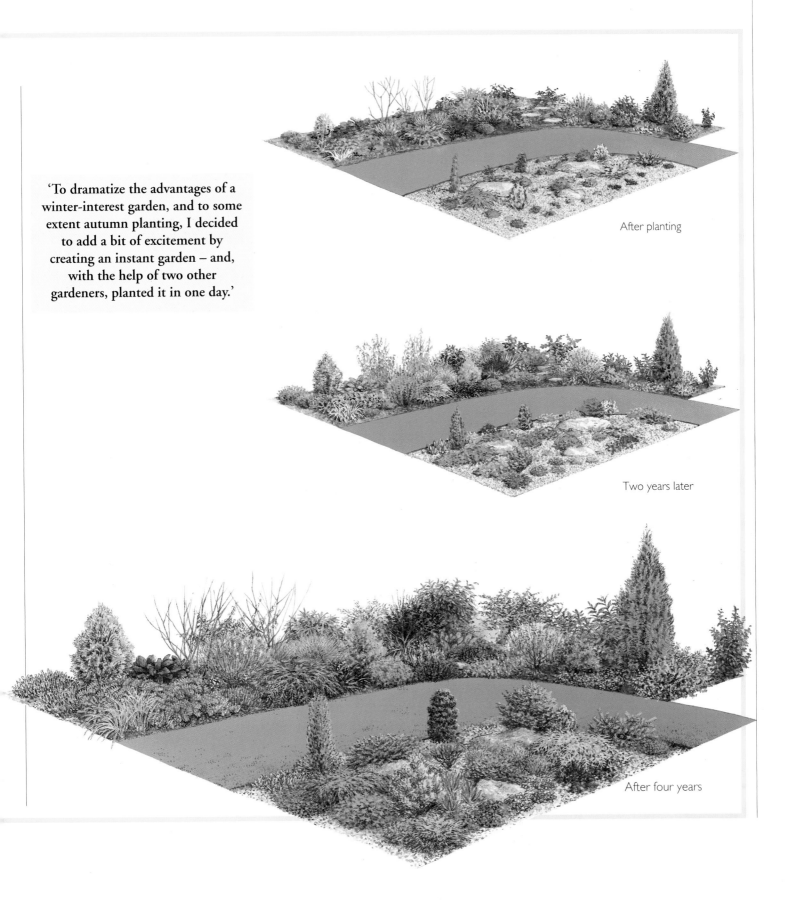

'To dramatize the advantages of a winter-interest garden, and to some extent autumn planting, I decided to add a bit of excitement by creating an instant garden – and, with the help of two other gardeners, planted it in one day.'

After planting

Two years later

After four years

A GARDEN WITHOUT A LAWN
THE JOHNSONS' DROUGHT-RESISTANT GARDEN

Bearing in mind that the soil in the Johnsons' tiny front garden was fairly well-drained and that water restrictions were regularly in force throughout the country, it seemed appropriate to consider a "drought-resistant" theme for this new venture. Since the Johnsons had already said how much they liked the small, shingle-covered scree bed that I had incorporated in their neighbours' front garden, I knew they would not object to a more Mediterranean look on their own patch.

I decided to completely strip off the grass and plant the entire garden with a blend of alpines, perennials and a few select trees, shrubs and conifers, covering up the earth with different shingles and small pebbles. This distinctive, interestingly patterned surface would enhance the dry theme and act as a mulch helping to retain valuable moisture during dry weather.

Colour, foliage, form and flower were to form the basis of this garden. The plan was to allow the plants freedom by not overcrowding them, although in some cases growth during the first couple of years was much more rapid than I had expected. The garden was also designed to illustrate how attractive plant associations can be made to work in a small area. If anything, perhaps because it was so different from most other front gardens, it excited more comment and interest from visitors and passers-by than the one I had already planted next door.

After removing the turf, we dug over the soil, adding some planting compost. Being dry and littered with builder's rubble the work was quite hard going in places. Before planting, I fashioned a curving "dry stream bed" through the centre of the garden simply by throwing some of the soil from the centre to the sides. This provided some slight undulation on the otherwise flat surface. Large flint stones, readily available in the locality, placed on the surface imitated rocks or pebbles, enhancing the dry stream bed effect.

When all is taken into consideration, this garden should take very little more time than would a grass lawn with a few shrubs scattered around it, if any, to keep it looking good. You have the cost of the plants, but you do not have the cost of the mower. And, if you choose carefully, the investment in the plants will pay great dividends in terms of interest and pleasure for many years to come, throughout both summer and winter months.

'I wanted to plant a completely different type of garden, something that, in view of all the dry summers we seemed to be getting, would be somewhat drought-resistant with a shingle surfacing. Next door to the Putts, the Johnsons' 6×6m/20×20ft plot seemed ideal. It would give a direct comparison of styles and would save me making two separate journeys to record and photograph the gardens' developments. It was to be planted in one day in early May, just two and a half years after we had planted the Putts garden.'

PERENNIALS AND GRASSES, planted in late spring, have already achieved results by the beginning of autumn. Geranium x riversleaianum *'Russell Prichard' and* Carex comans *'Bronze Form', with* Agapanthus *'Lilliput' to the right, create a pleasing association* (below)

LESS THAN A YEAR after being planted, the pulmonaria, (back left), and Chrysanthemopsis hosmariense (syn. Chrysanthemum hosmariense) (back right), are in flower in early spring. Bulbs planted in the autumn will heighten spring interest (left)

FORM AND TEXTURE provided by grasses and perennials in mid-autumn will last through most of the winter, as will the foliage interest of conifers and shrubs to the left of the bed, creating an arresting alternative to the common lawn (left)

DESIGN FOR HOT DRY SEASONS

THIS GARDEN IS PACKED with colour in summer. But in winter, apart from the brightly variegated leaves of *Elaeagnus pungen*s 'Maculata' and one or two conifers, the interest is sustained more in form and foliage. The wind and the frost on the grasses give movement and beauty and the contrast of light and shadow are more important because they are so much more noticeable during the duller months of the year.

Ornamental grasses, attractive the year round, add an architectural quality and look very natural on gravel, as do many of the sun-loving perennials such as the kniphofias and crocosmias. The perennials have been chosen to give as long a period of flowering as possible; plants such as *Geranium* 'Russell Prichard' and South African diascias fit the bill admirably. The few trees used in this garden are grown as shrubs; regular pruning – every year or every other year – keeps them small without making them look too stunted. *Acer negundo* 'Flamingo' will grow on most soils, providing a long period of interest with its attractively variegated summer leaves brightly splashed with pink. The area near the front of the garden is planted with dwarf alpine plants, their small size allowing a wider selection of interesting plants.

1 Pulmonaria saccharata 'Highdown'
2 Stachys byzantina (syn. olympica) 'Primrose Heron'
3 Platanus × acerifolia 'Mirkovec'
4 Miscanthus yakushimensis
5 Ajuga reptans 'Burgundy Glow'
6 Agapanthus campanulatus 'Isis'
7 Rosmarinus 'Jessop's Upright'
8 Chrysanthemopsis hosmariense
9 Crocosmia 'Jenny Bloom'
10 Festuca glauca 'Blue Glow'
11 Eryngium variifolium
12 Miscanthus sinensis 'Kleine Silberspinne'
13 Sempervivum arachnoideum 'Laggeri'
14 Heuchera 'Bressingham Bronze'
15 Hebe albicans 'Red Edge'
16 Diascia elegans
17 Molina caerulea 'Variegata'
18 Gaura lindheimeri
19 Geranium cinereum 'Ballerina'
20 Artemisia nutans (splendens)
21 Lysimachia nummularia 'Aurea'
22 Sisyrinchium macrodenum 'May Snow'
23 Ophiopogon planiscapus 'Nigrescens'
24 Crocosmia 'Spitfire'
25 Acer negundo 'Flamingo'
26 Carex testacea
27 Acorus gramineus 'Ogon'
28 Agapanthus campanulatus 'Albus'
29 Hakonechloa macra 'Alboaurea'
30 Kniphofia 'Little Maid'
31 Euphorbia wulfenii 'Humpty Dumpty'
32 Festuca cinerea 'Blue Seas'
33 Geranium 'Russell Prichard'
34 Artemisia schmidtiana 'Nana'
35 Lavandula stoechas 'Pedunculata'
36 Rhodiola rosea (syn. Sedum rosea)
37 Campanula carpatica 'Chewton Joy'
38 Sempervivum 'Royal Ruby'
39 Agapanthus 'Lilliput'
40 Geranium 'Russell Prichard'
41 Campanula turbinata 'Karl Foerster'
42 Geranium 'Ann Folkard'
43 Gypsophila 'Rose Beauty'
44 Mertensia asiatica
45 Hakonechloa macra 'Alboaurea'
46 Sagina subulata 'Aurea'
47 Origanum laevigatum 'Hopleys'

48 Campanula carpatica 'Chewton Joy'
49 Festuca cinerea 'Blue Seas'
50 Morisia monanthos 'Fred Hemmingway'
51 Hebe ochracea 'James Stirling'
52 Armeria maritima 'Dusseldorf Pride'
53 Sempervivum 'Cleveland Morgan'
54 Scabiosa graminifolia
55 Viola 'Molly Sanderson'
56 Campanula 'Dickson's Gold'
57 Hebe 'Caledonia'
58 Sisyrinchium macrodenum 'May Snow'
59 Eryngium bourgatii
60 Sempervivum 'Wollcott's Variety'
61 Pulsatilla vulgaris 'Rubra'
62 Pinus mugo 'Ophir'
63 Miscanthus sinensis 'Morning Light'
64 Carex buchananii
65 Geranium lancastrense 'Shepherd's Warning'
66 Scabiosa graminifolia 'Pincushion'
67 Euphorbia amygdaloides 'Rubra'
68 Dicentra 'Snowflakes'
69 Acorus gramineus 'Ogon'
70 Geranium 'Alan Bloom'
71 Artemisia lanata
72 Aster thompsonii 'Nanus'
73 Geranium × cantabrigiense 'Biokovo'
74 Kniphofia 'Bressingham Comet'
75 Stipa tenuifolia
76 Bergenia 'Bressingham Ruby'
77 Campanula poscharskyana 'Blauranke'
78 Lamium maculatum 'White Nancy'
79 Juniperus scopulorum 'Moonglow'
80 Deschampsia caespitosa 'Golden Dew'
81 Pulmonaria saccharata 'Leopard'
82 Elaeagnus pungens 'Maculata'
83 Ajuga reptans 'Burgundy Glow'
84 Carex 'Frosted Curls'
85 Hemerocallis 'Stella de Oro'

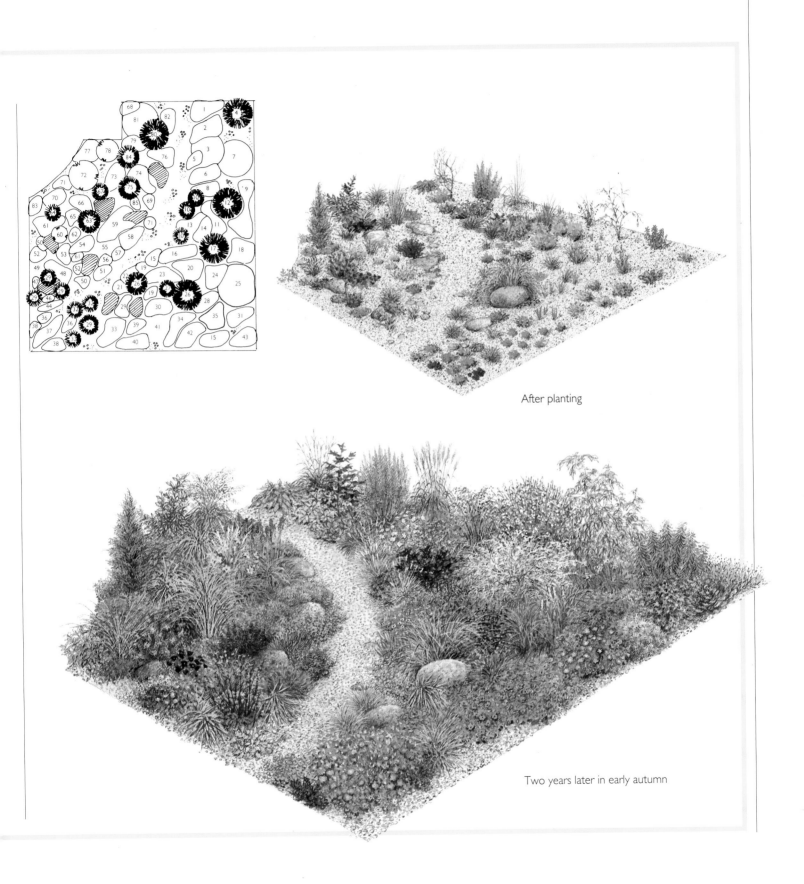

After planting

Two years later in early autumn

PLANTING ASSOCIATIONS FOR SEASONAL COLOUR

Perhaps the least understood or appreciated of plant associations are those that are most successful. One plant can make a striking specimen or show on its own, but if used in association with certain other plants it can produce some pleasing and often stunning scenes. The first thing to do when attempting a planting group is to decide in general terms what you require *before* you start planting.

Choice of plants and arrangements are very personal and the ideas shown on the next few pages can be used as guides as to what should work, but in fact the choice can be wider. There is undoubtedly less choice for winter than summer, so even if you wanted to, it would be difficult to create one-colour beds, although a white or silver winter arrangement using, for instance, a white-stemmed silver birch, *Rubus cockburnianus* or other with *Helleborus niger* and snowdrops could be quite stunning, particularly if given a light dusting of snow! But I think that most people like the idea of colour, and as some of the illustrations show, colour there is.

The seven plant associations shown here are for particular situations. There are associations for sun or shade, for walls and open beds, shrubs, trees, perennials, grasses, ferns, alpines and bulbs. Heathers, too, but no conifers, a conscious decision since they are featured so strongly elsewhere in the book, particularly in the Edens' garden (page 70). There are two illustrations each for autumn, winter and spring highlight, plus one featuring container-grown plants.

Each planting association has a note about when it would be best to plant for success. Climate, aspect and soil all have a bearing on what can safely be planted and the notes accompanying the illustrations are given as guidelines only.

All the plants have been grown in my own garden, and some of these associations used, too. I hope they will be a useful guide, but they also can be improved on. It is a good discipline to keep looking at new plants, new ideas, new associations to see how they might fit into your garden. Learn from both failures and successes!

AGAINST A DRAMATIC backdrop of Cortaderia selloana *'Pumila', the so-called dwarf pampas grass, and* Stipa calamagrostis, *a group of plants provides plenty of colour just outside the back door at Foggy Bottom on a sunny day in late winter.* Blue Chamaecyparis lawsonia *and fiery* Cornus sanguinea *'Winter Flame' front a prostrate, light yellow cedar* (right)

CONTAINERS FOR THE "QUIET" SEASON

For patios, terraces, courtyards or even balconies there are innumerable plants which can give autumn, winter or early spring interest. The selection in this group of containers offers year-round diversity and colour by including deciduous and evergreen shrubs and a few perennials and grasses. Of the plants illustrated here, the following will all do well in shady or semi-shady positions: *Hedera colchica* 'Dentata Variegata', *Acer palmatum* 'Senkaki', *Viburnum tinus* 'Eve Price', *Camellia* 'Donation' and the mixed planting of *Skimmia reevesiana*, *Euonymus fortunei* 'Emerald 'n' Gold' and *Sarcococca* x *confusa*. The remainder all prefer sun. Although all of these plants, except *Choisya ternata* 'Sundance' which must be put under cover during frosty periods, can stand light autumn frosts, the camellia, viburnum and prunus require protection during prolonged winter frost in exposed situations (see page 38). Other plants such as dwarf conifers and a wide range of evergreen shrubs, including heaths and heathers, can be equally successful and attractive, even more so when used in combinations.

Best potted from spring to late summer are: *Carex comans* 'Bronze Form', *Choisya ternata* 'Sundance', *Prunus incisa* 'Kojo-no-mai and *Camellia* 'Donation'. But all could be potted in early autumn if given the protection of a cold greenhouse. Advice for protecting containerized plants over winter is given on page 69.

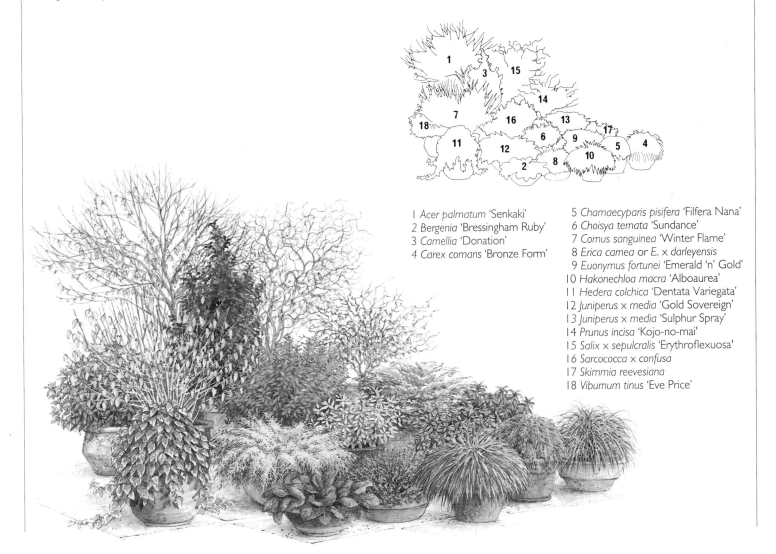

1 *Acer palmatum* 'Senkaki'
2 *Bergenia* 'Bressingham Ruby'
3 *Camellia* 'Donation'
4 *Carex comans* 'Bronze Form'
5 *Chamaecyparis pisifera* 'Filfera Nana'
6 *Choisya ternata* 'Sundance'
7 *Cornus sanguinea* 'Winter Flame'
8 *Erica carnea* or *E.* x *darleyensis*
9 *Euonymus fortunei* 'Emerald 'n' Gold'
10 *Hakonechloa macra* 'Alboaurea'
11 *Hedera colchica* 'Dentata Variegata'
12 *Juniperus* x *media* 'Gold Sovereign'
13 *Juniperus* x *media* 'Sulphur Spray'
14 *Prunus incisa* 'Kojo-no-mai'
15 *Salix* x *sepulcralis* 'Erythroflexuosa'
16 *Sarcococca* x *confusa*
17 *Skimmia reevesiana*
18 *Viburnum tinus* 'Eve Price'

SCENTED COLOUR FOR A SUNNY WALL

Offering year-round variety, this packed planting for a sun-facing wall is particularly colourful from late summer to early spring. The wall is covered by a thick mantle of lush evergreen foliage. At the base, the linear, silver-backed, dark green leaves of the rosemary contrast with the grey of *Santolina incana,* whose yellow summer flowers will have just finished, and the rush-like foliage of *Iris unguicularis.* With autumn come the beautiful pink flower heads of *Nerine bowdenii,* and the iris may produce a few of its charming and fragrant, light blue blooms although most appear in the middle of winter. Most visually striking is the free-fruiting pyracantha. Catkins decorate the garrya for weeks from early winter until early spring and are followed by the fragrant flowers of *Abelio-*

phyllum distichum (white forsythia) and of *Prunus mume* 'Beni-shidare', which are pink.

In summer the wall is less interesting but the evergreens show well and the rosemary has blue flowers in late spring, the pyracantha bears white flowers in early summer and the santolina yellow ones in late summer.

Apart from the self-clinging hedera, the taller shrubs may need tying to wall supports or brackets as well as pruning regularly to keep them neat. Widening the 1m/3ft bed would allow for finer touches to be added.

With the exception of the pyracantha, hedera and abeliophyllum, these plants are best planted from spring to early autumn. Use container-grown plants.

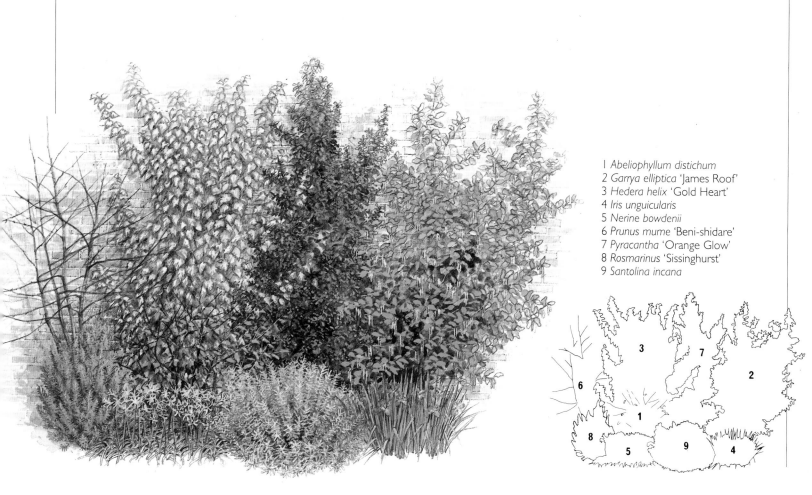

1 *Abeliophyllum distichum*
2 *Garrya elliptica* 'James Roof'
3 *Hedera helix* 'Gold Heart'
4 *Iris unguicularis*
5 *Nerine bowdenii*
6 *Prunus mume* 'Beni-shidare'
7 *Pyracantha* 'Orange Glow'
8 *Rosmarinus* 'Sissinghurst'
9 *Santolina incana*

A MIXED BED FOR AUTUMN, WINTER AND SPRING

This simple planting, shown here in mid-autumn, guarantees startling colour throughout autumn, winter and spring. It centres on one of the shrubby dogwoods, *Cornus sanguinea* 'Winter Flame', which is surrounded by a mixture of heaths, perennials and two types of bulb (snowdrop and winter aconite) that will play an important role in late winter and early spring. The bed should be sited in full sun, or at least in a position that receives sun for no less than half of the day and the plants will do best on any reasonable soil that becomes neither too wet nor too dry.

In autumn, the violet flowers of *Liriope muscari* and the bright blue foliage of *Festuca glauca* 'Blue Glow' contrast superbly with the startling transformation taking place in the dying leaves of the dogwood. Slower to change than most other dogwoods, these turn from pale green to pale yellow then gold, often finishing with russet hues. The naked, upright stems – yellow-orange at the base with fiery crimson tips – retain their striking colour, which deepens with frost, through the quiet season. They should be pruned almost to the ground in mid-spring. The pulmonaria's silver-spotted leaves will die away in winter to be renewed in early spring along with deep blue flowers which contrast with the bronze-green foliage and carmine blooms of *Erica carnea* 'Vivellii' which will flower until late spring. The snowdrops will have their perfect foil in the narrow, strap-like, black leaves of the evergreen ophiopogon which in turn contrast all year round with the silver-blue grassy foliage of the *Festuca glauca* 'Blue Glow'. It is against these that the bright, cheery yellow of the winter aconites will show up. In summer the grouping will be primarily sober shades of green. More summer colour could be introduced, perhaps by using a hardy geranium such as 'Russell Prichard' which flowers from early summer until well into autumn.

All the plants mentioned here can be planted from pots from spring to late autumn. Snowdrops can be planted "in the green" as divisions after winter flowers have finished, or as bulbs in late summer.

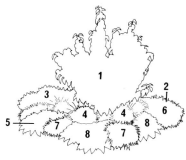

1 *Cornus sanguinea* 'Winter Flame'
2 *Eranthus hyemalis* (not in flower)
3 *Erica carnea* 'Vivellii'
4 *Festuca glauca* 'Blue Glow'
5 *Galanthus nivalis* (not in flower)
6 *Liriope muscari*
7 *Ophiopogon planiscapus* 'Nigrescens'
8 *Pulmonaria* 'Lewis Palmer'

CHEERING UP A SEMI-SHADY WALL

Based on foliage plants this planting, shown here in late winter/early spring, remains attractive all year, but it has particular appeal for autumn, winter and early spring. It consists of deciduous and evergreen shrubs and herbaceous perennials, including one evergreen fern, which represents an often neglected group of plants that adapt well to shade. The recommended width of the bed at the base of the wall is 1.2m/4ft, which allows for root development of the shrubs and space for the lower-growing plants.

The large-leaved hederas are invaluable for such a situation, and *Hedera colchica* 'Dentata Variegata' has year-round appeal. It may need some help to cling in its first year or two and tones well with the mahonia's dark green, behind which it may eventually grow, and in autumn, when 'Charity' opens its fragrant light yellow flowers, this will make a pleasing association.

The winter-flowering deciduous chimonanthus is a much treasured plant in winter once established. It usually bears enough waxy pendulous flowers for cutting. Climbing among its branches, but possibly also requiring supports on the wall, is the evergreen *Clematis cirrhosa* which has crimson-purple spotted flowers during mild periods from autumn to early spring. Classed as tender, it often seems hardy in well-sheltered spots.

Closer to the ground, the spreading dwarf evergreen *Sarcococca humilis* has shiny, dark green, box-like leaves and a profusion of small but delicately fragrant flowers in late winter. The pointed, dark green marbled leaves of the *Arum italicum pictum* emerge in autumn to last until spring. The mass of white flowers of *Pulmonaria* 'Sissinghurst White' last for weeks from early spring, while in summer it has hairy silver-spotted mid-green leaves. Arching above is *Dryopteris erythrosora* (Japanese wild fern), one of the most attractive of the hardy ferns. Its bronze-tinged fronds have a metallic sheen and are likely to be damaged only in severe winters. The rounded leathery leaves and sugar-pink spring flowers of *Bergenia* 'Baby Doll' complete the base planting.

The *Clematis cirrhosa* and possibly the *Dryopteris erythrosora* are best planted in the spring to late summer period, the remainder of the plants from spring to late autumn.

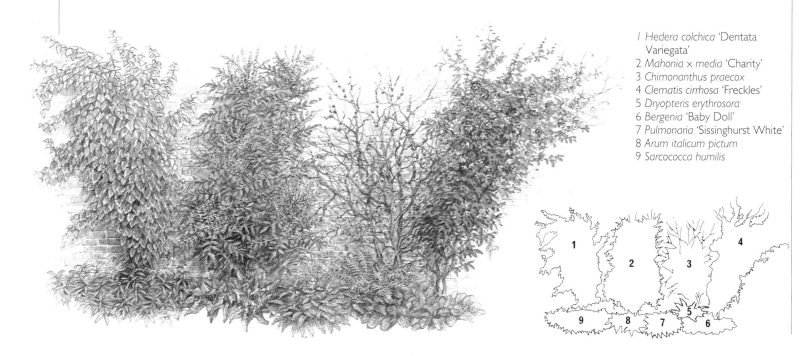

1 *Hedera colchica* 'Dentata Variegata'
2 *Mahonia × media* 'Charity'
3 *Chimonanthus praecox*
4 *Clematis cirrhosa* 'Freckles'
5 *Dryopteris erythrosora*
6 *Bergenia* 'Baby Doll'
7 *Pulmonaria* 'Sissinghurst White'
8 *Arum italicum pictum*
9 *Sarcococca humilis*

FOLIAGE AND BARK FOR WINTER

Silver and white are the predominant colours in this startling winter foliage combination. *Betula utilis* 'Jacquemontii' is one of the smallest of the silver birches, but will grow, perhaps over fifteen years, to over 10m/30ft. Its even branching habit and the bright silvery bark on its main stems and branches make it a superb specimen. Pruning away the lower branches reveals more of the trunk and lets light onto the plants growing beneath. The ones used here will thrive in all but the driest situations, but are best planted before the tree becomes large and competes for food and moisture. Mix in plenty of compost when you plant them and mulch well.

The black-leaved *Ophiopogon planiscapus* 'Nigrescens' contrasts impressively with the silver birch's trunk and the *Lamium maculatum* 'White Nancy'. Nestling against the trunk, *Epimedium pinnatum colchicum* provides evergreen cover for the summer and winter and bears yellow flowers in spring. There are a few other bergenias with red winter foliage, but 'Bressingham Ruby' appears to be tougher than most and turns from green to ruby-red in autumn reverting to green as the deep crimson flowers arrive in spring. Evergreen *Iris foetidissima* 'Variegata' reinforces the white-silver theme whilst sun-loving *Euphorbia myrsinites* with its long, prostrate, segmented blue stems contributes year-round foliage and large yellow spring flowers. Yet more colour could be added by planting crocus, snowdrops and other spring-flowering bulbs. All items can be planted from spring until autumn, particularly if they are pot grown.

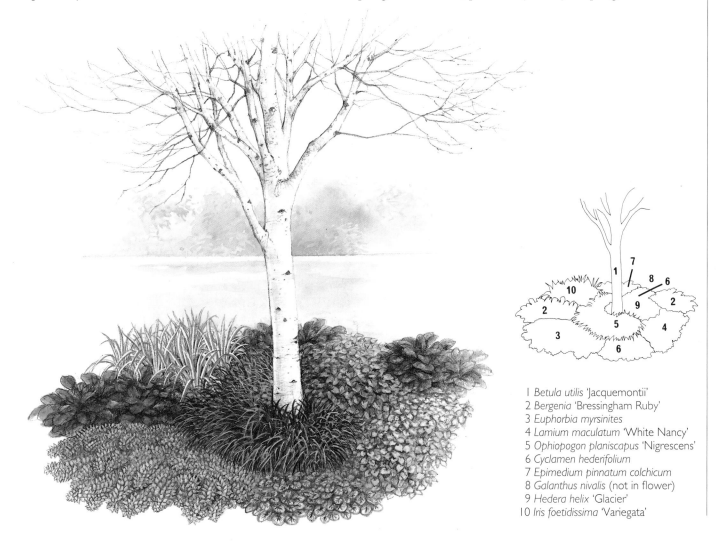

1 *Betula utilis* 'Jacquemontii'
2 *Bergenia* 'Bressingham Ruby'
3 *Euphorbia myrsinites*
4 *Lamium maculatum* 'White Nancy'
5 *Ophiopogon planiscapus* 'Nigrescens'
6 *Cyclamen hederifolium*
7 *Epimedium pinnatum colchicum*
8 *Galanthus nivalis* (not in flower)
9 *Hedera helix* 'Glacier'
10 *Iris foetidissima* 'Variegata'

WINTER STEMS, SUMMER COLOUR

This planting features a fast-growing willow – *Salix × sepulcralis* 'Erythroflexuosa' – as its centrepiece. None too remarkable in summer it can become a striking feature in winter if pruned to the ground each spring. It will take quite a few frosts to dislodge the last of the willow's leaves, but eventually these will all go, exposing spectacular curling, twisted, orange, brown and maroon stems. It grows well on all soils that are not too dry as do the other two shrubs. *Cornus alba* 'Kesselringii' is a black-stemmed dogwood which bears purplish black and green leaves in spring, summer and autumn. Quite different is the bramble *Rubus cockburnianus* 'Golden Vale' with arching stems that carry bright yellow leaves in summer which show up as ghostly white in winter. If this is placed on the shady side of the willow it is less likely to get scorched in very hot weather.

Winter aconites, snowdrops and the Christmas rose contrast well with the black stems of the dogwood. Additional colour for spring could be easily provided by a blue-flowered pulmonaria or *Muscari armeniacum.*

Pruning back the stems of the willow, dogwood and bramble should be done when shoots start to develop in mid-spring, the willow being a little earlier than the others. The later you prune the shorter the year's growth will be, but the willow will have grown to between 1.2-1.5m/4-5ft by midsummer and will be creating some shade. Summer foliage colour will be provided by the bramble and the dogwood, the pink flowers of the ground cover *Fragaria* 'Pink Panda', which last all summer, looking particularly good against the bramble. Additional summer colour could be added by planting something like a shrubby potentilla such as 'Goldfinger' or 'Kobold', yellow-flowered varieties, which could be placed close to the dogwood, but which would also complement the yellow of the bramble. The blue flowers of an *Aster amellus* would also set the bramble off.

All these plants can be planted from spring through autumn if they are purchased in containers. If available, snowdrops and aconites are best planted "in the green" as divisions after flowering, or they can go in as bulbs in autumn.

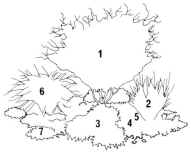

1 *Salix × sepulcralis* 'Erythroflexuosa'
2 *Cornus alba* 'Kesselringii'
3 *Helleborus niger*
4 *Eranthis hyemalis*
5 *Galanthus nivalis*
6 *Rubus cockburnianus* 'Golden Vale'
7 *Fragaria* 'Pink Panda'

BRIGHTENING UP A SEMI-SHADY SPOT IN EARLY SPRING

In this colourful planting, a witch hazel (hamamelis) provides the focal point. The witch hazels are among the aristocrats of shrubs yet could be more widely grown than they are. There are many selections to choose from, but those with yellow flowers are perhaps the most striking since their winter or early spring flowers light up the gloom more noticeably than those with darker orange or red ones. Contrary to general opinion, they do not have to have acid soil to succeed, but they do dislike thin, chalky soils. They grow well in sun or light shade, requiring a soil that is moist, yet well-drained and friable and to which ample humus in the form of well-rotted compost, leaf mould or composted bark is added.

For late winter and early spring, the yellow-flowered *H. mollis* 'Pallida' is one of the best. It has a spreading habit and fragrant, strap-like petals. The flowering period is determined by climate to some extent and in milder areas may be over before spring, in which case *H. × intermedia* 'Primavera' or *H. × i.* 'Westerstede', the latter among the latest, are worth looking for.

Any plants growing beneath the low-branching stems – here a selection of bulbs and perennials with winter and early spring interest – should make their show when the leaves are absent.

Snowdrops can surround the main stem, perhaps interspersed with *Chionodoxa luciliae* which has light blue, white-centred flowers, or the deeper blue flowers of *C. sardensis*. The nodding rose-pink flowers of *Helleborus orientalis* 'Winter Cheer' last for several weeks from late winter, depending upon the climate; there are many other choices among named or selected seedlings. Flowering at the same time is *Narcissus* 'February Silver', a dwarf cyclamineus daffodil with yellow trumpets and open, creamy white petals. Once the bulbs have finished flowering, they will not be seen until the following spring, but *Pulmonaria saccharata* 'Leopard' has leaves which are arguably the most spotted of all the lungworts and have summer-long attraction. In early spring its leaves take second place to the deep rosy-red flowers which continue for weeks. The *Dicentra* 'Snowflakes' will soon give a show of pendulous white lockets for many months. If space allows, this would be an ideal bed for a blue-leaved or variegated hosta for extra summer interest.

Snowdrops can be planted "in the green" as divisions after winter flowers have finished, or as with the chionodoxa bulbs in late summer. All the other plants can be planted from pots from spring to late autumn.

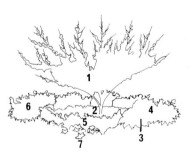

1 *Hamamelis mollis* 'Pallida'
2 *Chionodoxa lucilliae*
3 *Galanthus nivalis* (not in flower)
4 *Pulmonaria saccharata* 'Leopard'
5 *Narcissus* 'February Silver'
6 *Helleborus orientalis* 'Winter Cheer'
7 *Dicentra* 'Snowflakes'

DIRECTORY OF PLANTS

FOR AUTUMN, WINTER AND EARLY SPRING

Zones and Planting

This directory introduces hundreds of versatile plants that can add colour and interest to your garden in autumn, winter and spring as well as at other times of the year.

Most of the plants listed are hardy and adaptable to most soils, except where stated. A soil-testing kit will tell you whether your soil is acid or alkaline.

Unless you already have good, friable, fertile soil, you will probably need to dig thoroughly to a depth of 35-45cm/14-18in. Mix in organic material such as well-rotted compost or manure to help to retain moisture in light soils and aerate heavier types.

Before planting soak plants in their containers – for an hour or two if the compost is dry or a few minutes if it is moist. Make the hole deep enough so that the level of the soil in the container is just below the surface of the soil. Add some fertilizer – a slow-release type for conifers, shrubs or trees, but a quicker-acting, balanced one for perennials. Fill in with soil, firming gently on heavier soils but more firmly on lighter soils, and water in. Do not compact the soil too much. Mulch to retain moisture, protect new roots from frost and keep down weeds (page 71). Water regularly until established, for a tree at least a year.

Trees
Make the planting hole two or three times the width and depth of the rootball; on heavier soils break up the clay at the bottom. Provide a sturdy stake for anything over 90cm/3ft and use proper tree ties. Leave a circular ridge of soil just beyond the circumference of the rootball and fill with a good mulch.

Shrubs
Mulch around newly planted shrubs, particularly shallow- or fibrous-rooted ones, and then annually or every two years. Apply a general, slow-release fertilizer in spring if shrubs lack colour or vigour. Protect susceptible new shrubs from wind or frosts with close-woven or shade netting. More details on pruning etc. are given in the Directory section.

Conifers
Most conifers can be planted slightly deeper than the level of the soil in the container or the rootball. If the roots of containerized plants are congested or curled, prune away some and tease out others. Staking may be necessary for large specimens (1.8-3m/6-10ft high) but for abundant foliage a tripod of three stakes may be preferable. Although containerized conifers may be planted with care at any time of year, the beginning of autumn and towards the end of spring are best. If planting in a lawn leave a circle of soil at least 60cm/2ft in diameter.

Larger specimens or those grown in open ground, particularly if they have abundant foliage, will benefit when moving from one or two protective measures: use an anti-desiccant foliage spray or surround with a close-meshed shading material or netting, supported by four stakes. Many conifers benefit from pruning and shaping, but this must not be so overdone as to lose the natural shape of the tree. Upright conifers may be damaged by heavy falls of snow, so knock it off as soon as it builds up.

Perennials
Hardy perennials can be planted at almost any time unless soil conditions are poor and as long as they receive appropriate care – water in summer, drainage in winter. Tender plants must be planted in spring. Open-ground plants must be planted as soon after arrival as possible or temporarily in moist compost, sand or peat. If they arrive dry, soak them. Most early spring-flowering perennials are best divided and planted in late summer and early autumn, autumn-flowering ones are usually divided in early spring. Advice on protecting tender perennials in winter appears on page 38.

Grasses
Few open-ground grasses take kindly to being planted in late autumn and winter but most hardy containerized types can be planted at any time as long as they do not go into waterlogged conditions in winter.

Ferns
Hardy ferns appreciate a friable soil and, according to variety or species, sun, shade, moisture or good drainage; some can tolerate quite dry positions.

Heaths and Heathers
Summer-flowering heathers need an acid soil, although *Erica vagans* (Cornish heath) tolerates neutral soil. Winter-flowering heathers are all lime-tolerant and are the most valuable for winter colour. All heathers benefit from a generous 4-6cm/1½-2in mulch of medium- or large-grade composted bark.

Alpines
Many plants classed as alpines grow quite happily in any sunny spot with reasonable drainage. Many hardy alpines require well-drained soil which does not dry out in summer; consult specialist books for advice on creating an alpine or scree bed.

Bulbs
Seldom succeeding in heavy, wet soils, most bulbs prefer reasonably good drainage. Those flowering in winter and early spring must be planted in autumn, although if you can get them, both aconites and snowdrops are best planted after flowering in spring. Bulbs should go in places that are not likely to be disturbed.

Hardiness Zones
The plant hardiness zones given in this book are determined by the United States Department of Agriculture. They are based on the average annual minimum winter temperature for each zone. Climate variation is much less in the British Isles: Zone 7 covers the eastern Scottish Highlands; Zone 8 includes most of inland and eastern Britain and Ireland; and zone 9 includes the western coastal areas of Britain and Ireland. Each plant in the directories has been allocated a zone range within which it is likely to thrive. Within any one zone, however, several microclimates can occur, and other factors, such as site, aspect and soil, may also affect a plant's growth.

Key to Symbols
- ☼ full sun
- ☀ semi-shade
- ✹ shade
- ☐ dry soil
- ◪ moist soil
- ■ well-drained soil
- ⊕ alkaline soil
- ⊖ acid soil
- ☆ most soils
- ★ fertile soil
- ★ humus-rich soil

TREES DIRECTORY

THERE IS SOMETHING MAGICAL about the thought of planting trees, and for today's smaller gardens there are many suitable ones, including many that can be pruned regularly to keep within bounds. Listed here are some which give good autumn colour, show off outstanding bark or stems or bear early spring flowers. Most, with the exception of the silver birches, are small or slow-growing.

H: Approximate height after 10 years
W: Approximate width after 10 years
F: Months in flower
Z: Relevant hardiness zone(s)

Foliage colour in autumn

Alnus glutinosa 'Aurea'

Betula nigra 'Heritage'

ACER Maple

Deciduous. For more detail, see Shrubs Directory, page 96.☼ ✹ ■ ☆
A. griseum. Paper-bark maple. Year-round attraction. Slowly flaking, brown bark revealing orange-brown beneath. Leaves split into three smaller leaflets, often colouring well in late autumn. Very slow-growing. H3-4m/10-13ft, W1.5-2m/5-6ft. Z5. ☆
A. hersii (syn. *A. grosseri hersii*). Snake-bark maple. Small, shapely tree for autumn colour. Smooth, grey-green, silver-streaked or marbled bark. Broadly ovate leaves. On mature specimens pendulous greenish flowers in spring and greenish yellow fruits in autumn. Of similar value are *A. davidii* and its cultivars 'George Forrest' and 'Ernest Wilson', *A. rufinerve* and *A. capillipes*. H4-5m/13-15ft, W2-4m/6-13ft. Z7. ☆
A. pensylvanicum 'Erythrocladum'. Beautiful selection. In winter bright coral-pink young stems striped silvery white. Golden-yellow leaves in autumn. Can be difficult; dislikes chalk soils and is slow on all others. H3-4m/10-13ft, W2.5m/8ft. Z4-7.
A. rubrum 'Red Sunset'. Slender, vigorous. Glowing, scarlet leaves in autumn. 'Schlesingeri', eye-catching with similar colours. Both H8-10m/26-33ft, W5m/16ft. Z3-9.

ALNUS Alder

Deciduous. ☼ ◪ ☆
A. incana 'Aurea'. Slow-growing, golden-leaved, attractive in winter with orange-red young wood, reddish catkins fading to yellow followed by yellow shoots and leaves, which soon fade to light green, in spring. H5-6m/16-20ft, W2-2.5m/6-8ft. Z3.
A. glutinosa 'Aurea'. Faster growing than *A. incana*. Long pendulous catkins, brighter yellow leaves, the colour maintained well into summer. H10m/33ft, W3-4m/10-13ft. Z3.

AMELANCHIER

Small deciduous trees or shrubs with spring flowers and autumn colour. Neutral to acid soil. ☼ ✹ ■ ◪
A. lamarckii. Suckering, multi-stemmed shrub or tree. Massed stems with erect panicles of pure white flowers in spring, edible, blackish-purple fruits in autumn. Leaves turn orange to red in autumn. H5-7m/16-23ft, W4-5m/13-16ft. F3-4. Z4.

BETULA Birch

Deciduous. Most of the birches eventually make medium or relatively large trees but are so attractive for both foliage and bark that they warrant inclusion in any garden large enough. Relatively surface-rooting, reducing the availability of moisture to nearby plants. Mostly slower-growing types are listed here, all slower on drier soils. ☼ ◪ ■
B. costata. Eventually large but slow for some years. Stout trunk and branches with flaking creamy white bark revealing brownish inner skin. Good golden-yellow autumn colour. H7-10m/23-33ft, W4-5m/13-16ft. Z4.
B. nigra. River birch. From North America, grows well in damper ground. Brown peeling bark with age, brownish stems but variable from seed. The selection 'Heritage' is striking with glossy, dark green leaves, peeling bark revealing white then pinkish brown stems. Golden autumn colour. H6-10m/20-30ft, W4-5m/13-16ft. Z4.
B. pendula. Common silver birch.

Betula utilis jacquemontii

Pleasing white bark and graceful branching habit with pendulous twiggy branchlets. Usually good autumn colour, if brief. Does well on drier soils. 6-10m/20-33ft, W5-6m/16-20ft. Z4.

B. utilis jacquemontii. Perhaps the most striking white-barked birch, relatively slow-growing. Peeling bark, glossy green leaves, attractive catkins. The form '**Jermyns**' is more vigorous but quite stunning. H6-8m/20-26ft, W4-5m/13-16ft. Z5.

COTONEASTER

Several deciduous or evergreen forms can eventually make small trees. Often classed under the *watereri* hybrids these are mostly semi-evergreen, carrying abundant red or orange fruits into winter. Single stems are trained upright and side shoots removed until a trunk develops. Deciduous ☼; evergreen ☼ ☀; all ■

C. × watereri '**John Waterer**'. Clusters of red fruits show well against deep green leaves. H5-6m/16-20ft, W4-5m/13-16ft. F6. Z7.

CRATAEGUS Hawthorn, thorn
Deciduous. ☼ ☆

C. crus-galli. Cockspur thorn. Attractive small North American tree. Thorny branches, show of white flowers in late spring, abundance of persistent crimson fruits in autumn. Shiny dark green leaves turn yellow and red in autumn. H6m/20ft, W4m/13ft. F4. Z3-7.

C. monogyna. Common hawthorn or May. Attractive hedgerow or ornamental tree, tough and thorny. Good foliage takes clipping well. Fragrant white flowers in late spring, the mature tree generally well endowed with crimson autumn fruits. Several selections with cultivar names. H6-8m/20-26ft, W6-8m/20-26ft. F4-5. Z4-7.

Betula pendula

C. prunifolia. One of the most garden-worthy of the thorns. Small, round-headed tree with rich glossy green leaves, white flowers. Good display of deep red fruits and matching crimson autumn leaves, both falling early. H6m/20ft, W6m/20ft. F4. Z4-7.

EUCALYPTUS Gum tree
Evergreen trees with aromatic foliage. Need shelter. ☼ ★ ■

E. niphophila. Snow gum. One of the hardiest, most ornamental, and one of the few that can be classed as a small tree. Leathery, oval juvenile grey-green leaves become grey, narrow and lance-shaped as plant matures. Main stem usually develops

Eucalyptus niphophila

Liquidambar styraciflua 'Worplesdon'

a "lean", the smooth grey-green bark flaking to reveal creamy white, green and brown. Grown from seed, like all the gums, it is best planted as a young pot-grown plant so early roots quickly establish to support the rapid growth. The foliage is excellent for flower arranging and if cut back by hand or frost vigorous new shoots will emerge from the base. H10m/33ft, W5-6m/16-20ft. Z7-9.

LIQUIDAMBAR
L. styraciflua. Sweet gum tree. Eventually quite a large tree of upright habit. Often spectacular crimson autumn colours and corky bark. Seed-raised plants are unreliable for autumn colour, so look for selected cultivars, particularly for cooler climates. All prefer reasonably fertile soils which are not too dry and colour best in sunny position. Variable but expect H8m/26ft, W4m/13ft. ☼ ◪ ★

'**Worplesdon**', reliable for good display of rich crimson autumn colour and is slow enough for a

smaller garden. '**Lane Roberts**', also good. Both H7-10m/23-30ft, W5-8m/16-26ft. Z7.

MALUS Crab apple
Some of the most ornamental of flowering and fruiting deciduous trees, many suitable for the small garden. Any soil that is not too dry or wet. ☼ ☆

M. '**Evereste**'. Good value small tree, large white flowers, red in bud, deep green foliage, profusion of orange-yellow fruits in autumn. H 5-7m/16-23ft, W4-5m/13-16ft. F3-4. Z5.

M. '**Golden Hornet**'. White flowers followed by spectacular show of rounded, bright yellow crab apples well into winter. Can get straggly with age. H6-8m/20-26ft, W5-6m/16-20ft. F3-4. Z5.

M. '**John Downie**'. Considered the best of fruiting crabs. White flowers and attractive, comparatively large yellow and red fruits of good flavour, the best for making jelly. H8m/26ft, W6-7m/20-23ft. Z5.

M. '**Red Jade**'. Weeping shrub or

Malus 'Evereste'

Prunus serrula

small tree, bright green leaves, pink and white flowers, abundance of crimson fruits lasting into winter. H4-5m/13-16ft, W5-6m/16-20ft. Z5.

M. sargentii. Shrub-like, Japanese species of great merit making a rounded bush profusely covered in white, golden-anthered blossom in spring and abundant cherry-like, bright red fruits in autumn. H3-4m/10-13ft, W3-5m/10-16ft. Z5.

Populus alba 'Richardii'

POPULUS Poplar
Very fast-growing, deciduous trees with extensive roots. ☼ ▣ ■ ✭

P. alba '**Richardii**'. Slower-growing form of the white poplar. Maple-like leaves with white undersides, bright golden-yellow upper sides – a brilliant combination, especially where wind can ruffle the foliage giving flashes of silver and gold, the colour enhanced in autumn. Grey-green winter stems, eventually suckering habit. Can be pruned as a shrub or small tree. H8m/26ft, W4m/13ft. Z5.

PRUNUS Cherry
Large family of deciduous or evergreen trees and shrubs, the latter described in the Shrubs Directory, page 108. Some wonderful spring-flowering trees, including the Japanese cherries. Those listed here give good autumn colour, winter bark or early spring blossom. Deciduous ☼; evergreen ☼ ☀; all ☆

P. incisa. See Shrubs Directory, page 108.
P. maackii. Manchurican cherry.

Medium-sized, deciduous. Small, white flowers in spring, cinnamon-brown bark which flakes with age. Usually grown from seed and therefore variable; look for '**Amber Beauty**', a small-headed selection with amber bark. Excellent winter interest. H10-12m/33-40ft, W3-4m/10-13ft. F3-4. Z6.

P. serrula. The polished mahogany trunk and stems with peeling bark are a beautiful sight through winter, although the white spring flowers are of little note and autumn leaf colour is disappointing. H5m/16ft, W3m/10ft. F4. Z5-9.

P. subhirtella '**Autumnalis**'. Succession of small white flowers during mild periods from late autumn to early spring. Prolonged cold weather may inhibit flowers, giving more in spring. Eventually of some size with a broad, spreading habit and attractively pendulous branchlets. H5m/16ft. W5m/16ft. F11-4. Z4-8.

RHUS See Shrubs Directory, page 109.
SALIX See Shrubs Directory, page 111.

SORBUS Mountain ash
A great number of attractive, fruiting, deciduous trees many of which also have good autumn foliage colour. Smaller, shrubbier types are mentioned in the Shrubs Directory, page 112. ☼ ☀ ■ ▣ ✭

S. aucuparia. Mountain ash or rowan. Relatively small trees, growing widely throughout Britain. The pinnate leaves turn tints of orange-red and yellow in autumn. White, early-summer flowers are quickly followed by often heavy bunches of orange or red fruits. Many selections exist with somewhat different habits and fruits from crimson and red to orange and yellow. H5m/16ft, W2-3m/6-10ft. F5. Z3-9.

S. hupehensis. Large, prettily divided, almost bluish green leaves which turn reddish in autumn. Pendulous clusters of pink-tinged, white fruits often lasting well into winter. Selections with pink fruits such as var. *obtusa*, '**Rosea**' and '**Rufus**' are worth looking for. H5m/16ft, W3m/10ft. F5. Z3-8.

SHRUBS DIRECTORY

SHRUBS ARE EVERGREEN OR DECIDUOUS woody plants which do not die down to the ground in winter. Some shrubs remain dwarf, growing to only a few centimetres, while others can grow into small trees.

To provide interest and colour in autumn, winter and early spring there are innumerable shrubs to choose from. The problem in making this selection was not what to include, but what to leave out. Among the plants I have listed here are some first class but little known shrubs which will help to provide form, colour, flower, fruit, foliage and fragrance for all sizes of garden. Generally speaking, plants that are sited in sunny positions, as long as these are tolerated by the plant, give the best autumn colour.

The approximate size of each shrub after ten years is given at the end of its description. Remember that geographical situation, climate, soil conditions and pruning affect size, flowering times and sometimes even a plant's appearance. The hardiness zones allocated to each shrub are even more approximate, with local micro-climates, as well as protection provided by sunny walls, providing an exception to every rule.

H: Approximate height after 10 years
W: Approximate width after 10 years
F: Months in flower
Z: Relevant hardiness zone(s)

Acer palmatum 'Osakazuki' in autumn

Abeliophyllum distichum

ABELIA
Bright-foliaged evergreen or deciduous shrubs, late flowers. Best grown in a warm, sheltered position. Trim or prune as required in spring. ☼ ■ ☆
A. x *grandiflora* 'Francis Mason'. Yellow-variegated leaves, fragrant, blush-pink flowers. H1.2-1.5m/4-5ft, W1.2-1.5m/4-5ft. F7-10. Z7-9.

ABELIOPHYLLUM White forsythia
Deciduous. ☼ ■ ☆
A. distichum. Masses of small, almond-scented, blush-white flowers in early spring. Prune old wood after flowering, as for forsythia. Grow against sun-facing wall in cool climates. H90-150cm/3-5ft, W90-150cm/3-5ft. F3; occ. F8-9. Z5-9.

ACER Maple
Deciduous or evergreen. Some slow-growing species can be considered shrubs, others can be kept shrubby by annual pruning. Many produce best colour on neutral to acid soil; most Japanese maples tolerate non-acid soils if thoroughly prepared with humus or leaf mould. ☼ ❋ ■ ☆
A. japonicum. Japanese maple. Many excellent selections with coloured foliage and good autumn colour: 'Atropurpureum', purple; 'Aureum', light yellow; 'Bloodgood', reddish purple. All H1.2-1.5m/4-5ft, W90-120cm/3-4ft. F4-5. Z6-8.
Dissectum Group. Cascading branches, fern-like leaves. 'Atropurpureum', 'Garnet' and 'Inaba Shidare', purples. 'Viridis', bright green leaves, yellow, orange or red in autumn. Average H1.2-1.5m/4-5ft, W1.5-2.1m/5-7ft. Z5-8. 'Osakazuki', small, green-leaved tree, brilliant crimson in autumn. H2.1-3m/7-10ft, W1.8-2.1m/6-7ft. F4-5. Z5-8. 'Senkaki' (syn. 'Sango Kaku'), golden autumn leaves, coral-red stems. H1.8-2.4m/6-8ft, W1.2-1.5m/4-5ft. F4-5. Z5-8. 'Shishigashira', slow-growing tree, greenish stems, golden-yellow leaves with red tints. Good

Acer palmatum 'Garnet'

Berberis thunbergii 'Dart's Red Lady'

Aucuba japonica 'Crotonifolia'

container plant. H90-150cm/3-5ft, W60-90cm/2-3ft. Z5-8.

ARBUTUS Strawberry tree
Evergreen shrubs or small trees. ☼ ■ ☆
A. x andrachnoides. Hybrid similar to *A. unedo*, striking, cinnamon-red, peeling bark on older trees. H2.1-2.4m/ 7-8ft, W1.8-2.1m/6-7ft. F10. Z8-9.
A. unedo. Dark green leaves, clusters of white or pink autumn flowers, occasionally edible, orange or red fruits. 'Rubra', reddish flowers. Tolerates alkaline and seaside conditions. H2.1-2.4m/7-8ft, W1.8-2.1m/6-7ft. F10. Z7-9.
☼ ❋ ⊖

Arbutus unedo 'Rubra'

ARONIA Chokeberry
Flowering, fruiting, deciduous. Control size by hard pruning in late winter. Neutral or acid soil. ☼ ❋ ■ ☆
A. arbutifolia 'Erecta'. Upright, narrow habit, red autumn leaves, red fruits, white flowers. H1.8- 2.1m/6-7ft, W2.1-3m/7-10ft. F4-5. Z5-9.
A. melanocarpa 'Brilliant'. Red leaves and black fruits in autumn. H1.2-1.5m/4-5ft, W2.1m/7ft. F4-5. Z4-9.

ARTEMISIA Wormwood
Some retain their silvery foliage into winter, depending on climate. ☼ ■
A. 'Powis Castle'. Silver-grey mound. H90-120cm/3-4ft, W90-120cm/3-4ft. Z5-8.

Artemisia 'Powis Castle'

AUCUBA Spotted laurel
Evergreen. ☼ ❋ ❋ ☆
A. japonica. Japanese aucuba. A male plant, bearing panicles of purple-petalled flowers in spring, is necessary for females to set the red fruit. Easily pruned. 'Crotonifolia' (female) and 'Mr Goldstrike' (male), gold-speckled, green leaves. 'Picturata' (female), broad leaves, central gold splash. 'Variegata' (female), yellow-dotted leaves. H2.1-3m/7-10ft, W2.1-3m/7-10ft. F4-5. Z7-11.

BERBERIS Barberry
Wide range of deciduous and evergreen shrubs, many with good autumn colour and fruits. Some thorny types good for hedging. Most withstand pruning. Hardiness varies. Most ☼ ❋ ☆
B. × *carminea.* Deciduous. Thorny, arching branches. Good autumn foliage, startlingly colourful fruits. H1.2-1.8m/4-6ft, W1.2-1.8m/4-6ft. F4-5. Z6-9.
B. darwinii. Dense, evergreen. Arching branches, spiny, dark leaves. Racemes of orange-yellow flowers in late spring and often another flush in late autumn, plum-coloured fruit. Prune, if required, after flowering. H1.5- 2.1m/5-7ft, W1.2-1.5m/4-5ft. F4-5; occ. F9-10. Z7-9.

B. × *media* 'Red Jewel'. Dense, semi-evergreen. Thorny stems, bronze-purple leaves with brilliant autumn colours. H90-120cm/3-4ft, W90-120cm/3-4ft. F4-5. Z6-8.
B. × *ottawensis* 'Superba'. Vigorous, deciduous. Deep purple leaves, yellow flowers, sparse fruits. Prune hard every few years. H1.5-1.8m/5-6ft, W1.2-1.5m/4-5ft. F5. Z5-9. ■
B. thunbergii. Deciduous. Yellow spring flowers, excellent autumn colour, bright red fruits. Lightly prune taller cultivars every few years, or prune to the ground in early spring to rejuvenate. Purple-leaved forms need sun to colour well. H90-240cm/3-8ft, W90-240cm/3-8ft. F3-5. Z5-8. 'Atropurpurea Nana', compact bush, purple summer leaves, red fruits in autumn. H45cm/18in, W45cm/18in. F4-5. Z5-8. 'Dart's Red Lady', bushy, black-purple leaves turning crimson in late autumn. H60-75cm/24-30in, W75-90cm/30-36in. F4-5. Z5-8. 'Golden Ring', gold-margined reddy purple leaves, good autumn colour, red fruits. H1.5-1.8m/5-6ft, W1.2-1.5m/4-5ft. F4-5. Z5-8.

BUDDLEJA Butterfly bush
Deciduous, semi-evergreen or evergreen. Interesting form in winter,

Buddleja 'Pink Delight'

Camellia × williamsii 'Donation'

particularly if seed heads are left on. Many flower into autumn, especially if pruned late. Prune annually in late winter or early spring to within 15-30cm/6-12in of ground. Wide variety of shapes and sizes. All F7-9. Z5-9. ☼ ■ ☆

BUXUS Box, boxwood
Slow-growing, evergreen, many with coloured or variegated foliage. ☼ ✴ ✴ ■ ☆
B. sempervirens. Common box. Used for low hedging and topiary. '**Aurea Pendula**', broad; pendulous branches, leaves splashed creamy yellow. H90-120cm/3-4ft, W90cm/3ft. Z7-8. '**Elegantissima**', dwarf, dense, rounded; leaves margined creamy white. H45-60cm/18-24in, W30-45cm/12-18in. Z7-8. '**Latifolia Maculata**', rounded; large leaves splashed golden-yellow, bright yellow new shoots. H45-60cm/18-24in, W30-45cm/12-18in.

CALLICARPA
Deciduous. Startling, mostly lilac or purple, glossy fruit, abundant when three or more shrubs are planted together. Prune lightly annually for shape. Prefers a slightly alkaline soil. ☼ ✴ ■ ☆
C. bodinieri '**Profusion**'. The best for

cooler climates, fruits regularly as an individual, abundant pale violet berries. H1.5-1.8m/5-6ft, W90-120cm/3-4ft. F6-8. Z6-9.

CAMELLIA
Evergreen. Glossy green leaves, exotic flowers in late winter and spring. Ideal for pots or under glass. Best protected by a north or west wall or high shade in northern climates, but will not flower well in deep shade. Prune lightly for shape after flowering. Neutral or acid soil. ◩ ■
C. japonica. Japanese or common camellia. H1.5-1.8m/5-6ft, W90-120cm/3-4ft, but eventually, according to cultivar, much larger. F2-3. Most Z8-9.
C. sasanqua. Scented flowers in autumn and winter, likely to get frosted in cooler climates, eventually larger and more spreading than *C. japonica.* F10-2. Z7-9.
C. × williamsii. Blooms from an early age. '**Donation**', double, rich pink flowers. Both H1.8-2.1m/6-7ft, W1.5m/5ft. F2-5. Z7-9.

CARYOPTERIS Bluebeard, blue spiraea
Aromatic, deciduous, mostly dwarf or low-growing shrubs. Late bright blue flowers. Prune each spring to 10-

15cm/4-6in from the ground. In cold climates, grow against a sun-facing wall. Plant in spring. ☼ ■
C. x clandonensis '**Arthur Simmonds**'. Hybrid. Grey-green leaves, profuse bright blue flowers. '**Heavenly Blue**', more compact, deep blue flowers. '**Worcester Gold**', greeny gold leaves, bright blue flowers. All H60-75cm/24-30in, W60-75cm/24-30in. F8-9. Z6-9.

CERATOSTIGMA Hardy plumbago
The two species mentioned behave like perennials in cool, temperate climates. Both late-flowering, bright blue, periwinkle-like flowers. ☼ ■
C. plumbaginoides. Dwarf, spreading. Leaves turn reddish in autumn, contrasting with blue flowers. H15-20cm/6-8in, W30cm/1ft. F7-9. Z5-8.
C. willmottianum. Twiggy, upright stems, bright deep blue flowers. Prune to ground in late spring. H60-75cm/24-30in, W60-75cm/24-30in. F8-10. Z5-9.

CHAENOMELES
Japonica, flowering quince
Mostly very hardy, often sharply thorned, deciduous shrubs used as ground cover and on walls. Early, apple-blossom-type, crimson, pink, orange or white flowers often on bare

branches, often followed by bitter, apple-like fruits. Prune as required immediately after flowering. For wall shrubs, cut back all the previous season's growth to original shoot; late-summer pruning of fresh growth helps flower buds swell and exposes flowers. ☼ ✴ ✴ ☆
C. japonica. Japanese quince. Low-growing, spreading, dense, thorny stems, profuse bright scarlet, orange or red flowers before leaves on year-old wood. Yellow-green fruit. H60-90cm/2-3ft, W1.2-1.8m/4-6ft. F3-4. Z5-9.
C. speciosa. Common flowering quince. More upright than *C. japonica,* broad, spreading, densely congested, thorny branches. Scarlet flowers often in late autumn, especially if against a sunny wall, continue through winter, becoming more plentiful in spring, some even appearing in summer. H1.2-1.8m/4-6ft, W90-120cm/3-4ft. F11-4. Z5-9.
C. x superba. Hybrids of *C. japonica* and *C. speciosa.* Mounded or prostrate. All H1.2-1.5m/4-5ft, W1.5-1.8m/5-6ft. F12-4. Z5-9.

CHIMONANTHUS Wintersweet
Deciduous or evergreen, winter-flowering. ☼ ■ ☆
C. praecox (syn. *C. fragrans*). Upright, twiggy bush transformed by sweetly fragrant, waxy, bell-like, purple-centred yellow flowers. Excellent for cutting. Can be trained on walls. Prune to tidy, after flowering. '**Grandiflorus**', less fragrant but larger, clear yellow flowers. '**Luteus**', clear yellow, waxy flowers. All H1.5-1.8m/5-6ft, W1.2-1.5m/4-5ft. F12-1. Z6-9.

CHOISYA Mexican orange blossom
Evergreen foliage, fragrant flowers. Give shelter, particularly for young plants. Good patio or wall plants. Prune lightly in early summer, cut back harder if foliage is severely damaged by frosts. ☼ ■ ☆

C. 'Aztec Pearl'. Hybrid. Clusters of pink buds open to white flowers in late spring, lasting several weeks. Usually another show in late summer. H1.5-1.8m/5-6ft, W1.2-1.5m/4-5ft. F5-6; occ. F8. Z7-9.

C. ternata. Dense, slow-growing. Glossy leaves, white flower clusters in spring, sometimes autumn. H1.5-1.8m/5-6ft, W1.2-1.5m/4-5ft. F5-6; occ. F9. Z7-9. 'Sundance', compact, bright yellow, year-round foliage, flowers on older plants. Ideal for patios but protect from frost. H1.2-1.5m/4-5ft, W90-120cm/3-4ft. F5-6; occ. F9. Z7-9.

CLEMATIS

A few of these climbers have winter interest. Shade roots. ☼ ☀ ☀ ■ ☆

C. armandii. First of spring-flowering clematis. Dark green, ribbed leaves, masses of fragrant flowers. Sunny, sheltered wall or fence. 'Apple Blossom', flushed pink sepals. Prune only every few years to restrict growth. H5m/16ft, W5m/16ft. F4. Z7-9.

C. cirrhosa. Flowers through winter in mild areas. Pendent, bell-shaped, creamy yellow flowers. The form *balearica* has purple-spotted, yellow flowers, but is less hardy. 'Freckles', larger, crimson-purple splashed

Clematis tangutica

Cornus mas 'Aurea'

flowers. Provide shelter in cold areas. Perfect for conservatories. All H3m/10ft, W3m/10ft. F10-3. Z8-9.

C. orientalis. Vigorous. Finely dissected leaves and pendent, subtly fragrant, long-lasting, yellow flowers followed by fluffy seed heads. H2.1-3m/7-10ft, W2.1-3m/7-10ft. F8-9. Z6-9. 'Bill Mackenzie', larger-flowered, silvery seed heads. Both H5-6m/16-20ft, W5-6m/16-20ft. F8-9. Z6-9.

C. tangutica. Similar to *C. orientalis.* H5-6m/16-20ft, W5-6m/16-20ft. F7-9. Z6-9.

CORNUS Cornel, dogwood

Deciduous. Some of the most spectacular shrubs for winter stem colour, but many also provide autumn leaf colour, fruits and early flower. ☼ ☀ ■ ☆

C. alba. Siberian dogwood. Many good selections. Vigorous, spreading, with erect, flexible, dark red stems. Good autumn leaf colour, clusters of white flowers on two-year old wood, small, bluish white fruit. If grown for winter stems, site in sunny, open position and cut to the ground annually in late spring. Good beside water. 'Aurea', year-round appeal, bright yellow leaves particularly in autumn, deep red stems.

'Kesselringii', black-purple stems, purplish leaves, crimson-purple in autumn. 'Sibirica', the brightest red stems, green leaves, shorter and less vigorous than the species. 'Sibirica Variegata' and 'Elegantissima', variegated white and green leaves, red-tinged in autumn, red stems. Average H1.5-1.8m/5-6ft, W1.5-1.8m/5-6ft. F5-6. Z3-9.

C. mas. Cornelian cherry. Naked branches burst into yellow flower from buds that gradually swell through autumn and winter. Good against a dark background. 'Aurea', suffused yellow leaves in spring, greening in summer. Both H2.4-3m/8-10ft, W2.4-3m/8-10ft. F2. Z4-8. 'Elegantissima' and 'Variegata', slower-growing but offer summer interest, too. H1.8-2.4m/6-8ft, W1.2-1.5m/4-5ft. F3. Z6-8. ☀

C. sanguinea 'Winter Flame' (syn. 'Winter Beauty'). Superb golden-yellow autumn leaf colour for several weeks, stems are fiery orange-yellow at base and pink and red at tips. Prune as for *C. alba* cultivars. H1.5-1.8m/5-6ft, W1.5-1.8m/5-6ft. F5-6. Z4-8.

C. stolonifera 'Flaviramea'. Similar to *C. alba* but more erect, green leaves and yellowish green stems. H2.4-3m/8-10ft, W1.8-2.4m/6-8ft. F6-7. Z3-8. 'Kelsey's Dwarf', low-growing, narrow, upright stems and bright green, finely ribbed leaves. Good autumn colour. H60-75cm/24-30in, W60-90cm/2-3ft. Z3-8. 'White Gold', variegated gold leaves which turn creamy white. H1.5m/5ft, W1.5m/5ft. F6-7. Z3-8.

CORYLOPSIS Fragrant winterhazel

Choice deciduous shrubs. Upright or spreading habit, delicate, pendent yellow flowers on bare stems in early spring. Shelter from cold winds and spring frosts, away from early morning sun. Prune only to thin congested branches, immediately after flowering. Will grow on alkaline

Cornus stolonifera 'Flaviramea'

loam with peat or leaf mould added. ☀ ■ ◩ ☆

C. pauciflora. Dwarf, bushy, spreading habit, scented primrose-yellow flowers. H1.2-1.5m/4-5ft, W1.2-1.5m/4-5ft. F3. Z6-8.

C. spicata. Spreading, irregularly branched, long spikes of pale yellow, cowslip-scented flowers. H1.2-1.8m/4-6ft, W1.5-1.8m/5-6ft. F3. Z6-8.

CORYLUS Hazel, filbert

Easily grown deciduous shrubs or small trees, some with long-lasting, coloured foliage, all with catkins for winter and early spring interest. ☼ ☀ ■ ☆ ☆

C. avellana 'Contorta'. Corkscrew hazel or 'Harry Lauder's walking stick'. Contorted stems show well in winter, particularly if smaller branches are removed. Generously draped with long yellow catkins in spring which develop through winter. Remove suckers from base each winter. H1.8-2.4m/6-8ft, W1.8-2.4m/6-8ft. F2-3. Z5-9.

COTINUS Smoke bush, Venetian sumach

Deciduous, providing foliage colour well into autumn. Prune in late spring just before new growth

Cotinus 'Grace'

appears. To keep plants compact, prune annually to within 15-60cm/6-24in of the ground, at expense of flowers; for rejuvenation thin out a few older stems. ☼ ❋ ■ □ ☆

C. coggygria. Venetian sumach. Bushy. Oval, light green leaves turning yellow or red in autumn. Older plants, especially in open situations, are smothered in fluffy, beige-pink panicles in late summer, fading to beige or grey. H2.4-3m/8-10ft, W2.4-3m/8-10ft. F8. Z5-9. 'Foliis Purpureis', 'Notcutt's Variety' and 'Royal Purple', dark purple, oval leaves, colour best in full sun, going green in shade. All H2.4-3m/8-10ft, W2.4-3m/8-10ft. F8. Z5-9.

C. 'Grace'. Hybrid. Tall, open bush, distinct, soft red-purple leaves through which the sun glows. Imposing pinkish inflorescences. H3-3.6m/10-12ft, W2.4-3m/8-10ft. F8. Z5-9.

COTONEASTER

Extensive genera of invaluable deciduous and evergreen shrubs, ranging from dwarf to tree-like proportions. Most have white flowers, often spectacular displays of various coloured fruit in late summer and autumn, which attract birds. Prune only to shape or control vigour, in early spring. Many so-called evergreens are deciduous in

cold regions. Deciduous ☼; evergreen ☼ ❋; all ☆

C. 'Coral Beauty'. Excellent ground cover, taller in shade, dark, dense evergreen leaves, white flowers, coral-red fruit. H30-60cm/1-2ft, W1.5-1.8m/5-6ft. F5. Z6-8.

C. frigidus 'Cornubia'. Vigorous, deciduous or semi-evergreen, eventually a small tree. Large, dark green leaves, profuse bright scarlet fruit weighing branches down in autumn and winter. H3-4.5m/10-15ft, W2.4-3m/8-10ft. F6-7. Z7-8.

C. divaricatus. Dense, multi-stemmed, deciduous, spreading bush. Small, dark, glossy, green leaves turn crimson-red in autumn. Deep red fruit. Good as hedging. H1.5-1.8m/5-6ft, W1.5-1.8m/5-6ft. F6-7. Z5-8.

C. 'Exburiensis'. Tall, wide-spreading, semi-evergreen shrub or small tree, arching branches, profuse, pendulous clusters of pale yellow fruit well into winter. Very similar is *C.* 'Rothschildianus'. H2.4-3m/8-10ft, W2.4-3m/8-10ft. F6-7. Z6-8.

C. franchetii. Graceful, semi-evergreen shrub, arching branches, glossy, sage-green leaves, ovoid, orange-scarlet fruit. The form *sternianus* is similar but has round fruit and green foliage, silvery grey

Cotoneaster franchetti

beneath. Good autumn colour. Both H1.8-2.4m/6-8ft, W1.8-2.4m/6-8ft. F6-7. Z7-9.

C. horizontalis. Low, spreading shrub, often wall-trained where its herringbone branching pattern is effective. Dark green leaves, red in autumn, and bright red fruits. 'Variegatus', slower-growing, creamy white leaf margins, bright in summer, brighter in autumn with reddish tinges, less plentiful red fruit. Both H60-75cm/24-30in, W1.2-1.5m/4-5ft. F6-7. Z5-8.

C. 'Hybridus Pendulus'. Free-fruiting deciduous shrub, large, glossy, green leaves, graceful, open habit. Mostly trained up or grafted onto a stem with long, pendulous branches. Laden with bright red fruit in autumn. Non-grafted. H45-60cm/18-24in, W1.5-1.8m/5-6ft. F6-7. Z6-8.

C. simonsii. Vigorous, erect semi-evergreen used for hedging. Glossy leaves, white flowers, large scarlet fruit well into winter. H1.8-2.4m/6-8ft, W1.5-1.8m/5-6ft. F6-7. Z6-9.

C. 'Streibs Findling'. Controllable creeping habit, small-leaved, red fruit in autumn. Try on a bank, over a rock or a wall. H10-15cm/4-6in, W90-120cm/3-4ft. F6-7. Z6-8.

DAPHNE

Slow-growing, deciduous and evergreen shrubs, most with sweetly fragrant flowers. Often easier than reputed, requiring little or no pruning. Acccording to species flower in clusters or around stem, some from late winter until autumn, most in spring and summer. Poisonous berries, from golden-yellow to red and black. Add well-rotted leaf mould or peat when planting. Most ☼ ■ ◩ ☆; some ❋

D. blagayana. Evergreen, open, spreading habit. Terminal clusters of highly scented, creamy white flowers. Not easy but worth the effort. Peaty soil. H30-45cm/12-18in, W45-

Daphne mezereum

60cm/18-24in. F3-5. Z7-9. ☼ ◩

D. mezereum. Striking, deciduous shrub, stiff, upright branches. Fragrant, rosy purple flowers on naked stems. 'Alba', white flowers, yellow fruits. 'Rubra', deep purple-red flowers. All H75-90cm/30-36in, W60-75cm/24-30in. F2-3. Z5-8.

D. odora. Winter daphne. Bushy evergreen. Large, dark green leaves, terminal clusters of scented, rosy pink flowers. Shelter from frosts and cold winds. 'Aureomarginata', hardier; pale-centred rosy purple flowers, leaves margined creamy yellow. Both H60-90cm/2-3ft, W60-90cm/2-3ft. F2-5. Z7-9.

ELAEAGNUS Oleaster

Evergreen foliage, excellent for cutting for winter decoration. Dislikes thin, chalky soil. Resistant to heat and drought. ☼ ■ ☆ ☆

E. x ebbingei. Evergreen hybrid. Fast-growing, wind-resistant, useful for background. Dark, glossy green leaves, silver underneath, small, fragrant autumn flowers, orange fruits in spring. Hybrid and cultivars listed can suffer defoliation in bad winters, but usually recover. Prune dead wood and also to encourage bushiness, cutting back by a third or a half in spring. Slow-growing, variegated sports include 'Gilt Edge', deep green leaves irregularly

Euonymus planipes

margined golden-yellow, sometimes slow to establish; and '**Limelight**', central splashes of greeny yellow and gold. Both excellent for winter colour. All H1.8-2.4m/6-8ft, W1.5-1.8m/5-6ft. F10-11. Z6-9.

E. pungens. Cultivars include some of the best winter colour evergreens. Fragrant, silvery white flowers, seldom fruiting in cool climates. Prune as required in spring. Cut away any green shoots from variegated types at once. H1.8-2.4m/6-8ft, W1.8-2.4m/6-8ft. F9-11. Z6-10. '**Dicksonii**' (syn. 'Aurea'), slow, with mostly yellow leaves, the rest margined irregularly golden-yellow. H1.2-1.5m/4-5ft, W90-150cm/3-5ft. F9-11. Z7-10. '**Goldrim**', more reliable, dark green leaves banded with gold. '**Maculata**', dark green leaves splashed liberally with gold. '**Variegata**', similar to the species but with a thin, pale yellow leaf margin. All H1.8-2.4m/6-8ft, W1.8-2.4m/6-8ft. F9-11. Z7-10.

ELSHOLTZIA

Deciduous. ☼ ■

E. stauntonii. Interesting, mint-like, clump-forming sub-shrub. Erect stems, narrow, aromatic leaves and thin spikes of late, tiny, purplish flowers. Cut back to ground in late winter. H1m/39in, W60cm/2ft. F10-11. Z5-7.

EUONYMUS

Variable shrubs and small trees, evergreen grown for colourful foliage, deciduous types for fruits and autumn leaf colour. Several plants together required for cross-pollination. Good on chalk soil. ☼ ☀ ■ ☆

E. alatus. Deciduous, upright, later spreading habit. Dark green leaves, in favourable climates brilliant crimson in autumn. H1.8-2.4m/6-8ft, W1.5-1.8m/5-6ft. F5. Z4-9. '**Compactus**', smaller but colours equally brilliant, ideal low hedge. H1.2-1.5m/4-5ft, W1.5m/5ft. F5. Z4-9.

E. europaeus. Common spindle. Large shrub or small tree, unnoticed until autumn when bearing dangling red fruits surrounded by fleshy, yellow arils. '**Albus**', white-fruited, less robust. '**Atropurpureus**', purple leaves in spring. '**Red Cascade**', free-fruiting. Autumn foliage on above forms can be spectacular, varying from yellow to reddish purple. All H2.4-3m/8-10ft, W1.5-1.8m/5-6ft. Z4-8.

E. fortunei. Winter-creeper euonymus. Low-growing parent to numerous hardy, adaptable forms, many with coloured foliage, most excellent for ground cover, some self-clinging climbers. Prune occasionally in early spring to tidy bushes. Tolerates shade. As ground cover: H30-45cm/12-18in, W1.8-2.4m/6-8ft. Z5-9. '**Emerald Gaiety**', ground cover, low hedge or bushy shrub; round leaves, broadly margined in creamy white, sometimes tinged pink in winter. H90-120cm/3-4ft, W90cm/3ft. Z5-9. '**Emerald 'n' Gold**', small, glossy, green leaves, edged gold, tinged pink and cream in winter especially in exposed sites. Climbs. Several slightly different sports. H45-60cm/18-24in, W60-90cm/2-3ft. Z5-9. '**Sunspot**', deep green-margined, cream to yellow leaves. H30-45cm/12-18in, W60-90cm/2-3ft. Z5-9.

E. planipes (syn. *E. sachalinensis*). Large, upright, eventually spreading deciduous shrub or small tree. Purple winter buds open to light green

Fothergilla gardenii

leaves, usually turning crimson in autumn; yellowish green flowers, rosy red fruits in autumn. H3m/10ft, W2.4-3m/8-10ft. F4-5. Z6-9.

FORSYTHIA

Trouble-free, deciduous shrubs. Yellow flowers on bare stems in early spring. Larger forms make fine background with bright green summer foliage. Many can be wall-trained. To tidy, prune back some or all flowering stems in late spring as last flowers fade, or on mature plants remove a few older stems from the base. Severe late winter frost can damage buds. ☼ ■ ☀

F. '**Golden Nugget**'. Compact, densely branched, large, bright yellow flowers. Excellent for a small garden. H1.5-1.8m/5-6ft, W90-120cm/3-4ft. F3-4. Z5-9.

F. x *intermedia.* '**Lynwood**' (syn. 'Lynwood Gold'). A sport. Erect, branching habit. H1.8-2.4m/6-8ft, W1.2-1.5m/4-5ft. F3-4. Z5-9. '**Minigold**', compact, large, pale yellow flowers. H1.2-1.5m/4-5ft, W90-120cm/3-4ft. F3-4. Z5-9. '**Spectabilis**', profuse flowers hide the branches. Excellent for cutting. H1.8-2.4m/6-8ft, W1.2-1.5m/4-5ft. F3-4. Z5-9.

F. suspensa. This and its forms are graceful and informal, but difficult to control. The form *atrocaulis* has dark purple young stems. '**Nymans**', more erect, browny purple, arching branches, large, lemon-yellow flowers. All H1.5-1.8m/5-6ft, W1.8-2.4m/6-8ft. F3-4. Z5-8.

F. '**Weekend**'. Very free-flowering selection. H1.5-1.8m/5-6ft, W90-120/3-4ft. F3-4. Z5-9.

FOTHERGILLA

Slow-growing, deciduous shrubs. Fragrant flowers on bare branches, good autumn colour. Peaty soil. ☼ ☀ ◨ ■ ⊖

F. gardenii (syn. *F. alnifolia*). Dwarf, twiggy stems, small, fragrant, white bottlebrush flowers. Dull green oval summer leaves turn yellow, orange and fiery red in autumn. H45-60cm/18-24in, W45-60cm/18-24in. F5. Z5-9.

F. major (syn. *F. monticola*). Erect, picturesque shrub, can reach 3m/10ft. Congested branches, small, white, honey-scented, cylindrical flowers. Variable in habit, most have excellent autumn colour of yellow, orange and crimson, sometimes on the same leaf. H90-120cm/3-4ft, W75-90cm/30-36in. F5. Z5-9.

FUCHSIA

Many hardy varieties among this large group of shrubs provide flowers well into autumn, particularly in mild or coastal districts. Semi- if not evergreen in milder areas. In colder areas will be cut to ground, protect roots in winter. Plant in spring. All Z8-10. ☼ ◪ ■ ☆

GARRYA

Evergreen. Needs shelter. ☼ ■ ☆

G. elliptica. Silk-tassel bush. Fast-growing. Glossy, leathery leaves. Clusters of long, silvery, grey-green, pendulous catkins on established male plants, which on '**James Roof**', can reach 30-40cm/12-16in. Female catkins are less showy. Dislikes cold, desiccating winds, especially when young – leaves scorch easily. Best on a wall. Prune in late spring, removing unruly branches or to keep within

Garrya elliptica 'James Roof'

bounds. Both H3-4m/10-13ft, W3m/10ft. F11-2. Z8-10.

GAULTHERIA

A few of this large genus of evergreens are worth growing, all low-growing. Effective en masse as ground cover. Pendulous, bell-shaped flowers followed by coloured fruit. Can be invasive. Peaty soil. ☼ ☀ ◪ ⊖

G. procumbens. Slowly spreading prostrate carpet. Leaves are reddish purple in winter. White, urn-shaped flowers and numerous, bright red fruit, from late summer often lasting through winter. H10-15cm/4-6in, W60-75cm/24-30in. F5-6. Z3-8.

HAMAMELIS Witch hazel

Large deciduous shrubs renowned for autumn colour and winter flowers. Upright or spreading, twisting branches, broadly oval, hazel-like leaves. Mostly fragrant flowers with narrow, wavy, frost-resistant, strap-like petals on naked stems from autumn until well into spring, depending on type. Stems can be cut for indoor decoration. Most soils except thin chalk, with added humus, leaf mould, composted bark or peat, and a similar mulch every two or three years. ☼ ☀ ◪ ■ ☆ ★ ⊖

H. x intermedia. Hybrid group including some of the most colourful and varied forms. '**Arnold Promise**', free-flowering, upright, later spreading, branches. Yellow autumn leaves. Fragrant, deep yellow flowers, red sepals. F2-3. '**Diane**', crimson-red flowers, orange-red autumn colour. F2-3. '**Feuerzauber**' (syn. '**Magic Fire**'), bronze-red flowers, the most brilliant autumn leaves of all. F1-2. '**Jelena**' (syn. '**Copper Beauty**'), large, coppery orange flowers, lasting sometimes for months, orange-yellow autumn leaves. F12-2. '**Orange Beauty**', profuse, orange-yellow flowers, lasting for several weeks. F2-3. '**Primavera**', pale canary-yellow flowers, yellow-orange autumn

Hamamelis × intermedia 'Primavera'

colour, upright habit, good for small gardens. F1-2. '**Westerstede**', slightly later, canary-yellow, large flowers. F2-3. All H2.4-3m/8-10ft, W2.4-3m/8-10ft. Z5-9.

H. mollis. Upright, later spreading, bush. Downy, grey-green leaves turn butter-yellow in autumn. Clusters of fragrant, deep yellow flowers with bronze-red sepals for several months. '**Pallida**', copious, large, deliciously scented, bright sulphur-yellow flowers with bronze-red sepals. Site both against dark backgrounds to highlight their winter beauty. Both H1.5-2.4m/5-8ft, W1.5m-1.8m/5-6ft. F12-1. Z5-9.

H. vernalis. Variable, but tolerates a higher alkalinity and wetter soils than other species. Usually a multi-stemmed, compact bush. Yellow autumn colour and yellow-through-red flowers, lasting for several weeks, pungent rather than fragrant. '**Sandra**', purple young leaves, green in summer and rich flame-orange in autumn. Small, yellow flowers not always freely produced. Both H1.8-2.4m/6-8ft, W1.5-1.8m/5-6ft. F2-3. Z4-9.

HEBE

Large group of evergreen shrubs. Many are valuable garden plants,

others are borderline hardy in cold northern temperate zones. If cut back by frost, hebes often shoot from the base in late spring or early summer. Prune in late spring to tidy, remove faded flowers; rejuvenate old, woody shrubs by cutting back to 15cm/6in above ground. Late-flowering or good evergreen foliage types are mentioned here. ☼ ☀ ■

H. albicans '**Red Edge**'. Compact bush, glaucous leaves red-tipped in winter and spring. Pale lilac flowers. H45cm/18in, W45cm/18in. F6-8. Z8-11.

H. cupressoides. Upright, multi-branched, grey-green, scale-like leaves. Terminal clusters of pale blue flowers only in warm seasons. '**Nana**', seems identical. H60-120cm/2-4ft, W60-120cm/2-4ft. F7. Z8-10.

H. '**Great Orme**'. Compact, lance-shaped leaves, tapering racemes of bright pink flowers. H90cm/3ft, W90cm/3ft. F6-9. Z8-10.

H. ochracea. Dwarf, spreading habit, cypress-like, whipcord foliage, old gold in summer, bronzing in winter. White flowers, fewer in cool climates. Often confused with *H. armstrongii*, which has olive-green foliage. H75cm/30in, W75cm/30in. F7-8. Z8-10. '**James Stirling**', tidy, flat-topped, bright green in summer,

Hedera colchica 'Sulphur Heart'

and spring. Pale lilac flowers. H45cm/18in, W45cm/18in. F6-8. Z8-11.

HEDERA Ivy

Most are well-adapted to climb, some are excellent ground cover, especially large-leaved types, in dry shade, or can ramble over stumps; most are attractive in containers. ☀ ✲ ■ ☆ ⊕
H. canariensis 'Gloire de Marengo'. Used as a house plant, but is quite hardy in shelter of a wall and poor, dry soil. Variegation greener in shade. Its variegated leaves, grey, green and creamy white, are smaller than those of *H. colchica*. Excellent as a patio plant. H30cm/1ft, W2.4-3m/8-10ft. Z9-11.
H. colchica. This and variegated forms need help to climb a wall, but eventually grow up trees unaided; the species has leathery, dark green leaves. Variegated or coloured leaf forms are brighter in good light. 'Arborescens', shrubby mound of broad green leaves, free-flowering and fruiting at same time. H90-120cm/3-4ft, W1.2-1.5m/4-5ft. Z6-9. 'Dentata', lighter, larger green leaves. 'Dentata Variegata', broad, grey-green leaves, margined creamy yellow. 'Sulphur Heart' (syn. 'Paddy's Pride'), irregular

central splash. On older plants heads of rounded green flowers usually followed by black fruits. All H30cm/1ft, W1.8-3m/6-10ft. Z6-9.
H. helix. Common ivy. Innumerable selections, with variously shaped, coloured, marbled or variegated leaves for ground cover, climbing and containers. If they find no support upper stems become shrubby. Greenish flowers on older, arborescent stems in autumn followed by black fruits, leaves becoming rhomboid. 'Arborescens', classed as shrub, mound of dark green leaves, yellow flowers, black fruits. H90-120cm/3-4ft, W90-120cm/3-4ft. F9-11. Z4-9.

HYDRANGEA

Dwarf to large deciduous shrubs with varying types of flowers and foliage. Many flower well into autumn and flower heads turn to striking autumn colours, continuing to look attractive in winter when dry. Some are excellent for containers. According to species ☀ ✲ or ✲; most ◪ ■ ☆ ⊖ or slightly ⊕
H. arborescens. 'Grandiflora', large, round heads of creamy white, sterile flowers, or florets fading to green. Broad bush, the upright stems often weighed down by flowers, attractive even in winter. H1.2-1.5m/4-5ft, W1.5-1.8m/5-6ft. F7-9. Z3-9. 'Annabelle', similar, but more compact, enormous, domed flower heads, up to 30cm/1ft across. H90-120cm/3-4ft, W1.2-1.5m/4-5ft. F7-9. Z3-9. Both cultivars easy in any soil, sun or shade and flower on the same year's growth, prune by half or to ground in early spring. ☀ ✲ ☆
H. macrophylla. Includes mopheads and lacecaps, both dense bushes with erect branches, often weighed down by flowers, needing humus-rich soil. Buds can be damaged by winter or spring frost. Prune in spring, removing only the previous year's dead flower heads and, on older

Hydrangea arborescens 'Annabelle'

plants, a few woody stems from the base if congested. Good patio plants. In very acid soils some *macrophylla* and *serrata* types produce real blue, the same plant on neutral or alkaline soil can be pink or red. For blue flowers on neutral or alkaline soils, add aluminium sulphate. Lacecaps have small flowers surrounded by large, showy, flat ray. ☀ ✲
H. paniculata. Superseded by many selections, all erect, dense shrubs, with large, usually pyramidal, flower panicles, first light green, then white or cream, later often pink. Panicles grow on current season's wood, so escape spring frosts. To keep compact can be pruned in spring to just above where previous year's growth started – usually half the height of the shrub. 'Kyushu', glossy leaves, profuse, long panicles of creamy white flowers. 'Pink Diamond', large, creamy white heads, then pink, finally red-brown. 'Unique', with large, erect heads, rosy-pink in autumn. All, unpruned H2.4-3m/8-10ft, W2.4-3m/8-10ft. F7-10. Z4-8. ☀ ✲ ✲ ◪ ☆
H. quercifolia. Native to south-eastern U.S.A. Grows only half its natural height of 1.8m/6ft in climates with cool summers. Dark green 'oak' leaves turn bronze to purple in

autumn. Small, erect, long-lasting, greeny white panicles. 'Snowflake', double-flowered; requires warmth and shelter. Both H90-150cm/3-5ft, W1.2-1.5m/4-5ft. F6-8. Z5-9. 'Snow Queen', more vigorous, large, erect, white heads, later tinged pink. Needs a hot summer. Large leaves turn bronze in autumn. Prune back only if stems damaged in winter or if required as foliage shrub. H1.2-1.5m/4-5ft, W1.2-1.5m/4-5ft. F6-8. Z5-9.

HYPERICUM

Large genus containing herbaceous plants, semi-shrubby alpines, deciduous shrubs, evergreen in mild winters, all with yellow flowers. Most grow 60-150cm/2-5ft high and flower from midsummer onwards, some with colourful fruits in late summer and autumn. Prune for tidiness and flowering; cut back previous year's stems by a third, and every three to five years to the base, in early spring, to rejuvenate old plants. ☀ ☀ ■ ☆ ☆
H. androsaemum. Tutsan hypericum. Adaptable ground cover, dense, low-spreading bush, dark green leaves, small yellow flowers. Red-brown fruits turn black in autumn. 'Gladys

Brabazon', new shoots mottled cream and pink, yellow flowers, bright red berries. '**Gold Penny**', free-flowering and fruiting, maroon fruits. '**Hysan**', hardy, maroon fruits turning black lasting all winter, excellent for cutting. All H90cm/3ft, W90-120cm/3-4ft. F7-9. Z6-8.

ILEX Holly
Deciduous and evergreen species, miniatures as well as trees. Usually male and female flowers on separate plants, the females bearing fruit but usually requiring a male nearby for pollination. Most take well to pruning and are often improved by shaping early growth to increase density. Many are tolerant of pollution and maritime exposure, and make excellent hedges; prune in early spring or late summer. Often slow to establish. ☼ ❋ ■ ☆

I. x altaclerensis. Several selections. Mostly tall, pyramidal shrubs or trees, excellent for hedging. Large leaves, small, white flowers, large fruit. Some leaf drop in severe winters. '**Belgica Aurea**' (syn. 'Silver Sentinel'), lightly spined, green-grey leaves edged with creamy white to yellow, orange-red fruits. '**Golden King**', female,

Ilex x meserveae

spineless leaves edged yellow, abundant red fruit. '**Lawsoniana**', golden-centred, green-edged leaves, bright red fruit. '**Purple Shaft**', purple stems, free-fruiting. All H3-4.5m/10-15ft, W1.8-2.4m/6-8ft. F5-6. Z7-9.

I. aquifolium. Common holly. Numerous foliage and fruiting garden forms, all hardier than *I. x altaclerensis.* Mostly spiny leaves, small, white flowers, making large shrubs and eventually pyramidal trees. '**Amber**', bronze-yellow fruit. '**Argentea Marginata**', bushy and free-fruiting, broad leaves edged silvery-white. '**Fructu Luteo**' (syn. 'Bacciflava'), bright yellow fruit. '**Ferox**', slow, low-growing male, fiercely spiny leaves. Variegated forms include '**Ferox Argentea**', yellow and white leaf margins, and '**Ferox Aurea**', central gold splash. Growth rate of all 'Ferox' forms about a third of that given below. '**Flavescens**', female, needs sun to show its golden-yellow leaves best; young spring growth also very striking. '**Handsworth New Silver**', purple shoots, dark green leaves edged white, red fruit. '**J.C. Van Tol**', male, yellow-edged leaves, good for hedging. '**Madame Briot**', purple young stems, prickly leaves broadly edged golden-yellow, orange-red fruit. '**Silver Milkmaid**', striking, female, dark green, spiny leaves splashed with creamy white. Average H3-4.5m/10-15ft, W1.8-2.4m/6-8ft. F5-6. Z7-9.

I. crenata. Small-leaved, useful as dwarf, clipped hedge or container plant. Most are compact, evergreen shrubs with rigid branches, dense, small, dark, glossy, spineless leaves, inconspicuous white flowers, and black fruit on females. Most below, F5-6, Z5-8.

'**Golden Gem**', low and spreading, golden-yellow leaves in sun; female, but seldom flowers or fruits. H45-60cm/18-24in, W60-75cm/24-30in. '**Mariesii**', female, free-fruiting, erect, box-like leaves, ideal for troughs or bonsai. H45-60cm/18-24in, W30-45cm/12-18in.

I. x meserveae. Hybrids between *I. aquifolium* and *I. rugosa*, hardier and more adaptable than *I. aquifolium.* The following varieties are dense and bushy in habit, fruiting is less than spectacular in cool climates. All F4-5, Z4-5. '**Blue Angel**', dark green leaves, red fruits. H1.2-1.5m/4-5ft, W1.2-1.5m/4-5ft. '**Blue Prince**', male, shining dark green leaves, abundant flowers. H1.5-1.8m/5-6ft, W1.2-1.5m/4-5ft. '**Blue Princess**', blue-green leaves, free-fruiting. H1.5-1.8m/5-6ft, W1.2-1.5m/4-5ft.

I. verticillata. Common winterberry. Deciduous, broad, upright or spreading shrub or small tree. Dark green leaves, yellow in autumn. Small clusters of creamy white flowers in spring. A male is necessary for female to produce bright, long-lasting fruit. Unsuitable for chalk. All H1.5-1.8m/5-6ft, W1.5-1.8m/5-6ft. F3-4. Z4-9. ☼ ❋ ◩ ⊖

JASMINUM Jasmine
Deciduous or evergreen wall plants and climbers. ☼ ■ ☆

J. nudiflorum. Sprawling, eventually mounded habit, congested branches wreathed in yellow flowers in winter. Prune regularly after flowering, or the centre becomes woody and unsightly. H90-120cm/3-4ft, W2.1-3m/7-10ft. F11-3. Z6-9. As wall shrub, H2.1-3m/7-10ft, W2.1-3m/7-10ft.

J. officinale. True or common white jasmine. Vigorous, mostly trained as a wall climber, can reach 10m/33ft in mild areas. Also grown as semi-evergreen shrub over a support and kept bushy by annual spring pruning. Deliciously fragrant, white flowers. '**Aureum**', gold-splashed leaves. H60-90cm/2-3ft, W1.8-2.4m/6-8ft. As wall shrub H1.8-2.4m/6-8ft, W1.8-2.4m/6-8ft. F7-9. Z8-11.

KERRIA
K. japonica. Deciduous. Upright, graceful, arching branches, light green, serrated leaves, yellow, saucer-shaped spring flowers. Use free-standing, massed or against a wall. The only species in this genus has produced several forms. Green-leaved forms are suckering. All have distinctive green stems, attractive in winter, but these become congested; prune older branches from the base immediately after flowering. '**Golden Guinea**', similar to the species but larger, single, golden-yellow flowers. Both H1.5-1.8m/5-6ft, W1.5-1.8m/5-6ft. F3-5. Z5-9. '**Pleniflora**', showy, taller form, more upright stems, double, yellow flowers, needs regular pruning. H1.8-2.4m/6-8ft, W1.8-2.4m/6-8ft. F3-5. Z5-9. ☼ ❋ ■ ☆ ☆

LAURUS Laurel
Evergreen. Needs shelter. ☼ ❋ ■ ☆
L. nobilis. Bay laurel or sweet bay. Dense, pyramidal evergreen shrub or small tree. Dark, glossy, wavy-edged leaves, aromatic when crushed, culinary. Often container-grown as wall or conservatory plant, clipped into standards or formal pyramids.

Lonicera fragrantissima

Small, yellow flowers, black fruits on females if pollinated by a male. Half hardy in cooler temperate climates, thrives in milder ones. 'Aurea', golden-leaved, attractive in winter and early spring. Prune from late spring on as required, established shrubs breaking well from old wood. Good for coastal planting. Both H1.8-2.4m/6-8ft, W1.2-1.5m/4-5ft. F4-5. Z8-11.

LEUCOTHOE
Mostly evergreen. Leathery leaves, racemes of tubular or bell-shaped, often fragrant, flowers. Peaty soil. ☼ ☀ ◩ ⊖

L. fontanesiana (syn. *L. catesbaei*). Suckering. Long, arching stems, glossy leaves, dangling, pitcher-shaped, fragrant, white flowers. Bright green or red foliage in spring, turns glossy green in summer and purple-brown in winter. Ideal ground cover on acid soil. 'Rainbow', creamy yellow and pink new leaves. Occasionally prune old stems to the base in early spring to promote new shoots; reduce stem length to improve density. Both H1.2-1.5m/4-5ft, W1.5-1.8m/5-6ft. F4-5. Z5-8. 'Scarletta', compact, bright, glossy, reddish leaves from early summer, turning bronze-red in

autumn and winter. H30-60cm/1-2ft, W60-75cm/24-30in. Z5-8.

LONICERA Honeysuckle
Some worthwhile, fragrant, winter-flowering shrubs. Prune after flowering only to keep in shape or to restrict size. Climbers prefer their roots in shade. ☼ ☀ ◼ ☆

L. fragrantissima. Unremarkable in summer, this and similar forms, including *L. × purpusii*, provide winter interest. Depending on climate, its lemon-scented, creamy white flowers can last for many months. Usually deciduous, semi-evergreen in mild areas. Prune flowering stems by a third after

Magnolia stellata

flowering, if necessary; occasionally remove old stems from base of old shrubs. H1.8-2.4m/6-8ft, W2.4-3m/8-10ft. F12-4. Z5-9.

L. × purpusii. Hybrid between *L. fragrantissima* and *L. standishii*. Easy, hardy deciduous shrub. Both it and the cultivar 'Winter Beauty' are free-flowering plants with upright, spreading habit and fragrant, creamy white flowers. Both H1.8-2.4m/6-8ft, W2.4-3m/8-10ft. F12-4. Z5-9.

MAGNOLIA
Wide range of hardy spring-flowering shrubs or trees. Flowers, some fragrant, vary from the small, star-

shaped *M. stellata*, to goblet-like *M. × soulangeana* or the open saucers of *M. sinensis*. Early-flowering types may be hit by spring frosts, especially in northern Europe. Site near a tree or wall, to protect from early-morning sun. Prune only to shape young plants or thin, congested branches. Light pruning is best after flowering; leave severe pruning until late summer, painting large cuts with suitable dressing. Magnolias are relatively trouble-free, if chosen to match the site and soil; adding masses of enriched humus may help as will an annual mulch of composted bark, acid leaf mould or well-rotted compost. ☼ ☀ ◪ ◼ ☆

M. × loebneri. Hybrids between *M. kobus* and *M. stellata*, include beautiful free-flowering garden forms for all soils, including chalk. Flower young, each year becoming more floriferous, the multi-petalled, star-like, fragrant flowers appearing before the leaves. All eventually make large, broad shrubs or small trees. 'Leonard Messel', magnificent purple-pink flowers. 'Merrill' and 'Snowdrift', white. All H2.4-3m/8-10ft, W2.4-3m/8-10ft. F3-4. Z5-8.

M. × soulangeana. Most of these cultivars make tall, eventually wide-spreading shrubs or small trees. Goblet-shaped flowers on bare

branches. The species has profuse, large, creamy white, globe-shaped flowers stained rose-purple outside, flowering sometimes interrupted by spring frost. 'Alba Superba', fragrant, white flowers. 'Alexandrina', narrow, upright form, flowers rose-purple outside, white inside. 'Lennei', vigorous, large leaves, broad, goblet-shaped flowers, wine-purple outside, white inside. 'Lennei Alba', white flowers. All between H3-4m/10-13ft, W2.4-4m/8-13ft. F3-5. Z5-9.

M. stellata. Star magnolia. Automatic choice for a small garden. Free-flowering, rarely over 4.5m/15ft high, but eventually wide-spreading, broad, round bush; pruning can control size. Cloud of starry, white, multi-petalled, fragrant blooms, vulnerable to spring frost. Several clones may exist of the pink-flowered 'Rosea'. Other selections include 'Royal Star', hardy, floriferous, late-flowering, large, white flowers, and 'Water Lily', larger fragrant flowers, pink in bud, opening pinkish white. All H1.5-1.8m/5-6ft, W1.5-1.8m/5-6ft. F3-4. Z5-9.

MAHONIA
Hardier forms provide shape and substance in a winter garden, and flower and fragrance from autumn

Mahonia aquifolium 'Atropurpurea'

until spring. Erect clusters or graceful racemes of yellow flowers, glossy, generally prickly, evergreen leaves. Low-growing, dwarf to large shrubs or small trees, all preferring shelter from strong, cold, desiccating winds. Prune only to tidy, but straggly old plants, especially *M. aquifolium* and *M. pinnata*, can be cut to within 10cm/4in of the ground in spring to rejuvenate. Leaf drop may occur after severe frost, but if drop as a result of poor drainage, move plants. Any reasonable garden soil, where not too dry. ✸ ✷ ◪ ✬ ☆

M. aquifolium. Oregon grape. Clusters of blue-black fruits in summer and autumn. Glossy, green leaves tinged purple in winter, tight clusters of barely scented flowers. Specimen or ground-cover plant, good in shade. '**Apollo**', rich yellow flowers. '**Atropurpurea**', red-purple winter foliage, deep yellow flowers. Both H90-120cm/3-4ft, W1.2-1.5m/4-5ft. F3-5. Z5-8. '**Smaragd**', tall, hardy, reliable, bright yellow flowers, deep green leaves, tinged purple in winter. H1.2-1.5m/4-5ft, W1.2-1.5m/4-5ft. F3-5. Z5-8.

M. japonica. Eventually large, erect shrub. Long leaves divided into glossy, spiny leaflets. Terminal racemes of soft yellow, highly scented flowers for many weeks. Purple fruits

in summer. This and the similar '**Bealii**', shorter, more erect racemes, need shelter from cold winds. Both H1.8-2.4m/6-8ft, W1.8-2.4m/6-8ft. F11-4. Z7-9.

M. × *media.* Hybrids between *M. japonica* and *M. lomariifolia*. Deeply divided leaves, erect, later pendulous, racemes of dark yellow, lightly fragrant flowers. Less hardy than some, flowers can be damaged by early frost but light shade or the shelter of a wall helps. '**Charity**', '**Winter Sun**', '**Buckland**', '**Lionel Fortescue**' and '**Underway**', all good. All H2.4-3m/8-10ft, W1.5-1.8m/5-6ft. F10-2. Z8-9.

MYRICA

Deciduous shrubs with aromatic foliage, some growing in extremes of dry and wet. ⊖

M. gale. Bog myrtle or sweetgale. Aromatic, erect stems, small blue-grey leaves in summer, golden-brown catkins in spring on naked branches. Tolerant of very boggy conditions, succeeds in drier, acid soils, too. H90-120cm/3-4ft, W90-120cm/3-4ft. F4-5. Z1-8.

NANDINA

Evergreen. ✸ ◪ ■ ✬

N. domestica. Tall, multi-stemmed but unbranched. Divided, compound

leaves, red or purple in autumn and winter. Large, erect, white flower plumes in hot summers followed by red fruit, if climate allows. May be cut to the ground by severe winters but usually recover, if late. Tall and dwarf forms prefer moist soil, need warmth and shelter in cool climates. '**Moyers Red**' and '**Richmond**', crimson autumn and winter foliage, bright red fruit. H1.5-2.4m/5-8ft, W90-120cm/3-4ft. F6-8. Z7-9. '**Firepower**', dwarf, particularly colourful. '**Nana**', dwarf, low, green, leafy, non-flowering hummocks, pink, red, orange and purple through autumn and winter. '**Nana Purpurea**', shorter, purple-tinged summer foliage. These colour better in sun. All H30-45cm/12-18in, W30-45cm/12-18in. Z7-9.

OSMANTHUS

Evergreen trees and shrubs of varying hardiness. Usually small, white, fragrant flowers, although some grown for foliage. To shape or control large plants, prune just after flowering or as new growth begins, according to species. ✸ ✷ ■ ✬

O. × *burkwoodii* (syn. *Osmarea burkwoodii*). Robust hybrid between *Phillyrea decora* and *O. delavayi* often confused with latter, but has stiffer, stronger branches, larger, smoother-

Oxydendrum arboreum

edged leaves and clusters of small, white, fragrant, trumpet-shaped flowers on terminal shoots. H1.8-2.4m/6-8ft, W1.8-2.4m/6-8ft. F3-4. Z7-9.

O. delavayi. Dense, twiggy bush, eventually large in mild climates. Small, oval, glossy, toothed leaves, profuse, small, creamy white, scented, tubular flowers. Needs shelter. H2.4-3m/8-10ft, W2.4-3m/8-10ft. F3-4. Z8-10.

O. heterophyllus (syn. *O. ilicifolius*). Large, round, dense shrub or small tree in mild climates. Shining, holly-like leaves, some spined, but mature leaves smooth-edged and oval. Small clusters of fragrant, white flowers in hot climates, followed by blue berries. All selections can be tender, especially when young. H1.8-2.4m/6-8ft, W1.8-2.4m/6-8ft. F9-11. Z7-9. '**Aureomarginatus**', leaves edged in yellow. '**Aureus**', bright gold summer leaves, greeny yellow in winter. '**Gulftide**', compact, heavily spined leaves, fragrant autumn flowers. '**Latifolius Variegatus**', wide leaves edged silvery white. '**Purpureus**', striking, purple young shoots and leaves in spring. '**Tricolor**' (syn. '**Goshiki**'), dark green, white and pink leaves. '**Variegatus**', creamy white margins. Average H1.2-1.8m/4-6ft, W1.2-1.8m/4-6ft. F9-11. Z8-9.

Nandina domestica 'Firepower'

Osmanthus × *burkwoodii*

Parthenocissus henryana

OXYDENDRUM

O. arboreum. Deciduous. May reach
15m/50ft in its native eastern U.S.A.
but seldom more than a large shrub in
climates with cool summers. Open,
erect branches, long, narrow, graceful
leaves, turning yellow or crimson in
autumn, given an open situation.
Long, pendulous racemes of white,
fragrant flowers. H1.5-2.4m/5-8ft,
W1.2-1.5m/4-5ft. F7-8. Z5-9. ☼ ☀
◩ ⊖

PARTHENOCISSUS Ornamental vine

Deciduous climbers which attach
themselves by tendrils. Leaves often
colour well in autumn. Usually
insignificant flowers may be followed
by small, grape-like fruits, particularly
in warm summers. May need
controlling during the growing season
as most are vigorous. ☼ ☀ ■
P. henryana. Small, deep green leaves
veined with silver, occasionally flushed
with pink and turning bright red in
autumn. Blue-black fruit in autumn
after hot summers. Leaves show most
variegation in shade. Tying in and
training necessary. H6-8m/20-26ft,
W6-8m/20-26ft. F5-7. Z8.
P. tricuspidata (syn. *Vitis inconstans*).
Boston ivy. Vigorous, self-clinging
climber, glossy, dark green, variable,
maple-like leaves, which turn bright
fiery crimson in autumn. '**Veitchii**',

Pieris japonica 'Pink Delight'

smaller leaves, purplish green when
young, crimson-purple in autumn.
Both H5m/16ft, W5m/16ft. F5-7.
Z4.

PEROVSKIA Russian sage

Indispensable deciduous sub-shrubs.
Long, late display of shimmering blue
flower spikes. Quite hardy, but young
stems can die back in cold winters,
new shoots appearing from the base.
Prune to 15-30cm/6-12in from the
ground in spring to promote new
flowering growth. ☼ ■
P. atriplicifolia. Aromatic, downy,
grey-green, serrated leaves, white
stems and hazy panicles of lavender-
blue flowers. '**Blue Spire**', more
deeply cut leaves and larger flower
heads. H90-120cm/3-4ft, W90-
120cm/3-4ft. F8-10. Z6-8.

PHOTINIA

Large shrubs or trees, usually
depending on climate. In cool
summers, evergreens are shy to
flower, but make excellent foliage
plants. White, hawthorn-like flowers
borne in clusters or panicles, followed
by red fruits. Evergreens need shelter
in cold regions. For compact, dense

growth and ample new colourful
shoots, prune leading shoots back by
30-60cm/1-2ft in spring, as new
growth commences; hedges or screens
might need a summer trim.
Deciduous types dislike lime but
evergreens thrive in it, even on chalky
soil. Warm soil. ☼ ☀ ◩ ■
P. davidiana (syn. *Stranvaesia
davidiana*). Background shrub or
small tree. Irregular, erect branches,
glossy, lance-shaped, evergreen leaves,
a few turning red in autumn and
winter, small clusters of white
flowers, usually followed by bright
red fruit. It and some varieties are
susceptible to fireblight, a serious
fungal disease. H2.4-3m/8-10ft,
W1.8-2.4m/6-8ft. F7. Z7-9.
'**Palette**', variable, but relatively
bushy, leaves irregularly splashed
and variegated white, pink and
green, new shoots flushed reddish
pink. White flowers do not always
develop into impressive red fruit.
H1.5-1.8m/5-6ft, W1.2-1.5m/4-5ft.
F6-7. Z7-9.
P. x *fraseri* '**Birmingham**'. Robust
evergreen, dark, glossy green leaves,
copper-red when young. Denser and
hardier than the closely related, more

colourful '**Red Robin**', with an
almost continuous show of brilliant
red new growth all summer. Both
make outstanding focal points. Both
H2.4-3m/8-10ft, W1.8-2.4m/6-8ft.
F6. Z8-9.

PIERIS

Evergreen, attractive in flower and
foliage. Most make slow-growing,
mounded bushes, with lance-shaped,
glossy leaves. Racemes often develop
in autumn, opening in spring, with
mostly pendulous, fragrant, bell-
shaped, white flowers. New growth
can be vulnerable to spring frosts.
Prune only to tidy up bushes or
remove old flower heads as new
growth begins. Mulch with leaf
mould or composted bark every two
or three years. Peaty soil.
☼ ☀ ◩ ■ ⊖
P. '**Flaming Silver**'. One of several
selections with variegated foliage and
new growth of scarlet or crimson in
late spring. Leaves edged silvery
white. H1.2m/4ft, W1.2-1.5m/4-5ft.
F3-5. Z5-8.
P. '**Forest Flame**'. One of the best
hybrids. Dense flower sprays; scarlet
young growth turns pink and white,
then green. H1.5m/5ft, W1.5m/5ft.
F4-5. Z6-8.
P. japonica. Source of most new
European and North American
cultivars. Usually glossy leaves,
pendulous flower racemes, with waxy,
often fragrant, bell-like flowers,
showy even in winter as flowering
racemes develop. Most prefer an
open, sheltered spot. All F3-5. Most
Z6-8. '**Debutante**', dense trusses of
white flowers. H75cm/30in, W75-
90cm/30-36in. '**Flamingo**', carmine-
rose and white flowers, coppery
young growth. H1.2m/4ft, W1.2-
1.5m/4-5ft. '**Little Heath**', dwarf,
variegated form, compact, seldom
flowers; small white, pink and copper
leaves. H60cm/2ft, W60cm/2ft.
'**Mountain Fire**', coppery-red new
leaves, sparse, white flowers.

Polygala chamaebuxus 'Grandiflora'

H90cm/3ft, W90-120cm/3-4ft. **'Pink Delight'**, profuse, fragrant, rose-pink flowers on red stalks. H1.2m/4ft, W1.2m/4ft. **'Red Mill'**, glossy wine-red leaves, white flowers. H1.2m/4ft, W1.2m/4ft. **'Valley Valentine'**, deepest red flowers, free-flowering. H1.5m/5ft, W1.5m/5ft. **'Variegata'** covers a fast-growing form with white margins, also called **'White Rim'** (H90cm/3ft, W90cm/3ft), and a compact form, with creamy yellow variegations, which needs shelter. H45-60cm/18-24in, W45-60cm/18-24in.

PITTOSPORUM

Evergreen shrubs or small trees grown for foliage, useful for cutting. Few are hardy in cool temperate zones, but for mild and seaside areas there are good species and cultivars, the latter mostly belonging to *P. tenuifolium*. Leaves are rounded and undulating, pale or olive green with more recent variations purple, silver, gold or variegated. Purple or brown flowers, often small and fragrant, on mature plants in warmer climates. In cold, inland areas, grow against a sunny wall. Wet soil and cold, desiccating winds are fatal. If cut back by frost, most make new growth from old wood. Overwinter containerized plants in greenhouse or conservatory. Plant in late spring. All below F4-5, Z9-11. ☼ ❋ ■

P. **'Garnettii'**. Hybrid. Grey-green leaves, edged white and tinged pink. H3m/10ft, W1.5m/5ft.

P. tenuifolium. Bushy tree, columnar when young. Glossy, pale, wavy-edged leaves black stems. Good for hedging. Innumerable cultivars. H3m/10ft, W1.5m/5ft.

'Purpureum', red-purple leaves. **'Silver Queen'**, white-edged leaves. Both H1.8-2.1m/6-7ft, W1.5-1.8m/5-6ft. **'Tom Thumb'**, dwarf, purple-leaved form. H1m/39in, W1m/39in.

POLYGALA

Evergreen. ☼ ❋ ■ ☆

P. chamaebuxus. Dwarf, creeping. Bright, pointed leaves, profuse, large, long-lasting creamy white and yellow flowers a few centimetres above the ground. Good with alpines or in a peat bed. Any moist soil but chalk. H10cm/4in, W30-45cm/12-18in. F3-4. Z4-7. **'Grandiflora'** (syn. *rhodoptera*), taller and more lax in growth, deep green leaves, red and yellow, pea-like flowers. H15cm/6in, W30-45cm/12-18in. F2-3. Z5-7.

P. vayredae. Charming, creeping shrub. Glossy, green leaves, bright purple and yellow flowers, dense mat for moist positions. H2.5-5cm/1-2in, W30-45cm/12-18in. F3-4. Z8-10.

POTENTILLA Cinquefoil, shrubby cinquefoil

P. fruticosa. Among the most adaptable of hardy shrubs, often very long flowering period. Good for autumn flowers, wide range of colours, some best in cooler weather. Prune established plants annually as new shoots appear. Cut back by a third each year to improve vigour and flowering. Coloured forms may retain deeper hues in shade. ☼ ■ The following are hybrids mostly listed at one time under *fruticosa*, which is the parent of many. All F4-10. Most Z3-8. **'Abbotswood'**, the best white, profuse-flowering, blue-green leaves. H1.2m/4ft, W1.5m/5ft. **'Elizabeth'**, bushy, grey-green leaves, golden-yellow flowers, long-flowering. H90cm/3ft, W1.2m/4ft. **'Goldfinger'**, bright green leaves, golden flowers. H90cm/3ft, W1.2m/4ft. **'Goldstar'**, erect, open habit, huge, yellow flowers. H90cm/3ft, W1.2m/4ft. **'Hopleys Orange'**, orange flowers. H75cm/30in, W1m/39in. **'Kobold'**, dense, dwarf, small, yellow flowers. H30-45cm/12-18in, W40-60cm/16-24in. **'Pretty Polly'**, dwarf, low-growing, light rose-pink flowers. H35-50cm/14-20in, W45-65cm/18-26in. **'Princess'**, long-flowering, pale-pink, then paler, fading to white in heat. H75cm/30in, W1m/39in. **'Red Ace'**, bright vermilion-flame at best, fading to yellow in heat. **'Red Robin'**, similar but deeper red. Both H60cm/2ft, W80cm/32in. **'Snowbird'**, semi-double white flowers, light green leaves. H60-75cm/24-30in, W60cm/2ft. **'Tilford Cream'**, low habit, rigid branches, white flowers, can look scruffy. H60cm/2ft, W60cm/2ft.

Prunus × incisa 'Kojo-no-mai'

PRUNUS

Large family of trees and shrubs. Spectacular in flower. Deciduous ☼; evergreens ☼ ❋; all ■ ☆

P. × cistena (syn. 'Crimson Dwarf'). Deciduous. White flowers, reddish purple foliage. As a hedge, prune after flowering, then regularly through summer. H1.5-1.8m/5-6ft, W1.2-1.5m/4-5ft. F3-4. Z2-8.

P. incisa. Fuji cherry. Deciduous, many shrubby forms, eventually making small trees. Small leaves, lovely autumn shades. Brief small, white flowers, pink in bud, cluster on leafless stems. Small, purple fruits. **'Kojo-no-mai'**, slow-growing, contorted branches, ideal for bonsai, profuse flowers, year-round interest. H1.2-1.5m/4-5ft, W90cm/3ft. F3. Z4-7. **'Shidare'**, weeping, good winter outline and good as specimen for lawn, masses of pink-flushed flowers. H1.2-1.5m/4-5ft, W3-4m/10-13ft. F3. Z4-7.

P. laurocerasus. Cherry laurels. Evergreen. Generally vigorous and accommodating, dark green, useful as background or ground cover. Spring bottlebrush flowers. Plenty of cultivars. Prune only to control growth immediately after flowering; then trim hedges at regular intervals until late summer. Rejuvenate old, bare-stemmed plants by cutting to the ground in mid spring. Any soil except chalk, not too dry. F4-5. Most Z6-8.

P. lusitanica. Evergreen, dense bush or small tree. Glossy leaves good for winter foliage, usually profuse, small, white, fragrant flower spikes. Background shrub, screening or hedging. Prune as for *P. laurocerasus,* if required. 'Variegata', red young stalks, white-edged leaves, tinted rose-pink in winter in a sunny spot. H3m/10ft, W3m/10ft. F6. Z7-9.

P. mume. Japanese apricot. Deciduous, worth space, even in a small garden. Slender, erect or spreading branches. Winter blossom for several weeks. Prune just after flowering. 'Alba Plena', white, semi-double. 'Alphandii', semi-double, pink, 'Beni-shidare', profuse carmine, fragrant, saucer-shaped flowers. 'Omoi-no-mama', profuse, white. Give shelter. H3m/10ft, W3m/10ft. F2-4. F7-9.

PYRACANTHA Firethorn

Vigorous, evergreen or semi-evergreen, upright or spreading, thorny bushes with small, glossy leaves. Clusters of white flowers, followed by showy, round, 'fiery' yellow, red or orange fruit, attractive to birds. Can be used as specimens, hedge, screen or a wall shrub, even on shady walls. Most species have been superseded by hybrids. Prune after flowering, to remove extended, non-flowering shoots and repeat in early autumn on any subsequent new growths. Every five years, remove extended stems to within 10cm/4in of main branches for vigorous new growth, no flowering for a year, but a reborn plant! ☼ ❋ ■ ☆ ✶

P. coccinea 'Lalandei'. Erect habit, red fruits freely borne. H3m/10ft, W2.4m/8ft. F6. Z5-9.

Hybrids. The following are of complex parentage. All F5-6. 'Mohave', vigorous, upright, free-

Rhododendron 'Olive'

flowering and fruiting, red-orange fruits. H3m/10ft, W2.4m/8ft. Z6-9. 'Orange Glow', reliable, erect, dense habit, orange fruits. H3m/10ft, W2.4m/8ft. Z6-9. 'Red Cushion', low, dense, spreading ground cover, red fruits. H60-90cm/2-3ft, W1.8m/6ft. Z6-9. 'Soleil D'Or' ('Golden Sun'), broad, upright habit, spreading, large clusters deep yellow fruits. H2.4m/8ft, W3m/10ft. Z7.

RHODODENDRON

Vast range. Some, mostly deciduous azaleas, give autumn colour, a few offer considerable winter interest in foliage and flower, and many flower in spring – how early depends upon local climate. If rhododendrons will grow successfully in your garden, their early, exotic flowers are a welcome boost. Frost can damage winter and spring flowers; site plants facing away from early morning sun, under the shade of tall trees and out of a frost pocket. Severe winters or frosts can damage swelling buds. All, except those classed as tender, can be planted throughout the year as long as soil conditions are suitable, early autumn better than late spring for those less hardy for your area. Neutral or acid soil. ☼ ❋ ◩ ■

R. Bric-a-brac. Hybrid, early white flowers, dark green leaves. H1.2m/4ft, W1.2-1.5/4-5ft. F2-3. Z7-8.

R. dauricum. Semi-evergreen, small leaves, early rosy purple flowers. H1.2m-1.8m/4-6ft, W90-120cm/3-4ft. F2-3. Z4-8.

R. 'Golden Oriole'. Cheery sight in full flower, cinnamon-brown peeling bark, golden-yellow flowers. H1.2-1.5/4-5ft, W90-120cm/3-4ft. F2-3. Z8-9.

R. moupinense. Parent of many excellent hybrids, dwarf, narrow tubular fragrant flowers, light or rose-

Rhus glabra 'Laciniata'

pink or white often speckled with red. H60-90cm/2-3ft, W60-90cm/2-3ft. F3-4. Z7-8.

R. 'Nobleanum'. Eventually large-growing hybrid, striking early flowers, trumpets of deep rose-pink open from bright red buds. Needs woodland or shelter. 'Album', white flowers and 'Venustum', pink, are generally put in this 'Nobleanum' group and have equally early flowers. 'Nobleanum' H1.5-1.8m/5-6ft, W1.5-1.8m/5-6ft. F1-2. Z6-9.

R. 'Olive'. Ample trusses of pale mauve flowers. H1.2-1.5m/4-5ft, W90-1.2m/3-4ft. F2-3. Z6-9.

R. 'P.J. Mezitt'. Hardy, free-flowering, small, dark green leaves, purplish in winter, striking, rosy purple flowers with darker spots. H90-120cm/3-4ft, W60-90cm/2-3ft. F3-4. Z4-9.

R. 'Silkcap'. Compact shrub, white flushed pink flowers with prominent brown anthers. H60-90cm/2-3ft, W60-90cm/2-3ft. F2-3. Z7-9.

R. 'Tessa'. Hybrid between *R.* 'Praecox' and *R. moupinense.* Purplish pink, spotted crimson, brighter than violet purple 'Praecox'. 'Tessa Roza', more striking, rosy pink flowers. Both H90-120cm/3-4ft, W60-90cm/2-3ft. F2-3. Z7-9.

RHUS Sumach

Deciduous. A few species grown for their summer and autumn foliage, some have striking fruit. Can be invasive. Their sap can be an irritant: wear gloves and avoid touching cut stems with bare skin. ☼ ■

R. glabra. Smooth sumach. Erect, spreading, deciduous shrub, smooth, purplish stems and bright green, pinnate leaves turning glorious orange and red in autumn. 'Laciniata', deeply dissected leaflets, brilliant autumn colour. Dense, erect panicles of greenish flowers followed, on female plants, by bright crimson seed heads in autumn, often remaining long after leaf fall.

H2.4-3m/8-10ft, W2.4-4m/8-13ft. F6-8. Z3-9.

R. typhina. Stag's-horn sumach. Striking, unruly shrub or small, flat-topped tree, erect, spreading stems, gaunt in winter. Large, pinnate leaves usually turn bright orange and scarlet in autumn. Modest, greeny male and female flowers on separate plants, the female flowers followed, if a male is present, by hairy, crimson seed heads. 'Dissecta' (syn. 'Laciniata'), deeply cut leaves, orange and yellow autumn colours, is more garden-worthy. Both H3-4.5m/10-15ft, W3m/10ft. F6-8. Z3-9.

RIBES Currant

Deciduous or evergreen, among the first shrubs to flower, just before or as the new leaves appear. Pendulous, graceful flower racemes, although the broadly lobed leaves often detract, as does the pungent aroma emitted by *R. sanguineum.* Prune back older stems, at the same time shortening unruly stems as required. Pruning can be formal, but I prefer their more irregular, natural shape. ☼ ❋ ■ ☆

R. laurifolium. Lax evergreen, glossy, dark green, leathery leaves, small, pendulous clusters of greenish white flowers. Prune after flowering to improve density. H90-120cm/3-4ft, W1.2-1.5m/4-5ft. F3-4. Z7-8.

Ribes sanguineum 'Red Pimpernel'

R. sanguineum. Flowering currant. Stiff, upright habit; pendulous flower clusters on naked stems quickly joined by emerging, downy, bright green leaves. Coloured forms are brightest in bud. Unless otherwise indicated, all below H1.8-2.4m/6-8ft, W1.5-1.8m/5-6ft. F4-5. Z5-7. 'Carneum', best pink, softly coloured blooms. 'King Edward VII', best red for small garden, compact with large racemes of deep crimson flowers. 'Porky's Pink', white flushed with pink. 'Pulborough Scarlet', vigorous (eventually up to 3m/10ft), rose-red, white-centred flowers. 'Red Pimpernel', long-flowering, dense racemes of rose-red flowers. 'Tydeman's White', pinkish buds, masses of silver-white flowers on long trusses. 'White Icicle', large, white flowers, flushed pink with age.

ROSA Rose

A great many roses of most groups – shrub, species, ground cover, climbing and rambling, bush roses (hybrid teas and floribundas) patio roses (dwarf cluster roses) – flower well into autumn and in milder districts into winter. Take care when making a selection – some roses are either too large for most gardens or sucker and become invasive. Those mentioned have colourful autumn foliage and fruits or striking stems, and can be used as shrubs to mix with other plants. Prune in late winter or early spring only to shape or control size. Old or untidy stems of ground cover types can be pruned to 15cm/6in above the ground every two or three years.

R. 'Canina'. 'Dog Rose'. Variable, fragrant white or pink flowers, shining red fruits. H3-4m/9-13ft, W3-4m/9-13ft. F6-8. Z5-9.

R. damascena. Damask rose. Non suckering, spiny stems. Fragrant pink or white flowers used traditionally for perfume. Red, egg-shaped fruits last into autumn. H1.8-2.1m/6-7ft, W1.5-1.8m/5-6ft. F6-7. Z5-9.

Rosa virginiana

R. eglanteria (syn. *R. rubiginosa*) 'Sweet Briar'. Vigorous, upright species, thorny stems, scented leaves, fragrant pink flowers in summer followed by a generous show of oval, scarlet fruits lasting until winter. H1.8-2.4m/6-8ft, W1.8-2.4m/6-8ft. F6-8. Z5-9.

R. glauca (syn. *R. rubrifolia*). Excellent summer foliage, bristly reddish purple stems, greyish purple leaves until well into autumn. Single, cerise pink flowers, white centres followed by rounded bright red fruits in late summer and autumn. H1.8-2.1m/6-7ft, W1.5-1.8m/5-6ft. F6-7. Z5-9.

R. nitida. Low-growing suckering shrub, good ground cover. Reddish prickly stems attractive in winter. Single, rosy red flowers, glossy green leaves turn purplish red then crimson in autumn, accompanied by bright scarlet hips. H45-60cm/2ft, W1.2-1.5m/4-5ft. F6-11. Z5-9.

R. 'Penelope'. A musk rose. Salmon pink buds open to fragrant, semi-double, blush-pink flowers which continue into winter in mild areas. Coral-pink hips with greyish bloom. H1-1.5m/3-5ft, W1.5m/5ft. F6-11. Z4-9.

R. rugosa. Suckering shrubs good for ground cover and hedging varying from 90-150cm/3-5ft in height. Double-flowered cultivars flower well into autumn. Abundant tomato-like hips, as foliage turns to gold. Look for dwarf selected forms or hybrids. 'Alba', single white, fragrant flowers, orange hips in autumn. H1.8-2.4m/6-8ft, W1.2-1.8m/4-6ft. F6-10. Z4-9. 'Blanche Double de Coubert', intensely fragrant semi-double, white flowers into autumn. H1.5m/5ft, W1.5-2.1m/5-7ft. F6-10. Z4-9. 'Frau Dagmar Hastrup', compact, bushy hybrid, single, pink flowers, crimson hips. H90-120cm/3-4ft, W1.2-1.8m/4-6ft. F6-10. Z4-9. The form *rubra*, fragrant wine-red flowers, orange-scarlet hips in autumn. H90-120cm/ 3-4ft, W1.5-2.1m/5-7ft. F6-10. Z4-9.

R. virginiana. Impressive shrub, can become invasive. Glossy green leaves in summer, lightly fragrant pink flowers. Foliage turns bronze and purple in autumn, rounded red fruits. H1.5m/5ft, W1.5-2.4m/5-8ft. F6-10. Z4-8.

ROSMARINUS Rosemary

Aromatic evergreen, good dark green winter foliage and light blue spring flowers. Prune if necessary after flowering. ☼ ■

R. officinalis. 'McConnell's Blue', prostrate mound, useful for tumbling over a sunny wall. H45cm/18in, W1.2m/4ft. F4-6. Z7-9. '**Miss Jessopp's Upright**' (syn. 'Fastigiatus'), good hedging, erect but informal habit. H1.2-1.5m/4-5ft, W90-120cm/3-4ft. F4-6. Z7-9. '**Sissinghurst Blue**', erect habit, rich blue flowers. H90-120cm/3-4ft, W90-120cm/3-4ft. F5-6. Z7-8.

RUBUS Bramble
A few of this genus are useful for their winter stems, displaying a silver-white bloom, although most require space. Most have spines or thorns, some vicious. Prune winter stems back to ground in late spring. ✿ ❋
R. biflorus. Twisted, spreading branches, thick stems. White flowers on previous season's stems, followed by edible yellow fruits. H1.8-2.4m/6-8ft, W3-4m/10-13ft. F5-6. Z5-9.
R. cockburnianus. Spreading habit, thorny, erect stems. In winter, purple stems are overlaid with a brilliant white bloom. H2.4-3m/8-10ft, W2.1-3m/7-10ft. F6-7. Z5-9. '**Golden Vale**', year-round interest, golden yellow leaves, silver-white arching branches in winter. H90-120cm/3-4ft, W1.2-1.5m/4-5ft. F6-7. Z5-9. ❋
R. thibetanus '**Silver Fern**'. Suckering shrub, grey-green, finely cut leaves, arching bright white stems in winter. Prune annually in late spring, to maintain a height of 90-120cm/3-4ft. Purple flowers only on two-year-old wood. Unpruned H1.8-2.4m/6-8ft, W1.5-1.8m/5-6ft. F6-7. Z6-9.

RUSCUS
Unusual evergreens, attractive foliage and winter fruits. ❋ ☆
R. aculeatus. Butcher's broom. Slow-spreading clump of rigid, green, erect stems clothed in dark green cladodes, which resemble leaves. Tiny, white flowers in the centre of the cladodes, followed on females, if males are present, by bright red fruit, excellent

Salvia officinalis 'Berggarten'

for winter decoration. Rare, self-fertilizing, hermaphrodite forms in cultivation. H60-75cm/24-30in, W60-90cm/2-3ft. F3-4. Z7-8.

SALIX Willow
Some excellent forms for winter stems and spring flowers or catkins, male and female catkins on separate plants, usually the male is showier. Most grow and look well beside water. ✿ ☆
S. alba. Little summer appeal, but rewarding in winter. '**Britzensis**' (syn. 'Chermesina'), shining, orange-red stems. '**Vitellina**', bright yellow stems. Prune both hard each year when new leaves appear, to the ground for a multi-stemmed shrub, or allow them to make a trunk (will reach 10m/33ft unpruned). Prune back to the same point each spring; annual stems of 1.8-2.4m/6-8ft. W1.8-2.4m/6-8ft.
S. gracilistyla '**Melanostachys**' (syn. *S.* 'Kurome'). Striking shrub, shiny, deep purple stems, black catkins. Prune every other year when catkins have finished. H1.8-2.4m/6-8ft, W1.5-1.8m/5-6ft. F3. Z5-8.
S. irrorata. Blackish purple winter stems with a whitish bloom, small catkins before bright green leaves, blue-grey beneath. Prune annually in late spring for best stem colour. Height

then 1.2-1.8m/4-6ft. Unpruned H3m/10ft, W3-5m/10-16ft. F4. Z5-9.
S. x *sepulcralis* '**Erythroflexuosa**' (syn. *S. erythroflexuosa*). Hybrid, small tree with curiously twisted branches and leaves. In winter orange-yellow, contorted stems are striking. Pruned to ground each spring it forms a fascinating dwarfer shrub for winter colour. H10m/33ft, W5-6m/16-20ft. F4. Z6-9.

SALVIA Sage
S. officinalis. Common sage. Indispensable evergreen. Plants are best kept young, prune back if required in spring every two or three years. Various coloured-foliage forms, but shy to flower in cool climates. '**Berggarten**', hardy, felted grey leaves. '**Icterina**' (syn. 'Variegata'), leaves splashed and variegated with creamy yellow, golden-yellow and light green. '**Purpurascens**', purple younger shoots, older leaves turning soft grey-green. '**Tricolor**', most tender but colourful, grey-green leaves boldly marked white and pink, new shoots purple-tinged red. All ✿ or ❋ ■ H45-60cm/18-24in, W75-90cm/30-36in. F6-7. Z7-9. ✿ ■ ★

SANTOLINA Cotton lavender
Dwarf, evergreen shrubs, cypress-like,

grey or green foliage on soft, semi-woody stems, making low, spreading mounds. Profuse, yellow, button flowers. Prune annually or every other year in mid-spring to keep tidy. Prune all branches away to just above newly developing shoots. ✿ ■
S. chamaecyparissus (syn. *S. incana*). Bright silver-grey, woolly foliage in summer, dull grey in winter, yellow flowers which last for several weeks. H45-60cm/18-24in, W60-90cm/2-3ft. F7. Z6-9.
S. virens. Bright green foliage, deep yellow flowers. H45-60cm/18-24in, W45-60cm/18-24in. F7-8. Z7-9.

SARCOCOCCA Sweet box
Related to box, glossy, evergreen shrubs. Insignificant flowers providing heady winter and spring fragrance commend them for garden use and indoor decoration. Spread slowly as clumps or suckers. Trim back tall forms which get untidy immediately after flowering. Best in light shade. ✿ ❋ ❋ ◪ ★
S. confusa. Clump-forming, dense, erect branches, pointed, dark, glossy leaves, clusters of fragrant, creamy white flowers, often black, shiny fruit. H1.5-1.8m/5-6ft, W1.5-1.8m/5-6ft. F2-3. Z7-8.
S. hookeriana digyna. Untidy habit, spreading by suckers, lance-shaped leaves, useful for fragrance. Pinkish flowers followed by black berries. H1.2m/4ft, W1.2m/4ft. F12-3. Z6-8.
S. humilis. Low-growing, dense shrub, glossy leaves, small, creamy white, winter flowers fill a garden with lovely fragrance, excellent near a door. Grows well in deep shade. H30-45cm/12-18in, W45-60cm/18-24in. F1-2. Z6-8.

SKIMMIA
Slow-growing, dwarf to medium-sized shrubs, evergreen leaves, mostly fragrant spring flowers, bright red fruit from late summer through winter. Except for hermaphrodite, or

Skimmia reevesiana

self-fertilizing, *S. reevesiana*, a male form is needed to fertilize fruiting females. Female flowers are usually less showy than those of males. Benefit from fertilizer and an annual mulch of well-rotted compost. Little or no pruning is needed. Tolerate some lime on heavy soils, and sun if moisture is available. ✳ ✳ ◪ ✬ ⊖

S. × *confusa* 'Kew Green'. First-class, male form, mounded bush of glossy, bright green leaves, darker with age and in shade. Large, pyramidal, freely produced heads of sweetly fragrant, creamy white flowers with golden anthers rival any spring-flowering evergreen. H90-120cm/3-4ft, W90-120cm/3-4ft. F2-4. Z7-9.

S. japonica. Choose named selections. 'Bronze Knight', male, similar to 'Rubella'. 'Fructo Albo', dense clusters of white flowers, white fruit, but can be difficult. 'Nana Femina', female, dark green leaves and large heads of bright red fruit. 'Nymans', one of the best, free-fruiting female types, narrow leaves, open habit, bright red fruit. 'Rubella', one of the best male forms, often seen as a pot plant. Dense bush of dark green leaves, reddish brown in winter, as are the leaf stalks and flower spikes. Bronze-red buds in winter open to

reveal pink-flushed petals and yellow anthers; very fragrant flowers. 'Rubinetta', similar to 'Rubella' but more compact. All H60-90cm/2-3ft, W60-90cm/2-3ft. F3-5. Z7-8.

S. reevesiana. Hermaphrodite, often seen containerized and laden with bright red fruit in garden centres, but not always so free-fruiting in the garden. Low, spreading, open plant with panicles of fragrant, white flowers. Dislikes lime. H45-60cm/ 18-24in, W60-90cm/2-3ft. F4-5. Z7-8.

SORBUS Rowan, mountain ash

Some excellent shrubs in this large genus of mostly trees, for attractive foliage, often with good autumn colour, and late summer and autumn fruit, popular with birds. ✳ ✳ ◪ ■ ✬

S. cashmiriana. Beautiful, slow-growing, open, shrubby habit. Graceful, deeply divided leaves. Panicles of pink buds open white and, on older plants, reliably produce clusters of large, succulent, white fruit in late summer. H2.4-3m/8-10ft, W1.8-2.4m/6-8ft. F5. Z5-7.

S. koehneana. Easy-going shrub or small tree, dark green leaves, crimson-purple in autumn. Clusters of pure white flowers, bunches of small, porcelain-white fruit in late summer, even on young plants. H1.8-2.4m/6-8ft, W1.8-2.4m/6-8ft. F5-6. Z6-7.

SPIRAEA

Useful and hardy ornamental shrubs some with good autumn colour, others early spring flowers. Dislikes thin chalky soil. ✳ ◪ ■ ☆

S. betulifolia aemeliana. Dwarf, twiggy shrub, reddish brown stems, oval, bright green leaves which darken, with excellent autumn colour, flat heads of white flowers. H60-75cm/24-30in, W60-75cm/24-30in. F6. Z5-8.

S. prunifolia 'Plena'. Arching stems, serrated, oval leaves, brilliant orange-red in autumn, white, densely

Sorbus koehneana

petalled, double flowers. Prune after flowering by a third. H1.5-1.8m/ 5-6ft, W1.5m/5ft. F4-5. Z5-8.

S. thunbergii. Free-flowering, dense, twiggy bush, arching branches. Profuse, white flowers display along the stems before the leaves. On established plants, prune away older and weakest stems after flowering. 'Mt. Fuji', leaves edged with white, pink shoots, longer interest. Both H90-120cm/3-4ft, W1.2m/4ft. F3-4. Z5-8.

STEPHANANDRA

Spiraea-like in habit, leaf and flower, some are useful for winter stems. ✳ ✳ ◪ ✬

S. tanakae. Large, oval leaves, good autumn colour, dull, creamy yellow flowers on widely arching, pendulous branches. Rich brown stems are of great value in winter. Prune oldest wood to the base in late winter or early spring. H1.5-1.8m/5-6ft, W1.5-1.8m/5-6ft. F7. Z6-8.

STRANVAESIA See under *PHOTINIA*

SYMPHORICARPOS Snowberry

Large-scale, colonizing ground cover, often spectacular autumn fruits, should be used with care. Many are vigorous so growth may need to be

restricted. Remove spreading suckers, prune old stems to base and shorten others by half in winter. Tolerate dryish shade. ✳ ✳ ◪ ✬

ULEX Gorse

Almost leafless shrubs appearing as evergreens. ✳ ■ ⊖

U. europaeus. Prickly common gorse. Some forms are ornamental and were it not so often seen in the wild the species would be considered garden-worthy. Profuse, golden-yellow, pea-shaped flowers, in mild weather some flower at Christmas, and often on and off almost all year. To restrict size, prune immediately after flowering on younger, softer wood with shears, but older, straggly plants can be cut to the ground in spring as growth begins. H1.2-1.5m/4-5ft, W1.5-1.8m/5-6ft. F3-6. Z8-9. 'Aureus', greeny yellow stems, spines and leaves turn clear yellow in summer. H1.2-1.5m/4-5ft, W1.5-1.8m/5-6ft. F4-5. Z8-9. 'Plenus', denser, double flowers, ideal with heathers. H60-90cm/2-3ft, W90-120cm/3-4ft. F4-6. Z8-9.

VACCINIUM

Evergreen and deciduous shrubs. Ornamentals are mostly grown for fruit and foliage, not the modest flowers. Deciduous types have good

Stephanandra tanakae

autumn leaf-colour; the evergreens, often showy, mostly edible berries. Peaty soil. ☼ ❊ ◪ ■ ⊖

V. corymbosum. Blueberry. Ornamental. Upright, multi-stemmed, dark bluish green leaves, turning scarlet and bronze in autumn. Clusters of white-tinged pink, urn-shaped flowers before the leaves in spring, followed in summer by blue-black fruits covered in a blue bloom. The tasty fruits are much loved by birds. H1.5-1.8m/5-6ft, W1.2-1.5m/4-5ft. F4-5. Z4-8.

V. vitis-idaea. Cowberry. Dense, creeping shrub, dark, glossy green leaves, pinkish white, bell-shaped flowers, followed by abundant, shiny, red, edible fruit. H15-20cm/6-8in, W60-90cm/2-3ft. F6-8. Z4-7. 'Koralle', pink, bell-shaped flowers, larger, if sparser, fruit than the species. Slightly more vigorous, making a carpet of small leaves; excellent ground cover in shade. H10-15cm/4-6in, W60-90cm/2-3ft. F6-8. Z4-7.

VIBURNUM

Among this varied group of deciduous and evergreen shrubs and small trees are many valuable for autumn colour, fruits and flowers, winter and early spring foliage and flower. Many have fragrance as an added bonus. Most grow in any soil, including chalk, some need moist soil; others, especially evergreens, may need shelter from cold, desiccating winds.
☼ ❊ ◪ ❀

V. × bodnantense. Erect, eventually large, bushes, fragrant flower clusters along the stems, even before the last leaves fall. Pink in bud, they open light pink, fading to white, and being frost-resistant, they last for many weeks. Perhaps the most striking is 'Charles Lamont', deep rose-pink flowers. 'Dawn', deeper pink in bud. 'Deben', pink in bud, opening white flushed with pink. All H1.8-2.4m/6-8ft, W1.5-1.8m/5-6ft. F10-3. Z5-8.

V. davidii. Evergreen, low, spreading

Viburnum tinus 'Gwenllian'

shrub, leathery, narrow, corrugated leaves, dull flowers, but bright metallic-blue fruit in autumn and winter, not always freely produced. Plant several to ensure cross-pollination – many nurserymen offer fruiting female plants with an identifiable male. Protect from severe frost and wind. H60-75cm/24-30in, W90-120cm/3-4ft. F6-7. Z8-9. ☼ ◪

V. farreri (syn. *V. fragrans*). Large, deciduous, erect shrub, bronze young leaves, fragrant flower clusters, pink in bud and opening white, continuing spasmodically through all but severe winters. 'Candidissimum', light green leaves, white flowers. Both H1.5-1.8m/5-6ft, W1.2-1.5m/4-5ft. F11-3. Z5-8.

V. opulus. Guelder rose, European cranberry-bush viburnum. Deciduous, outstanding in late summer when hung with clusters of succulent, bright red fruit. Flat, white, lacecap flowers in early summer. Some have good autumn leaf colour, but fruit appears when leaves are green. 'Aureum', bright yellow leaves which can scorch in full sun, but which stay yellow well through summer. Red fruit and reddish brown autumn tints. H1.5-1.8m/5-6ft, W1.2-1.5m/4-5ft. F6-7. Z3-8. 'Compactum', dwarf,

free-flowering, red fruit persisting after leaves have dropped. H90-120cm/3-4ft, W90-120cm/3-4ft. F6-7. Z4-8. 'Notcutt's Variety', large, red fruit, often purple autumn leaves. H2.4-3m/8-10ft, W1.8-2.4m/6-8ft. F6-7. Z4-8. 'Xanthocarpum', bright green leaves, white flowers and golden-yellow fruits, becoming translucent with age. H2.4-3m/8-10ft, W1.8-2.4m/6-8ft. F6-7. Z4-8.

V. tinus. Valuable evergreens, winter form, dark, glossy leaves. Fragrant flower clusters can continue on and off for months, bright blue fruit are rare except in warm climates. For hedging or to retain density, prune immediately after flowering; to rejuvenate old, woody or open plants, prune to the ground in mid- to late spring when hard frosts are finished. Most plants sold are selected clones. Can be damaged in severe winters inland, especially when young. Exposed foliage is vulnerable to frost and freezing winds, although even if apparently killed, new shoots often break from the base in late spring. Flowers less in shade. H1.8-2.4m/6-8ft, W1.8-2.4m/6-8ft. F10-4. Z8-10. 8 'Eve Price', lower, more spreading, smaller leaves, rose-red flower buds, opening white, fragrant. 'Gwenllian', compact habit, small leaves, pinkish

white flowers, deep pink in bud, free-fruiting. Both H1.2-1.5m/4-5ft, W1.2-1.5m/4-5ft. F11-4. Z7-8.

VITIS Vine

Ornamental grape vines are self-supporting, most are vigorous, ideal for covering walls, climbing up trees or training over pergolas, creating leafy shade. Most have maple-like leaves spectacular autumn colour, panicles of insignificant greenish white flowers followed by bunches of grapes, varying in ornamental and edible value. Prefers chalky soil.
☼ ❊ ■

V. coignetiae. Vigorous, probably the most spectacular ornamental vine for autumn leaf colour. Large green leaves in autumn turn from purple-bronze to bright crimson and scarlet, the best colour on poor, dry soil. Needs tying in before it becomes self-supporting, later requires considerable space, although it can be pruned. Purple-black grapes. H5-6m/16-20ft, W5-6m/16-20ft. F6-7. Z5-9.

V. vinifera 'Purpurea'. Teinturier grape. Slow to establish, eventually makes a striking display of reddish purple leaves and, on older plants, deep purple, bloomy grapes, excellent autumn colour. Both H3-4m/10-13ft, W3-4m/10-13ft. F6-7. Z6-9.

Vitis coignetiae

CONIFERS DIRECTORY

CONIFERS COME IN ALL SHAPES *and sizes and may be slow or fast growing. They may be low, bushy and bun-shaped, narrow, upright, prostrate or semi-prostrate, wide-spreading, or any shape in between, and they are available in many shades of green, blue, gold or yellow as well as variegated colours. Some have soft, feathery foliage, others have sharp, prickly or needle-like foliage.*

Since the majority of conifers are evergreen, most give colour and form throughout the year. The selection that follows concentrates on those that are particularly attractive during the autumn, winter and early spring period. It is a personal selection that includes primarily dwarf and slow-growing types.

An indication of the approximate size, after ten years, appears after each description; inevitably, this is an estimate, since growing conditions, soils and climate can differ widely. The most important point to take into consideration when selecting conifers, however, is their rate of growth. For the best colour in both summer and winter, plant conifers in full sun.

H: Approximate height after 10 years
W: Approximate width after 10 years
G: Propagated by grafting
Z: Relevant hardiness zone(s)

Conifers contribute valuable colour and form in winter

Abies procera 'Glauca Prostrata'

ABIES Silver fir

The genus includes attractive, smaller cultivars. Cones usually stand above the foliage, and on some species, such as *A. procera* and *A. koreana*, can be most impressive. Generally prefer temperate zones, with cool winters. Most species are hardy; some dislike shallow, chalky soils and industrial atmospheres. ☼ ☀

A. lasiocarpa '**Compacta**'. Superb compact form of Arizona cork bark fir. Slowly makes a broadly pyramidal, dense, silvery blue bush with light brown winter buds. Foliage turns intense silver in midsummer. H60-90cm/2-3ft, W45cm/18in. G. Z6-7.

A. nordmanniana '**Golden Spreader**'. A form of Caucasian fir. Excellent winter colour. Slow and prostrate when young, eventually forming an irregular, compact bush with light gold summer leaves turning glowing, deep gold in winter. In hot climates, best in part shade. H45-60cm/18-24in, W45-60cm/18-24in. G. Z5-7.

A. procera '**Glauca Prostrata**'. Dwarf or prostrate form of noble fir. Bright, silver-blue foliage, deep crimson male flowers in spring. Very irregular, spreading bush unless pruned, ideal for the larger rockery or heather garden. Occasional upright shoots can be pruned, or left to make a small, controllable tree, occasionally

Calocedrus decurrens 'Aureovariegata'

with cylindrical cones. Unsuitable for chalk. H30-45cm/12-18in, W75-120cm/30-48in. G. Z6-7. ☀ ◪

CALOCEDRUS Incense cedar

C. decurrens '**Aureovariegata**'. Slow-growing, eventually forming a broadly conical tree. Deep green foliage, irregularly splashed golden-yellow. Pruning branch tips in early years promotes density. The species, with rich green foliage, is also attractive in winter. H2.1-3m/7-10ft, W90cm/3ft. G. Z6-8. ☀ ◪ ☆

CEDRUS Cedar

Genus of four species, most becoming large trees, pyramidal in mid-life, some flat-topped with age. Needle-like leaves spirally arranged in clusters along the branches. The upright cones often take two or three years to ripen. Deep soil.

☼ ☀ ◪ ■ ☆

C. deodara. 'Cream Puff', small pyramid, creamy white foliage, brighter in summer. Pruning will enhance density. H1.5-1.8m/5-6ft, W90cm/3ft. G. Z7-8. 'Golden Horizon', bright, golden-yellow needles in summer, golden-green in winter. Varies considerably in habit, perhaps according to grafting; in its best form low and prostrate, but can become semi-prostrate and sometimes throws up a leading shoot which, if not cut out, will develop into a large upright form. Approximate H45-60cm/18-24in, W1.5-1.8m/5-6ft. G. Z7-8. 'Karl Fuchs', distinctive pyramid, striking, blue-grey foliage. H3-5m/10-16ft, W1.5-2.1m/5-7ft. G. Z6-8. 'Nana Aurea', one of the best, although unexciting when young and perhaps prone to spring frost damage. Slowly develops into a dense, golden-yellow bush, keeps its colour throughout the year in a sunny position. If allowed to make a leading shoot, it forms a narrow, conical tree. For the smaller garden, prune the leading shoots to create a dome shape with pendulous branch tips. H (unpruned) 1.8-3m/6-10ft, W1.5m/5ft. G. Z7-8.

CHAMAECYPARIS False cypress
The selection below is but a fraction of the choice available for winter colour. ☀ ◩ ☆

C. lawsoniana. Most cultivars are hardy to Zone 6 but young golden- and cream-foliaged forms need shelter from cold winds and intense sunlight. 'Aurea Densa' and its sister plant, 'Minima Aurea' are two of the finest dwarf conifers. 'Aurea Densa' makes a very compact bush of stiff, golden-yellow foliage, eventually rounded in habit. Best in full sun. H30-45cm/12-18in, W30cm/1ft. Z7. 'Golden Pot', soft, feathery, upright branching foliage, slow-growing, year-round bright yellow colour. Excellent with contrasting foliage shrubs or heathers.

H90-120cm/3-4ft, W30-45cm/12-18in. Z7. 'Lane', a taller-growing Lawson, also known as 'Lanei', golden-yellow summer foliage, turning brighter, clearer yellow in winter. Eventually makes a broad pyramid, and can make an effective and colourful screen. H2.4-3m/8-10ft, W1.2m/4ft. Z6-7. 'Minima Aurea', rigid branches, dense sprays of bright golden-yellow leaves which appear brighter in winter. Eventually makes a dwarf pyramid; 'Aurea Densa' is more ovoid, but both are equally desirable. 'Moonshine', outstanding for bright yellow winter foliage, broad pyramid of soft, feathery foliage. Quite slow. H1.5-1.8m/5-6ft, W75-120cm/30-48in. Z6-7. 'Pygmaea Argentea', bright, year-round show, creamy white-splashed foliage. Needs sun but shelter from cold winds. H30-45cm/12-18in, W30-45cm/12-18in. Z7-8.

C. obtusa. 'Fernspray Gold', golden-leaved selection of fernspray cypress (*C. obtusa* 'Filicoides'), often straggly or open in habit unless trimmed from an early age. Fern-like foliage clothes the branches exposed to sunlight, giving bright, year-round colour. H1.5-1.8m/5-6ft, W90-120cm/3-4ft. Z6-8. 'Nana Lutea', dwarf, golden-yellow in summer and clear yellow in winter in an open position. Gradually forms a broad, irregularly pyramidal bush. H45-60cm/18-24in, W30-45cm/12-18in. Z5-8. 'Pygmaea', vigorous cultivar, belying its name. Bronze-green, glossy foliage, becoming deeper bronze in winter, grows in flat tiers, ending in thin, twisted, whipcord shoots. H30-45cm/12-18in, W60-75cm/24-30in. Z5-8.

C. pisifera. 'Filifera Aurea', first class for winter form and colour, eventually grows large but is extremely slow in early years. All 'Filifera' types have long, thin, thread-like foliage; on this plant it is

Cryptomeria japonica 'Elegans'

bright yellow all year round. It may be slow to produce upright shoots and pruning side shoots may help – hardly natural but most effective pruned as a narrow pyramid. H90-120cm/3-4ft, W90-120cm/3-4ft. Z5-8. 'Filifera Aureovariegata', sprawling and untidy when young but slowly forms a mounded bush of cascading, string-like, dark green foliage, irregularly splashed golden-yellow. H75-90cm/30-36in, W60-90cm/2-3ft. Z5-8. 'Squarrosa Lombarts', soft, heather-like foliage, grey-blue in summer, turning deep purple in winter, large bush in time. Dislikes extremely heavy or alkaline soils. H1.2-1.5m/4-5ft, W1.2-1.5m/4-5ft. Z5-8.

C. thyoides. Some attractive dwarf selections with juvenile foliage turning from greyish green in summer to shades of purple in winter. 'Heather Bun', 'Purple

Heather' and 'Rubicon', distinctive purple winter foliage, oval-shaped bushes, a little tender in exposed positions. H1.2-1.5m/4-5ft, W60-75cm/24-30in. Z7-8.

CRYPTOMERIA Japanese cedar
C. japonica. 'Elegans', finely cut, feathery foliage, soft to the touch. Eventually becomes broadly conical, varying according to climate and situation. Fresh-green summer foliage turns deep purple-bronze in late autumn and winter. Ideal for the winter garden, although not hardy in very cold climates. H1.8-3m/6-10ft, W1.2-1.5m/4-5ft. Z7-8. ☆ 'Sekkan-sugi', superlative, broad column of upright branches from which hangs looser, pendulous green inner foliage, which where exposed to the light is sulphur-yellow in winter and the most startling creamy white in summer. Shelter from

strong sun and cold winds in early years. H1.5-1.8m/5-6ft, W90-120cm/3-4ft. Z6-9. **'Vilmoriniana'**, dwarf, very tight ball of dense, congested foliage, bright green in summer and bronze in winter, particularly in exposed situations. H30-45cm/12-18in, W30-45cm/12-18in. Z6-9.

× CUPRESSOCYPARIS
× C. leylandii. Leyland cypress. Fastest-growing conifer, popular for hedges (for which it is often unsuitable) and screening. Dark green foliage is useful in winter, but its windbreak qualities are greater than its ornamental value. Some attractive, garden-worthy selections with golden or variegated foliage. ☼ ■ ☆
'Golconda', one of the brightest golden conifers, excellent in winter. Open in habit when young, it fills in nicely with age. H5-6m/16-20ft, W1.5-2.1m/5-7ft. Z6-10. **'Gold Rider'**, similar. **'Silver Dust'**, vigorous, splashes of creamy white on dark green foliage. H5-6m/16-20ft, W2.4-3m/8-10ft. Z7-9.

CUPRESSUS Cypress
C. glabra. Hardy cypress, formerly considered a form of *C. arizonica*. ☼ ☆
'Conica', **'Glauca'** and **'Pyramidalis'**, slow-growing, eventually large conical or pyramidal forms of striking blue-grey foliage, enhanced with large, round 'nuts' or cones. **'Blue Ice'** and **'Silver Smoke'**, two new cultivars worth looking for. Ensure when planting that roots are not 'corkscrewed' within the pots. Often grafted. H3-5m/10-16ft, W1.2-1.5m/4-5ft. Z7-9.
'Sulphurea', striking column of densely packed, sulphur-yellow foliage, brighter in summer, as hardy as blue forms. Often grafted. H2.1-3m/7-10ft, W90-120cm/3-4ft. Z7-9.

JUNIPERUS Juniper
The junipers are among the most ornamental and adaptable conifers for garden use. Some have colourful winter foliage and an added bonus on mature specimens of attractive berries. Many are extremely hardy, surviving low and high temperatures, and thin and impoverished soils, including limy ones. ☼ □ ■ ☆
J. chinensis. **'Aurea'**, golden Chinese juniper, lovely but difficult to propagate and grow as a young plant. Prickly whitish yellow juvenile foliage and non-prickly golden-yellow adult foliage, eventually a narrow cone of deep golden-yellow, especially bright in winter. Hardy, but protect from cold winds and hot sun in early years. Often grafted. H1.2-1.5m/4-5ft, W60-75cm/24-30in. Z5-9. **'Japonica Variegata'**, often mistakenly sold as 'Kaizuka Variegata'. Semi-prostrate, almost vase-shaped, with juvenile foliage or, more commonly, an upright, irregular pyramid of mostly adult foliage, in each case splashed creamy white. H1.5-1.8m/5-6ft, W90-120cm/3-4ft. Z5-9. **'Kaizuka'**, upward, spreading bush with several leading stems, forming a plant of great character. Attractive clusters of blue-grey fruits on older plants. Excellent for specimen planting in a lawn or heather garden. To train it as a wall shrub or espalier, start early! H1.2-1.8m/4-6ft, W1.2-1.5m/4-5ft. Z4-9. **'Keteleeri'**, annual autumn and winter display of bluish grey berries, long-lasting when cut. Upright, grey-green, columnar form. H2.1-3m/7-10ft, W90cm/3ft. Z5-9.
J. communis **'Depressa Aurea'**. Unusual semi-prostrate conifer, bronze-green in winter, changing to greeny yellow in spring, transformed in early summer when golden-yellow new shoots appear. The whole bush becomes butter-yellow, toning down

Juniperus chinensis 'Kaizuka'

later in summer. Full sun essential. At its best superb; excellent for ground cover. H30-45cm/12-18in, W1.2-1.5m/4-5ft. Z3-7. Many other *J. communis* forms have winter interest in foliage and habit – look for them in specialist books, nurseries and garden centres.
J. horizontalis. Creeping juniper. The many forms take some beating for year-round cover. However, most are duller in winter and few can be specifically recommended for autumn, winter or spring interest. Prune as necessary to keep a denser habit. Easy to grow on any well-drained soil. Semi-prostrate **'Plumosa Compacta'** and **'Youngstown'** change colour after first frosts from soft blue-grey to distinctive bronze-purple, effective next to a golden-foliaged heather, conifer or shrub. Both H30-45cm/12-18in, W75-90cm/30-36in. Z4-9.

Juniperus chinensis 'Aurea'

Juniperus communis 'Horstmann'

J. x media. Broad group includes first-class, mostly semi-prostrate cultivars of great ornamental value. **'Gold Coast'**, one of the best of many selections, keeping a good winter colour. Low-growing and wide-spreading habit with bright, mostly adult, golden-yellow foliage, less brilliant in winter. Takes pruning well. H60-90cm/2-3ft, W1.5-1.8m/5-6ft. Z4-9. **'Gold Sovereign'**, very compact cultivar, ideally suited to the smaller garden, with brilliant golden-yellow juvenile and adult foliage in summer, and in a sunny situation remaining bright in winter. Can be kept quite dwarf with annual pruning. H45-60cm/18-24in, W75-90cm/30-36in. Z5-9.
'Sulphur Spray', vigorous, semi-prostrate bush of striking, sulphur-yellow adult foliage, particularly in summer. Needs sun to produce the best colour. Regular pruning will keep it within bounds. H90-120cm/3-4ft, W1.2-1.5m/4-5ft. Z4-9.
J. scopulorum. Rocky Mountain juniper. Appealing upright, fastigiate forms. Perhaps most outstanding are **'Blue Moon'**, **'Gray Gleam'** and **'Wichita Blue'**, all with silvery grey winter foliage, silver blue in summer and maintained well into autumn. All are of narrow, upright habit with tiny, scale-like leaves. Best in open positions in sun. Often grafted. Average H1.5-2.1m/5-7ft, W30-45cm/1-2ft. Z4-7.
J. squamata. **'Blue Star'**, quickly makes a compact bush, deep blue in winter, changing to a brilliant, silvery blue in summer. H30-45cm/12-18in, W45-60cm/18-24in. Z5-8.
J. virginiana. Most cultivars have thin, scale-like leaves, are generally very hardy and adaptable to a wide range of soil and climatic conditions. Among the many selections are some with columnar habits, whilst others are prostrate or semi-prostrate, their colour maintained well in winter. **'Grey Owl'**, one of the best junipers for ground cover where little else will grow. Thin, wide-spreading branches, smoky grey, scale-like leaves, blue-grey in winter. Its vigour and adaptability to sun, shade, flat ground, banks and heavy or light soils are remarkable! Lacy, overlapping foliage can be kept in check with regular trimming. H60-90cm/2-3ft, W1.8-2.4m/6-8ft. Z3-9. Similar but slower-growing is **'Blue Cloud'**, with curled and twisted branch tips. **'Helle'**, slowly forms a broad column of rich green foliage, maintained well in winter. Distinct but considered by some authorities to be the same as *J. chinensis* 'Spartan'. H1.5-1.8m/5-6ft, W45-60cm/18-24in. Z3-9.

LARIX **Larch**
L. decidua. European larch. One of the few deciduous conifers, along with *Ginkgo*, *Metasequoia* and *Taxodium*. In spring it bursts into clusters of bright green leaves, which darken through the summer before turning golden in late autumn. A beautiful tree, but rather large for average gardens, and not good on chalk soils. H8-10m/26-33ft, W3-5m/10-16ft. Z3-6. ☆
'Pendula', beautiful, if variable, with weeping branches. Often sold as a standard with shoots of 'Pendula' top-grafted onto the stem of a seedling of the species. Height is difficult to estimate, but growth can be vigorous, 30-45cm/12-18in a year. Pruning may be necessary. G. Z3-6.
L. kaempferi. Japanese larch. Grows to 30m/100ft or more. Broader, almost sea-green leaves and reddish winter twigs. Several forms have been selected from witches' brooms. H6-8m/20-26ft, W3-4m/10-13ft. Z5-7. **'Diana'**, peculiarly twisted and curly branches and long, light green leaves similarly curled. Estimated H90-120cm/3-4ft, W90-120cm/3-4ft. G. Z5-7. **'Nana'**, rare, in its best form it is truly dwarf, with shortened and congested branches and bright fresh-green leaves turning light gold in autumn. H30-45cm/12-18in, W45-60cm/18-24in. G. Z5-7.

Larix kaempferi 'Diana'

Picea glauca 'Coerulea'

METASEQUOIA Dawn redwood
M. glyptostroboides. Dawn redwood. Rapid-growing, deciduous, conical conifer. Delicate-looking, fresh-green feathery foliage clothing erect branching stems. In late autumn the dying leaves turn pink, russet or gold. Tolerates wide range of soils and climates. H5-8m/16-26ft, W1.2-1.5m/4-5ft. Z5-10. ❋ ◿ ■ ☆

MICROBIOTA
M. decussata. Sole species of this genus. Attractive ground cover of gently overlapping lacy sprays of foliage. Bright green in summer changing to a deep rust-purple in winter, a good contrast to golden and variegated evergreens and excellent with heaths and heathers. It is adaptable to sun or shade. H15-30cm/6-12in, W1.2-1.5m/4-5ft. Z2-8. ✿ ❋ ☆

PICEA Spruce
There are attractive ornamental species, but mainly the dwarf forms, usually arising from selected seedlings or witches' brooms, are grown in the smaller, modern-day garden. Although fairly adaptable to a wide range of conditions, they are less happy on very dry or thin chalky soils and most dislike alkaline soils
P. abies. Norway spruce. '**Aurea Magnifica**', brighter all year than '**Aurea**' which is much less ornamental, light yellow in summer and much brighter in winter and spring. Needs sun to colour well. H2.1-3m/7-10ft, W1.5-2.4m/5-8ft. G. Z3-7. '**Inversa**', totally prostrate, but training the main stem to 2.1-3m/7-10ft eventually produces a weeping form of long, dark green shoots cascading down. As a specimen this creates a plant of considerable year-round interest. Annual growth rate 10-15cm/4-6in. G. Z3-7. '**Will's Dwarf**' (syn. 'Wills Zwerg'), pyramid of short, rigid branches, clothed in rich green foliage, rather open at the top but colour maintained throughout winter. H1.2-1.5m/4-5ft, W60-90cm/2-3ft. Z3-7.
P. glauca '**Coerulea**'. Slower-growing in early years and more

Picea pungens 'Globosa'

compact than the species, making a narrow pyramid with upward-angled branches of short, soft, blue-grey needles. Small green cones on quite young trees on the branch tips, maturing to light brown. Eventually quite tall. H1.5-1.8m/5-6ft, W90cm/3ft. G. Z3-7. ❋ ◿
P. omorika '**Nana**'. Attractive form of Serbian spruce. Small for first ten years, eventually forms a broad pyramid 3-5m/10-16ft or more high. Slow to develop leading shoots, initially dome-shaped with dark green upper leaves, bright

silver-blue beneath. H90-120cm/3-4ft, W60-75cm/24-30in. Z5-8. ❋ ◿ ☆
P. orientalis '**Skylands**'. Beautiful when well grown, one of the brightest for colour. Prone to sunscorch when young and slow to make a leading shoot, hence its other name, 'Aurea Compacta'; unless trained when young it is almost semi-prostrate. When established it grows strongly, as much as 30cm/1ft a year, into a narrow conical tree with a rather open branching system. The leaves are bright golden-

Picea orientalis 'Skylands'

yellow on the upper surface, but green underneath. Occasionally prune the more vigorous side shoots. H1.2-1.8m/4-6ft, W90-120cm/3-4ft. G. Z5-7. ☀ ◪

P. pungens. Colorado spruce. Some of the finest and most striking garden conifers for year-round colour. Nearly all cultivars are propagated by grafting, often using side shoots from upright trees, so young plants generally need their main shoot trained upwards on a cane for several years. Pruning vigorous side shoots in early spring helps maintain a better form and removes competition from the leading shoot. Species average: H2.1-3m/7-10ft, W1.2-1.5m/4-5ft. Z3-8. ☀ ■ ☆

'**Globosa**' (syn. 'Glauca Globosa'), closely set, congested branches slightly angled up from the centre, gradually forming a neat but irregular bush. Stiff, prickly needles are grey-blue in winter; in late spring soft, bright blue new leaves transform the colour for the whole summer. Unless grown from

cuttings (not easy) grafted plants may, within four or five years of planting, make one or more leading shoots. Prune away in early spring, unless you want an equally desirable compact pyramid. Mostly grafted. H45-60cm/ 18-24in, W45-60cm/18-24in. Z3-8.

'**Hoopsii**', soft, broad, bright silver-blue needles in summer, silver-grey in winter. Narrow pyramidal or broadly conical form, eventually large. Prune side shoots when young to improve habit. H1.8-2.4m/6-8ft, W90-120cm/3-4ft. G. Z3-8.

'**Koster**', difficult to train a leading shoot in early years, and even later the main terminal tends to bend or snake. Side shoots are irregular and need annual pruning to make a balanced specimen. Branches are angled sharply upwards from the

main stem. Good year-round silver-blue. Cones freely. H1.8-2.4m/6-8ft, W1.2-1.5m/4-5ft. G. Z3-8.

'**Prostrata**' (syn. 'Glauca Prostrata' and 'Procumbens'), covers any prostrate blue spruce but completely flat ones are rare, since most sooner or later try to make angled or vertical shoots. Cut these away to maintain a low-growing habit if required. These will make broad, spreading specimens, their bright silver-blue foliage showing brilliantly against golden heathers or conifers. Annual growth 15-30cm/6-12in. H30-45cm/12-18in, W1.5-1.8m/ 5-6ft. G. Z3-8. '**Thomsen**', one of the best, narrow, with branches angled upwards and soft, thick needles, distinctive silver-grey in winter, bright silver-blue in summer. Difficult to propagate. H1.8-2.4m/ 6-8ft, W90-120cm/3-4ft. G. Z3-8.

P. sitchensis '**Papoose**'. Eventually forms a dense, broadly conical bush whose blue-green leaves have showy silver undersides. H45-60cm/ 18-24in, W45-60cm/18-24in. G. Z4-8.

PINUS Pine

Extremely varied and valuable. All have needles growing in bunches of two to five. In spring many have cone-like male flowers which shed pollen, whilst female flowers produce cones. A great many offer colour, form and cones for winter interest, some turning from green to gold. Some cultivars root readily from cuttings but most must be grafted. ☀ □ ■ ☆

P. aristata '**Sherwood Compact**'. Compact replica of its parent, erect branches forming a tight, conical, blue-green bush, the needles' scales much less and sometimes not at all noticeable. H45-60cm/18-24in, W20-30cm/8-12in. G. Z4-7.

P. cembra. Arolla pine. Excellent for garden and landscape. Formal column of upright branches, densely

Picea pungens 'Hoopsii'

Pinus mugo 'Winter Gold'

Pinus parviflora 'Glauca'

clothed young shoots in sets of five dark blue needles, with bright bluish white insides, covered with thick, orange-brown down. Most plants offered are from seed and may be variable. ◪ 'Glauca', attractive selection with dark blue needles, is grafted, as is the slower-growing 'Aurea', or 'Aureovariegata', which needs full sun, has paler foliage and gold-tipped needles, particularly in winter. *P. cembra* and 'Glauca': H1.5-1.8m/5-6ft, W75-90cm/30-36in. G. Z4-7.

P. koraiensis 'Silveray'. Correct name for plants listed as *P.k.* 'Glauca'. Very attractive selection of the rare, five-needled Korean pine. Hardy, adaptable, fairly slow when young. Rather open column of grey-green branches, clusters of blue-green needles, bright silver-grey underneath. Red male and female flowers often appear in spring, later on older plants. Quite large olive-green cones hug the stems, ripening brown. A distinctive pine for garden and landscape. H1.5-1.8m/5-6ft, W60-75cm/24-30in. G. Z5-7.

P. leucodermis (syn. *P. heldreichii leucodermis*). Bosnian pine. Some first class seedlings and witches' brooms, which although a dark, rich green are invaluable in winter in association with gold, yellow and blue conifers. Distinctive for long, dark green, paired needles which in their first years press forward close to the branches. Bright blue cones ripen brown. Very useful on dry, poor and alkaline soils. Slow when young but eventually tall. H2.4-3m/8-10ft, W90-120cm/3-4ft. Z6-8. ☼ ◪ 'Compact Gem', compact and quite slow-growing when young, dense clusters of lustrous, deep green needles. My eighteen-year-old specimens are 3m/10ft tall and 1.8m/6ft across, so allow for its future development! H90-120cm/3-4ft, W60-90cm/2-3ft. G. Z6-8.

P. mugo. Numerous selections of the two-needled mugo pine, some very similar to each other. They take kindly to pruning and many nurserymen prune them with shears just as they develop new shoots in early summer, still early enough for them to bush out and form buds for the following year. Most succeed in inhospitable conditions, including alkaline soils, as long as good drainage exists. Z3-7.

'Humpy', one of the most compact and attractive dwarf pines, forms a neat cushion with branches densely clothed in short, dark green needles. Prominent brown-purple winter buds. H30cm/1ft, W60cm/2ft. G. Z3-7. 'Ophir', nondescript in summer, but in winter its green needles gradually turn golden-yellow. An open, sunny position gives best colour. H60cm/2ft, W90cm/3ft. G. Z3-7. 'Winter Gold' differs from 'Ophir' in that its needles turn completely golden-yellow where light does not reach, while 'Ophir' needles remain green. Neither suffers sun- or frostburn. 'Zundert', similar but more compact. All H60-75cm/24-30in, W90cm/3ft. G. Z3-7.

P. parviflora 'Glauca'. One of many selections made from seedlings of the Japanese white pine, popular in Japan for their form and outline, particularly when pruned to allow light and air in. Widely used for bonsai. Bright blue-green needles, silvery beneath, borne in clusters at ends of branches and branchlets. Eventually attains 6-10m/20-33ft or more, although often sold as a dwarf. Prune if required to form a narrower outline, or for bonsai. Cones freely. H1.8-2.4m/6-8ft, W1.8-2.4m/6-8ft. G. Z5-8. ☼ ◪

P. strobus. Generally unsuitable for small garden use, but many cultivars have been selected and introduced from seedlings and witches' brooms. ☼ ◪ ■ 'Minima', dense, low, neat, round bush of thin, blue-green needles. Similar but even slower are 'Horsford' and 'Reinshaus'.

H30cm/1ft, W60-75cm/24-30in. G. Z4-9.

P. sylvestris. Scots pine. Two-needled, the only pine native to the British Isles. Old specimens reach 30m/100ft or more, so it is hardly suitable for the smaller garden. Slightly twisted needles, dark blue in winter, brighter in summer. Small rounded cones. A pine of picturesque outline as a mature specimen. Most soils and sites, including acid and alkaline ones. H3-5m/10-16ft, W2.1-3m/7-10ft. Z3-7. ■ ☆ 'Aurea' covers several forms in cultivation, including a fairly rapid-growing one similar to the species, but with light grey-green leaves in summer changing to pale yellow in winter. Although grafted and starting a bit slower, estimated H3-4m/10-13ft, W2.1-3m/7-10ft. G. Z3-7. A much better and initially slower-growing form, sometimes referred to as 'Nisbets', has needles that turn a bright, deep golden-to-orange yellow in winter. Estimated

Taxodium distichum

Taxus baccata 'Standishii'

H1.8-2.4m/6-8ft, W1.5-1.8m/5-6ft, developing more strongly each year. G. Z5. The so-called dwarf '**Gold Coin**' and '**Gold Medal**' have probably been grafted from small, secondary shoots or weak plants and, given time or rich, heavy soil, they soon want to become grown up, too! Unless continually pruned, with age they become much taller, with deep golden winter needles, exposure to sunlight producing the strongest colour. For a golden dwarf Scots pine, prune new growth with secateurs or shears each spring, just as the plant develops 5cm/2in or so of soft foliage. It will still bush out and make attractive winter buds by late summer, as though it had not been trimmed at all. Place against contrasting conifers and underplant with hardy cyclamen. Your plant could be kept for many years at, say, H60cm/2ft, W60-75cm/24-30in by this method. G. Z4-7.
'**Moseri**' (formerly *P. nigra* 'Pygmaea'), distinctive, long needles,

twisted and congested around the top of the branches, and buds surrounded by a sheaf of short green leaves. The needles are nondescript green but turn green-gold in winter, the colour in some winters more extreme than others. H75-90cm/30-36in, W60-75cm/24-30in. G. Z3-7.

PODOCARPUS

Some Australian species have produced forms of note for winter colour and fruit. The few dwarfs of note are similar to yews in appearance. Male and female plants must be in close proximity for the females to produce attractive, berry-like, brightly coloured, seed-holding receptacles, similar to *Taxus*. Like most yews they do well on chalky soils. ☼ ✳ ☆
P. alpinus. Slowly forms a prostrate bush of dark green needles, a few leading branches spreading beyond the mass of foliage. With age becomes a larger shrub. Provide shelter in early years from severe

frosts. Excellent as ground cover or in a rock garden. H20-30cm/8-12in, W60-90cm/2-3ft. Z8-11.
P. lawrencii. Similar to *P. alpinus*, but deeper blue-green needles, attractive against golds in winter.
P. nivalis. Recent breeding and selection by Graham Hutchins in England has resulted in a fascinating range of forms which turn bronze and purple in winter and which fruit readily. All are low-growing forms suitable for smaller gardens. Average H20-30cm/ 8-12in, W60-90cm/2-3ft. Z8-11.

TAXODIUM

Deciduous, for the larger garden. Thrive on moist, swampy soils, but dislike alkaline ones. ☼ ◪
T. distichum. Swamp cypress, bald cypress. Pyramidal habit, wide-spreading or ascending branches. Bare winter stems make picturesque outline, broken in spring by new, bright green shoots. Leaves turn a deep reddish brown in late autumn,

remaining for several weeks. Older trees have reddish brown bark. Beautiful at pond side. H4-6m/13-20ft, W1.5-2.4m/5-8ft. Z5-10.

TAXUS Yew

Useful conifers because of their adaptability. Many introductions have colourful foliage. Succeed in dry, dense shade. ☼ ✳ ▢ ☆
T. baccata. Common yew, known outside Britain as English yew. Variable from seed but leaves are glossy dark green, lighter green beneath; male and female flowers on separate plants but red-capsuled fruits borne only on females. Berries and foliage are poisonous, and one should be aware of possible dangers if children use the garden; avoid yew on boundaries accessible to livestock. Ideal for topiary and hedges, taking pruning, even hard pruning, well since shoots will develop from old wood. Growth rate per annum once established 15-30cm/6-12in. Z6-7.
'**Fastigiata Robusta**', outstanding accent plant, narrower than 'Fastigiata', dark green foliage untouched by severe frosts. Perfect where formality is required. H1.5-1.8m/5-6ft, W20-30cm/8-12in. Z6-7. '**Repens Aurea**', slow and low-growing when young, wide-spreading branches raised at tips. Orange-yellow shoots turn golden-yellow in spring, the foliage gracefully drooping along the outer branches. Colours best in sun. H45-60cm/18-24in, W1.2-1.5m/4-5ft. Z6-7. '**Semperaurea**', erect semi-spreading habit, intense orange-gold shoots in spring, and bright golden-yellow leaves the rest of the year. Excellent winter colour. Prune as necessary. H1.2-1.5m/4-5ft, W1.2-1.5m/4-5ft. Z6-7. '**Standishii**' (syn. 'Fastigiata Standishii'), best upright golden yew for the British climate. Slower and narrower than golden-leaved 'Fastigiata' types, also much brighter in summer and winter. In

Thuja orientalis 'Elegantissima'

open, sunny positions needle tips are deep old-gold. Often fruits. H1.2-1.5m/4-5ft, W30cm/1ft. Z6-7.

THUJA Arbor-vitae

Important ornamental conifers related to, and closely resembling, chamaecyparis. Most form conical trees with flattened foliage sprays, scale-like foliage, noticeably aromatic on certain species and cultivars. Most are hardy, although *T. orientalis* and some of its cultivars are much less so. ✿ ✳ ■ ☆

T. occidentalis. 'Holmstrup Yellow', more open in habit than the narrowly pyramidal, dark green 'Holmstrup', forming a broad column of yellow-green summer foliage, bright yellow in winter, perhaps the brightest of any thuja. Can scorch when young in exposed positions. H1.5-1.8m/5-6ft, W90-120cm/3-4ft. Z4-8. 'Lutea Nana', grows to 8m/26ft or more. Broad column of loose foliage sprays,

bright yellow in summer, deep golden-yellow in winter. H1.8-2.4m/6-8ft, W90-120cm/3-4ft. Z3-8. 'Marrison Sulphur', slow-growing and broadly pyramidal with delicate, lacy, creamy-yellow foliage, even in winter. H1.5-1.8m/5-6ft, W90-120cm/3-4ft. Z3-8. 'Rheingold', attractive bush of lacy, bright golden-yellow summer foliage, rich coppery bronze in winter. Excellent with heathers but colours best in an exposed spot. Prune as necessary, since with age it often gets too broad and untidy. Variable size but approximate H90-120cm/3-4ft, W90-120cm/3-4ft. Z3-8. 'Smaragd', narrow column of bright, rich green foliage, loose, soft and, rare among the green-foliaged cultivars, maintaining its rich colour through winter. Excellent as a specimen or for suburban garden hedge, needing only occasional clipping. H1.8-2.4m/6-8ft, W60-75cm/24-30in. Z3-8. 'Sunkist',

slower-growing and more densely pyramidal than 'Lutea Nana', soon forms a bush with several leading shoots, the flattened foliage sprays golden-yellow in summer, bronze-gold in winter. H1.2-1.5m/4-5ft, W90-120cm/3-4ft. Z3-8.

T. orientalis. Although considerably less hardy than the others, it provides attractive, colourful cultivars, most of which vary in hardiness. Z6-9. 'Collen's Gold', narrow column of open foliage, bright golden-yellow in summer, well maintained in winter. H1.5-1.8m/5-6ft, W30-45cm/12-18in. Z6-9. 'Elegantissima', stiff, upright habit, flat foliage sprays on curving branchlets. Deep golden-yellow leaves in summer, deep bronze in winter, particularly in an open sunny spot. Although slow when young, may reach 5m/16ft or more. H1.2-1.5m/4-5ft, W60-75cm/24-30in. Z6-9. A recent selection, 'Flame', turns almost orange-red in winter in full sun. 'Purple King', narrowly oval habit, green laminated foliage in summer, startling deep purple-brown in winter. Site against brighter foliage. H60-75cm/24-30in, W30-4cm/12-18in. Z6-9.

T. plicata. Fast-growing, tall, eventually broad-based pyramid, foliage flattened in fern-like sprays, from mid- to dark green, scale-like leaves glossy above and pale green beneath with silver markings. Excellent for hedges and screens, stands clipping well, and is one of the few conifers to produce new growth from its centre. The species has a most pleasant, fruity odour when the foliage is brushed or rubbed. Prefers areas of high rainfall. 'Atrovirens', more formal, conical shape, erect branches clothed in deep, rich, glossy green foliage all year round. H4-5m/13-16ft, W90-120cm/3-4ft. Z6-8. 'Irish Gold', one of the brightest conifers in winter, prone to sunscorch when

young. Pyramidal, creamy white foliage lightly flecked with green if grown in full sun. Shelter from cold, desiccating winds. 'Zebrina', much denser and more yellow-green. H1.5-2.4m/5-8ft, W90-120cm/3-4ft. Z7-8. 'Rogersii' (syn. 'Aurea Rogersii'), slowly forms a dense, round bush of congested foliage, dark green inside, deep golden-yellow to bronze at the tips. Cut away growths that break surface if they begin to grow too strongly. Good year-round colour, ideal for the rock garden. H30-45cm/12-18in, W30cm/1ft. Z6-8. 'Stoneham Gold', one of the best plants in the winter garden. Slow-growing, often with several leading shoots to start with. Stems are reddish brown, especially in winter, foliage dark green inside, golden-yellow and green where exposed to sunlight, and orange-yellow, often bronze, at the tips. Excellent winter colour in exposed spots. Trim occasionally. H60-90cm/2-3ft, W45-60cm/18-24in. Z6-8.

TSUGA Hemlock

Not always easy to grow or establish. Need shelter from wind when young, even though the forms listed here are perfectly frost-hardy. ✿ ✳ ◢ ■ ⊖

T. canadensis. 'Everitt Golden' (syn. 'Aurea Compacta'), very slowly forms an upright bush, eventually a small tree, upright, stiff branches, the small leaves golden-yellow all year round. Colours best in full sun but prone to damage from drying winds. H45-60cm/18-24in, W30cm/1ft. Z4-8. 'Gentsch White', slow-growing, bushy, dark green foliage at its centre but the new season's brown stems bear startling white leaves still attractive in winter. Trim annually once well established. 'Dwarf Whitetip' is similar. H60-90cm/2-3ft, W60-90cm/2-3ft. Z4-8.

PERENNIALS DIRECTORY

MOST HARDY PERENNIALS HAVE THE GOOD SENSE to disappear below ground in winter, hopefully to pop up and surprise us each spring. Luckily though, there are many that are evergreen, providing flower and foliage in winter and early spring. There are also many perennials that flower well into autumn. In large genera such as asters and dendranthemas (chrysanthemums) only a few of the vast range available can be mentioned here. Local and regional climates have a bearing on what can be grown successfully, what will flower and for how long in any area.

H: Approximate height
W: Approximate width
F: Months in flower
Z: Relevant hardiness zone(s)

Autumn flower and foliage

Aconitum carmichaelii 'Arendsii'

Adonis amurensis

ACONITUM **Aconite, monkshood**
One or two species are excellent for late flowers, their blues welcome among autumn foliage colours. Tall types may need staking. Roots are poisonous, in the unlikely event of being eaten. Adaptable to heavy soil. ☼ ☀ ■ ☀
A. carmichaelii (syn. *A. fischeri*). Rich green summer foliage, light blue flower heads in autumn. H1.2m/4ft, W30cm/1ft. F9-10. Z3-8. **'Arendsii'**, deeply divided leaves, erect stems topped in autumn with short spikes of deep amethyst-blue flowers. H1.8m/6ft, W30cm/1ft. F9-10. Z3-8. ◪

ADONIS
Indispensable for late winter flowers. Long-lived with fibrous roots, best lifted and divided for replanting when dormant, from mid-summer to late autumn. Provide shelter. ☀ ◪ ■
A. amurensis. Glistening, green-tinged, yellow flowers open from bronze-green shoots which become verdant, ferny foliage. H15cm/6in, W25cm/10in. F1-3. Z4-7. **'Plena'**, large, double, green-centred yellow flowers. H15cm/6in, W25cm/10in. F3-5. Z4-7.
A. vernalis. Choice species. Erect little bushes, single, bright yellow, buttercup-like flowers. Green until late summer. H30cm/1ft, W30cm/1ft. F4-5. Z4-7.

AGAPANTHUS **African lily**
Sterling plants for summer flowers, and even if only a few flower into autumn, their strap-like leaves turn golden and the seed heads remain attractive on slender stems. The newer, hardy kinds, mostly selections from the narrow-leaved Headbourne hybrids, are deservedly popular. Best covered with litter over winter in coldest areas. Move in spring, when new growth is about to begin. Most are Z8-10. Good, deep soil. ☼ ◪ ■

ANAPHALIS **Pearl everlasting**
A. triplinervis **'Summer Snow'**. Best form of the species with neat habit. Silvery, woolly leaves; flowers freely, close to pure white. H25cm/10in, W60cm/2ft. F7-9. Z7-10. ☼ ☀ ◪ ■

ANEMONE
There is some confusion in the naming of the very garden-worthy "Japanese anemones" which are all listed under *A.* x *hybrida.* Their beautiful, delicate flowers are enchanced by golden stamens. ☼ ☀ ■ ★
A. × *hybrida.* None needs staking, and they revel in limy soil. **'Alba'**, strong growers, pure white flowers with contrasting yellow stamens. H75cm/30in, W45cm/18in. F8-10. Z5-8. **'Bressingham Glow'**, rich deep pink, semi-double flowers. H60cm/2ft, W45cm/18in. F8-10.

Anemone x hybrida 'Lady Gilmour'

Z5-8. **'Hadspen Abundance'**, deep rose-pink, almost semi-double flowers, prominent golden-yellow stamens, very free-flowering. H60cm/2ft, W30cm/1ft. F8-10. Z5-9. **'Lady Gilmour'**, large, ivy-type basal leaves, large, semi-double, clear pink flowers. H60cm/2ft, W45cm/18in. F7-10. Z5-8. There are many others.

ARTEMESIA

Good foliage plants until winter. ☼ ■
A. canescens. Delicate, silvery, almost hoary or filigree leaves. Compact, somewhat shrubby, a good foil to other plants. H30cm/1ft, W30cm/1ft. Z5-9.
A. stelleriana. Quite large, deeply cut, felted, silver leaves on ground-hugging stems. Good ground cover. **'Mori'** (syn. 'Boughton Silver'), more compact. H30cm/1ft, W60cm/2ft. Z4-8.

ASARUM Wild ginger

Evergreen, ground-covering plants forming mounds of rounded leaves but with insignificant flowers.
❋ ◪ ■ ★
A. europaeum. Neat, clump-forming, highly glossy, kidney-shaped leaves, brownish flowers. H20cm/8in, W30cm/1ft. F5-6. Z4-7.

Aster amellus 'King George'

ASTER

Among this enormous family are some excellent late-flowering types for all sizes of garden. Most are easy to grow; many are valuable for cutting. ☼ ❋ ■ ★
A. amellus. First-rate, trouble-free plants. Single rayed, yellow-centred flowers seldom needing support. Long-lived, no faults or diseases, slow-growing, long-flowering. For autumn planting, pot-grown plants are best. All F8-10, Z5-8. **'King George'**, violet-blue. H60cm/2ft, W45cm/18in. **'Nocturne'**, rich lilac-lavender. H75cm/30in, W45cm/18in. **'Pink Zenith'**, the most prolific pink variety. H75cm/30in, W45cm/18in. **'Violet Queen'**, masses of deep violet-blue flowers. H60cm/2ft, W45cm/18in.
A. cordifolius. Heart-shaped leaves, wiry stems and graceful sprays of silvery blue flowers. **'Blue Heaven'**, deep blue. 120cm/4ft, W45cm/18in. **'Photograph'**, light blue. H1.3m/51in, W45cm/18in. **'Silver Spray'**, some need staking. H1.6m/63in, W45cm/18in. All F9-10.

Z3-8.
A. ericoides. Shapely bushes, tiny leaves and profuse, tiny flowers. Trouble-free, largely self-supporting, need dividing only after several years. **'Blue Star'**, light blue. **'Brimstone'**, soft creamy yellow. **'Pink cloud'**, delicate lilac pink. **'White Heather'**, white. All H70-90cm/28-36in, W30cm/1ft. F7-9. Z3-8.
A. x *frikartii* **'Wunder von Stäfa'** (syn. 'Wonder of Stäfa'). Taller, more branching and leafier than the type. Clear lavender-blue flowers. H1m/39in, W40cm/16in. F7-9. Z5-8. **'Mönch'**, similar, less branching, very long-flowering.
A. lateriflorus **'Horizontalis'**. Slender, twiggy, upright stems, horizontal sprays of small white or bluish flowers with pink stamens. Foliage turns purple-bronze in early autumn. H1.5m/5ft, W38cm/15in. F9-11. Z4-8.
A. novae-angliae. New England asters. Stout clumps from fibrous roots giving startling colour in late summer and autumn. Sturdy stems carry loose heads of single, yellow-

centred, ray-petalled flowers. Most soils, not too wet. All F9-10, Z4-8. **'Alma Pötschke'**, striking, warm salmon-rose. H1.5m/5ft, W60cm/2ft. **'Autumn Snow'** (syn. 'Herbstschnee'), large white flowers in bushy heads. H1.5m/5ft, W50cm/20in. **'Purple Dome'**, dwarfest to date, intense glowing purple. H60cm/2ft, W45cm/18in. **'Rosa Sieger'** and **'Harrington's Pink'**, similar, clear, clean pink. H1.5m/5ft, W60cm/2ft.
A. novi-belgii. Michaelmas daisy. Many varieties well worth including for their autumn colour. Some are prone to mildew and wilt; avoid tall kinds. Lift and divide in spring every two to three years. All Z4-8. **'Ada Ballard'**, large mauve-blue flowers. H90cm/3ft, W45cm/18in. F8-10. **'Carnival'**, intense, semi-double, cherry-red, erect-growing. H60cm/2ft, W45cm/18in. F9-10. **'Coombe Rosemary'**, fully double violet-purple flowers. 3-5cm/1¼-2in across. H90cm/3ft, W45cm/18in. F9-10. **'White Ladies'**, strong-growing, white flowers, dark foliage. H1.2m/4ft, W45cm/18in. F9-10.

Dwarf hybrids, sometimes listed under *A. dumosus*, are less prone to diseases, grow vigorously and do not need support. **'Audrey'**, mauve-blue single, one of the best. H30cm/1ft, W45cm/18in. F9-10. **'Jenny'**, double red. H30cm/1ft, W45cm/18in. F9-10. **'Little Pink Beauty'**, the best semi-double pink. H40cm/16in, W45cm/18in. F9-10. **'Snow Cushion'**, low-growing, compact, with white flowers. H30cm/1ft, W45cm/18in. F9-10.
A. pringlei **'Monte Cassino'**. Very late-flowering cut-flower variety, a mass of white. H1.2m/4ft, W60cm/2ft. F9-11. Z4-8.
A. spectabilis. Dwarf, mat-forming. Dark, leathery foliage, wiry stems and late sprays of blue, yellow-centred flowers for several weeks. Disease-

resistant. H30cm/1ft, W25cm/10in. F8-10. Z4-9.

A. thomsonii 'Nanus'. Shapely, bushy habit, greyish foliage, rayed, light blue, starry flowers for weeks on end. Best left undisturbed. H40cm/16in, W25cm/10in. F7-10. Z4-9.

BERGENIA
Useful and attractive for both foliage and flowers, although both can be damaged by late spring frost. Mainly evergreen, shiny leaves vary in size up to 25cm/10in across. Surface-expanding from shallow-rooting rhizomes. Many listed here notable for leaves which turn purple, bronze and red in late autumn. ☼ ☀ ■

B. purpurascens. Narrow leaves turning almost beetroot-red in winter, brownish red underneath. Good ground cover among shrubs. Deep pink flowers. H30cm/1ft, W30cm/1ft. F3-5. Z3-8.

Hybrids. 'Abendglut' (syn. 'Evening Glow'), slow-spreading, almost prostrate purplish leaves, purple-red stumpy spikes. H25cm/10in, W30cm/1ft. F3-5. Z3-8. 'Baby Doll', close-set spikes of sugar-pink flowers. H20cm/8in, W30cm/1ft. F3-5. Z4-8. 'Bressingham Ruby', outstanding intense, deep red flowers and almost beetroot-red leaves in winter, which seem to withstand both winter frosts and summer heat. H35cm/14in, W30cm/1ft. F3-5. Z3-8. 'Bressingham White', white flowers, handsome, rounded leaves. H30cm/1ft, W30cm/1ft. F3-5. Z4-8.

Bergenia 'Bressingham Ruby'

'Eric Smith', glossy, rounded leaves turn bronze-purple in winter, reddish beneath. Red flowers. H45cm/18in, W30cm/1ft. F3-5. Z4-8. 'Wintermärchen', small, pointed, somewhat upright leaves turn bronze-purple, carmine beneath, in winter. Rose-red flowers. H30cm/1ft, W30cm/1ft. F3-5. Z4-8.

CHRYSANTHEMUM
C. nipponicum see *Nipponanthemum nipponicum*
C. rubellum see *Dendranthema rubella*
C. uliginosum see *Leucanthemella serotina*
C. yezoense see *Dendranthema yezoense*

CIMICIFUGA Bugbane
Beautiful, trouble-free plants, some late-flowering. Slender, graceful stems, bottlebrush spikes of often scented, small white or cream flowers in late summer or autumn. Leaves often turn yellow in autumn. Support not necessary. Appreciates a good deep soil that is not too limy. ☼ ☀ ◪

C. ramosa. Large, divided leaves and lofty, tapering, branching spikes, creamy white, late in the season.

Cimicifuga simplex 'Elstead'

H2.1m/7ft, W60cm/2ft. F8-9. Z4-8. 'Atropurpurea', purplish leaves and stems, white flowers. H2.1m/7ft, W60cm/2ft. F8-9. Z4-8. 'Brunette', black-purple foliage. H1.8m/6ft, W60cm/2ft. F8-10. Z4-8. *C. simplex* 'White Pearl'. The latest to flower, with full, arching spikes of pure white to brighten the autumn scene. Deservedly popular. 'Elstead', similar, but with purplish buds. H1.2m/4ft, W60cm/2ft. F9-10. Z4-8.

COMMELINA
C. coelestis. Tuberous, tender plant that can be treated as *Cosmos atrosanguineus* with which it associates well. Spreading habit. Azure blue flowers in autumn. H60cm/2ft, W60-90cm/2-3ft. F6-10. Z8-9. ☼ ■ ☆

COREOPSIS Tickseed
Yellow daisies, with yellow or orange central discs, some flowering into autumn. ☼ ■ ☆

C. verticillata. Shapely bushes of finely divided leaves. Studded with small, bright yellow flowers for many weeks. H40cm/16in, W45cm/18in. F7-9. Z4-9. 'Golden Gain', larger flowers, more clump-forming habit.

H60cm/2ft, W38cm/15in. F7-9. Z4-9. 'Grandiflora', larger, deeper yellow flowers. H50cm/20in, W45cm/18in. F7-9. Z4-9. 'Moonbeam', light lemon-yellow flowers, scented foliage, multi-branched growth. H40cm/16in, W30cm/1ft. F7-9. Z3-9. 'Zagreb', clear yellow flowers, dwarf bushy growth. H35cm/14in, W30cm/1ft. F7-10. Z3-9.

COSMOS
C. atrosanguineus (syn. *Bidens atrosanguinea*). Long succession of chocolate-scented, rich deep crimson, single, dahlia-like flowers above bushy, dark green, divided foliage. Tuberous root. Survives outdoors only if covered to prevent frost penetration; roots may be lifted and stored as for dahlias. H80cm/32in, W38cm/15in. F7-10. Z8-9. ☼ ◪ ■

CROCOSMIA
Some of these South African plants create vivid splashes of colour in late summer and into autumn. Parentage is very mixed; montbretia types, indicated with (M), are less hardy and more tender. Best planted in spring and either protected by leaves or dug up for winter. ☼ ◪ ■

C. 'Citronella' (M). Masses of small, soft yellow flowers. H60cm/2ft, W15cm/6in. F7-8. Z6-9.
C. 'Emily MacKenzie' (M). Large-flowered late variety, deep orange petals and mahogany-crimson throat. H50cm/20in, W15cm/6in. F8-10. Z6-9.
C. 'Jenny Bloom'. Soft butter-yellow flowers, strong-growing and prolific. H80cm/32in, W15cm/6in. F7-10. Z5-9.
C. 'Star of the East' (M). Large, warm orange, turning apricot-yellow. H90cm/3ft, W30cm/1ft. F7-9. Z5-9.

DENDRANTHEMA
To many gardeners these will always be chrysanthemums, but the name

Epimedium pinnatum colchicum

Eupatorium purpureum 'Glutball'

change is being followed by all nomenclature authorities. For cheery autumn colour, there is little to beat the "crysanths" or "mums", and now breeders are producing an amazing range of both hardy and pot-plant varieties. Only a few of the hardy species and hybrids that flower reliably late in the year can be mentioned. Some shade where not too dry is acceptable. ☼ ■ ☆

D. rubella (syn. *Chrysanthemum rubellum*). Some excellent garden-worthy cultivars which look natural among other perennials and grasses. All are single ray-petalled, with yellow eyes. Replant every year or two to avoid congestion. '**Apricot**', glowing orange-yellow. H75cm/30in, W45cm/18. F9-10. '**Clara Curtis**', clear pink. '**Duchess of Edinburgh**', bright bronzy crimson. '**Mary Stoker**', yellow. All H60-90cm/2-3ft, W60cm/2ft. F8-9. Z5-9.

Hybrids. Much confusion as to parentage exists, but singles, doubles and pom pom flowers are available in all colours, heights, shapes and sizes. Taller, larger-flowered hybrids have a tendency to flop and need staking. Here are a few well-tried varieties. All Z7-9. '**Anastasia**', compact, double, rose-pink, button flowers.

H75cm/30in, W45cm/18in. F10-11. '**Brennpunkt**', brilliant cherry-red. H75cm/30in, W45cm/18. F10-11. '**Mandarin**', bushy, double, orange-yellow. 60cm/2ft, W30cm/1ft. F9-10. '**Mei Kyo**', double, rose-pink. H5cm/18in, W30cm/1ft. F10-11. '**Peter Sare**', fully petalled, single, clear pink. H60cm/2ft, W30cm/1ft. F9-10. '**Pink Procession**', masses of single, bright pink flowers. H90-120cm/3-4in, W45cm/18. F9-10. '**Sunbeam**', bushy, double pom pom, golden yellow. 60cm/2ft, W30cm/1ft. F9-11.

ECHINACEA **Purple coneflower**
Reliable, daisy-like perennials. Radiating crimson-magenta petals, often with lighter tips and dark centres. Good, light soil. ☼ ■ ★

E. purpurea '**Magnus**'. Outstanding for flower size, almost 10cm/4in across. Warm purplish rose. H90cm/3ft, W38cm/15in. F7-10. '**Robert Bloom**', a selection from the more variable Bressingham hybrids. Sturdy stems, rounded, dark brown cones and flattened, deep rose-pink petals. H90cm/3ft, W38cm/15in. F7-10. '**White Lustre**'. Yellow-centred, ivory-white flowers. H90cm/3ft, W45cm/18in. F7-10.

EPIMEDIUM **Barrenwort**
Ground cover, some forms are virtually evergreen, whilst others have veined and rose-tinted leaves. Trim back semi-evergreen foliage in winter to display spring flowers. Only evergreens are listed as most flowers appear in late spring. ☼ ☀ ◪ ■ ★

E. x *perralchicum*. Evergreen hybrid. Quite large, yellow flowers. H30cm/1ft, W30cm/1ft. F3-5. Z5-9. '**Fröhnleiten**', neater, yellow flowers and marbled foliage. Evergreen. H25cm/10in, W25cm/10in. F4-5. Z5-9.

E. perralderianum. Strong-growing evergreen. Glossy leaves, bright green and bronzy red when young, copper-bronze in winter, and yellow flowers. H35cm/14in, W35cm/14in. F3-5. Z5-9.

E. pinnatum colchicum. Semi-evergreen foliage is brightly coloured in autumn and winter. Profuse, large yellow flowers. H25cm/10in, W25cm/10in. F3-5. Z5-9.

EUPATORIUM
Small, fluffy flower heads. Easy in most conditions. ☼ ☀ ◪ ■

E. fraseri (syn. *E. ageratoides*). Dense, bushy clumps of light green leaves and effective heads of puffy white

flowers. H1.2m/4ft, W60cm/2ft. F8-10. Z4-9.

E. purpureum. American Joe Pye weed. Stately, late-flowering background plant. Stiff stems with whorls of pointed leaves carry wide, flat, rose-purple flower heads. '**Atropurpureum**', deep purple heads. '**Album**', white flowers. H1.8-2.1m/6-7ft, W90cm/3ft. F8-10. Z3-9. Some new selections of dwarfer habit are worth noting, particularly '**Glutball**' with large heads of intense purple-red. H150cm/5ft, W60cm/2ft. F8-10. Z3-9.

EUPHORBIA **Spurge**
Among the spurges are some evergreen species with attractive winter foliage and early spring flowers. Most of these: ☼ ☀ ◪ ■

E. amygdaloides '**Rubra**'. Purple-leaved form of the wood spurge. Free-seeding evergreen foliage plant, with contrasting greenish yellow spring flowers. H30cm/1ft, W30cm/1ft. F4-5. Z7-9.

E. characias. Still confused with *E. wulfenii*. The former has brown centres to the greenish yellow flowers; the latter has yellow-centred flowers, carried in broader spikes and with broader leaves. Both have evergreen, glaucous foliage and bushy growth habits; if stems die back to the base after flowering, prune away. H1.2m/ 4ft, W90cm/3ft. F3-5. Z7-10.

E. dulcis 'Chameleon'. Early spring growth. Clumps of purple leaves, followed by greenish yellow flowers. Foliage throughout year with good autumn colour. H45cm/18in, W30cm/1ft. F5-6. Z7-9.

E. myrsinites. Blue-grey, fleshy leaves closely set along trailing stems which carry heads of sulphur-yellow flowers. H15cm/6in, W30cm/1ft. F5-7. Z5-8.

E. robbiae. Evergreen ground cover. Rounded leaves forming attractive basal rosettes, and flattish heads of almost green flowers. Roots spread quite rapidly but are easily curbed. H50cm/20in, W50cm/20in. F3-5. Z8-9.

E. wulfenii. Yellow-green flowers, no brown centres, carried in broader spikes than *E. characias.* Sturdy habit, with glaucous leaves. Several named cultivars. Some dwarfer with nodding heads in early spring like 'Humpty Dumpty', compact blue-grey stems. H75cm/30in, W75cm/30in. F3-5. Z7-10. Some tall with enormous heads like 'Lambrook Gold' and 'Spring Splendour'. H1.5m/5ft, W90cm/3ft. F3-5. Z7-10.

Euphorbia wulfenii 'Humpty Dumpty'

GAURA

G. lindheimeri. Willowy, branching stems carry a long succession of small, pinkish white flowers. H1.2m/4ft, W90cm/3ft. F7-10. Z6-9. ☼ ■

GENTIANA Gentian

Some valuable perennials for late summer and autumn colour.
☼ ❋ ◨ ■ ★

G. asclepiadea. Willow gentian. Wiry stems, willow-like leaves, terminating in many pairs of deep blue trumpets. Colour varies a little; the form 'Alba' is white. H60-70cm/24-28in, W60cm/2ft. F8-10. Z6-9. ❋

GERANIUM Crane's bill

Deservedly popular perennials. Most flower in summer but some make quite a show in autumn. See also Alpines Directory, page 141. Most ☼ ☆

G. 'Ann Folkard'. Wide-spreading, with magenta-purple, saucer-shaped flowers. Yellow-tinged leaves early in the year. Excellent if allowed to scramble among other plants. H30cm/1ft, W30cm/1ft. F6-9. Z5-8.

G. macrorrhizum. Semi-evergreen sweet briar-scented leaves, colouring well in autumn, somewhat woody stems and short sprays of magenta flowers, 4cm/1½in across. The form

Geranium 'Russell Prichard'

Helianthus salicifolius

album is white, 'Ingwersen's Variety', is soft pink, and 'Variegatum' has variegated leaves. 'Bevan's Variety', deep rose-pink flowers. Good, quick-spreading, weed-proof ground cover for sun or shade. All H25cm/10in, W60cm/2ft. F6-7. Z4-8.

G. procurrens. With self-rooting runners forms rapid ground cover of light green leaves and pale magenta flowers. H15cm/6in, W60cm/2ft. F6-10. Z5-8.

G. × *riversleaianum.* Long-flowering on wide-spreading stems, greyish leaves. 'Mavis Simpson', masses of light pink flowers. H30cm/1ft, W60-90/2-3ft. F 6-10. Z7-8. 'Russell Prichard', vivid magenta-rose, slightly greener foliage. Good for frontal or sloping positions with full sun. H15cm/6in, W45cm/18in. F6-10. Z6-8.

G. wallichianum 'Buxton's Variety'. Wonderful for a frontal position. Dense, deep green summer growth studded for weeks with lavender-blue, saucer-shaped flowers, white at the centre. H30cm/1ft, W90cm/3ft. F6-10. Z4-8. ☼ ■

HACQUETIA

H. epipactis. Uncommon, spring-flowering plant. Tight umbels of tiny,

sulphur-yellow flowers set in leafy bracts, followed by a mound of tufted, deeply lobed, dark green leaves. A rare form with variegated leaves is attractive. Humus-rich soil. H15cm/6in, W23cm/9in. F3-5. Z5-7. ❋ ◨ ★

HELIANTHUS Perennial sunflower

Many species and varieties, all with golden-yellow flowers, mostly in late summer and early autumn. ☼ ■

H. salicifolius (syn. *H. orygalis*). Distinctive for its long, willow-like stem, foliage and sprays of yellow flowers. Tall and for the larger garden. H2.1m/7ft, W60cm/2ft. F9-10. Z6-9.

HELLEBORUS Christmas rose, Lenten rose

One of the most important groups for winter and early spring colour. Cup- or bowl-shaped flowers with prominent stamens and thick petals. Subtle range of colours and colour combinations. Ideally a north-facing position without excessive competition from tree roots. Light mulch of humus to retain moisture. Hellebores resent disturbance, so young plants are most successful, flourishing for years if left alone.

Helleborus foetidus

Divided plants of *H. niger* are apt to sulk, producing only occasional flowers and little foliage thereafter, but it seldom varies from seed. A healthy plant remains evergreen at least until early winter. Most *orientalis* types make new sets of leaves after flowering, providing a shady canopy for the seeds to ripen slowly. Recent developments have produced some excellent, sought-after strains. ✿ ❈ ◪ ■ ☆

H. argutifolius (formerly *H. corsicus*). Evergreen, rather lax in habit, grey-green, attractively veined, divided leaves and large clusters of pale apple-green flowers. H60cm/2ft, W90cm/3ft. F3-5. Z7-9.

H. foetidus. Deep green, upright growth, fingered, dark evergreen leaves and greenish flowers with maroon-edged petals in spring. Not a long-lived plant but naturalizes by self-seeding freely. 'Wester Flisk', reddish stems, even more attractive. H60cm/2ft, W60cm/2ft. F2-4. Z6-9.

H. niger. Christmas rose. Nodding white flowers, often tinged greeny pink, and dark green, leathery leaves, usually flowers after Christmas until early spring. Resents being moved or divided. All H25-30cm/10-12in, W45cm/18in. F1-3. Z4-8.

H. x *nigercors.* Cross between *H. argutifolius* and *H. niger.* Handsome,

dark leaves, rather loose stems carrying sprays of open, creamy flowers. H30cm/1ft, W45cm/18in. F2-4. Z6-9.

H. orientalis. Lenten rose. Scarcely obtainable now in the true species, but hybrid strains are excellent, including white, greenish yellow, pink, maroon and blue-black shades, with many flowers delicately spotted crimson or pink. Some forms almost come true from seed, but there are named selections which must be grown from division. All are virtually evergreen, with new leaves following the flowers, and they make good ground cover. Cut away any tatty leaves before flowers start. H30-60cm/1-2ft, W30-60cm/1-2ft. F2-4. Z4-9.

HEUCHERA

Those with coloured foliage are useful for autumn, winter and early spring. Selection and breeding is beginning to show results with some – purple, cream, bronze and marbled leaves. When replanting, discard old woody sections; fibrous roots encourage free flowering.
✿ ❈ ◪ ■ ☆

H. micrantha. 'Palace Purple', excellent garden-worthy form with large, glossy, richly coloured, almost beetroot-red leaves, but is variable from seed. 'Bressingham Bronze', a reliable selection with large bronze-surfaced crinkled leaves, whitish flowers. H70cm/28in, W30cm/1ft. F6-8. Z4-8.

HOSTA Plantain lily

Many hostas remain interesting in late summer, if left alone by slugs! Dying leaves are often attractive, turning to gold and beige before collapsing. All Z3-9 ❈ ◪ ■ ★

IRIS

A few are certainly worthy plants for autumn, winter and early spring interest, although the majority are

Iris foetidissima 'Variegata'

Iris stylosa

summer flowering. Requirements depend on type.

I. foetidissima. Gladwyn or gladdon iris. Insignificant, buff-yellow flowers followed in autumn by decorative scarlet or orange seed pods, valued in dried-flower arranging. Grows almost anywhere, including dry shade under trees. H60-70cm/24-28in, W45cm/18in. Z5-9. 'Variegata', evergreen, creamy white variegated form, shows up brightly in winter, although seldom flowers. H50cm/20in, W45cm/18in. Z5-9.

I. pallida. Two variegated forms have year-round interest because their sword-like leaves remain attractive until frosts and start growing again in early spring. Rich, slightly alkaline soil. 'Argentea' (formerly *I. p.* 'Variegata'), white and grey striped leaves, and 'Variegata' (formerly *I. p.* 'Aurea Variegata'), golden-yellow stripes. Both have clear blue flowers. Both H60-75cm/24-30in, W30cm/1ft. F6-7. Z4-8.

I. stylosa (syn. *I. unguicularis*). Mainly winter-flowering iris, good for sunny, sheltered spot. Flowers occasionally in early autumn but freely through to mid-spring. Fragrant light blue flowers, deeper in 'Mary Barnard'. H30cm/1ft, W30cm/1ft. F1-3. Z8-9.

KNIPHOFIA Red hot poker

Indispensable for their architectural value, but some need plenty of space. Vary from 35cm/14in to 1.8m/6ft in height, flower from late spring to mid-autumn according to type. Plant in spring; pot-grown plants can be planted in autumn if protected in their first winter. Moist soil in summer.
✿ ■ ☆

K. 'Bressingham Comet'. Bright orange, red-tipped spikes, grassy leaves. H60cm/2ft, W45cm/18in. F8-10. Z6-9.

Kniphofia rooperi

K. caulescens. Large, yucca-like glaucous-leaved rosettes; stumpy, yellow-tipped red flower spikes. H70cm/28in, W60cm/2ft. F9-10. Z6-9.

K. 'Cobra'. Upstanding, long-flowering. Tight leaves, deep bronze in bud, changing through copper to creamy white. H90cm/3ft, W60cm/2ft. F8-10. Z6-9.

K. 'Little Maid'. Charming, narrow leaves, profuse, ivory-white spikes. H60cm/2ft, W45cm/18in. F7-9. Z5-9.

K. rooperi (syn. *K.* 'C.M. Prichard'). One of the latest to flower. Deep orange spikes rise from broad foliage. H1.5m/5ft, W60cm/2ft. F9-10. Z6-9.

LAMIUM Deadnettle

This genus includes useful ground cover, a few of greater garden value, some with evergreen leaves. ☀ ◩ ■

L. galeobdolon 'Florentinum' (syn. 'Variegatum'). Semi-evergreen, surface-rooting, rapid spreader good for wild garden. Silvery green leaves on straggly stems, brief, patchy show of yellow flowers in spring. H25-30cm/10-12in, W30cm/1ft. F5-6. Z4-8.

L. maculatum. Shallow-rooting ground cover, easy to curb if necessary. Silver-pink speckled leaves, purplish pink flowers. **'Beacon Silver'**, excellent for leaf colour, silvered, semi-evergreen leaves, H15cm/6in deep pink flowers in early summer. **'White Nancy'**, similar foliage, pure white flowers. H15-30cm/6-12in, W60cm/2ft. F4-7. Z4-8.

LIRIOPE

Slow-spreading evergreen perennials. Broadly grassy, mostly deep green, leaves, erect spikes of bead-like lilac flowers from midsummer to mid-autumn. Some make good ground cover even in shade, but flower more freely in the open. Drought-resistant. ☀ ☀ ■

Lamium maculatum 'White Nancy'

L. muscari (syn. *L. macrophylla*). Most reliable selection for cooler temperate zones. Tussocks of deep green, blade-like leaves, fading slightly in winter. Bright display of short spikes set with grape hyacinth-like flowers of lilac-purple from late summer to late autumn. H30cm/1ft, W30cm/1ft. F8-10. Z6-10.

OMPHALODES Navelwort

Dwarf perennials for shade and ground cover. ☀ ☀ ◩ ■

O. cappadocica. Mounds of green leaves, pretty sprays of forget-me-not-type, bright blue flowers; several selections are similar. H13cm/5in, W30cm/1ft. F3-5. Z6-9.

O. verna. Blue-eyed Mary. Spreading mats, bright blue flowers, good under trees. **'Alba'**, white. H10cm/4in, W60cm/2ft. F3-4. Z6-9.

ORIGANUM Marjoram

Several worth growing as ornamentals, each very different. ☀ ■ ⊕

O. 'Herrenhausen'. Mauve-pink hybrid, rather lax habit. H60cm/2ft, W30cm/1ft. F7-10. Z5-8.

O. laevigatum. Dense, twiggy sprays of tiny, deep purple-violet flowers from late summer, small, rounded, glaucous leaves. **'Hopleys'**, brighter, deep blue flowers. H40cm/16in, W30cm/1ft. F8-10. Z5-9.

O. vulgare. Culinary marjoram. Insignificant flowers. Good ground cover. **'Aureum'**, more or less evergreen, golden-leaved form. H15cm/6in, W30cm/1ft. Z4-8.

PENSTEMON

Some hybrids have good, late display and are a deservedly popular group of semi-hardy perennials, which need protection in cold regions. Leafy spikes, continuous show of tubular flowers in many colours. Best planted in late spring or early summer; autumn-purchased plants need protection under glass. All F6-10 unless noted otherwise.

All Z9-10. ☀ ◩ ■ ✬

Hybrids include the following. **'Firebird'**, bright red. H40cm/16in, W45cm/18in. **'Garnet'**, wine-red. H50cm/20in, W45cm/18in. **'King George'**, salmon-red, white throat. H60cm/2ft, W45cm/18in. **'Hewell's Pink'**, light pink. H45cm/18in, W30cm/12in. **'Hidcote Pink'**, pink and red. H60cm/2ft, W45cm/18in. **'Rubicunda'**, large, warm red, white centre. H60cm/2ft, W45cm/18in. **'Sour Grapes'**, large, pale purple flowers, strong-growing. H70cm/28in, W45cm/18in. F6-9. **'Snowstorm'**, distinctive white flowers. H70cm/28in, W45cm/18in. F6-9.

Physalis franchetii

PHYSALIS Cape gooseberry, Chinese lantern

P. franchetii. Rapid, invasive spreader needing to be planted with care. Insignificant white flowers followed by bright orange inverted cones, or 'lanterns', in autumn, within each is a gooseberry-sized, orange berry. Excellent for drying and effective in patio container. H60-80cm/24-32in, W90cm/3ft. F8-10. Z5-8. ☀ ☀ ■

PHYSOSTEGIA Obedient plant

Useful, late-flowering. Squarish

stems, tubular flowers. Spreading but easy to curb. Frequent lifting, dividing and replanting advisable. ☼ ◪ ■ ☼

P. virginiana (syn. *P. speciosa*). 'Rose Bouquet', rosy lilac. H80cm/32in, W60cm/2ft. F7-10. 'Summer Snow', white. H70cm/28in, W60cm/2ft. F7-10. 'Variegata', quite tall, lilac-pink spikes, variegated leaves. H50cm/20in, W45cm/18in. F8-10. 'Vivid', much dwarfer and later, deep pink. H50cm/20in, W45cm/18in. F8-10.

POLYGONUM (syn. PERSICARIA) Knotweed

Some members of this family have a bad name, overshadowing the fact that there are many good garden plants, many with a very long flowering period. ☼ ❋ ◪ ■

P. affine. Good ground cover with shallow roots. Narrow, leathery leaves, bottlebrush flowers. H15-23cm/6-9in, W38cm/15in. F6-7. Z3-9. 'Darjeeling Red', deep pink. H20cm/8in, W45-60cm/18-24in. F6-10. Z3-9. 'Dimity', fuller, long-lasting pink, more reliable, good

autumn colour. H15cm/6in, W45cm/18in. F6-10. Z3-9. F6-7. Z3-9.

P. amplexicaule. Abundant, bushy growth, long succession of thin terminal spikes before dying back to a sturdy but not invasive root. H1.2m/4ft, W75cm/30in. F6-9. Z5-9. 'Arun Gem' (syn. 'Pendula'), distinct bright pink tassels dangling above a leafy, compact base. H30cm/1ft, W75cm/30in. F6-10. Z5-9. 'Atrosanguineum', deep crimson. H1m/39in, W60cm/2ft. F6-9. Z5-9. 'Firetail', outstanding bright red. H1.2m/4ft, W1.2m/4ft. F6-10. Z5-9. 'Taurus', deepest crimson, larger, longest-lasting. H75cm/30in, W1.2m/4ft. F6-11. Z5-9.

P. campanulatum. Dense, leafy growth, light pink flower heads for weeks until the frost, from shallow, spreading roots. Good for dampish place. 'Rosenrot', deep rose-pink. 'Southcombe White', white. All H90cm/3ft, W90cm/3ft. F7-11. Z5-9.

P. milletii. Clumps of narrow leaves, intensely crimson-red pokers on and

Pulmonaria officinalis 'Sissinghurst White'

off all summer. Choice plant. Good, deep soil. H30cm/1ft, W30cm/1ft. Mainly F6-10. Z5-9.

POTENTILLA Cinquefoil

P. x tonguei. Flowers freely into autumn. Low clump of bronze-green leaves, prostrate rays of crimson-centred, apricot flowers for months. H10cm/4in, W45cm/18in. F6-10. Z5-7. ☼ ■

PRIMULA

Only a few of this enormous family can be selected for early spring flowering. Requirements depend on type.

P. denticulata. Drumstick primula. Dense, round heads of flowers on single stalks in spring. Colours range from white to mauve, lilac, lavender-blues and deep pink. Deep-rooting and long-lived. Propagate named selections by root cuttings. 'Alba', many white forms. 'Rubin', many with red drumstick flowers. 'Bressingham Beauty', free-flowering powder-blue. H30-45cm/12-18in, W25cm/10in. F4-5. Z6-8. ☼ ❋ ◪ ■

P. rosea. Short sprays of bright pink flowers in early spring. Leaves open as these lengthen. 'Delight', best cultivar. H25cm/10in, W25cm/10in. F3-5. Z6-8. ☼ ❋ ◪

P. vulgaris. Primrose. Cheerful yellow spring flowers. Divide regularly. Heavy soil. ☼ ◪ ■

Singles: 'Garryarde Guinevere', purple-red; 'Wanda' and 'Wisley Red', bright red; 'Schneekissen', brilliant white; the form *sibthorpii* is pink. Doubles: 'Alan Robb', apricot; 'Dawn Ansell', white; 'Easter Bonnet', prolific, large, lilac-blue flowers; 'Miss Indigo', compact, purple-blue, edged white; 'Sue Jervis', shell-pink. 'Sunshine Susie', golden-yellow. All H10-15cm/4-6in, W15-25cm/6-10in. F3-5. Z5-8.

PULMONARIA Lungwort

First class early spring display. Ground-covering foliage, prettily spotted on many, lasts until the first hard frost. Good infill between deciduous shrubs. ☼ ❋ ◪ ■ ☼

P. angustifolia. Almost the first to flower in early spring. Narrow leaves follow the flowers. The form *azurea* is the earliest, intensely blue. 'Munstead Blue', a shade deeper. All H15cm/6in, W30cm/1ft. F3-4. Z3-8.

P. longifolia. Conspicuously spotted leaves 15cm/6in long, blue flowers on terminal sprays; white in the form *alba*. 'Bertram Anderson', deep violet-blue flowers. 'Roy Davidson', lighter blue flowers. All H25cm/10in,

Polygonum amplexicaule 'Atrosanguineum'

W45cm/18in. F4-5. Z5-8.

P. rubra. Early flowering, coral-red blooms, evergreen leaves softer than most. 'Bowles' Red' is usually listed, but 'Redstart' is superior. H30cm/1ft, W60cm/2ft. F3-4. Z5-8.

P. saccharata. Bethlehem sage. Widest range of choice. Overlapping evergreen leaves. Almost all have pink flowers which fade to blue on short sprays. All Z4-8. 'Argentea', almost entirely silvered leaves. 'Highdown' (syn. 'Lewis Palmer'), outstanding for deep blue flowers, vigour and attractive foliage. 'Leopard', spotted summer leaves, deep rose-pink spring flowers. 'Pink Dawn', spotted silver all summer. 'Sissinghurst White', white sprays, white-spotted leaves. All H25cm/10in, W60cm/2ft, F3-5, except 'Highdown', H30cm/1ft.

RUDBECKIA Cone flower, black-eyed Susan

Daisy-like flowers with central cone and rayed petals. ☼ ☀ ◨ ■ ☆

R. deamii. Wide clumps of grey leaves, masses of yellow flowers. H80cm/32in, W38cm/15in. F7-9. Z4-9.

Leucanthemella serotina

R. 'Goldsturm'. One of the finest plants ever raised. Rayed, deep yellow, black-centred flowers for weeks. Dark green leaves on slow-spreading plants. H70cm/28in, W30cm/1ft. F6-10. Z4-9.

R. laciniata 'Goldquelle'. Leafy, deep green bushy growth covered in fully double, chrome-yellow flowers, 8cm/3in across. H1m/39in, W60cm/2ft. F7-10. Z3-9.

SALVIA

Some good garden plants in this vast genus, many of which flower non-stop until frosts. Some tender salvias are worth the extra care required to keep them over winter: the dwarf red *S. blepharophylla*, the silver-leaved, blue-flowered *S. farinacea*, the carmine-red *S. involucrata* 'Bethellii' and the taller red *S. neurepia* give a bright display. Most are best lifted, divided and replanted every three or four years. ☼ ■ ☆

S. ambigens (syn. *S. guaranitica* 'Blue Enigma'). Shapely bushes, small, deep green leaves, short spikes of royal blue flowers. Protect by covering with leaf mould, bark or

Saxifraga fortunei 'Rubrifolia'

litter in cold districts. H1.1m/43in, W45cm/18in. F7-10. Z5-8.

S. uliginosa. Tall, distinctive, late species. Delicate sprays of long-lasting, sky-blue flowers above deep green foliage. Warm, sheltered spot; needs supporting. H1.5m/5ft, W45cm/18in. F9-11. Z8-9.

SAXIFRAGA

Other saxifrages are described in Alpines Directory, page 142.

S. fortunei. Shallow-rooting rosettes of round, glistening leaves, red beneath, in spring and, in mid-autumn, airy sprays of starry white flowers. Light soil; give shelter, a light spring mulch and, in cold areas, some winter cover. H30-45cm/12-18in, W30cm/1ft. F10-11. Z4-7. 'Rubrifolia', reddish foliage. H25cm/10in, W20cm/8in. F10-11. Z6-7. 'Wada's Variety', almost beetroot-red leaves. H25cm/ 10in, W20cm/8in. F10-11. Z6-7. All ☀ ◨ ☆

SCABIOSA Scabious, pincushion flower

Many species and cultivars continue to flower well into autumn, particularly if dead flower heads are removed. Plant in spring. ☼ ■ ☆

S. 'Butterfly Blue'. Deep blue flowers all summer. Similar, but with pink

flowers is *S.* 'Pink Mist'. H30cm/1ft, W25cm/10in. F5-10. Z5-8.

S. caucasica. Valued for cutting. 'Blansiegel' ('Blue Seal'), vigorous light blue. 'Bressingham White' and 'Miss Willmott', good whites, the latter more ivory. 'Clive Greaves', prolific mid-blue. All H60-80cm/24-32in, W45-60cm/18-24in. F6-9. Z4-9.

S. graminifolia. Excellent for frontal groups. Dense mats of narrow, silver-grey leaves, long show of light blue flowers. H30cm/1ft, W30cm/1ft. F6-10. Z7-9. 'Pink Cushion', light pink, less robust. Light soil for both. H25cm/10in, W25cm/10in. F6-9. Z7-9.

SCHIZOSTYLIS Kaffir lily

Valuable for late flowering. Mats of spreading foliage, rush-like leaves, bright gladioli-like flowers. Cover with leaves or bark in cold districts, to protect in winter. ☼ ☀ ◨ ☆

S. coccinea. All Z6-9. The form *alba* has clean white flowers on slender stems. H60cm/2ft, W25cm/10in. F9-11. 'Major', fine crimson-red. H60cm/2ft, W25cm/10in. F9-11. 'Fenland Daybreak', bright green foliage, satin pink blooms. H60cm/2ft, W25cm/10in. F8-11. 'Mrs Hegarty', pale pink. H50cm/20in, W25cm/10in. F9-11. 'November Cheer', clear pink. H50cm/20in, W25cm/10in. F9-11. 'Snow Maiden', white. H50cm/20in, W25cm/10in. F10-11. 'Sunrise', almost salmon. H60cm/2ft, W25cm/10in. F9-11.

SEDUM Stonecrop

Some of these succulent-like perennials are indispensable for late summer and autumn colour, attracting bees and butterflies. Their flat heads remain interesting throughout winter. ☼ ■ ☆

S. 'Autumn Joy' (syn. 'Herbstfreude'). One of the best of all perennial plants. Spring growth of

glaucous, fleshy stems and leaves remaining attractive all summer. Glistening pink flower heads widen to 25cm/10in across, turning a deep bronze, then coppery red. Divide and replant regularly. H50cm/20in, W50cm/20in. F8-10. Z3-10.
S. spectabile. Fleshy glaucous foliage all summer before wide heads of bright pink flowers appear. **'Brilliant'**, wide, bright pink heads; **'Iceberg'**, pale foliage, creamy white flowers; **'Indian Chief'**, smaller heads, deeper rose-pink; **'September Glow'**, broad, glowing pink heads. All H30-40cm/12-16in, W30-40cm/12-16in. F8-10. Z4-9.

SERRATULA
Late fluffy flowers on stiff, branching stems, and deeply divided deep green leaves. ☼ ■ ☆
S. macrocephala. Shapely, bushy growth, profuse, small violet flowers. H30cm/1ft, W25cm/10in. F7-9. Z5-8.
S. seoanei (syn. *S. shawii*). Similar to above, more delicate leaves. H25cm/10in, W25cm/10in. F8-10. Z5-8.

SOLIDAGO Goldenrod
Wide range of easily grown perennials, some lasting into autumn and giving a splash of golden yellow. Ideal with blue asters. All Z4-9. ☼ ☀ ■

TRADESCANTIA
Easy growing with long-flowering season into autumn, although apt to be untidy by then. Bright, three-petalled flowers amid copious narrow foliage. Cultivars listed are hybrids of *T. virginiana* and other species.
☼ ☀ ☆
'Caerulea Plena', double light blue flowers. **'Carmine Glow'**, crimson flowers, neat habit. **'Iris Prichard'**, white flowers stained azure-blue. **'Isis'**, warm Oxford blue. **'Osprey'**, white, lilac-centred flowers. **'Pauline'**, light lilac-pink flowers. **'Purple**

Sedum spectabile 'Brilliant'

Dome', rich velvety purple flowers. All approx. H50cm/20in, W50cm/20in. F6-9. Z5-9.

TRICYRTIS Toad lily
Late show of distinctive flowers, most of which are spotted and bell-shaped.
☼ ☀ ◪
T. formosana. Clumpy plant, erect leafy stems carrying open heads of mauve, yellow-throated flowers with a hint of brown. H75cm/30in, W45cm/18in. F8-10. Z5-9. ☼
T. hirta. Near white, heavily spotted lilac flowers along stems; hairy leaves. The form **alba** is less vigorous, pleasing white. Both H90cm/3ft, W60cm/2ft. F8-10. Z4-9.
T. macropoda. Purple-spotted, greenish yellow flowers, broad leaves. H1m/39in, W60cm/2ft. F9-10. Z5-9.
T. stolonifera. Vigorous spread, a little paler than *T. formosana.* H90cm/3ft, W60cm/2ft. F8-10. Z5-9.

VERBENA
Although long-flowering and useful, few verbenas are hardy. ☼ ■
V. bonariensis. Hardy plant making late contribution of form and colour. Little heads of lavender-blue, fragrant flowers above slender, sparsely leaved, branching stems. Pretty as a group. Not very long-lived, but self-seeds

freely. H1.5m/5ft, W60cm/2ft. F6-9. Z7-10.

VINCA Periwinkle
Evergreen ground cover, useful for foliage, and in *V. minor* for early flower. Some are invasive and wide-spreading. ☼ ☀ ☆
V. major. Greater periwinkle. Larger, rounded leaves and taller than *V. minor.* Blue flowers are sparse, but the bright foliage throughout winter in the cream-variegated **'Variegata'** (syn. 'Elegantissima') makes up for this. Both H30cm/1ft, W90cm/3ft. F4-5. Z7-9.
V. minor. Lesser periwinkle, trailing myrtle. Flowers more freely than *V. major.* Small dark green leaves. Many colours. **'Argenteovariegata'**, creamy white-edged leaves, blue flowers. **'Atropurpurea'**, reddish purple. **'Aureovariegata'**, golden-edged leaves, white flowers. **'Azurea Flore Pleno'**, double blue. **'Bowles' Variety'** (syn. 'La Grave'), the best, least rampant single, free-flowering blue. **'Gertrude Jekyll'**, free-flowering white, better than *alba.* **'Multiplex'**, double reddish purple. All H15cm/6in, W60-90cm/2-3ft. F3-7. Z4-9.

YUCCA
Often listed as shrubs, these evergreen

plants, with their sword-like foliage, have considerable character and appeal through the winter. They are generally hardy and long-lived. ☼ ■
Y. filamentosa. Adam's needle. The most reliable species. Almost stemless, has evergreen, greyish foliage with hair-like fibres along the edges. Few variations, all with basically ivory-white, bell-shaped flowers most years. H1.5m/5ft, W1.5m/5ft. F7-8. Z5-10. **'Bright Edge'**, dark green, narrow leaves edged yellow. **'Golden Sword'**, light yellow-centred leaves with green edges. **'Variegata'**, covers perhaps more than one selection with green-centred, white- or yellowish-edged leaves, sometimes tinged pink. Variegated forms are less free to flower. Foliage reaching 60-90cm/2-3ft, W60-90cm/2-3ft. F7-8. Z5-9.

ZAUSCHNERIA
Showy, late-flowering, semi-shrubby perennials, fuchsia-like flowers. ☼ ■
Z. californica 'Glasnevin'. Grey-green leaves, intensely red flowers. H35cm/14in, W35cm/14in. F8-10. Z8-10.
Z. canescens. Twiggy summer growth, small grey leaves, brilliant, trumpet-shaped, orange-scarlet flowers. H35cm/14in, W35cm/14in. F8-10. Z8-10.

Yucca filamentosa

FERNS DIRECTORY

HARDY FERNS ARE SELDOM CONSIDERED as plants which have autumn and winter interest, but both the deciduous ferns, whose foliage often turns golden in autumn, and the evergreen ferns provide colour and form throughout winter. The latter, like the ornamental grasses, can be quite magical in their appearance as mist and frost play on their foliage. Hardy ferns are relatively easy to grow in the garden, some requiring some shade where not too dry, others being quite happy in sun. Only a few can be selected for inclusion in this book

H: Approximate height after 2 years
W: Approximate width after 2 years
F: Months in flower
Z: Relevant hardiness zone(s)

ADIANTUM Maidenhair fern
A. pedatum. American or northern maidenhair. Branching fronds made up of many toothed lobes on slender black stems. H45cm/18in, W30cm/1ft. Z3-8. ☀ ◪ ★

ASPLENIUM
Hardy, easily grown evergreens (formerly *Phyllitis* and *Scolopendrium*) growing well on lime soils. ☀ ◪
A. scolopendrium. Hart's tongue. British native. Long, leathery leaves. Given shade it is easy to grow, even in crevices or on walls. H up to 35cm/14in, W40cm/16in. Z4-8. 'Cristatum', curiously dissected crests on the light green fronds. H35cm/14in, W40cm/16in. Z4-8. 'Undulatum', narrow fronds with attractive wavy edges. H30-40cm/12-16in, W30-45cm/12-18in. Z4-8.

BLECHNUM Hard fern
B. spicant. Common hard fern, or deer fern. Produces two types of pinnate frond: arching, spreading, sterile ones and erect, spore-bearing, deciduous ones; both deep glossy green and highly ornamental. A clump-forming species for humus-rich soil but once established will succeed in less. H30-60cm/1-2ft, W45cm/18in. Z3-8. ★
B. tabulare. Shade lover, reliably

hardy only in mild districts or sheltered gardens. Forms a spreading mass of deep green leathery fronds. H30-100cm/1-3ft, W30-60cm/1-2ft. Z7-9. ☀ ◪

Blechnum tabulare

CYRTONIUM
C. falcatum. Holly fern. Attractive clump of erect, glossy deep green fronds. H60cm/2ft, W45cm/18in. Z7-9. ☀ ◪

DRYOPTERIS Buckler fern
In milder climates or winters many remain evergreen until spring or severe frosts. ☀ ◪
D. borreri (syn. *D. affinis* and *D. pseudomas*). 'Crispa' is a select form with arching, deep green, crisped fronds. The form *cristata* 'The King', a selection of the golden-scaled male fern, has evenly crested, arching fronds from a symmetrical

Dryopteris borreri 'Pinderi'

central crown. Tolerates dry soil. 'Pinderi' has narrow, deeply pinnate fronds of dark green, an attractive form. All H80-90cm/32-36in, W80-90cm/32-36in. Z4-8.
D. erythrosora. Japanese shield fern. Unusual pink- or bronze-tinged young fronds that mature to light green. Evergreen according to weather. H60cm/2ft, W30cm/1ft. Z5-9. ☀ ★

MATTEUCCIA Ostrich fern, shuttlecock fern
M. struthiopteris. Spectacular, with large, shapely fronds forming shuttlecock-like rosettes from stout stocks and spreading runners which are likely to colonize in rich, moist soil. The fertile fronds are dark brown in winter. H1m/39in, W60-90cm/2-3ft. Z2-8. ☀ ◪

POLYPODIUM Common polypody
P. cambricum. Mass of evergreen fronds in mounded clumps. Adaptable to fairly dry soil. H25cm/10in. W45-60cm/18-24in. Z5-8. ☀ ◪ ■
P. vulgare 'Pulcherrimum'. Good for ground cover and for rock gardens or wall crevices. The evergreen fronds are fresh green, tinted in autumn. Tolerant of dry soil but less vigorous in alkaline soil. H25cm/10in, W40cm/16in. Z5-8. ☀ ◪ ■

POLYSTICHUM Shield fern, holly fern
Evergreen ferns with large, broad fronds, many variations in their intricate form. Most are adaptable even where soil is poor, dry or limy, if given a good start. ☀ ☀ ◪ ■
P. aculeatum. Hard shield fern. Bold, deep, lacy, feathery fronds. H60-75cm/24-30in, W60cm/2ft. Z4-8.
P. polyblepharum. Year-round, elegant greenery with broad, shining fronds from hairy central crowns. Hardy and reliable. H50cm/20in, W30cm/1ft. Z5-8.
P. setiferum. Soft shield fern. Produces bulbils, or potential babies, along its midrib, adding to its charm. The several forms differ in the pattern of the broad, deeply cleft fronds, arching from a stout central crown. H up to 90cm/3ft, W90-120cm/3-4ft. Z5-8. 'Divisilobum', finely divided fronds, tolerates fairly dry conditions. H50cm/20in, W50cm/20in. Z5-8.
'Herrenhausen', dense clumps of spreading fronds of finely feathered, mid-green foliage. H45cm/18in, W75cm/2.5ft. Z5-8. 'Plumosum', soft, semi-prostrate, densely clothed, evergreen fronds. H30cm/1ft, W50cm/20in. Z5-8.

Polystichum setiferum 'Herrenhausen'

GRASSES DIRECTORY

ONE OF THE GREATEST ATTRIBUTES of ornamental grasses, an increasingly appreciated group of plants, is their interest and beauty during autumn, winter and early spring. They can be planted with many different groups of plants, but they associate particularly well with perennials, conifers, heathers and shrubs, softening harsh or bright colours and adding their own in summer, with more subtle whites, browns and beiges in winter. Most of the grasses listed here are hardy and none of them is invasive. Container-grown plants can be planted at any time of year in free-draining soil, but most field-grown plants, which are sent out bare rooted, may not establish so it is best to purchase and plant these in spring. Although generally they tolerate a range of conditions, they mostly prefer well-drained soil.

H: Approximate height
W: Approximate width
F: Months in flower
Z: Relevant hardiness zone(s)

Bouteloua gracilis seen here in winter

ACORUS
A. gramineus 'Ogon'. Not strictly a grass but looks like one with rush-like foliage. Narrow, gold and green leaves arching in fan-like sprays are almost brighter in winter than summer. '**Variegatus**', less showy with white and green striped leaves. Both H20cm/8in, W30cm/1ft. Z4-10. ☼ ❄ ◪

ANDROPOGON
A. scoparius. Upright, shapely, slow-growing evergreen, with narrow blades of a bluish coppery hue particularly in autumn. Light soil. H60cm/2ft, W60cm/2ft. Z5-8. ☼

BOUTELOUA Mosquito grass
B. gracilis (syn. *B. oligostachya*). Short sprays of curious, brownish flower spikes, at right angles to the stems, resembling hovering mosquitoes, above a tufty, semi-evergreen, deep green base. Attractive in winter frost. H25cm/10in, W20cm/8in. F6-8. Z5-9. ☼ ◪ ★

BRIZA Common quaking grass
B. media. Small clump with panicles of tiny, greenish purple, locket-like flowers which nod in a breeze. The flowers are popular for drying. Best where not too dry. H60cm/2ft, W30cm/1ft. F6-8. Z5-9. ☼ ■ ★

CALAMAGROSTIS
C. x *acutiflora*. 'Karl Foerster'. Attractive hybrid with erect habit, rich green foliage followed by plum-brown spikes which remain until spring. H1.5m/5ft, W60cm/2ft. F7-8. Z5-9.

CAREX Sedge
Low-growing, mostly clump-forming plants with much year-round interest. ❄ ◪ ★
C. buchananii. Leatherleaf sedge. Evergreen, erect tufts of unusual, coppery brown, thin, needly blades,

reddish towards the base. H60cm/2ft, W20cm/8in. Z6-9.
C. comans. More mounded, wide-spreading habit. The thin, dense growth has a decidedly light brownish hue, held all year round. Flowers are not conspicuous. There are various forms of the species. '**Bronze**', deep bronze-green foliage. Very similar in form but classed as a hybrid is '**Frosted Curls**' which looks, even in summer, as though its narrow foliage is frosted with creamy white. All H45cm/18in, W60cm/2ft F6-8. Z6-9.
C. morrowii (syn. *C. oshimensis*). '**Evergold**' is one of the brightest year-round plants, forming large clumps with narrow, shiny, dark green leaves, striped golden-yellow. H25cm/10in, W60cm/2ft. Z7-9.
C. testacea. Another hummock type, similar to *C. comans* but with wide-spreading leaves, yellow-green in summer, bronze-green in winter. H45cm/18in, W90cm/3ft. F6-8. Z6-9.

CHIONOCHLOA
C. rubra. Finely spaced, arching leaves rounded and graceful in habit, olive-green in summer, bronzed in winter. H60cm/2ft, W60cm/2ft. F7-8. Z7-9.

CORTADERIA Pampas grass
Spectacular flowering grasses, unsuitable for the smaller garden. Evergreen in mild climates, but die back to ground in cold ones. Plumes excellent for drying. ☼ ◪ ★
C. selloana. Several variations, from 1.5m/5ft to 3m/10ft high, making large clumps and silvery white plumes in autumn which, particularly in '**Pumila**' and others in sheltered situations, last until spring. '**Gold Band**', narrow, golden-green striped leaves and silvery plumes. H1.8m/6ft, W1.2m/4ft. F9-10. Z8-10. '**Silver Comet**', leaves margined white and a good display of flowers,

Deschampsia caespitosa 'Golden Dew'

Festuca glauca 'Blue Glow'

Cortaderia selloana 'Pumila'

but needs a warm, sheltered spot. H1.5m/5ft, W90cm/3ft. F9-10. Z8-10. '**Sunningdale Silver**', strong-stemmed, finely plumed, free-flowering. H2.5-3m/8-10ft, W1.8m/6ft. F9-11. Z7-10.

DESCHAMPSIA Tufted hair grass
D. caespitosa. Large tufts of narrow, deep green leaves and sheaves of very graceful spikes, valuable for autumn and winter interest. Self-seeds freely. ✿ ✴ ◪ '**Bronze Veil**' (syn. 'Bronzeschleier'), effective bronze plumes. '**Gold Veil**' (syn. 'Goldschleier'), strong, clumpy

evergreen with plumes of green stems and flowers which turn a warm golden-yellow. H90cm/3ft, W90cm/3ft. F6-8. Z4-9. '**Golden Dew**' (syn. 'Goldtau'), similar growth with fountains of green stems and flowers which mature to a rich golden-brown. Good, compact form. H70cm/28in, W50cm/20in. F6-9. Z4-9.

FESTUCA Fescue
F. glauca. Blue fescue. Neat, bluish evergreen tufts, useful as edging, ground cover or frontal groups. Several selections worth looking for: '**Blue Glow**' (syn. 'Blauglut'), striking silver-blue leaves and a good show of flowers; '**Elijah Blue**', compact, silver-blue. Colour good into winter. Best divided every two or three years. Average H25cm/10in, W25cm/10 in. F6-7. Z4-8. ✿

HAKONECHLOA
H. macra '**Alboaurea**'. One of the best dwarf grasses. Although not evergreen has winter interest in beige pendulous foliage. Spring brings a lovely show of green- and yellow-striped leaves, gradually ageing to reddish brown and effective until late autumn. Plants spread slowly,

appreciating good soil. Excellent in a container as a patio plant. H25cm/10in, W38cm/15in. F8-9. Z7-9. ✿

LUZULA Woodrush
L. sylvatica. Greater woodrush. Bright green leaves, slow-spreading, tufted habit, and open heads of greenish flowers. Good ground cover for dry shade. '**Marginata**' (syn. 'Aureomarginata'), white leaf margins. Attractive in winter. Both H30cm/1ft, W30cm/1ft. F5-6. Z5-9.

MISCANTHUS Silver grass
Some first class selections with great autumn and winter appeal through flower and foliage. Heights range between 60cm/2ft and 3m/10ft, nearly all are clump-forming, making annual growth of bladed leaves, some green-silver or variegated. Although none is evergreen, the foliage remains attractive over winter. Cut back foliage in spring. They flower best in hot summers. Some good selections, mainly raised by Ernst Pagels in northern Germany, flower regularly in cooler, northerly climates. A number are quite dwarf. ✿ ▢ ★
M. sinensis. Chinese silver grass.

Miscanthus sinensis 'Cascade'

Ample green- and silver-striped foliage but seldom planted. H1.8m/6ft, W90cm/3ft. F7-9. Z5-10. Its many erect-growing and non-invasive cultivars are more garden-worthy. All Z5-10. '**Cascade**' (syn. 'Kaskade'), pendulous, silvery white flowers. H1.2m/4ft, W60cm/12ft. F8-10, '**Flamingo**', deep crimson flowers fading white. H1.2m/4ft, W60cm/2ft. F8-10. '**Gracillimus**', elegant, narrow leaves, a shapely habit, seldom flowers in autumn. H1.5/5ft, W45cm/18in. F7-9. '**Kleine Fontane**', tall, free-flowering with pendulous, silver

heads. H1.5/5ft, W90cm/3ft. F7-10.
'**Malepartus**', vigorous, broad, silver-striped leaves, crimson flowers fading pink then beige. H1.8m/6ft, W90cm/3ft. F8-10. '**Morning Light**', outstanding variegated Japanese selection, compact, densely foliaged, silver and white. Needs heat to flower. H1.2m/4ft, W60cm/2ft. F9-10. '**Purpureus**', reddish leaves, profuse but small flowers. H1.2m/4ft, W60cm/2ft. F8-9. '**Silver Feather**', sprays of white flowers arching above luxuriant green foliage. Majestic where space allows. H2.4m/8ft, W90cm/3ft, F8-10. '**Variegatus**', stately and brightly variegated with vertical white stripes. H1.5m/5ft, W90cm/3ft. '**Zebrinus**', or zebra grass, lateral bands of gold across green leaves. H1.5m/5ft, W90cm/3ft.
M. yakushimensis. Dwarf, late-flowering with erect, beige plumes. H90cm/3ft, W60cm/2ft. F9-10.

MOLINIA Moor grass
M. altissima.(syn. *M. litoralis*). Strong-growing, free-flowering, good autumn colour as stems fade. The terminal flower sprays are greenish purple, turning brown in autumn. Some good selections: '**Fontane**', pendulous heads; '**Transparent**', slender stems, wispy flower heads; '**Windspiel**', smaller heads, all turning golden brown autumn colours. All 1.5-1.8m/5-6ft, W45cm/18in. F8-10. Z5-9.
M. caerulea. Purple moor grass. British native for damp, acid soils. '**Moorhexe**', a good green-leaved selection with purplish flower heads, brown in autumn. H40cm/16in, W40cm/16in. F8-9. Z5-9. '**Variegata**', stout clumps of soft, deciduous, creamy yellow-green leaves and long-lasting, small, purplish buff flowers. Prefers a light, deep soil and sun. H60cm/2ft, W60cm/2ft. F7-10. Z5-9.

Molinia altissima 'Transparent'

Stipa gigantea

PANICUM Switch grass
P. virgatum '**Rubrum**'. Clump-forming, narrow, erect reddish autumn foliage, panicles of airy reddish brown seed heads. H1.2m/4ft, W60cm/2ft. F8-9. Z5-9. ☼ □ ★

PENNISETUM
Large, deciduous tussocks, but not all produce their bottlebrush flowers freely. Long, arching and narrow grey-green leaves. ☼ □ ☆
P. alopecuroides (syn. *P. compressum*). Shy to flower in cool temperate zones but '**Hameln**' and '**Woodside**' are much freer, and their flowers attractive well into winter. All H90cm/3ft, W60cm/2ft. F8-10. Z5-10.
P. orientale. Hairy leaves, tufty growth. Its bottlebrush, silvery pink flowers are long-lasting and reliable fading to grey. H45cm/18in, W30cm/1ft. F7-9. Z6-9.

STIPA Feather grass, needle grass
S. arundinacea. Compact clump of narrow-leaved, arching, bronze-green stems, diffuse, brownish flowers. Foliage tinged red, bronze, yellow and orange in winter. H45cm/18in, W60cm/2ft. F7-9. Z7-9. ☼ ◪ ☆
S. calamagrostis. Clump-forming species which flowers freely with dense, buff-white plumes which arch gracefully. H1.2m/4ft, W60cm/2ft. F7-9. Z5-10.
S. gigantea. Imposing specimen clumps. Narrow green leaves above which tall stems remain erect, carrying oat-like flowers for months which are still attractive in winter. H1.8-2.1m/6-7ft, W60-75cm/24-30in. F6-10. Z5-10.
S. tenuissima. A beautiful ornamental grass forming a dense, grassy, deep green clump which is topped in mid-summer by fluffy plumes which turn from beige to white. H60cm/2ft, W45cm/18in. F6-9. Z7-10.

HEATHS AND HEATHERS DIRECTORY

ALTHOUGH THEY ARE CLASSED AS EVERGREEN SHRUBS, heaths and heathers stand alone as a group which, where they can be grown successfully, can have a tremendously colourful impact the year round but especially in winter. Even for those who do not have acid soil and therefore are not able to grow the summer-flowering types, there are many lime tolerant winter-flowering ones to choose from.

Heathers have a wide selection of flower colour as well as a vast range of foliage colour – shades of green, bronze, gold, yellow, orange, crimson, grey and silver – which often changes with the seasons and, given sunny situations, lights up the winter garden. They can be used as frontal groups to shrub beds or borders, as edging for paths or as a heather garden. Smaller-growing cultivars are ideal with alpines or dwarf shrubs in rock gardens. They can be used in window boxes, containers and raised beds. Heathers and slow-growing conifers complement one another particularly well, the various forms, textures and colours of the latter providing dramatic contrast. Heathers work well with ornamental grasses, too.

Well over 500 cultivars are currently in cultivation and wider selections can be found from specialists. Those described here are some of the most outstanding in my experience. As a guide to planting densities, the approximate widths of heathers after only 3-4 years are given, this being the period within which plants will have matted together. All require well-drained, humus-rich soil.

H: Approximate height after 8-10 years
W: Approximate width after 3-4 years
F: Months in flower
Z: Relevant hardiness zone(s)

Massed heathers make a striking display in early spring

Calluna vulgaris 'Anne Marie'

CALLUNA **Common heather, ling**
C. vulgaris. Hundreds of cultivars of this heathland plant offer an amazing range of colours, shapes and sizes. Prune all except the dwarfest and very prostrate types in early to mid-spring, before growth really begins. All flowers are single unless otherwise stated. All Z5-7. ☼ ⊖
'Allegro', profusion of deep red flowers, dark green foliage. H45-60cm/18-24in, W45cm/18in. F8-10.
'Anne Marie', bushy habit, dark green foliage. Flowers open bright pink, gradually deepening to brilliant carmine-rose. H23-30cm/9-12in, W45cm/18in. F8-11. **'Beoley Gold'**, one of the best yellow-foliaged cultivars, bushy year-round foliage, contrasting white flowers. H30-45cm/12-18in, W45cm/18in. F8-9. **'Boskoop'**, superb, dense, feathery foliage, golden-orange in summer, bronze-red in winter. Light mauve-purple flowers. H30-45cm/12-18in, W45cm/18in. F8-9. **'Dark Beauty'**, compact, bushy

Calluna vulgaris 'Boskoop'

plant, dark green foliage, bright crimson flowers over long period in autumn. H30cm/12in, W30-45cm/12-18in. F8-10. '**Golden Carpet**', low, prostrate mat of golden-yellow foliage, tinged bronze and red in winter. Mauve flowers often sparse. H10cm/4in, W40cm/16in. F8-9. '**Golden Feather**', first-class foliage form, bright gold, feathery summer foliage, turning reddish orange in winter. Occasional mauve flowers. H30-45cm/12-18in, W45cm/18in. F8-10. '**H.E. Beale**', vigorous, with strong, erect spikes of soft, double, silver-pink flowers lasting for weeks. H30-45cm/12-18in, W50cm/20in. F9-11. '**Peter Sparkes**', similar to 'H.E. Beale', but with double, much deeper, pink flowers on sturdy, erect spikes. H45-60cm/18-24in, W45cm/18in. F9-10. '**Robert Chapman**', changes from gold to yellow, orange to bronze and red. Lower winter temperatures enhance the colour intensity. Purple flowers. H30-45cm/12-18in, W45cm/18in. F8-9. '**Sir John Charrington**', arguably the best foliage cultivar, compact and bushy, golden-yellow foliage, orange with bright red and crimson tips in winter. Excellent in bloom, with short spikes of crimson flowers. H30-45cm/12-18in, W40cm/16in. F8-9.

DABOECIA **Irish bell heather**
Summer-flowering. ⊖
D. cantabrica. Long flowering period, glossy green leaves and bell-shaped flowers. Resent drought almost as much as severe frost, but where they can be grown offer a contrast to other heathers. Stronger-growing cultivars can get straggly with age and should be pruned each year, either lightly once the flowers have finished in late autumn, then more severely in spring, or, preferably, leave it all until spring. All Z7. ☼ ❋ ◪

Calluna vulgaris and *Erica* × *darleyensis* 'Ghost Hills'

Erica carnea 'Pink Spangles'

'**Atropurpurea**', one of the hardiest and most reliable. Bronze-green leaves, rich purple flowers. H60cm/2ft, W50cm/20in. F6-10. '**Snowdrift**', bright green foliage, masses of white bell flowers. H45cm/18in, W45cm/18in. F6-10. *D.* x *scotica* '**William Buchanan**'. One of several dwarf hybrids between *D. azorica* and *D. cantabrica*. Glossy green leaves, masses of crimson flowers. One of the hardiest cultivars. H30cm/1ft, W30cm/1ft. F5-10. Z7.

ERICA **Heath**
E. carnea (syn. *E. herbacea*). Winter heaths are among the most valuable garden plants. Most cultivars are low-growing with a bushy or spreading habit, and flower from late autumn to late spring, some lasting several months. Very few need pruning, except to prevent spreading into other plants or to tidy them occasionally. All Z5-7. All ⊖; some ⊕ '**Ann Sparkes**', superb foliage sport of 'Vivellii', slowly makes a compact bush of deep orange-yellow foliage, tipped bronze-red. Deep carmine-red flowers. H15cm/6in, W25cm/10in. F2-4. '**Eileen Porter**', reputedly less hardy than some, but has endured temperatures of -20°C/-4°F in my garden. Out-performs all others in length of flowering. Rich carmine flowers, producing a bicoloured effect. H15-20cm/6-8in, W25cm/10in. F10-5. '**Foxhollow**', low-growing, spreading habit. One of the finest foliage heathers, brilliant golden-yellow foliage in late spring and summer, deep gold in winter, often flecked with red. In low-lying areas, new growth can be caught by late spring frost. Pale pink flowers, rarely borne. H15-25cm/6-10in, W45cm/18in. F2-4. '**King George**', compact, bushy habit, dark green leaves, bright pink flowers, rose-red with age. Always reliable, one of the best. H20-25cm/8-10in,

W30cm/1ft. F12-3. '**Myretoun Ruby**', magnificent, smothering display of deep ruby-red flowers. Dark green foliage. H30cm/1ft, W35cm/14in. F3-4. '**Pink Spangles**', first-class spreader, large, bicoloured, pink and cream flowers, deepening to rose-pink. H20-30cm/8-12in, W35cm/14in. F1-3. '**Springwood White**', excellent ground cover, spreading, bright apple-green foliage. Roots as it goes, may need curbing. Smothered in pure white blooms. H20-30cm/8-12in, W60cm/2ft. F2-4. '**Vivellii**' (syn. 'Urville'), attractive for foliage and flower. Dark, bronze-green foliage, ideal against gold, silver or blue evergreen plants. Deep carmine-red flowers. H10cm/4in, W35cm/14in. F2-3. '**Westwood Yellow**', similar to 'Foxhollow' but more compact, flowers more freely. H15cm/6in, W40cm/16in. F2-4.
E. cinerea. Bell heather. Grows on cliffs by the sea, on moorlands and mountains, surviving with less moisture than most species. Long flowering period, as with some of the cultivars. Late flowers, attractive in winter even when flowering has finished and some with colourful foliage. Prune in spring, just as new growth begins. All Z7. ☼
'**Eden Valley**', bushy and compact, soft lavender and white bicoloured flowers. H15-20cm/6-8in, W25cm/10in. F7-10. '**Purple Beauty**', easy and reliable, with bushy, spreading habit, dark green foliage, large, bright purple flowers, one of my favourites. H30cm/1ft, W40cm/16in. F6-10. '**Rock Pool**', low, spreading form, deep golden-yellow foliage in summer, rich copper-bronze, often with red tints, in winter. Occasional purple-red flowers. Excellent contrast to blue spruce. H15cm/6in, W25cm/10in. F7-9. '**Windlebrooke**' similar to 'Rock Pool' but brighter yellow foliage in summer, orange-yellow in

Erica arborea 'Albert's Gold' with *Erica carnea* 'Pink Spangles'

winter. Purple flowers. H25-30cm/10-12in, W30cm/1ft. F7-9.
E. x *darleyensis*. First-class cultivars from an original cross between *E. carnea* and *E. erigena*. Excellent ground cover in broad drifts or on banks. Prune only to tidy up any unkempt growth, if necessary. All Z7-8. Tolerate ⊕
'**Arthur Johnson**', reputedly a hybrid between *E. erigena* 'Glauca' and *E. carnea*, taller than others, making a looser plant with long, narrow stems, dark green foliage and pink flowers. Superb garden plant, useful for cutting. H60-75cm/24-30in, W60cm/2ft. F11-4. '**Darley Dale**', robust, spreading dark green bush, profuse pale mauve-pink flowers, untroubled except by severe frosts. Somewhat similar are '**George Rendall**' (F12-3), '**Furzey**' (F1-4) and '**Ghost Hills**' (F11-4). All H30-45cm/12-18in, W50cm/20in. '**Jack H. Brummage**', bright golden-yellow foliage in summer in full sun, orange-gold in winter. Bright pink flowers. H30-45cm/12-18in, W40cm/16in. F1-4. **Kramer's Red**, deep green leaves, long-flowering truly red flowers. H25-30cm/18-12in. F10-4. '**Silberschmelze**' (syn. 'Molten Silver'), formerly appeared

under various names such as 'Silver Beads', 'Silver Bells' and 'Silver Mist'. Similar to 'Darley Dale' but has silvery white, sweetly scented flowers over long period. H30-45cm/12-18in, W50cm/20in. F12-4.
E. erigena. Irish heath. Useful garden plants, although less hardy than some winter-flowering species. Long flowering period, honey-scented. The species varies in height from 60cm/2ft to 2.4m/8ft, although most modern cultivars are compact and bushy. All Z8. Tolerate ⊕
'**Golden Lady**', a sport of 'W.T. Rackliff'. Dense bush, year-round bright yellow, colours well in light shade. Sparse white flowers. Shoots can revert to green. Prone to sunscorch in exposed situations. H45-60cm/18-24in, W35cm/14in. F4-5. '**Irish Dusk**', compact and bushy, erect branches of dark to mid-green foliage and deep salmon-pink flowers. Older plants can get open and woody. H45-60cm/18-24in, W40cm/16in. F12-5.
'**W.T. Rackliff**', dense, rounded rich green bush, white flowers. H60-75cm/24-30in, W40cm/16in. F3-5.

E. vagans. Cornish heath. Old flower heads remain attractive through winter and although frost damage can occur plants usually sprout from the base in spring. Prune in spring just as new growth begins. All Z7-8. ☼ ❄ Tolerates some ⊕
'**Cream**' and '**Cornish Cream**', creamy white flowers, the latter with longer spikes. H45cm/18in, W50cm/20in. F8-10. '**Lyonesse**', light green leaves, reliable annual show of white flowers with golden anthers. The faded, buff heads are equally attractive. H45cm/18in, W45cm/18in. F8-10. '**Mrs D.F. Maxwell**', perhaps the most outstanding of all the cultivars, neat, mounded habit, sprays of deep cerise-pink flowers. H45-60cm/18-24in, W40cm/16in. F8-10. '**Valerie Proudley**', slow-growing, compact, bright yellow bush. Good in light shade; can scorch in exposed positions. Flowers white but seldom occur. H15-20cm/6-8in, W35cm/14in. F8-9.

TREE HEATHS
Provide the height lacking in most other heathers, and have a flowering period that knits together the late winter- and spring-flowering types with the earliest summer ones. In exposed spots and colder regions can suffer damaged or broken foliage. In sheltered positions make magnificent, free-flowering plants, useful for cutting. Some are sweetly scented. All ☼ ❄; most ⊕ ⊖
E. arborea. '**Albert's Gold**', remarkably hardy, upright branches, bright golden-yellow foliage, tolerant of cold winds and frost. White flowers a bonus. Ultimate H1.5-1.8m/5-6ft, W60-75cm/24-30in. F3-5. Z8. '**Estrella Gold**', slow-growing, less bright bush, greeny yellow foliage, white flowers. H90-120cm/3-4ft, W60-75cm/24-30in. F3-5. Z8.

ALPINES DIRECTORY

USUALLY REFERRED TO AS ALPINES OR SOMETIMES AS ROCK PLANTS, this group of plants is a diverse one that can be confusing to beginner and expert alike. Many of the plants offered by garden centres in this category are not necessarily native to mountainous regions, but are usually of dwarf or compact stature and really can be classed as dwarf perennials. In their natural habitat, most either die back in autumn or spend the winter covered by snow, and flower from early spring onwards. The majority, therefore, are somewhat limited in appeal during the winter months.

In addition to those that do flower early enough to be included here, I have included those that have some interesting foliage during the quiet season, such as houseleeks, sempervivums, dianthus, raoulias and thymes. All of these have an invaluable contribution to make to alpine or scree gardens when interplanted with dwarf shrubs and dwarf conifers. They all have another season of interest as well. Most alpines prefer reasonable drainage and all those mentioned can be safely planted in autumn unless otherwise indicated.

H: Approximate height after 2 years
W: Approximate width after 2 years
F: Months in flower
Z: Relevant hardiness zone(s)

A group of alpines, perennials and dwarf shrubs add colour in spring

ACAENA **New Zealand burr**
Creeping, semi-evergreen plants with finely cut leaves, small flowers and rounded burr-like seed heads. Best as ground cover or between paving as can be invasive. Several forms. ☼ ❋ ■
A. 'Blue Haze'. Good foliage, bluish grey leaves, brown burrs. H10cm/4in, W60cm/2ft. F7-8. Z6-8.
A. microphylla. One of the best. Coppery bronze mats, reddish flowers and burrs. H2.5cm/1in, W60cm/2ft. F7-9. Z5-8.

Ajuga reptans 'Braunherz'

AJUGA **Bugle**
Creeping, semi-evergreen, flowering plants, colourful ground cover between taller plants. ☼ ❋ ◪ ☆
A. reptans. Common bugle. Green leaves. Best foliage selections are 'Braunherz', glossy purple-bronze leaves, blue flowers, and 'Burgundy Glow', wine-red, bronze and cream leaves, pale blue flowers. H15cm/6in, W30-45cm/12-18in. F5-6. Z3-9.

ALYSSUM **Gold dust**
A. saxatile (correctly *Aurinia saxitalis*). Early spring-flowering alpines, ideal for banks, walls and frontal groups. 'Citrinum', grey-

green leaves, lemon-yellow flowers; 'Dudley Neville', compact, silvery leaves, primrose-yellow flowers. 'Dudley Neville Variegated', creamy edges to leaves. All H25cm/10in, W45cm/18in. F4-6. Z3-7. ☼ ■

ARABIS **Rock cress**
Showy, spring-flowering, taller forms, good for banks or over walls. ☼ ■
A. caucasica. White flowers well above grey-green leaves. 'Plena', double white flowers. 'Corfe Castle', deep magenta. 'Variegata', single white flowers, creamy-edged white foliage. H20cm/8in, W45cm/18in. F3-5. Z4-7.
A. ferdinandi-coburgii. Mat-forming rosettes, white flowers. Best are 'All Gold', gold and green leaves, and 'Variegata', creamy variegations. H10cm/4in, W20cm/8in. F4-6. Z5-7.

ARMERIA **Thrift**
Evergreen, grassy-leaved hummocks, flowers in late spring. ☼ ■
A. caespitosa (syn. *A. juniperifolia*). First alpine thrift to bloom, pink. 'Alba', white. 'Bevan's Variety', bright pink. H10cm/4in, W15-20cm/6-8in. F4-7. Z4-8.

Aubrieta 'Bressingham Pink'

AUBRIETA

Wonderfully coloured flowers in spring for frontal groups, slopes or over walls, but of no value for rest of the year. Clip back after flowering. Seed-raised varieties are less effective than good named cultivars. '**Alix Brett**', double, carmine-purple. '**Bob Saunders**', double, reddish purple. '**Bressingham Pink**', single, bright pink. '**Dr. Mules**', single, violet-purple. '**Red Carpet**', best single red. '**Silver Edge**', leaves narrowly margined with cream, blue flowers. Average H10-15cm/4-6in, W30-45cm/12-18in. F4-6. Z5-8. ✷ ■

AZORELLA

A. trifurcata (syn. *Bolax glebaria*). Dense mats of glossy evergreen rosettes with small, yellow flowers. H5cm/2in, W25cm/10in. F6-7. Z6-7. ✷ ▢

DIANTHUS Rock pinks

Includes perennial and alpine types. Although few of the alpines flower in the autumn to spring period, many provide attractive mats or hummocks of silver or grey foliage for the scree garden. Many suitable for troughs. Slightly alkaline soil for most. Average H5-15cm/2-6in, W10-30cm/4-8in. F5-7. Z4-8. ✷ ■

DRABA

Cushions of green foliage, bright yellow flowers in early spring. Good for alpine house. Gritty soil. All Z4-6. ✷ ■
D. aizoides. Easy to grow from seed. H5cm/2in, W20cm/8in. F3-5.
D. bruinifolia. Miniature hummocks. H8cm/3in, W20cm/8in. F3-5.

ERIGERON Dwarf fleabane

E. karvinskianus (syn. *E. mucronatus*). Long-flowering, self-seeding, dwarf perennial with masses of small, daisy-like pink flowers for months. H15-20cm/6-8in, W30cm/1ft. F6-10. Z5-7. ✷ ■

GENTIANA Gentian

Classic alpines flowering in summer or autumn. Acid soil for autumn-flowering types, slightly alkaline for spring-flowering. ✷ ✸ ▢ ■ ★
G. acaulis. Trumpet gentian. Large, deep blue flowers nestling above green mats. H10cm/4in, W30-45cm/12-18in. F3-5. Z4-7.
G. verna. Spring gentian. Small, deep azure blue flowers. H8cm/3in, W15cm/6in. F3-5. Z4-7.

G. x *macaulayi* '**Kingfisher**'. Brilliant deep blue trumpets in autumn on bright green mats. H10cm/4in, W20cm/8in. F8-10. Z5-7.
G. sino-ornata. Deep sky blue flowers in autumn. '**Alba**', white. '**Angel's Wings**', bright blue, striped white. H10cm/4in, W20cm/8in. F8-10. Z5-7.

GERANIUM

Some forms repeat bloom in autumn until frosts arrive. See also Perennials Directory, page 127. Most ✷ ☆
G. cinereum. '**Ballerina**' and '**Laurence Flatman**', lilac-pink flowers veined with darker colour; the latter is much deeper, at times crimson. H15cm/6in, W30cm/1ft. F5-10. Z5-8.

IBERIS Candytuft

Sub-shrubby, glossy, evergreen foliage. Brilliant white flowers in early summer. Good for banks and walls. ✷ ■
I. '**Little Gem**' (syn. 'Weisser Zwerg'). Compact shrub for alpine scree, not always long-lived. H15cm/6in, W30cm/1ft. F5-7. Z3-9.

Iberis sempervirens 'Snowflake'

I. sempervirens (syn. *I. commutata*). Vigorous, ground cover. H15cm/6in, W60cm/2ft. F4-6. Z3-9. '**Snowflake**' is less spreading.

LYSIMACHIA Loosestrife

L nummularia '**Aurea**'. Golden form of creeping Jenny. Spreading mat of yellow foliage, attractive from early spring to late autumn. Yellow, buttercup flowers are hardly noticeable. H5cm/2in, W60cm/2ft. F6-7. Z3-8. ✷ ✸ ▢ ■

POLYGONUM

P. vacciniifolium. Rapidly spreading mats, masses of short spikes bearing light pink flowers in autumn. Good for hanging over walls. H10cm/4in, W60cm/2ft. F9-10. Z4-8. ✷ ✸ ▢ ■

PRIMULA See Perennials Directory, page 130.

RANUNCULUS

R. ficaria. Lesser celandine. Comes into leaf in spring, followed by bright yellow flowers, dies back in mid-summer. Several selections. '**Alba**', white. '**Aurantiacus**', coppery orange. '**Brazen Hussey**', brightest of all, coppery leaves, golden flowers. All H10cm/4in, W20cm/8in. F3-5. Z4-8. ✷ ✸ ▢ ■

RAOULIA

Carpeting evergreens grown for their tiny leaves rather than their miniature flowers. Peaty soil; good drainage in winter. ✷ ✸ ▢ ■
R. australis. Silver leaves, insignificant, yellow flowers. H1cm/½in, W30cm/1ft. F6-7. Z7-8.

SAGINA

S. subulata '**Aurea**'. Bright, evergreen carpeter. Creamy yellow foliage in winter, bright yellow in summer, white flowers. Good for screes or paving. H1cm/½in, W20cm/8in. F6-7. Z6-8. ✷ ▢ ■

SATUREJA **Winter savory**
S. montana 'Pygmaea'. Pretty semi-evergreen bush, deep blue autumn flowers. H20cm/8in, W15cm/6in. F9-10. Z6-9. ☀ ■

SAXIFRAGA **Saxifrage**
Indispensable genus for evergreen foliage and early flowers. The range and variety is immense.
Kabschia or cushion group. Rosettes of lime-encrusted, grey-green or silvery foliage, often large, saucer-shaped pink, white or yellow flowers, generally in early spring. Excellent

Saxifraga 'Pixie'

for troughs. H5-25cm/2-10in, W8-25cm/3-10in. F2-4. Z4-6. ☀ ◩ ■
Aizoon or encrusted group. Similar to the Kabschia types, but much larger leaves, often evergreen, and flowering in late spring. H5-30cm/2-12in, W 13-40cm/5-16in. F5-6. Z4-7. ☀ ■ ⊕
Mossy group. Moss-like, green or coloured foliage, masses of white, pink, crimson, even yellow flowers on slender stems. **'Cloth of Gold'**, bright golden leaves. **'Hi-Ace'**, delicately variegated foliage. **'Pixie'**, compact, bright pink flowers. H10-25cm/4-10in. W15-30cm/6-12in. F3-5. Z5-6. ☀ ◩
S. juniperifolia. One of the earliest to flower. Green hummocks festooned with clusters of bright yellow flowers. H5cm/2in, W15cm/6in. F3-4. Z5-7. ◩ ■
S. oppositifolia. Showy, small, lilac-like flowers then dark green mats – early in spring. **'Florissa'**, bright rose-pink. All H5cm/2in, W45cm/18in. F3-4. Z2-6. ☀

Sedum spathulifolium 'Purpureum'

Sedum lidakense

SEDUM **Stonecrop**
There are some good evergreen foliage types among these succulents and a few late-flowering species. ☀ ■ ☆
S. kamtschaticum 'Variegatum'. Attractive, pink-tinged, yellow and green leaves give a long period of interest. Deciduous. Golden flowers. H15cm/6in, W20cm/8in. F6-8. Z3-8.
S. lidakense. Bluish grey leaves, a good show of bright, rosy red flowers. Deciduous. H10cm/4in, W15cm/6in. F8-10. Z4-8.
S. spathulifolium. Dwarf, mat-forming. Silvery grey spathe-like leaves, yellow flowers. **'Capo Blanco'**, dwarfer, powdery white leaves. **'Purpureum'**, larger, purple-tinged leaves. All H5cm/2in, W25cm/10in. F6-7. Z4-7.

SEMPERVIVUM **Houseleek**
Rosette-forming succulents offering wide range of size and colour. Foliage can be red, purple, grey or green with colourful leaf tips. Flowers are often spasmodic, curious, sometimes spectacular. Gritty soil. The plants vary in size, but all F6-7, Z5-9. ☀ ■

S. arachnoideum 'Laggeri'. One of the best silvered, "cobwebby" types. Dense cushion webbed with silver threads. H2.5-8cm/1-3in, W20-30cm/8-12in. F6-7. Z5-9.

THYMUS **Thyme**
Popular aromatic plants, some creeping, some more shrubby. Carpeters, good for paving. ☀ ◩ ■
T. 'Bressingham Pink'. Grey-green carpet, pink flowers. H2.5cm/1in, W15cm/6in. F5-6. Z4-7.
T. x citriodorus. Bushy, lemon-scented, evergreen. **'Silver Posie'** and **'Silver Queen'**, prettily variegated forms. Similar is the hybrid **'Anderson's Gold'**, bright, golden foliage all year round. All 15cm/6in, W30cm/1ft. F5-6. Z6-8.
T. 'Doone Valley'. Deep green foliage flecked with gold. H15cm/6in, W30cm/1ft. F5-6. Z6-8.
T. nitidus. Erect, twiggy bush, grey-green foliage, clear pink flowers. **'Peter Davis'**, perhaps the best form. Both H20cm/8in, W30cm/1ft. F5-6. Z7-8.
T. serpyllum. Grey-green carpet, white, pink and red flowers. H2.5cm/1in, W10-25cm/4-10in. F5-7. Z4-8.

Bulbs Directory

To most gardeners bulbs are the true harbingers of spring, starting with snowdrops and aconites which appear in late winter according to region and season. As with most other groups of plants, once you investigate you realize that the variety available is greater than you originally thought. The selection below concentrates on some of the best plants for autumn, winter and early spring interest, but there are also lots of later spring-flowering bulbs available.

The majority of bulbs are sold dry in late summer and autumn and most, crocus, narcissus and tulips in particular, can be planted up until early winter if they are stored in a dry atmosphere meanwhile. Most bulbs prefer a reasonably well-drained soil. Plant them at a depth twice that of their height.

Some bulbs – snowdrops (Galanthus) and aconites (Eranthis) – are best planted "in the green", just after flowering, if you can obtain them like this. More bulbs are now being offered in pots at their time of flowering in winter or early spring. These are more expensive but are a good way of acquiring some choice or well-grown plants; it is by far the best way to buy hardy cyclamens, for example, as these seldom grow satisfactorily from older, dry corms.

Spring-flowering bulbs bring early colour

Colchicum agrippinum

Crocus sieberi

CHIONODOXA Glory-of-the-snow
Late winter- and spring-flowering bulbs related to scilla. Naturalize freely, even in grass. ☼ ❋ ■
C. luciliae. Brilliant show of white-centred, bright blue, star-like flowers in early spring. Similar are **C. 'Pink Giant'**, slightly taller, and **C. sardensis**, almost gentian-blue flowers but a little later. H10-15cm/4-6in, W10-15cm/4-6in. F3-4. Z4.

COLCHICUM
Open, trumpet-shaped flowers on naked stems in late summer and autumn. Use as frontal groups among shrubs, but not where their large leaves will smother smaller plants. ☼ ❋ ■
C. agrippinum. Star-shaped, lilac-purple flowers spotted with white. H10-15cm/4-6in, W30cm/1ft. F 9-10. Z6.
C. autumnale. Mauve-lilac flowers in early autumn. The form *roseum plenum*, with showy double, reddish violet trumpets is later. Both H10-15cm/4-6in, W30cm/1ft. Z5.
C. speciosium. Probably the most showy of the genus. Large lily-like flowers, shades of mauve, purple and lilac with creamy centres and golden anthers. The form *album* is white. Both H15-20cm/6-9in, W30cm/1ft. F 9-10. Z5.
Hybrids between *C. speciosium* and *C. autumnale* are equally showy, including the double '**Waterlily**', pinkish lilac flowers, and '**Atrorubens**', single, crimson-lilac.

CROCUS
Many autumn-, winter- and early spring-flowering species but only a few can be selected here. Field mice and voles enjoy the bulbs as winter food. Like high shade under trees. ☼ ■
C. ancyrensis. Small, orange-yellow flowers rising above needle-like, deep green foliage in winter. H5-8cm/2-3in, W5-8in/2-3in. F1-2. Z5.
C. chrysanthus. Indispensable for early spring flowers. Mostly represented by named varieties from light blue to purple, white to striped, yellow to bronze. Small-flowered, they are better for naturalizing than the equally showy large-flowered, so-called Dutch crocus. Similar are selections of *C. sieberi* and *C. etruscus* and *C. tommasimianus*. All H9-12cm/3-4in, W3-4cm/9-12in. F2-3. Z5.
C. speciosus. Excellent autumn-flowering species with many variants from violet-blue to mauve to lilac and white. Naturalizes freely. H15cm/6in, W15cm/6in. F8-10. Z4.

CYCLAMEN
Worthy garden plants for flower, foliage and some for fragrance, during autumn, winter and early spring. Some naturalize very freely, self-seeding on surface mulch or undisturbed leaf mould. Apply a light mulch of composted bark or leaf mould when dormant. ☼ ❋ ■
C. coum. Brightest crimson to pink and white mid-winter flowers, unfurl

Cyclamen coum

from rounded, kidney-shaped leaves. Many selections with silver or marbled foliage. H9-12cm/3-4in, W15cm/6in. F11-3. Z6.
C. hederifolium. Pink or white flowers from late summer into autumn as marbled leaves appear, these making a total ground cover which once established lasts through winter. H10-15cm/4-6in, W15cm/6in. F8-1. Z6.

ERANTHIS
E. hyemalis. Winter aconite. The easiest and most popular of the genus. Early, cheery, golden-yellow, buttercup flowers followed by fresh green foliage. More a tuber than a bulb but can be treated in the same way; when planting in late summer or early autumn, do not plant too deep, add a leafy, peaty mulch and keep moist. Self-seeds once established. Plant beneath trees or shrubs. H5-10cm/2-4in, W8-12cm/3-5in. F1-2. Z4. ☀ ❋ ◪ ▪

ERYTHRONIUM Dog's tooth violet
Pretty woodland plants with trumpet-shaped flowers, some with mottled leaves. Resent disturbance so plant in autumn as dry bulbs. ☀ ◪ ▪ ★
E. californicum. Californian fawn lily. Clusters of creamy yellow flowers, purple-mottled leaves. H25-30/10-12in, W15cm/6in. F4-5. Z4.
E. 'Pagoda'. Pale yellow flowers. H30-45/12-18, W20cm/8in. F4-5. Z5.

GALANTHUS Snowdrop
Larger family than many realize,

Galanthus nivalis

with more than a hundred species and varieties in cultivation, available only from specialists. All have pendulous, white flowers some in autumn but most in winter. Best moved and planted immediately after flowering whilst leaves are still green. ☀ ❋ ◪ ★
G. nivalis. Common snowdrop. Simple, single flowers, green leaves. Seems to do well anywhere and naturalizes easily in grass, woodland or gardens. 'Plenus', pretty double. 'Viridapicis', green-tipped outer petals. All H10-15cm/4-6in, W15cm/6in. F1-3. Z4.
G. reginae-olgae. Autumn-flowering, best grown in the open. H10-15cm/4-6in, W15cm/6in. F 9-11. Z6. ▪
G. 'S. Arnott'. One of the best of all and one I grow widely at Foggy Bottom. Large flowers, abundant foliage and good vigour. H15-25cm/6-10in, W15in/6in. F1-3. Z4.

IRIS
Some early spring-flowering species and varieties. Useful in containers, with alpines or nestling between dwarf shrubs or conifers. ☀ ❋ ▪
I. danfordiae. Beautiful early species with deep yellow flowers on sturdy stems. Best planted 2.5cm/5in deep. H10-12.5cm/4-5in, W10cm/4in. F2-3. Z4.
I. histrioides 'Major'. Best form of the species. Deep blue flowers speckled white. H8-10cm/3-4in, W10cm/4in. F1-2. Z4.
I. reticulata. Early, mostly fragrant flowers on sturdy stems. Blue to purple, the falls marked with yellow. 'Cantab', pale blue and yellow.

Eranthis hyemalis

Erythronium californicum

'Harmony', sky blue, yellow markings. 'J.S. Dijt', reddish purple. All H12-15cm/5-6ins, W10cm/4in. F2-3. Z4.

LEUCOJUM Snowflake

L. vernum. Spring snowflake. Larger flowers than snowdrops, with overlapping, green-tipped white petals, in late winter and early spring. Good for naturalizing in grass. Plant 10cm/4in deep. H10-15cm/4-6in, W15cm/6in. F2-3. Z5. ☼ ◩ ■

MUSCARI Grape hyacinth

Showy plants adding blue, poker-like flowers to the predominant yellows of mid-spring and mixing well with conifers and heathers. Plant 8cm/3in deep. Colours range from pale blue to azure and deep indigo as well as white. All 15-20cm/6-8in. Z4. ☼ ☀ ◩ ■

NARCISSUS

Large genus with just a few early flowering types suitable for rock gardens, naturalizing or general planting. ☼ ☀ ■

N. asturiensis. Perfect miniature for rock or alpine garden with small, pendent, golden-yellow trumpets. H8-10cm/3-4in, W8cm/3in. F2-3. Z4 .

N. bulbocodium. Distinctive species with nodding, petticoat-shaped flowers from pale lemon to golden-yellow, and grassy leaves. Naturalizes well in grass. H15-30cm/6-12in, W15cm/6in. F3-4. Z5. ◩

N. cyclamineus. Golden-yellow, swept back or recurved petals, the corona long and tubular. H10-20cm/4-8in, W8cm/3in. F2-3. Z3. ☼ or ☀ ◩

Hybrids. Early flowering, smaller types worth obtaining are as follows. 'February Gold', nodding, deep yellow trumpets. 'February Silver', yellow trumpets, white petals or perianth. Both H20-25cm/8-10in, W15cm/6in. F2-3. Z3. 'Peeping Tom', bright green foliage enhancing nodding, deep yellow, tubular corona and swept back perianth. H30cm/1ft, W15cm/6in. F3. Z3. 'Tête-à-Tête', early, deep yellow trumpet, lighter perianth, usually two or more flowers per

Narcissus 'Tête-à-Tête'

stem. H15cm/6in, W10cm/4in. F2-3. Z3.

NERINE

Strap-like leaves for most of the year. showy terminal flower clusters on leafless stems in autumn. Plant bulbs shallowly, against a wall or as edging. Easy and reasonably hardy, except in cold regions. Light, sandy soil. ☼ ☀ ■

N. bowdenii. Late-autumn display of clear pink, lily-like trumpets. H35cm/14in, W23cm/9in. F9-11.

Z8-10. 'Fenwick's Variety', taller and larger-flowered. H40cm/16in, W23cm/9in. F9-11. Z8-10.

PUSCHKINIA

P. scilloides. Striped squill. Early white flowers striped pale blue, closely allied to *Chionodoxa* and *Scilla*. The form **alba** is white. Plant 8cm/3in deep. Both H10cm/4in, W8cm/3in. F3. Z4. ☼ ☀ ◩ ■ ★

SCILLA

The early spring-flowering squills or wild hyacinths grow happily among shrubs, on alpine or rock gardens. Plant 8cm/3in deep. ☼ ☀ ◩ ■

S bifolia. Often variable but mostly turquoise, star-like flowers. H5-8cm/2-3in, W8cm/3in. F3-4. Z4.

S. sibirica. Siberian squill. Brilliant deep blue flowers. 'Spring Beauty', similar blue flowers but more vigorous, good for naturalizing in grass. H10-15cm/4-6in, W10cm/4in. F3-4. Z4.

S. tubergeniana. Very early, pale blue, star-like flowers with darker blue veins on backs of petals. H10cm/4in, W10cm/4in. F1-2. Z4.

Muscari armeniacum

Nerine bowdenii

The "Busy" Seasons

INTRODUCTION

As a garden enthusiast, I often get asked which is my favourite season in the garden. The answer is invariably spring, summer, autumn and winter – which is telling the truth, but avoiding the question! Every season is to be enjoyed in the garden and every season should be planned for interest and pleasure. With the amazing range of plants now available to choose from, this can be achieved in even the smallest garden. And yet, despite the obvious appeal of the garden in high summer, it is perhaps easier to find reasons to consider winter a favourite season, since the garden and our activities are then much quieter, more reflective of simple pleasures, and the interest of the fewer flowering plants, foliage, stems, bark and twigs more treasured. Time seems more plentiful and one can appreciate the changing light and the frost on foliage transforming the appearance of individual plants and the whole garden scene.

Undoubtedly, therefore, it was easier to create a strong theme and a more direct message when writing the first half of this book. Having spent the last thirty years creating a six-acre garden with year-round interest at Foggy Bottom, I had some reason to encourage other gardeners to give more thought to planning for winter interest. But summer garden glory? Doesn't everyone plant their garden for summer colour? What can I have to say that will be any different from hundreds of other books on the subject? This was certainly a question I asked myself when I sat down to write the following chapters.

This section starts from where the previous one finishes, so while the seasons of autumn, winter and early spring are covered in the first half of this book, they are followed by late spring, early, mid- and late summer in the second. And since it is set in the same garden, Foggy Bottom at Bressingham in Norfolk, the book as a whole enables you to follow in words and photographs some of the changes and moods of the garden through a complete year.

Foggy Bottom is one of the few gardens whose main structure is provided by conifers, among which are interplanted hundreds of other plants, including trees, shrubs, perennials, ornamental grasses, bulbs, alpines and ferns. The conifers provide colour in both winter and summer and have a different effect on the plants around them.

All too often, garden writers dismiss conifers and claim that if used anywhere they should be used on their own, but I believe they can be assimilated and used to great effect with a wide variety of plants. The conifers themselves of course may change colour from summer to winter and the background colour they provide offers many opportunities for striking

THE ACER BED in late spring. A 30-year old specimen Japanese maple, Acer shirasawanum *'Aureum' creates leafy shade for a wide variety of bulbs and perennials. Golden-leaved hostas highlight (centre foreground)* Phlox divaricata *'Blue Dreams',* × Heucherella *'Bridget Bloom' and to the right* Dicentra *'Pearl Drops'* (left)

A VIEW FROM the patio at the rear of the house frames the distant acer bed. On the right, standing on the driveway, is a large ten-year-old container-grown Wisteria sinensis *in full flower at the end of spring* (right)

plant associations. For instance, a witchhazel, such as *Hamamelis mollis* 'Pallida', will hardly be noticeable against the shaded side of a dark blue conifer in summer, but when the leaves have dropped in winter and the golden, strap-like flowers emerge, the contrast is dramatic. Some stunning combinations can be created by planting a bright blue agapanthus against the background of a golden-leaved conifer, or the shimmering scarlet of *Crocosmia* 'Lucifer' against a steel-blue juniper, at its brightest in mid- to late summer.

As in the previous chapters, I have tried in the photographs to capture the feel of the garden, as well as the beauty of its plants, though these have surprisingly been more difficult to portray in the better light available in the "busy" seasons.

SOME THOUGHTS ON GARDENING

In the first half of this book, I described autumn, winter and early spring as the "quiet" seasons, compared to the time of the year from late spring to late summer which, by contrast, comprise the "busy" or "noisy" seasons in the garden. As gardeners we all know that there is some truth in this for, with the warmth of the later spring sunshine and the mowing of the first new grass, we know we are in for a roller-coaster ride of activity, which will be unlikely to finish until early autumn.

Gardening is enjoyment and we should not complain once the warmer weather arrives at last and our garden plants burst into frenetic activity to create the display we have planned for. Now, in the busy seasons, we can expect to plant and to prune, to weed and to trim, to water and feed – and to mow the grass. We appear to be driven by events happening too fast to catch up with, and it seems as though the garden is in control, rather than its owner – a feeling most gardeners are familiar with.

The quiet seasons, on the other hand, with little or no growth taking place, give us the chance to catch up and prepare for the following year, to see in what ways we may be able to plan new features and prepare the ground for planting, perhaps move other plants around to create better associations, or just to give prized specimens more room. Autumn is the time when I usually go round making notes of all the projects that we would like to get done, knowing full well that at best only half will be achieved.

A garden is of course a series of living organisms brought together to create an artistic effect, and there is every reason, without pretension, why one should consider creating a garden or a plant association an art form. Yet what you

create in year one will, as plants grow, have changed in years two, three and four and, without constant adjustment, may well not be what was planned for by year ten.

THE TIME SCALE

Planning a garden can be done on paper, with the correct spacings and positionings carefully worked out, and of course that is the guidance you would expect from a professional garden designer. But at what stage in its life cycle is it planned for perfection? Five years after planting, or ten? Some plants do not change form and size as dramatically as others. My

LATE SUMMER IN a corner of Foggy Bottom: the yellow black-eyed Susan, Rudbeckia *'Goldsturm', is backed by the waving wands of* Stipa gigantea *and the almost luminous lilac flowers of* Phlox *'Franz Schubert'* (above)

father Alan Bloom, who created his famous perennial island beds in the six-acre Dell Garden at Bressingham, can still see today much the same perennial plants and associations as when he planted them nearly forty years ago. Perennials, though in need of replanting and rejuvenating at regular intervals, will mostly reach their ultimate height, with little variation, within two years' growth.

SPLASHES OF COLOUR are timed to appear through the seasons, with some plants, such as Hosta 'Frances Williams' (in the foreground), lasting longer than the Knaphill azaleas, which make their startling contribution in early summer (above)

A NEW BED of mainly perennials and ornamental grasses creates interest and colour from June until October, the structure of conifers and trees providing a more mature vertical backdrop to the flatness of the former meadow. There are fifteen varieties of Miscanthus sinensis in this "Snake Bed" to continue the interest into winter (left)

Trees, shrubs and conifers are somewhat different. When I started planting the slightly sloping meadow in what was to become Foggy Bottom, I put in few plants that were higher than 1.5-1.8m/5-6ft. Thirty years later, some have reached over 18m/60ft, while others have made a considerable spread. With six acres that may not seem much of a problem, but plants and specimens will spoil as they become overgrown or overcrowded in a large garden as well as in a smaller one. In some ways, I see the development of Foggy Bottom as a microcosm of the experience many gardeners have, either with their brand-new garden on an open site, or dealing with an existing garden with reasonably well-established trees.

GARDEN STYLES

Each type of garden is a challenge and can be an adventure, with size a determining factor in the plants you might select, but not necessarily a restriction when it comes to what imagination and application might achieve. But we often approach our gardening from different perspectives. Starting with an open meadow around a new house would suggest to me an informal, natural garden because I like vistas and distant views, but someone else may wish to create "rooms" surrounded by hedges. When the well-known gardener and writer Christopher Lloyd visited Foggy Bottom for the first time, when the garden was about twenty years old, having previously been rather damning about conifers and heathers as garden plants, he walked round the garden with me, eventually saying politely, "I can see we have quite different approaches to garden styles." As I wondered what was coming next, he graciously added, "There is room for both."

A LATE SUMMER'S EVENING shows conifers and heathers in the foreground, with flowers still left on Buddleja davidii *'Pink Delight'* (above)

CONIFERS, SHRUBS, PERENNIALS and ferns create an early summer picture. The white-flowered shrub is Viburnum plicatum *'Cascade';* Geranium sylvaticum *'Mayflower' and* Pulmonaria longifolia *the other flowers* (left)

Although I knew of his own garden at Great Dixter, my first visit was not made until the following summer and I could see immediately what he meant. There was not a heather in sight and although he had conifers, they were old yew hedges. The ancient house at Great Dixter already had an established garden and any development called for something in keeping with the traditions of the place; this is what Christopher was carrying on, while at the same time making his own individual mark on the garden. Even if you are bound by certain restrictions, established trees, walls or hedges, it is still possible to make your own unique contribution to the style of a garden.

And what of garden fashions? Well, there are some people who are led by what others create or suggest, but while it is fun to obtain the latest plants to be introduced, it is quite something else to create a whole garden as a fashion. Cottage gardens, formal gardens, single-colour-theme gardens or borders, conifer and heather gardens, even Mediterranean gardens – all have their merits, but once planted they are not so easy to change. More modern gardens make much of hard landscaping and tend to be designed without really considering the plants, beyond their use in creating the correct form and colour. I would perhaps go to the other extreme and suggest that such is the diversity of plants that you can create almost any effect you want with them alone. This does not necessarily rule out structures such as walls, fences or pergolas, which are used to support and display plants, but plants can offer so much potential pleasure throughout the year that it seems a pity not to use every possible area of the garden to achieve this.

LATE SPRING/EARLY SUMMER

Spring is always an exciting time in the garden, from the early spring when flowers such as snowdrops and aconites create natural dashes of colour, to the later, more bold-looking daffodils and tulips. But bulbs are not the only flowers of early spring – shrubs, perennials and trees all have their role to play.

Towards the end of April would be called late spring in most of the British Isles because spring is so drawn out, snowdrops having appeared as early as January. We can go through the whole of the month of January in fact without a frost, and then receive some stinging spring frosts in May when plants, now in full soft growth, are least prepared for them. In parts of Canada and the northern, eastern and central United States, winter never seems to end. And when it does, it often changes to summer within a few weeks, so that the spring season can be even more frantic, and there is seldom time for this lovely period to be enjoyed to the full. Having spent two springs in Maryland, I can vouch for the fluctuations that can be experienced there, with temperatures of 24°C/75°F following on from frosty weather, then plunging back to snow or frost again, but late spring frosts are less of a danger. If spring frosts seem like a recurrent theme in my narrative, I suppose it is because, having waited all year for a favourite plant to flower or come into leaf in Foggy Bottom, one night's frost can spoil it all.

A VIEW BETWEEN two upright conifers just coming into new growth highlights bright contrasts between flower and foliage. In the centre one of the most striking hostas, H. fluctuans *'Variegated' is flanked by the scarlet flowers of* Rhododendron *'Morgenrote' in the foreground and* Acer palmatum *'Garnet' behind.*

VALUABLE SPRING PERENNIALS

Some spring plants seem more or less impervious to frost while in flower. Take those two excellent herbaceous perennials, epimediums and pulmonarias. Some of the latter, commonly known as lungworts, start into flower in late winter and continue to flower until the late spring. They are low-growing and very accommodating as to soil and situation, flourishing either in full sun or shade where it is not too dry – and when the flowers are finished, many selections have attractively silvered or spotted leaves. They are excellent subjects to plant among shrubs or roses, providing early flowers then attractive ground cover foliage. Like certain groups of plants, they have become better appreciated in recent years, particularly since some excellent new selections have been introduced. Fifteen years ago you would have been lucky to find more than twenty varieties of lungworts being offered, even by a specialist. Now it is more like seventy, so the advice is as always to select the best, ideally those which offer both distinctive flowers in the spring and attractive foliage all summer. Once the flowers are finished, the new leaves start to grow, so it is best to cut off the old flowerheads, unless you want to allow seed to drop, which may produce some interesting progeny.

Epimediums are also becoming more widely appreciated. New introductions from China seem certain to lead to some important new developments in these generally tough perennials which not only have striking flowers, particularly in close up, but stunning leaves, in terms of their delicate patterns and markings, thereafter performing an admirable ground-covering role in sun or shade where it is not too dry.

SOME PLANTS FOR FOLIAGE EFFECT

Epimedium × perralchicum *'Frohnleiten' in mid-spring*

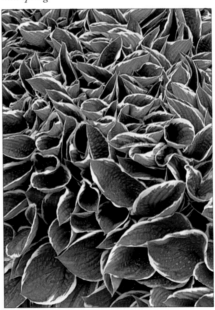

Hosta *'Francee' in late spring*

As gardeners we are fortunate to have such a wide range of plant material at our disposal, allowing us to create almost any effect we want. Plants of course need to be selected to suit the soil type, aspect, hardiness and general climatic conditions where we garden and we should bear in mind that foliage, as well as flowers, has an important role to play in our gardening schemes – and our enjoyment of the garden.

Rodgersia podophylla *in late spring*

Whether the foliage is evergreen or deciduous, attractive leaves can be a feature of any plant, from bulbs, alpines, perennials and ferns to shrubs, conifers and trees. Indeed, whole gardens or plant associations can be made from plants with interesting or handsome leaves and many plants, such as some hostas and pulmonarias, have attractive foliage as well as flowers. The foliage of a plant can be used to contrast with that of other plants or to accentuate the flowers, or it can become a focal point in its own right, particularly on those plants with purple, gold, silver or variegated leaves; it can be equally effective seen in close-up or from a distance.

CORYDALIS FLEXUOSA 'China Blue' is a choice but generally easy spring-flowering perennial (above)

DICENTRA SPECTABILIS 'Alba', a white "bleeding heart", looks cool against the ostrich fern, Matteucia struthiopteris (*above right*)

POLEMONIUM CAERULEUM 'Brise D'Anjou', a Jacob's ladder with brightly variegated leaves, extends the interest well beyond its early summer flowering period. Behind is Phlox divaricata *'Blue Dreams'* (right)

Using a camera as much as I do makes one appreciate the close-up detail of both foliage and flower, and in both respects the epimediums can be quite exquisite, though flowers are often hidden.

Generally known as bleeding hearts, the dicentras are indispensable spring perennials. *Dicentra spectabilis* from Japan (also known as lady-in-the bath) has soft, delicate foliage which, however, can be singed by a spring frost, though it is otherwise totally hardy. The species has dangling lockets of pink and white, and there is a pure white form too. Of equal or even better garden value are the North American species and selected cultivars, *D. formosa* from the west coast and *D. eximea* from the east. These make spreading clumps of finely cut foliage above which emerge a succession of pretty, pendulous flowers which continue for weeks; on younger plants, for months. Thriving in most soils which are not too dry, they may require dividing every few years. Three of my favourite forms are *D.* 'Luxuriant', with rich green foliage and bright crimson flowers, *D.* 'Pearl Drops', a selection my father made many years ago, whose glaucous foliage makes an attractive carpet set off by white flowers, and the lighter-green leaved and free-flowering *D.* 'Snowflakes'. My father also named a red-flowered variety which he called 'Adrian Bloom' – and I see mentioned in one nursery list a *D.* 'Adrian Bloom Variegated', which sounds sickly to me!

Early spring offers a medley of choice bulbs and perennials. Usually choice-looking plants are exactly what they seem, and remain choice and rare because they are difficult or slow to propagate. It was thought when it was first introduced from Western Sichuan in China that *Corydalis flexuosa* would for this reason take years to become available to the average gardener. But here was a plant for light shade whose bright electric blue flowers would make keen gardeners crawl over hot coals to get one, which in peaty soils seemed to romp away, making mats of foliage which by autumn could easily be divided and propagated. To date, four clones or selections have been introduced and are now easily found, which have given pleasure to a great many gardeners.

Not all choice plants are difficult to grow, by any means. Take the trilliums or blood lilies, for instance. Most are native to North America, although there are Asian species too. They are bulbous plants whose leaves unfurl in spring, followed by intriguing and striking flowers. They, like the related erythroniums, ideally need cool shade and a humus-rich soil, but they will survive with less than the ideal. With care, these conditions can usually be found or provided for in most gardens. Perhaps not the most natural, but one of the most sought-after forms is the large-flowered, spectacular *Trillium grandiflorum* 'Flore Pleno', a plant with perfect, fully double pure white flowers, which usually times its flowering for mid-spring and holds on for a prized position in our Chelsea Flower Show exhibit.

The Chelsea Flower Show at the end of May each year is where many new plants are launched – and at Bressingham we have always tried to find something new which would appeal at that time of year. One recent introduction seemed to fit the criteria for the perfect plant *and* be out just at the right time for Chelsea, but time will eventually tell how adaptable it is. This is a Jacob's

THOUGH THE FLOWERS ARE SMALL, the North American native, Trillium erectum, *makes a striking woodland or shade-loving plant* (right)

LATE SPRING at Foggy Bottom shows the morning sun shining on new leaves of maple and birch, a rhododendron and, to the right, Prunus *'Amanogowa' in full bloom (above)*

THE DWARF BROOM Cytisus ardoinii *makes a perfect contrast to the fresh green shoots on* Picea glauca *'Laurin' on the right of the picture (left)*

ladder with variegated leaves, named *Polemonium caeruleum* 'Brise D'Anjou' – French because it originated in France and the translation 'Breeze of Anjou' sounds as refreshing as the plant itself. Best in half shade where it is not too dry, this plant creates excellent foliage to which the spikes of blue flowers seem almost an unnecessary accessory. It looks good in a container too.

SPRING-FLOWERING SHRUBS

With a garden of six acres there can always be surprises (including sometimes a patch of weeds that has been overlooked!) and certain plants which one has hardly noticed for a whole year since they were last in flower, suddenly shout for attention as they burst into full bloom. Such plants include the brooms – the cytisus and genistas – for instance, both easily grown on a wide range of well-drained soils, including alkaline. Their narrow evergreen stems carry flower buds which in spring erupt into colour, mostly yellows but also red, pink and white and some in between. In hot weather they are gone within two or three weeks, but in late spring they are well worth their space in the garden. After flowering, cut back cytisus to half their length with a sharp knife rather than with secateurs. These are plants which are usually bought in flower from garden centres when they have little flowering period left, whereas it is much better to plant them in early spring, buying them with the promise of the colour offered in the description or photograph on the label. Again, position them in the garden where they will brighten up a dull spot during this part of the year.

There is little doubt that we are in the era of the impulse purchase – perhaps we always have been if the item is

IN MID-SPRING the scarlet new shoots of Pieris japonica *'Flaming Silver' erupt into growth* (top), *gradually toning down to pink, cream and white* (above) *before finally becoming variegated, like the rest of the foliage.*

tempting enough – but it is certainly true of plants now that buying from garden centres is rather like shopping at the supermarket. Such plants as the acid-loving pieris, a group of shrubs from Asia, many of which have bright crimson new shoots in late spring, can so tempt the customer that he or she must have it, no matter that the label may say "unsuitable for alkaline soils". It used to be the green-leaved *Pieris* 'Forest Flame' which drew the gardener's eye as fresh scarlet shoots emerged in spring; now, more selections are available and if you have acid soil or a container to put in ericaceous compost, *Pieris* 'Flaming Silver' offers year-round interest, with white-margined leaves and bright red shoots which fade to pink.

Plants with such pulling power are of course favourites with the public, the garden centre and the grower alike. As with any new product, nurserymen these days scour the world looking for new plants which the consumer will want to purchase. This is a necessary business and good economics too, and it makes the world of gardening and horticulture an exciting one to be in, but for the keen gardener it is only the icing on the cake. Some of these plants have not been tried and tested sufficiently and may not enter the hall of fame until after ten years or so of trial by the discerning gardener. But, although the commercial promotion of new plants may be looked upon askance by certain plantspeople, in reality the public is generally getting good new garden plants. If the nurseryman is reacting to public demand, he will be looking for a plant which is ideally compact in habit, free-flowering, fragrant, which has a long period of interest and is easy to grow on most soils! Now, isn't that just what most gardeners want?

RHODODENDRONS AND AZALEAS

Gardening on acid soil has led me into the temptation of growing quite a selection of hardy rhododendrons and azaleas, subjects vulnerable to spring frost damage but, when untouched, as bright and spectacular as you could wish. They can be difficult to position among other plants, but I have placed some singly and others in groups where, as they come into flower, they make a relatively brief but bright contribution to spring but where, surrounding them or nearby, are other plants to continue the interest. Combinations using the strongly coloured rhododendrons may not be remembered for their subtle colour tonings, but they certainly create an impact that can make you draw breath. One such is a hardy hybrid, *Rhododendron* 'Amethyst' which in late spring vies for attention beside the striking golden-needled dwarf fir *Abies nordmanniana* 'Golden Spreader'. I believe the person who called this conifer by such a descriptive name was rather premature in doing so, for although it is initially flat and spreading in growth, within ten years or less its desire to become a tree overcomes it and its growth becomes increasingly upward.

The foliage on many rhododendrons is attractive, particularly the new growth, but I think that the deciduous azaleas fit in better with most other garden plants, and among my favourites are the late spring- and early summer-flowering Knaphill hybrids. Attractive in bud, they burst into wonderful brash colours, but subtle pastel shades are among them, and the flowers are seldom caught by late frosts. If you garden on acid soil they are a challenge, not so much to grow but to find plants with which to associate them. *Geranium*

VIBURNUM PLICATUM 'MARIESII' has flowers on branches resembling the icing on a wedding cake (top left)

THE FOGGY BOTTOM cat surveys the scree bed on an early summer morning (top right)

AVOIDING A SPRING FROST on the west side of tall conifers, Rhododendron *'Amethyst' and* Abies nordmanniana *'Golden Spreader' form a strong focal point in the spring garden* (above)

THE PINK TINGES ON
the flowers of
Rhododendron
'Loders White' is
quite typical of this
old variety, so far
enjoying a frost-free
spring (left)

sylvaticum 'Mayflower', a deep blue flowered woodland geranium, is a good choice since its flowering is timed to make a striking contrast to bright orange or yellow. In Foggy Bottom the rhododendrons and azaleas follow on nicely as the winter-flowering heathers finally run out of flower in mid-spring – though the erigena varieties carry on into late spring – and before other flowering shrubs and perennials start coming out in numbers.

ALPINES

Late spring and early summer is the peak flowering time for alpines. The term "alpine" is really a misnomer, as is the American term "rock plants", for almost the same subject. True alpine plants come from high alpine regions and true rock plants, one assumes, from rocky alpine sites. In Britain the term alpine covers dwarf perennials such as armerias, many campanulas, plants like erysimums or perennial wallflowers, ajugas and dwarf astilbes besides many others. The term also covers some dwarf shrubs like helianthemums (the rock roses) and shrubby thymes.

For many years at Foggy Bottom there was no situation or feature that could accommodate alpine plants in the garden, the soil in the top part of the garden being too wet and heavy and the lower part subject to flooding. Such a feature would also have been somewhat incongruous among larger conifers, shrubs and perennials.

Eventually, in 1989, we created an alpine or scree bed in front of the house, which had previously contained conifers and heathers. Additional drainage was put in and gravel mixed with the soil. I then planted a few dwarf shrubs and conifers for a mature effect, interplanted them with alpines, and covered it all

with sharp grit. This scree garden has been a joy, yet also frustrating and much work. We put in too little grit initially and the clay soil and grit made a pretty stiff mix, though every new alpine now goes in with handfuls of grit and a good gravel mulch. Many will know from experience what I mean when I say that some plants – and weeds – have tried to take over, and it is a constant battle to keep everything in balance. When you purchase plants from a specialist nursery or garden centre you need to be absolutely sure it has no perennial or annual weed in it; some of the oxalis are particularly rampant. Undoubtedly, as Rosemary and I know to our cost, this area requires the most intensive attention of any part of the garden.

But, despite the hard work, this garden in miniature has great rewards, with the bulbs, alpines, shrubs and conifers

SYMPHYTUM GRANDIFLORUM 'Hidcote Blue', although, like some other comfreys, it can be invasive, makes ideal ground cover beneath a cherry tree (above)

THE SCREE GARDEN – seen in early summer with dwarf shrubs, alpines and bulbs in flower, and the sun flooding its light over the distant trees (above left)

AN OLD SPECIMEN OF Abies koreana 'Aurea', the golden-leaved Korean fir, makes a magnificent display of cones held above the branches (below left)

providing some startling displays in spring and summer particularly. Once again, the challenge should be to make such a garden furnish more year-round interest, but this involves careful selection of the plants to make it work – while making sure you are the one in control!

At the peak of the alpine season we know for sure that we are into the busy season and the "mid-summer surge" is upon us. The warmer nights and longer days create a burst of activity and growth – in ornamental plants, lawns as well as weeds. There is so much happening in the garden now: all the trees and shrubs still have fresh growth, giving pure colour contrasts, the conifers are breaking their winter buds into bright new foliage, and perennials such as hostas are making the greatest impact with their fresh leaves, a wonderful foil

for other flowers. And how can anyone say that conifers are dull, as new shoots and needles are produced, giving a contrast between new and old, and candles of new growth appear on the pines? Everything is changing so rapidly, you can almost hear the plants growing, but while you do not want to miss anything that happens, you are also very busy catching up on late planting, keeping up with the weeds and cutting the grass, a task now necessary twice a week.

MAKING THE BEST CHOICE

Nowadays, with the advent of smaller specialist nurseries and national collections, the choice of plants is impossible to keep up with. Twenty years or so ago, a garden collection of thirty hardy geraniums would have been impressive. Now that these plants are in high fashion, new varieties and hybrids are being introduced at an alarming rate. In 1989 *The Plant Finder*, that indispensable gardeners' guide to what is in cultivation, listed 189 species and cultivars of geranium. Five years later there were 350. As a nurseryman, you can only hope to keep up by being a specialist.

For the gardener, what is important of course is to consider garden worthiness, colour, leaf, habit, rate of growth and length of flowering. The latter is particularly important and there are varieties like *G. riversleanum* 'Russell Prichard' and 'Mavis Simpson' which flower from early summer until the frosts, as does the popular spreading and climbing hybrid between *G. procurrens* and *G. psilostemon* called 'Ann Folkard'. This has golden-tinged leaves and purple-magenta flowers, which is quite a combination, but for summer-long colour it also takes some beating.

There are geraniums for sun and shade, for moist soils as well as dry. The ground-covering *G. macrorrhizum* and its cultivars and hybrids are indispensable plants for sun or quite deep shade and although some people dislike its pungent fragrance, to me that is the essence of summer itself, its aroma quite pervasive as you walk by on a summer's evening. Geraniums come in some good blues as well as the more obvious pinks and reds, none more popular than 'Johnson's Blue', of which thousands are sold each year. It is perhaps a truer blue than that of *G. himalayense* but no better plant. Could it just be the name? – though few gardeners will relate it back to the original Mr. A.T. Johnson after whom it was named around 1950.

I have extended the range of perennials used in Foggy Bottom in recent years partly because I have always had a liking for plants I grew up with, but also because perennials are so truly adaptable to the modern garden and to mixed planting. The structure established at Foggy Bottom with trees, conifers and shrubs and my experimentation with heathers, has somewhat run its course, and though I will always find room for some, the garden needed the colour, the foliage and the changing interest that perennials can give. The more you get involved with plants and gardening, the more you want to experiment and to change. I believe that, all things being equal and if space is available, most gardeners would probably prefer to have a selection of woody plants, bulbs and perennials rather than be restricted to a single group. The challenge to me is to continue to change and adapt, to create pleasing plant associations, knowing that what is planted today will need readjusting to some extent within a year or two.

I am lucky enough, too, to travel and find new plants from all over the world,

GERANIUM HIMALAYENSE is a reliable blue-flowered hardy geranium for sun or shade (above)

A DECIDUOUS KNAPHILL azalea times its bloom perfectly to contrast with Geranium sylvaticum *'Mayflower'* (left)

DODECATHEON PULCHELLUM 'Red Wings' lives up to its name "shooting star", an eye-catcher in a moist spot in semi-shade (left)

EQUALLY EYE-CATCHING AND also a shade lover is the aptly named Omphalodes cappadocica *'Starry Eyes'* (below left)

as well as keeping an eye open for what is new in the U.K. New plants have to be tested and what better place (so my argument goes) than at Foggy Bottom? But it can sometimes be difficult to reconcile being a collector with attempting to create dramatic effects. To make large drifts of colour, be it heathers, ornamental grasses or perennials, means using fewer varieties, therefore there is less space for "testing". I know this will be a recurring problem, but it is not one I am too anxious about, except that the number of plants I collect which stand waiting in pots or containers "in the wings", waiting to be planted, never seems to diminish.

I believe I have inherited my father's suspicion and certainly initial dislike of roses. In the days of hybrid teas and floribundas, roses of course did not seem to fit in too well with conifers and heathers. In recent years, however, there has been a resurgence of interest in species and hybrid shrub roses as well as ground-cover types. Rose breeders have done a marvellous job in creating whole new ranges of plants that are repeat-blooming and relatively trouble-free. Roses are now generally accepted, as they should be, as flowering shrubs which can fit into mixed plantings, rather than necessarily being a feature on their own. And I have certainly come round to the idea that ground-cover roses like 'Surrey' and 'Kent', to name but two varieties, do in fact fit in very well with conifer and heather plantings.

But roses and perennials make pretty good bedfellows too. Most roses look dreadful in winter and spring, but underplanting them with various perennials, such as the pulmonarias, gives early spring flowers and summer foliage at the base of the rose, turning a loss into a gain with "companion planting".

MID-SUMMER

The period from late spring to mid-summer is undoubtedly that of the greatest change in the garden, and for most gardeners the most active and exciting time. This is the period of peak activity for garden centres and nurseries which, over the years, have encouraged gardeners to continue planting well into summer by growing and offering nearly all plants as container-grown. But though it is perfectly safe to plant right through the summer – and many shrubs or perennials will give an immediate flowering performance – great care should be taken to ensure their establishment in hot or dry conditions. Soak the plants well before planting, prepare the ground thoroughly and then water in and mulch with well-rotted compost, composted bark, or other inert or weed-free material after planting.

I continue to plant at Foggy Bottom throughout the summer, but in a six-acre garden it is difficult always to remember exactly which plants need specific spot watering, so I generally concentrate on only one or two areas so that these get more attention than longer-established plants. Sometimes these summer plantings, particularly if I have only a single specimen, are only temporarily domiciled and will, as they grow, provide more young plants which can be replanted the following spring.

THIS IS ALMOST THE MOST EXCITING point of the year in the garden at Foggy Bottom – the June surge of plant growth brings fresh, clean colours and vitality. A background of shrubs, including the white Viburnum plicatum *'Cascade', shows off the varying textures of hostas, ferns and grasses. The flowering perennial is* Geranium sylvaticum *'Mayflower'.*

FLOWERING SHRUBS

During the late spring and early summer there have been some marvellous displays of flowering shrubs in the garden. Apart from those mentioned individually below, the acid-loving pieris and rhododendrons, magnolias, berberis, camellias, cherries and crab apples as well as lesser-known plants like exochorda and kalmia, add superb early splendour. By mid-summer, the range becomes more limited, but nonetheless there are a great many excellent flowering or foliage shrubs which should be better known and more widely used. Over the years I have been an avid collector of shrubs both large and small, at times being unable to resist trying out some that were probably quite unsuitable for our soil and the frost pocket of our garden.

If you look at almost any garden planted thirty or more years ago, whether in town or country, you will often see very mature shrubs and, depending upon location, in a fairly limited range. Shrubs were looked upon as the mainstay of the garden and as spring turned to summer the progression of flowering would generally be forsythia, *Ribes sanguineum,* the flowering currants, viburnums perhaps and lilac, then in early to mid-summer, weigela, deutzia and philadelphus. On acid soils, rhododendrons would fill in the gaps. But many of these more traditional summer-flowering shrubs have such a short period of flower that any modern gardener, particularly with a smaller plot, would be right in questioning whether they deserve garden space.

There are of course smaller-growing selections and shrubs with coloured or variegated foliage which have a longer appeal. But there is also a range of other good flowering or foliage shrubs now available at most garden centres, which were simply not available thirty years ago. The public has in a way demanded innovation by flocking to buy the more dwarf shrubs with a long period of interest into which category I would put berberis, *Potentilla fruticosa*, hebes, perovskias and spiraeas, as well as the grey- and silver-leaved shrubs such as santolina, lavender and senecio. Among these groups – as with shrubs such as the escallonias and fuchsias, not forgetting roses – there are some to give a continual succession of flower, but it is at this time of year that foliage is increasingly important, and it becomes more so as the summer draws on. Selecting shrubs for several seasons of interest is good sense, particularly if you garden in a small space.

Garden worthiness is a subject one can come back to time and again, and I believe each plant has to earn its place in the garden, for there are so many good plants to choose from. When you get to mid-summer, it is time to start evaluating your garden's performance. If we could choose our weather in summer, most would go for warm, perhaps hot days and cool nights, with occasional evening rains, which would help to keep our plants looking happy – but of course it seldom works out that way. In Britain and in northern Europe we can expect no real extremes, but sometimes we will have a wet summer, sometimes a dry one and this will vary considerably from east to west and north to south. In North America and in southern Europe, hot summers are the rule, as are droughts, and this will dictate what plants can be grown successfully. The fact that the term "shade tree" hardly exists in Britain says much about our climate.

When choosing plants which will become permanent for many years in

LAVANDULA 'BLUE CUSHION' is aptly named for its rounded dwarf habit and flowers as close to blue as any Lavender. Like all lavenders, it is both fragrant and a friend to bees (above)

DEUTZIA × HYBRIDA 'PINK POMPON' seemed aptly descriptive of this showy summer-flowering shrub, but after many years under this name it now seems it must be called Dentzia × hybrida *'Rosea Plena'* (right)

your garden – the trees, shrubs and the larger-growing conifers – look for potential garden worthiness in terms of your climate and your soil. It is easy to be tempted by pictures in books or even plants at a garden centre by something which is not suitable and will therefore never thrive.

LARGER SHRUBS AND TREES

Trees, shrubs and conifers provide the structure in any garden and are essential on the flat piece of ground now called Foggy Bottom. But, like many people, I

IT IS OFTEN SAID that conifers look the same all year round but in fact some of them can change as dramatically as any flowering shrub when new growth begins in early summer. In the right foreground is a 30-year-old specimen of Thuja orientalis *'Aurea Nana', and in the centre the beautiful blue of* Picea pungens *'Globosa', which both show up against the purple-leaved* Acer palmatum *'Garnet' and* Acer shirasawanum *'Aureum' (above)*

did not always make the best choice when selecting the initial range of trees, nor did I always plant them in the most suitable position. But trees chosen for flower, foliage, fruit or autumn colour can have considerable impact at their particular moment – the Japanese cherries in spring, silver-leaved willows, purple or variegated foliaged maples, golden poplars in summer, sorbus, cotoneaster and thorn trees (*Crataegus* species) in autumn, along with colour from the maples, sweetgums, silver birch and many others.

THIS FIVE-YEAR-OLD Acer negundo *'Flamingo' sits quite happily in a container, given food, water and some annual pruning.* Campanula *'Stella' contrasts with the colourful leaves* (top)

A MIXED PLANTING of mostly low-growing shrubs and conifers accentuates the taller blue spruce, Picea pungens *'Globosa' in the background* (above)

Trees do need space, but there are trees which can be pruned as shrubs or grown in containers. *Acer negundo* and its coloured foliage forms is one of those and, whether grown in a container on the patio or as a plant in the open garden, it makes a superb small tree with summer-long colour provided it is pruned back in the early spring, then the new soft growth pinched out during the summer. The best selection is the aptly named *Acer negundo* 'Flamingo' with pink, green and cream shoots, but *A. n.* 'Elegans' is another quite bright cultivar with golden variegated leaves. The Japanese maples make excellent container subjects too.

Conifers provide the real backbone to the structure in Foggy Bottom which becomes truly noticeable only in winter, when all the leaves have fallen from deciduous shrubs and trees. But during the summer the intensity of the East Anglian light creates dazzling reflections from the bright silver-blue of the blue spruce *Picea pungens*, and the golden foliage of many of the lawsons, the *Chamaecyparis lawsoniana* varieties. Among these I have placed either deciduous trees or other conifers of contrasting colours, the pines being a real favourite of mine. When we have to move or remove some of the larger conifers it is amazing how dry the soil is beneath them, and following dry summers some larger lawsons visibly suffer. Originating in the northwest of North America, where rainfall is at least twice the British average, this is perhaps not surprising.

In assessing a maturing garden, deciding what to remove is as important a decision as choosing what to plant. And removing a large conifer or tree is no easy task and may, for the average gardener, call for expert help from either

Clematis *'Dr Ruppel'*

Tropaeolum speciosum

THE VERSATILE CLIMBERS

Climbing and scrambling plants have become increasingly popular in recent years as gardeners come to realize that they have a wider use than covering walls and pergolas. One can add to the background tapestry of conifers, trees and taller shrubs, each with its own moment of glory, by planting climbers or scramblers such as honeysuckles, roses, clematis or vines. Sometimes planting too close to the base of a conifer or tree will prevent climbers from getting established, so always plant as much as 1m/3ft or more away and train it in the right direction. Though it may take time to establish, Tropaeolum speciosum, *with its bright scarlet flowers, makes a spectacular summer show scrambling among and over spent rhododendrons and conifers.*

For clothing boundary walls, not only can such freestanding shrubs as pyracantha, chaenomeles and Carpenteria californica *be used, but also a wide range of natural climbers, like vines, ivy and* Euonymus fortunei. *There are some herbaceous climbers which die back to the ground in winter, for example the climbing dicentras and tropaeolums as well as one or two geraniums. Here are some suggestions worth considering:*

Clematis The clematis family cover such a wide range of colour as well as flowering periods that they are indispensable. Whether scrambling over heathers, up conifers or up trees, they can add colour and contrast at times of the year when it is most needed, from the early-flowering species – *C. alpina, C. macropetala* and *C. montana* – then the larger-flowered hybrids which can also be used as ground cover over low-growing shrubs or heathers, to, later in the season, *C. viticella, C. orientalis* and *C. tangutica.* I have a quite spectacular show from *C. orientalis* 'Bill Mackenzie' which I planted beneath a purple-leaved silver birch, *Betula pendula* 'Purple Splendour'.

Campsis The trumpet vines, which need a warm climate to perform.

Dicentra scandens and **D. macrocapnos** With glaucous green leaves and yellow lockets in summer, these perennials can make nearly 3m (10ft) of growth in a single year.

Euonymus fortunei The variegated forms more usually grown as shrubs make good climbers on walls, through other shrubs or up tree trunks.

Fremontodendron Though not a true climber and not very hardy, this is an excellent wall shrub which, with sun and good drainage, has a long flowering season.

Geranium procurrens and **G. 'Ann Folkard'** Ideal for use in front of spring-flowering shrubs, these geraniums will climb into them, flowering later in the summer.

Hedera Ivy is as useful on walls as it is as ground cover; there is a wide choice of small-leaved *H. helix helix* varieties and the large-leaved *H. colchica* is also attractive, doing well in shade.

Hydrangea petiolaris The climbing hydrangea is useful for walls, trees or as a freestanding shrub.

Jasminum Several species and cultivars ideal for walls and fences provide evergreen-looking foliage and mostly fragrant flowers.

Lonicera The climbing, usually fragrant, honeysuckles are indispensable.

Parthenocissus These ornamental vines with good autumn colour are excellent for clothing walls.

Roses A wide range of climbers and ramblers with an equally wide usage; training and pruning are important.

Vitis Some ornamental selections of note include *V. vinifera* 'Purpurea', with purple leaves, and *V. coignetiae*, with large leaves and good autumn colour.

Tropaeolum There are several species, some tender, but *T. speciosum* is reliable and looks striking grown through conifers and over contrasting foliage.

Wisteria Several selections can be grown, either as a climber or a small tree.

Geranium *'Ann Folkard'*

landscapers or tree surgeons. If a tree, shrub or conifer has given twenty or thirty good years and simply outgrown its welcome, it is perhaps time to say goodbye. And the space it creates will leave you with all sorts of exciting possibilities. This will increasingly become necessary at Foggy Bottom but fortunately, "head gardener" Michel Boutet, who does most of this clearing work, loves such challenges, leaving me the opportunity to create another plant association, or to try out new plants.

PERENNIALS

From mid-summer onwards, perennials and ornamental grasses come into their own and provide the colour, movement and variety which most woody shrubs cannot offer at this time of year. The growing popularity of hardy perennials and ornamental grasses in Britain, Europe and North America appears to be unstoppable. From being the Cinderellas of the garden plant world,

A SLIGHTLY MISTY mid-summer morning is lightened by the sun's rays slanting onto Acer shirasawanum *'Aureum', and the "kitchen beds", seen here from the roof of the house* (right)

THE STILL FRESH green leaves of Alchemilla mollis, *lady's mantle, are enhanced by the droplets from a recent summer shower and make a good companion for* Euphorbia griffithii *'Fireglow'* (below)

despite the efforts of my father Alan Bloom back in the 1960s, they have, from a slow start, become exceedingly fashionable. It was thought when the perennial craze started to hit the United States in the early 1980s that within ten years, like many other fads, perennials would be back where they started. Not a bit of it: in fact, I would say that the interest there has only just begun. Why then is there such an abiding interest in this group of plants? The answer lies in their versatility. But to that quality should be added those of adaptability and diversity, with flower and foliage in an amazing range.

Because of their low-lying habit and because they were originally found in the wild, the majority of perennials were in the past often viewed by gardeners as weeds – and indeed some still are! Even within my memory, they were still considered so by a great number of gardeners fed on a diet of "trouble free" woody trees and shrubs and by others on the more highly cultivated annuals. But such times are past and perennials are now at their peak of popularity. And in reality aren't perennials the ultimate group of plants that every gardener has been looking for? Perennials can be found in every size and scale, from ground-hugging ajugas to eupatoriums and helianthus 2m/6ft or more high; they can be found with narrow leaves and broad leaves, with yellow, green, red or variegated foliage; and there are plants for moist shade as well as for dry sun. With this selection and the amazing variety of colour, shape and form of perennials from all over the world, it is hardly surprising that there is always a perennial to fit every garden, however inhospitable it may seem.

Because my father's nearby Dell Garden had over 5000 species and varieties of perennial flourishing in it before I even started our garden at Foggy Bottom, I felt I should try woody plants first. But as the trees, conifers and shrubs began to grow, the conditions in the garden changed to such an extent that, fifteen years on, there was shade and tree roots where there had been sun, and south-, west- and east-facing beds where once they had all been south-facing. The garden was in a state of constant change and trial. First, great blocks of heathers began to deteriorate in the shade and the ground-cover plantings of junipers had their stems ringed by field mice in winter. So it was time for a change, and it has continued thus ever since, giving the opportunity to introduce new plants, new schemes and new ideas. So perennials and grasses have now become the underplanting and the interplanting between the conifers, trees and shrubs, creating the scope for pattern, movement and more rapid seasonal change, as well as greater variety.

DAYLILIES AND OTHER PLANTS

Perennials and grasses combine to produce textures and colours which create visual diversity. What brighter surprise could be created than by using the vibrant scarlet *Crocosmia* 'Lucifer', whose bright nodding flowers are even attractive when holding green, then brown, seeds in their beak-like heads? When in full flower, 'Lucifer' shows up vividly against the steely blue foliage of *Juniperus chinensis* 'Blue Alps' and other contrasting perennials at its base.

Softer in tone for a more moist spot is a "purple loosestrife", except that this plant is not purple. I came across *Lythrum salicaria* 'Blush' in Canada, where the nurseryman who gave it to me explained that it was now forbidden in his country to grow these mostly Asian

and European imports because they seeded too freely, escaping the captivity of gardens to roam freely in the wild. His loss was our gain, and I have a high regard for these long-flowering perennials which, until this variety was discovered, had been mostly in colours of rose-red to purple. 'Blush' is the softest, most delicate pink you could wish for.

But if lythrums as introduced plants in North America are environmentally suspect, perhaps the hemerocallis, or "daylilies" should also be considered so,

ORNAMENTAL GRASSES ARE becoming ever more popular as are variegated leaved plants. The two features are combined in Miscanthus sinensis *'Variegatus' whose softer tones and vertical habit provide a contrasting background for the short spiked orange flowers of* Crocosmia *'Spitfire' (above)*

at least in certain conditions, though in some quarters it would be heresy to suggest it. The species – small-flowered and often fragrant – are all native to Asia, mostly Japan and China, but these lowly subjects have largely become "Americanized" in recent years and, through breeding, transformed beyond recognition. Their flowers have become larger and more varied in colour, shape and form. The breeding programme has developed multitudes of varieties, not all of which turn out to be good garden plants. But they are adaptable to both heat and drought, from Minnesota to Louisiana, and while many look out of place among other perennials, some do earn their place in any garden. Of the 150 or so American-raised varieties we imported at Bressingham some years ago, some did not adapt to the cooler British summers, but others, such as 'Stella d'Oro', the first dwarf yellow long-flowering selection, has added immeasurably to their value.

The intensity of breeding work will undoubtedly continue because of the demand, and more long-flowering types are continually being produced following the commercial success of 'Stella d' Oro', whose sales must now run into several millions of plants. Though the popularity of the daylilies is assured in the United States, where I am told that at least several hundred varieties are introduced each year, the term "daylily" bemuses many British gardeners who are not quite sure how many days the flowers will last! The answer is of course that although each flower lasts but one day, flowering on most varieties will continue for four to six weeks, while 'Stella d' Oro' and other repeat-bloomers will flower from early summer into the autumn with a few rests in between. That represents very good value in the

LYTHRUM SALICARIA 'BLUSH', an import from Canada, is far removed in colour from the original purple loosestrife but it has struck a chord with many gardeners (left)

HEMEROCALLIS 'WHICHFORD' is a classic daylily, with rich green, grassy foliage and fragrant yellow flowers (below left)

PLANTS WITH SUMMER FRAGRANCE

Fragrance is a real bonus in the winter and there are some shrubs which stand out for their sweet fragrance – such as the mahonias, viburnums, hamamelis, sarcococcas, skimmias and many daphnes. In the summer, fragrance adds immeasurably to the enjoyment of gardening and being close to plants when sitting out in the garden. When considering plants for the summer garden, therefore, scent should be considered along with other attributes. Fragrance can be a subjective matter, however: while most of us would agree on the enjoyment of scented roses or lilacs, other plants, such as the scented leaf geranium, Geranium macrorrhizum, *are far too pungent for some.*

Shrubs and climbers
Aesculus parviflora
Buddleja davidii
Carpenteria californica
Choisya ternata
Clethra alnifolia
Cytisus battendieri
Daphne (many)
Erila arborea
Fothergilla
Jasminum (some)
Lonicera (some)
Philadelphus (many)
Rhododendron, (many)

Perennials, alpines and bulbs
Clematis heracleifolia
Cosmos atrosanguinea
Dianthus (many)
Dictamnus albus
Hemerocallis (some)
Hosta (some)
Iris (some)
Lavandula (most)
Origanum (many)
Paeonia (many)
Phlox paniculata

Syringa vulgaris *'Sensation' in early summer*

Clematis heracleifolia *var.* davidiana *'Wyevale'*

Iris germanica *'Patterdale'*

PENSTEMON DIGITALIS 'HUSKER'S RED' is an easy plant, as attractive for its purple foliage as for its summer flowers (above)

garden, though the plants will need splitting every couple of years to keep them young and performing well.

AMERICAN INTRODUCTIONS

Plants from North America are of course part of the British gardening heritage. While American collectors may have been introducing hostas and hemerocallis and many other plants from Japan, we British were combing parts of North America for new and interesting species to introduce to Britain – and not only trees, shrubs and conifers, but also standard American wildflowers like *Phlox paniculata* as well as many asters and solidagos (the goldenrods). We too have hybridized species and varieties and introduced new selections for British gardeners. It used to be said by some American gardeners that a plant had to come to Britain or Europe to become "civilized" before being sent back to the United States, when it would immediately become accepted! Now there is much more awareness of the value of the North American flora and the richness that still exists there, as well as the potential for commercial opportunities. Nonetheless it is nice to record that two of my father's selections of *Phlox paniculata*, 'Eva Cullum' and 'Franz Schubert', have recently been well received by American gardeners.

One recent brash introduction which we were delighted to trial and to introduce into Britain was a hardy verbena called 'Homestead Purple'. The story of its discovery is an interesting one. Two good friends of mine, both professors of horticulture at the University of Athens, Georgia, Michael Dirr and Allan Armitage, were driving along a back road in the state of Georgia, when they suddenly spotted a patch of bright purple in an old homestead garden. On closer investigation it proved to be a verbena, which in time turned out to be hardy enough to withstand temperatures of -10°C/14°F, perhaps even lower. They called it 'Homestead Purple' and it made its debut appearance at the 1994 Royal Horticultural Society's prestigious Chelsea Flower Show, where it was acclaimed by British gardeners. Its bright purple flowers will hit you between the eyes from early summer until the frosts. For sheer summer colour this perennial has a well-deserved place in the garden at Foggy Bottom. We have also used it in a hanging basket and a window box where it looks most attractive.

SUCH VIBRANT COLOUR MAY BE too much for some, but Verbena *'Homestead Purple' flowers all summer and makes a strong focal point in garden or window box. It has come through three winters with temperatures as low as -10°C/14°F in the author's garden* (above)

Plants Enjoyed by Bees

*In collecting nectar to make honey, the bees
are doing all gardeners an enormous favour.
Not only do they provide enjoyment for us as
they go about their business, but some of the
best garden plants have arisen from the
accidental hybridizing created by bees as
they carry pollen from one plant to another.
This can certainly lead to new seedlings
being distinctly different from either parent
plant – though it is sometimes difficult to be
sure which both parents were. Some plants
will be almost certain to come true from
seed, while others vary tremendously. Plants
such as the spring-flowering pulmonaria
and many of the foxgloves and aquilegias are
notorious for their promiscuity. But if you
plant the beautiful white foxglove* Digitalis
purpurea *'Alba' near the species or seedlings
of the pink- or red-flowered foxglove, you
will almost certainly find within a few years
that the resulting crosses of these
indispensable biennials are almost all red or
pink. To prevent this degeneration, at
Foggy Bottom we pull up most of the pink-
flowered seedlings as soon as the first
flowers open.*

*All the plants shown opposite are herbaceous
perennials, but there are many other plants
enjoyed by bees and butterflies too.*
Main picture: Delphinium belladonna
'Peace' (syn. 'Volkerfrieden')
Top left: *Both butterflies and bees are
attracted to* Allium senescens *'Glaucum'*
Top centre: Digitalis purpurea albiflora
Top right: Heuchera *'Rosemary Bloom'*
Centre left: Erigeron *'Vanity'*
Centre centre: Eryngium *'Jos Eijking'*
Centre right: Eryngium alpinum
'Superbum'
Bottom left: Centaurea macrocephala
Bottom centre: Gaillardia *'Goblin'*
Bottom right: Helenium *'Waltraud'*

THE FREE-FLOWERING penstemons provide a summer-long show with a wide range of colours. Penstemon 'Blackbird' (foreground) is backed by 'Mother of Pearl' and 'Hidcote Pink' (above)

VARIED ORIGINS

Plants for summer colour will seldom be found among British natives, so for summer-colour plants we generally need to turn to more exotic locations. That said, the callunas or lings and other heathers, where they will grow, can create sheets of colour when seen from a distance. And members of the mallow family, particularly *Lavatera olbia* and *L. thuringiaca*, which are European natives, have become exceedingly popular since new colours and strains have been introduced. The lavateras come in pink, white and burgundy colours and most of them bloom from mid-summer onwards, depending on their location, and produce countless flowers for

LAVATERA 'PINK FRILLS' is a dwarf shrubby mallow whose flower petals are prettily frilled (above left)

CAMPANULA PERSICIFOLIA 'Chettle Charm' flowers on tall spikes, its subtle colouring silhouetted against a purple beech in the background (above right)

months on end. Some, like *Lavatera* 'Barnsley', can grow very tall, and with its soft, semi-woody stems can blow over or break unless it is in a sheltered spot, but the unceasing show of white, pink-centred flowers is worthy of garden space if it can be found. Even though they may not survive severe climates, the lavateras are valuable enough to be considered or used as annuals.

The same might also be said of the

diascias, a group of perennials introduced from South Africa many years
ago, but which have recently become
extremely popular. Though many
species are annual, several others are
perennial, these mostly originating from
the Drakensberg Mountains and generally hardy to -10°C/14°F, sometimes
lower. As always when a group of plants
becomes popular, new varieties will be
almost certain to follow, and some of
the new diascias are very good in terms
of summer-long flowering on soils that
are not too dry. Small- and large-flowered, with heights from 10cm/4in to
40cm/1ft 3in, and in colours from light
pink to rose-pink and lilac, all will give a
flowering performance over many
weeks, if not months.

One of my current favourites is
'Blackthorn Apricot' which makes a carpet of colour among which I have
spread seed of the biennial *Eryngium
giganteum*, the notorious 'Miss Willmott's Ghost'. This group has been
planted in what we call our Mediterranean bed, a sunny, south-facing area
backed by tall conifers. I am gradually
planting in it a selection of perennials
and shrubs which will happily grow and
survive the rather dry but heavy soil.
The conifers have provided shelter for a
Melianthus major, another South African
plant of great merit for its foliage. I
would not have even tried it a few years
ago, before I had sufficient shelter, for it
is unlikely to take more than -10°C/14°F
in winter, and even then would need

MISS WILLMOTT'S GHOST, Eryngium
giganteum, *always seems to have a ghost-like
quality. It is planted here between an olearia
and in the foreground the soft-toned* Diascia
'Blackthorn Apricot' (left)

*GERANIUM CINEREUM 'Laurence Flatman'
nestles on a low Norfolk flint wall, determinedly
making a summer-long show even if it is
squeezed by the yew behind* (above)

A GOLDEN LAWSON'S CYPRESS, Chamaecyparis
lawsoniana *'Stewartii',* provides the
background to the contrasting lilac, Syringa
vulgaris *'Sensation',* Euphorbia characias *ssp.*
wulfenii *and* Veronica armena *in early
summer* (far left)

*THE SUN FILTERS through the glowing carmine
flowers of* Rosa moyesii *'Geranium' on a mid-
summer morning* (left)

some protection. But even if the foliage dies back each year, or you have to keep it in a container as a patio plant, its blue-grey, deeply cut overlapping leaves provide a dramatic foliage effect in summer. It grows to 3m/10ft or more in its native Southern Cape Province, but only to 1.2-1.5m/3-4ft in a season in Britain.

This Mediterranean bed also contains olearias, *Euphorbia characias* ssp. *wulfenii, Eucalyptus niphophila, Spartium junceum,* rosemary and ceanothus – plants which come from Mediterranean climates in Europe, California, New Zealand and Australia – with a Chilean native, an azara, thrown in. I'm no purist when it comes to using plants, although those that fit best together visually often do prefer similar conditions, even though they may come from different continents. This example underlines just how international our gardening palette has become, and how much we owe to both old and new plant hunters for their endeavours over the years.

BALANCED COMBINATIONS

Foggy Bottom is quite an open garden and has developed along natural, meandering lines – or at least that has been the intention – against structural backbones around which beds and borders have been created. As you walk round, you will see some interesting cameos or plant associations which might fit into a smaller garden, but you will also hopefully look up to enjoy the broader view and the vistas, since there is always something in the distance to draw the eye. Colour combinations can start from the ground and work upwards, but they might also work in reverse, starting from the top with a cone-laden blue spruce, for example, or a purple-leaved silver birch. As the eye runs along, the colours and contrasts will appear too bright for

some, particularly on a sunny day – the blues with golds and purples. Thank goodness for green, you might say!

As tastes change and adapt, so will our gardens but, above all else, the theme running through should be to create year-round colour for our climate. In the British climate, the sun can be a relatively rare commodity, especially in winter. There are some beds in Foggy Bottom which are considerably brighter in winter than summer, and I have been making a concentrated effort to provide more summer colour in recent years, which means bright foliage and long-flowering plants if one is to be achieved without sacrificing the other. I have made good use of such plants as *Cornus alba* 'Sibirica Variegata' or *Cornus alba* 'Aurea', the dogwoods which have summer-long foliage contrast and winter stems, as well as the long-flowering shrubby potentillas, ground-cover roses and *Polygonum affine* 'Dimity' (now called *Persicaria*), which makes leafy ground cover from which arise a succession of bottlebrush spikes, white, pink and deepening to red as summer progresses to autumn.

So when does mid-summer end and late summer begin? Though some topics and plants have been included in the period from mid-summer to late summer, a great many more have been left out altogether. What, no iris, paeonias and poppies, you may well ask? The answer is that while some of the plants I recommend can be found in the Directory (see page 218), this trundle through the summer seasons is inevitably selective, as one must be in an individual garden, and this allows me to be more discursive. But do not think, as we come to the late summer period, that all is over in the garden, for some of the best is yet to come.

LATE SUMMER

More than one gardening journalist I have read has made the point that August should be written off as a gardening month. I suppose that if you take a full month's holiday at this time and go away to a summer retreat, that is perhaps an understandable point of view. In climates where summers become unbearable in August, this would be understandable too. But for those that wish for it, the garden in August can be as colourful and interesting as any time of the year. Apart from the range of plants that exist among the perennials and ornamental grasses to give late summer colour and interest, also to be considered are the elements of water and the use of containers. These will adorn the terrace, patio or other favourite spots, when you can sit in the shade sipping iced tea or lemon and enjoy the rewards of your earlier labours.

THE VALUE OF WATER

Water can of course be a crucial element in any garden in more ways than one. It is vital to the survival of your plants although most, if well planted and mulched, will survive without additional watering provided they are given conditions approximating to their requirements – which is not as much gobbledegook as it sounds. You will choose sun lovers for a sunny position – but take advice or read to see how much moisture is required; you will select shade lovers for shade, but is it dry shade or moist shade those plants want? Plantings in their first year will require more attention than those which are more established, and new plants, particularly the more valuable trees or shrubs, may require a large hole prepared and filled with quantities of thoroughly mixed in, well-composted humus in the form of farmyard manure,

BLACK CLOUDS highlight the background to this view of Foggy Bottom on a late summer's afternoon, the dipping sun casting light and long shadows from west to east. Buddleja davidii *'Pink Delight' is in the left foreground, rising above a patchwork of heathers and conifers*

SUMMER SPECTACULAR

The perennials and alpines in these photographs (alpines mostly being dwarf perennials) show the brilliance and diversity that can be obtained from early to late summer.

Top row, from left to right: Dendranthema weyrichii, *a dwarf early-flowering chrysanthemum.*

Geranium subcaulescens 'Splendens', *an undeniably striking dwarf hardy geranium. Early summer.*

Lupinus *'Russell Hybrids', universally popular perennials. Mid-summer.*

Phlox paniculata *'Flamingo', a "border phlox" with fragrance and colour for late summer.*

Second row, from left to right: Geranium × oxonianum *'Bressingham's Delight' an easily grown free-flowering hardy geranium. Mid-summer.*

Hemerocallis *'Holiday Mood': summer colours on this brightly coloured daylily. Mid-summer.*

Campanula cochleariifolia, *an alpine miniature campanula ideal for rock or scree gardens. Mid-summer.*

Achillea *'Anthea', the second flowering on this compact grey-leaved yarrow. Late summer.*

Bottom row, from left to right: Helenium *'Coppelia', a first-rate sneezeweed for late summer colour.*

Phlox divaricata *'Blue Dreams', a late spring and early summer flowering garden-worthy phlox. Early summer.*

Mimulus *'Puck': striking bicolor effect for many weeks with this "monkey musk". Early summer.*

Rudbeckia fulgida *var.* deamii: *few perennials are more valuable for late summer than this black-eyed susan.*

*TWO EARLY MORNING VIEWS highlighting the
pond at Foggy Bottom in late summer.
Early morning sun lightens the* Rudbeckia
fulgida *var.* sullivantii *'Goldsturm', happy at
the water's edge (left). A slight mystery surrounds
the shadows close to the pond as the first rays of
light filter onto plants in the distance (below).*

leafmould, or even straw which will hold moisture. When Rosemary and I visited that great garden, La Vasterival in Normandy, created and run by the indefatigable Princess Sturdza, she explained to us that she never watered new shrubs again once they were planted, having given such thorough preparation as I have described, followed by watering them in well, and giving them a thick top mulch of leafmould or pine needles to retain the moisture.

A water feature, such as a pool or a fountain, brings another dimension to the garden and can provide interest particularly in the late summer period. The pond at Foggy Bottom – for one can hardly consider it a lake – was created towards the lower part of the garden, which seemed to make eminent sense but, although it might fill up in winter, without a butyl liner it would empty in summer. After two years with a dry pond we managed in 1978 to get a patchwork butyl liner made to cover the island and fit the rather uneven natural shape. Remarkably, within a few years the pond became the natural feature which an informal garden of six acres needed. What I failed to do at the time, however, was to allow sufficient liner to overlap the adjacent moisture beds which I was to plant three or four years later. When the time came to plant, it was obvious that there was little to hold the moisture in these beds adjoining the pond – the soil is so well drained in summer that many plants have been disappointing and in due course we will need to tackle the problem properly by adding an extension to the liner.

I learned another lesson when planting down near the pond. I was anxious to have in the garden a rather unusual spring-flowering moisture-loving perennial, *Peltiphyllum peltatum*, with its large summer leaves; thinking that my father would let me have some from his group

in the Dell Garden, I dug up a fair-sized chunk in mid-winter (with his permission, I hasten to add). Only later did I realize that it contained some all too healthy roots of a dreaded weed, the perennial horsetail. Despite all our efforts, we have so far failed to stop its establishment, so that is another problem to be tackled before it gets totally out of hand. There must be a moral there somewhere.

Despite these problems, the water feature has given year-round appeal as well as a place for fish to breed, herons to feed and wild duck to shelter and nest. Summer, winter and other seasons are reflected in the water, and on occasion we have taken a canoe out on it, and also skated round the island on thin ice in winter. In the late summer of 1987 the bottom third of the garden was flooded which, despite its serious after-effects in terms of loss of plants, had some benefit in that it enabled us to canoe around the garden. And some say that nothing happens in the garden in August!

This flooding in particular highlighted the adaptability of one of the best of the hardy perennials, *Rudbeckia* 'Goldsturm' or, to give its true title, *Rudbeckia fulgida* var. *sullivantii* 'Goldsturm'! This black-eyed susan is a North American native which brightens up the late summer garden with its deep yellow flowers highlighted by a black central cone, over the abundant deep green foliage. When the rains came, the group of rudbeckia was in full flower in a reasonably well-drained sunny spot, but soon only the flowers were showing above the flood level. Throughout the ten days the plants were under water, the flowers continued to bloom, and for another month afterwards as the water receded. To me, brought up in the knowledge that this was a sun lover, if not for dry soil then for ordinary, well-drained conditions, its performance was remarkable. It was only after I looked it up in reliable botanical reference books that I learned that it was native to low-lying, moist meadows.

Though 'Goldsturm' is a popular perennial in North America, it is surprising how little used this glorious plant is in Britain. There is also a quite different, but lesser known rudbeckia which deserves a place in more gardens. *Rudbeckia laciniata* 'Goldquelle', like 'Goldsturm', was raised in Germany, and its finely cut, light green leaves produce 60cm/2ft high stems with fully double heads of clear yellow, with overlapping petals. I have these two rudbeckias close to each other beside some contrasting ornamental grasses. Blue with yellow always seems to work well and *Festuca glauca* 'Blueglow' ('Blauglut'), another German selection, has the brightest blue leaves or needles; 'Elijah Blue' is another example. I have found these fescues invaluable in creating low-growing groups for the front of a border to enhance other, contrasting plants; they look their best if they are divided every few years.

ORNAMENTAL GRASSES

Ornamental grasses have certainly added a whole new dimension to gardening as far as I'm concerned. I have not only developed a passion for collecting them to try out at Foggy Bottom, but I have also experimented by using them in different situations in the garden where they seem to give greater impact to many other types of planting. Ornamental grasses fit in perfectly well with hardy perennials and generally have a much longer period of interest than most individual types of perennial.

Take *Stipa gigantea*, for instance: I have copied a combination found in the Dell Garden using this majestic yet airy grass with *Phlox paniculata* 'Franz Schubert', a pleasing soft lilac phlox which grows to 120cm/4ft. The stipa in spring makes a large, grassy hummock with narrow, dark green leaves, whose early flowers emerge on panicles like delicate heads of oats, but much more widely spaced. The plumes turn from green to beige in early to mid-summer, then to golden brown later in the summer, at the time *Phlox paniculata* 'Franz Schubert' reaches the peak of its flowering performance. The plumes of the stipa have by now reached 180-240cm/6-8ft and the burnished golden heads make a stunning contrast to the phlox – as though both had come to the harvest festival together. I have no qualms about copying combinations or ideas from other gardens or gardeners and am only too pleased to give credit as to where an idea came from. Some of the best ideas, so we are told, happen by chance and of course this may well be true at times.

Ornamental grasses are undoubtedly now nearing a peak of popularity and as more gardeners realize how they can use them, and how wide the range is, the more widely they will be grown and appreciated. Twenty-five years ago we listed nearly forty varieties of grasses in our Bressingham Gardens catalogue but, although there was some interest, we gradually had to reduce the list through

ORNAMENTAL GRASSES ARE at their most dramatic when light plays on their flowers and foliage. Early morning sun touches the plumes of Molinia altissima *'Transparent' before lighting up the plants around it* (left)

lack of sales. However, following the lead by German nurserymen and gardeners and some innovative work in the U.S.A. in using and publicizing this group of plants, British gardeners are now developing a new interest. This is largely due to the ever-increasing range of newly discovered, bred or selected species and varieties available.

Many of these grasses come from Japan originally and one, with a name once heard, never forgotten (though remembering it is the difficult part) – *Hakonechloa macra* 'Alboaurea' – has been in demand ever since its introduction to Britain thirty or more years ago. Growing to only 30cm/1ft at most, this slow-growing, clump-forming grass has narrow golden-yellow leaves, striped irregularly with green, which arch gracefully over each other, giving the appearance of a golden sea. We grew it in the garden for a number of years, where it needs a friable soil which does not dry out, but it wasn't until I had seen it growing in a large container in a garden centre in Japan, that I realized its true vocation was probably as a patio or container plant. Back in England I potted plants up for our patio and for the last several years this plant has been one of the star exhibits of our Chelsea Flower Show stand.

Some grasses are at their best in early summer, such as *Calamogrostis × acutiflora* 'Overdam', with striking pink-flushed, variegated leaves and *Deschampsia flexuosa* 'Tatra Gold', whose tussocks of foliage shine with gold early in the season, followed by wispy flowers. Others with variegated foliage, like some of the miscanthus, make a pleasing foil to other plants. In this respect few can match the adaptability of *Miscanthus sinensis* 'Variegatus' which seems happy in half shade or full sun and can make as good a combination with a hosta or a fern as it can with a sun-loving kniphofia or crocosmia. Of narrower leaf but every bit as effective is the graceful 'Morning Light'. However, for me the outstanding "finds" in recent years are some of the miscanthus hybrids, bred and selected by Ernst Pagels. Until Herr Pagels' numerous introductions, many of which are listed in the Directory of Plants (see page 218), very few cultivars of *Miscanthus sinensis* flowered in the cooler summers of northern climates. We are only recently aware of what we have been missing, and although other excellent foliage forms have recently come from Japan and North America, we certainly owe a debt to this German nurseryman.

These strains, of which there are now almost too many to choose from, offer interest from early summer to the following spring, though they are most spectacular from late summer until late autumn. With heights ranging from 1m/3ft to 2.4m/7ft, with grassy foliage of green and silver and plumes of varying sizes and forms, and with colours ranging from crimson to silver and changing from one to the other, they are plants which have come to add an exciting new form to the garden. And, as will be seen in the chapter on the smaller garden (see page 200), they are suitable not only for the large plot.

MISCANTHUS SINENSIS 'Morning Light' lives up to its name as the morning sun strikes its narrow variegated leaves, gracefully arching out from an upright centre. It looks equally effective through winter as its leaves and stems turn light brown (right)

LATE-FLOWERING PERENNIALS

Just as the ornamental grasses have in themselves brought a new dimension to summer colour (and autumn and winter too), so they have highlighted so many other good plants with which they can be associated. Some of those I have used include plants with South African origins – the kniphofias, agapanthus and crocosmias, plants with mostly bold colours and interesting flowerheads. Late- or long-flowering broad-leaved perennials such as *Polygonum* (now *Persicaria*) *amplexicaule* 'Taurus' can be equally striking.

The common name for kniphofias – red hot pokers – is certainly a misnomer these days, for recent breeding and selection has widened the range from the original South African species to include sizes from 30cm/1ft to over 2m/6ft and colours which range from white through yellow, orange and pink as well, of course, as all shades of red. Some have tight buds which open from green, brown or bronze, then change as the flowers open to yellow, then white, so that it can be an oversimplification to describe a cultivar by one colour only. Take *Kniphofia* 'Innocence', for instance; it starts tight in bud with true poker-like heads in green and bronze, the flowers as they open turning to orange, then yellow and lastly fading to white from the base. The bees can't wait to dive into the opening flower buds to draw out the nectar – another attraction of kniphofias as garden plants.

A FINE CONTRAST IN colour and form is provided by two plants in close proximity. Scabiosa caucasica 'Blue Seal' and Kniphofia 'Bressingham Comet' provide colour from late summer into early autumn (left)

THE VOLCANO BED

I believe one should try and have some fun with garden plants and I recently had the opportunity to experiment with an idea I had had for creating an association of kniphofias with grasses. In the late spring I dug up some failing heathers which had been badly damaged by spring frosts as well as by recent dry summers. This left a slightly sloping area between conifers and heathers, into which I planted a meandering line of glowing orange-red flowered *Kniphofia* 'Bressingham Comet' to represent a stream of lava, while the wavy ornamental grasses *Stipa tenuissima* on either side were the land through which it flowed. This, which we named the volcano bed, has been surprisingly effective with other plants being added later to continue the year-round appeal.

This species of stipa is a marvellous plant, with bright green, narrow leaves in spring producing delicate sprays in summer which, en masse, reflect the light and movement of every breeze. In autumn the faded plumes are bleached white, but dew and frost settling on them continue their attraction into winter. Though it seeds itself happily around, this is never a nuisance and indeed often a bonus.

Provided you select carefully, you can achieve enough colour to see you through the late summer months without difficulty, though in areas with extremely hot summers the flowering periods are often reduced. But I believe that wherever you live there is a plant or several plants that can be found to fit a purpose.

Late summer in the early years at Foggy Bottom meant almost exclusively summer-flowering and foliage heathers, which were planted in large groups among the winter-flowering types and contrasting conifers, to provide ever more colour as well as height, scale and structure. But nothing is for ever, and although many of these original plantings are still effective others, which have given of their best for twenty years or so, have gradually been replaced by perennials and shrubs.

In late summer the bergamots (the monardas) are good value, their mop-like heads in brilliant colours attractive to bees. And in recent years penstemons have also come back into fashion, helped along by milder winters, since most of the hartwegii types will not take severe winter temperatures. These plants produce stems in mid-summer from which hang developing buds, opening to both brash reds, crimson and purple flowers often with white or speckled throats, as well as delicate pastel shades. They will flower for most of the summer, and if they are cut back after the main flush, they will repeat-bloom until the autumn.

Good blues are not always easy to come by at this time of year, but plants like *Aster × frikartii* and its dwarfer cousin, *Aster × thompsonii* 'Nana' flower for several weeks at the end of the summer and will continue into the autumn. These trouble-free asters are essential ingredients for creating colour and contrast, so I make no apology for having two or three groups in the garden. The *Aster × frikartii* selections have proved themselves over many years to be one of the best groups of perennials, let alone of asters – and I will always have a particularly soft spot for them because they were introduced not long before I worked at the Frikart nursery in Stafa in Switzerland, by the shores of Lake Zurich, during the spring and summer of 1961.

SEDUM 'AUTUMN JOY' can always be relied on to produce a beautiful show. In the foreground is Ajuga reptans *'Braunherz' (above)*

PHLOX PANICULATA 'MOTHER OF PEARL' shows delicate toning in both sun and shade (above)

THIS GROUPING HAS a warm glow on a late summer's afternoon: the Joe Pye weed, Eupatorium, *on the left surrounded at the base by* Rudbeckia fulgida *var.* sullivantii *'Goldsturm'. Ripening seedheads of* Stipa gigantea *tower behind, partially obscuring* Phlox paniculata *'Franz Schubert'* (above top)

ASTER X FRIKARTII, with a similar hybrid Aster x frikartii *'Monch', are among the finest perennials ever raised. Hardy, free- and long-flowering, they are very useful for late colour* (above)

LATE FLOWERING SHRUBS

In late summer there are still shrubs to provide colour, though they are fairly limited in number – until you start to list them! Many hebes are at their best now and shrubby potentillas start to rebloom more strongly as cooler nights arrive. The blues of ceratostigma, perovskia and caryopteris are welcome alongside those of abelia, lavatera and lesser-known plants such as lespedeza, while many roses will continue to flower for weeks yet.

Buddlejas are a group of popular shrubs enjoying something of a revival. This revival was started, as is often the way, by the introduction of a new variety. In this case it was *Buddleja davidii* 'Pink Delight' which arose from a breeding programme in Boskoop, Holland; it has proved a winner, being compact in habit, and the closest to pink yet seen. Hypericums used to be relied upon to give us flowers throughout the summer, followed by mostly crimson, red or black fruits. Unfortunately some have become susceptible to rust which can ruin, and sometimes kill, the plant. A dwarf and admittedly free-seeding North American species, *H. prolificum*, which is very hardy and seems immune to this disease, deserves to be more widely used. It grows to .1m/3ft or so and has small, bright green leaves and masses of tufted golden-yellow flowers all summer long.

Hydrangeas should also be mentioned, both for the garden and for containers. Unfortunately, in Foggy Bottom spring frost seems to damage the flowering shoots of the mophead and lacecap forms of *Hydrangea macrophylla*, so I have increasingly been using those that flower on the new season's growth. *Hydrangea arborescens* and *H. paniculata*

BUDDLEJA DAVIDII 'PINK DELIGHT' is flowering away in the background, standing above the heathers or lings in the foreground. One can almost hear the bees going about their work on this late summer's day (above)

are the species to look for: though limited in flower colour, if pruned back each spring they will produce heads of white flowers in late summer. *H. arborescens* 'Annabelle' is a favourite, with large, green rounded heads opening to brilliant white, while *H. paniculata* 'Kyushu' and 'Pink Diamond', whose white florets turn pink with age, are some of the worthiest selections.

We are still skimming the surface in selecting plants to provide late summer colour which will drift into early autumn. In Foggy Bottom we may start to get autumn colour even before autumn begins, once the cooler nights arrive, bringing mist and sometimes fog with the still evenings. At this time the conifer background is at its most colourful, the heathers at their best and, being low-lying, the cooler air gathers to bring some wonderful misty mornings, with the dew hanging onto leaf surfaces and the plumes of the grasses.

The flowers of asters, rudbeckias, sedums, kniphofias, some crocosmias and agapanthus, solidagos, ceratostigmas, perovskias and many, many more are there to brighten late summer and take us into autumn. The coloured foliage of many shrubs – cotinus, berberis, cornus and corylus – can create striking backgrounds, quite apart from the conifers. Flashes of light come through the waving grasses as the sun takes a lower arc in the sky. There are fruits on the sorbus (the mountain ashes), cotoneasters and pyracanthas, while crimson autumn colour is already appearing on the leaves of *Euonymus planipes*, its yellow seedheads held enticingly open for the birds to collect from the crimson capsules that surround them. Colour is all around – summer garden glory may be over, but autumn and winter garden glory are about to begin.

AS A FINE FOLIAGED and free-fruiting shrub, Sorbus koehneana *has considerable merit, with bunches of glossy white fruits in late summer* (above)

HYDRANGEA ARBORESCENS 'Annabelle' makes quite a spectacular show for much of the summer with its large ball-shaped flowerheads (left)

SUMMER COLOUR

Summer Colour in the Smaller Garden

At Foggy Bottom I am continually attempting to change and develop the garden and to fill any seasonal gaps with plants of interest, whether for the effect of their flowers or their foliage. In a six-acre garden there is of course room to grow a much wider range of plants than in the small garden and I can create cameos or scenes in one area without even disturbing the rest of the garden.

In the smaller plot it is essential to be selective in the use of plant material to create year-round interest and a careful choice needs to be made according to the length of display. Although there may be fewer varieties of plants that give winter colour, many of those plants will give a longer period of interest than plants selected for summer colour. Shrubs like the dogwoods – *Cornus alba* and *Cornus sanguinea* – will offer leaf colour in autumn then, when the leaves have dropped, will provide coloured stems until spring when new growth begins.

Structure and scale

For late spring and summer we need another selection of plants, a different balance; it is important to remember that part of the structure of the garden, including many of the plants which have given winter colour, will remain, though by now they mostly provide a supporting role. Certain evergreen foliage plants, such as hollies, elaeagnus, euonymus and conifers, continue to be invaluable. And the ornamental grasses like carex and perennials such as bergenias and ophiopogons are equally attractive in summer as they are in winter.

This dwarf birch, Betula 'Trosts Dwarf', has many of the attributes of a dwarf Japanese maple: slow growing with finely cut foliage and able to take full sun. Viola 'Boughton Blue' grows beneath it in mid-summer (left)

Scale is another important consideration in the small garden. In Britain many gardeners seem frightened of planting trees – and in a garden 5m x 5m (20ft x 20ft) or less, one can understand that reluctance. In North America, where gardens are usually larger and most summers considerably hotter, "shade trees" are often a necessity. But there are trees which can give structure to the small garden: trees with a fastigiate habit will not give much shade, but won't take over either, while other trees can be pruned to keep them within bounds. These days it is popular to plant pendulous "top worked" trees where, for example, a weeping willow or cotoneaster is grafted onto a stem to cascade down. But although there are more dwarf trees which will provide periods of flower or fruit – crataegus, prunus and sorbus, to name but three – it is true to say that most of the flower power in a small garden will be provided by shrubs and perennials (here I include plants like crocosmias which are strictly bulbs).

Though they look nothing in winter, shrubby potentillas, especially *P. fruticosa*, are generally good value, most being relatively dwarf and flowering from late spring until autumn, depending on the climate. Many of the more common shrubs, such as philadelphus and deutzia, have a limited period of flower, but there are selections with mottled or variegated foliage to extend their interest. Spiraeas too are one of the most trouble-free shrubs and many of the *S. japonica* cultivars, like 'Gold Mound' and 'Golden Princess', not only have a display of pink flowers, but offer summer-long colour with their golden or yellow leaves. Foliage is all-important for providing colour in the smaller garden, both in its own right and as effective contrast to other plants.

BENEATH THE ACER BED a moist, shady area offers a home for Dicentra *'Pearl Drops',* Corydalis flexuosa *'Purple Leaf' and* Trillium ovatum, *whose white flowers have faded to a pretty pink (above)*

In selecting plants for the small garden a useful exercise is to go through books and catalogues and initially to list far more plants than you will probably need; then, against each name, note when the flowering period is and how long it lasts, plus any other features it may have at other times of the year. Make sure that your selection covers the seasons adequately and in this way you will start to whittle down your selection to those plants that will give you most value throughout the year. Always include a few of your favourite plants, albeit it those which last but a moment. Gardening should not all be done on a scientific basis: impulse and flair must be allowed for if it is to be enjoyed.

THE STAR PLAYERS

Against the more static trees, shrubs and conifers, we have already seen that perennials, alpines and ornamental grasses provide not only the ebb and flow of the garden but also the summer highlights. There are vast numbers of species and varieties to fit almost any site or situation – though extremes of shade, drought and moisture will narrow down the choice significantly. As with structural planting, look for plants which give a long period of interest, preferably with a mixture of foliage and flower – there are good examples of multi-purpose plants in the two small suburban front gardens featured later in this section, while others are described in the Directory of Plants (see page 218).

SOME SMALL-GARDEN PLANTS WITH A LONG PERIOD OF INTEREST

DWARF SHRUBS

Shrubby potentillas are deciduous, but give months of flower; dwarf hebes such as 'Red Edge' *have flowers and attractive foliage;* Choisya ternata 'Sundance' *has bright yellow leaves and fragrant flowers.* Ceratostigma willmottiana *flowers for weeks late in the summer.* Berberis thunbergii 'Dart's Red Lady' *has deep purple leaves and crimson autumn colour, 90-120cm/3-4ft in height;* 'Bagatelle', *reddish-purple, is more dwarf. Useful variegated evergreens include euonymus, pieris, cotoneaster, ivy; for certain areas, the larger growing aucubas, elaeagnus and ilex can be used and pruned accordingly. Deciduous shrubs which have flowers and coloured leaves include spiraeas such as* S. japonica 'Gold Mound' *and* 'Golden Princess', S. thunbergii 'Mt. Fuji' *and* 'Pink Ice', Weigela florida 'Praecox Variegata', Caryopteris 'Worcester Gold' *and* Fuchsia genii. *Some of the dwarfer ground cover roses are excellent value for long flowering periods in summer.*

Weigela florida 'Praecox Variegata'

HEATHS AND HEATHERS

Remember that summer-flowering heathers need an acid soil. The lings, callunas and bell heathers (Erica cinerea) *all have dwarf varieties which have flowers in summer and golden foliage in winter.* Calluna vulgaris 'Sir John Charrington' *is outstanding and* Erica cinerea 'Rock Pool' *or* 'Windlebrooke' *can be recommended.* Erica carnea 'Aurea', 'Westwood Yellow' *and* 'Foxhollow' *have golden foliage in summer, pink flowers in winter. All are best in sun.*

Calluna vulgaris 'Allegro'

PERENNIALS

Most spring-flowering perennials may have a long period of flower, but most summer-flowering perennials, depending on climate, are over relatively quickly. The pulmonarias are an exception and flower for weeks in spring, then many have attractive leaves later in summer, lasting well into autumn. My recommendations include Pulmonaria angustifolia 'Highdown' *(also known as* 'Lewis Palmer') *with strong blue flowers and large spotted leaves;* P. officinalis

'Sissinghurst White', *smaller, with silver-spotted leaves;* P. rubra 'David Ward' *has variegated, white-margined leaves and red flowers;* P. saccharata 'Leopard', *red flowers, dark green silver-dotted foliage;* P. longifolia 'Roy Davidson' *has smaller, narrower, spotted leaves and light blue flowers;* P. saccharata argentea, *with almost fully silver-grey leaves.*

Perennials with evergreen foliage include the Japanese "black mondo grass", Ophiopogon planiscapus 'Nigrescens', *with narrow black leaves, sparse lilac-white flowers and black berries in autumn; planted against blue, silver or yellow, it can make a stunning year-round combination. Some bergenias with broad, cabbage-like leaves are a bright green in summer but turn purple or ruby in winter providing a show of flowers in late winter.* Bergenia purpurascens, B. 'Bressingham Ruby', 'Eric Smith' *and* 'Wintermarchen' *are all recommended. In recent years new heucheras have been introduced with coloured leaves – purple, bronze or silver – which give summer-long foliage attraction, adding to the briefer season*

Diascia rigescens × integerrima lilacina

SUMMER COLOUR IN THE SMALLER GARDEN 203

of flower: 'Palace Purple', 'Bressingham Bronze' and 'Pewter Moon' fit into this category. Hostas give ample choice for shade; some excellent smaller-leaved varieties give foliage effect in the small garden.

Perennials with longer periods of flower are much in demand. New varieties of diascia will flower for most of the summer, including D. 'Blackthorn Apricot', D. 'Salmon Supreme' and D. rigescens × integerrima lilacina'. Several hardy geraniums can be relied upon to flower for months; best for a small garden are: G. 'Ann Folkard' which is vigorous but can climb less attractive shrubs in late summer, G. × riversleanum 'Russell Prichard' and 'Mavis Simpson', and G. oxonianum 'Bressingham's Delight', 'Little Gem' and 'Sea Spray'. Dwarf scabious have a succession of flowers in sunny spots; recommended are S. 'Pink Mist' and 'Butterfly Blue', lesser-known but equally attractive S. graminifolia and S.g. 'Pincushion'. Certain coreopsis, dicentras and rudbeckias have long flowering periods. Other perennials, such as euphorbias, sedums, ajugas, artemisias, thymes and dianthus, have a worthwhile mixture of flower and foliage.

ORNAMENTAL GRASSES

Ornamental grasses should have a place in most gardens, however small, provided they are sunny. In summer the grasses and sedges act as a foil to other plants, their brown, bronze, green, silver and blue leaves contrasting well with flowering and foliage plants. Grasses such as pennisetum, deschampsia, stipa and miscanthus have dwarf or compact selections with plumes or panicles which develop and ripen through the summer, going on to create wands which dew and frost can enhance in autumn and winter. One of the most valuable grass-like plants for year-round colour is Acorus gramineus 'Ogon', whose low, mounded habit of golden leaves is actually brighter in winter than summer.

CONIFERS

Conifers of course give year-round colour and a selection for the smaller garden must be made on the basis of habit, colour, scale and suitability to climate. Rate of growth is another important factor, so always study books or seek advice from garden centres. There are many fascinating and colourful dwarf conifers to choose from, and they can be fitted in with other plants, as I have shown at Foggy Bottom and in the small front gardens featured on pages 208-11.

Geranium sanguineum *var.* striatum *'Splendens'*

Pennisetum orientale

THROUGH THE SEASONS IN THE ACER BED

MID-APRIL. The shade provided by the acer creates the right environment for some woodland plants from North America and China. In the foreground is Corydalis flexuosa *'Purple Leaf', the purple-flowered* Trillium sessile *and white* Trillium ovatum. *Behind and under the stems of the tree are the white lockets of* Dicentra *'Pearl Drops' and the yellow heads of daffodils*

LATE APRIL. Acer shirasawanum *'Aureum' is sheltered from the morning sun, which protects it from spring frosts as it comes into leaf. The snowdrops at the base of the tree are in full growth. Daffodils, pulmonarias and violas show flower as well as dicentras, bergenias and* Phlox × divaricata

Over the years, as our garden at Foggy Bottom developed, I have tried to remain aware of the need to create smaller areas and plant associations which could be readily 'transported' to smaller gardens. In fact, going back to 1975 when I created my first year-round garden, mostly using conifers and heathers, I have attempted to show by example that almost all gardens, however small, can benefit from displays of plants carefully used and designed. One of the best examples of this at Foggy Bottom is the area we have called the acer bed, an oval-shaped bed about 3 x 4m (10 x 13ft), first planted in 1967. It began with two main plants, *Acer shirasawanum 'Aureum'*, a wonderful Japanese maple, and *Picea pungens* 'Globosa', the dwarf blue spruce which we surrounded by heathers.

For nearly twenty years this bed was a picture from the house, providing glorious colour all year round, the maple with its golden leaves in summer contrasting brightly with the blue-grey needles of the spruce. But inevitably, as the plants grew, it became obvious that unless both were to spoil, one tree would have to be moved. It was decided it should be the picea, by now less of a dwarf than the books had indicated! On a frosty mid-winter morning in 1985 the operation began to remove the picea, with a good rootball, to another site. It was hoisted on a large fork lift and successfully established elsewhere. I then replanted the bed, using a much wider range of plants that would adapt to shade and sun to create a new effect. In this small area choices had to be made to give year-round interest without using evergreen shrubs and conifers. Some of the plants and planting associations are shown on these pages as the seasons develop through the year of 1994.

MID-MAY. Seen from another angle, the acer is now in full fresh golden leaf, sparkling in the midday sun. A mound of greenery and flowers cover the ground and there is a strong contrast from the Acer palmatum *'Garnet' behind. Golden-leaved hostas contrast vividly with* Phlox divaricata *'Blue Dreams'*

MID-JUNE. The foliage plants in the centre foreground now take a lesser role than in March, the Bergenia *'Bressingham Ruby' now with leaves turned green. A seedling white foxglove lights up the left foreground and* Geranium × oxonianum *'Bressingham's Delight' the right*

EARLY AUGUST. The flowers have diminished with just the geranium showing touches of colour, but now the foliage of ferns, bergenias, ophiopogons, pulmonarias and hostas becomes more important

DECEMBER. The framework of branches of Acer shirasawanum *'Aureum' are momentarily clothed with hoar frost, giving it an ethereal appearance. The evergreen bergenias, ophiopogons and acorus hardly show but the old flower sprays of* Stipa tenuissima *are also lit up with frost*

Summer Colour in Containers

Patio plants have never been more popular, but the selection used is often quite limited. There are far more plants which will grow in containers than most people imagine: many trees, shrubs, perennials and ornamental grasses all make excellent patio subjects and there is sufficient choice to suit both sun and shade. I remember the reaction we had when people saw a *Wisteria sinensis* in full flower in a container in our garden. Grafted wisterias, trained and pruned, will within a few years make impressive container specimens.

Containers are essentially versatile – they can be moved to front or back, to produce new arrangements and different effects, to create their own plant associations. Depending on the size of plant or container, they can be transported from sun to shade, and be taken to a less prominent spot once their main season is over in order for others to be put in the limelight. We use a sack barrow to transport larger pots, which takes some of the physical strain out of this task. Over the years the more established container-grown specimens will tend to get bigger and may need either repotting or root pruning.

One of the most important considerations when growing plants in containers is to adapt the compost to the subject. If you garden on alkaline soil, here is your chance to grow plants which like acid soils – camellias and pieris, for instance – by potting into an ericaceous mix. Clay or terracotta containers will dry out much more quickly than plastic, but on the other hand it is more difficult to overwater plants in them, which is a risk when first planting in a plastic pot, before the plant grows large enough to take up all the moisture in the compost. Feeding and pruning are equally important; knowing how easy it is to forget to keep up a regular liquid feed, I would always recommend incorporating a slow-release fertilizer which should last the plant a whole season.

Besides the traditional summer-colour subjects for containers– such as pelargoniums, fuchsias and annuals – trees, shrubs, conifers, climbers, perennials and grasses, as well as bulbs, ferns, alpines and even bamboos, can all offer something different and yet will be long-lasting container subjects. Planted as single specimens or as part of a group planted to create an association in a pot, there is no limit to the versatility and effects one can achieve. Pendulous or prostrate-growing plants are particularly attractive when they cascade over the side of the container.

Individual plants such as hostas can give summer-long interest and when grown in containers they are less subject to slug damage. The new American cultivars – 'Francee', 'Wide Brim' and

WISTERIAS ARE MOSTLY *seen growing against walls or over pergolas but they can also be trained as a small tree or shrub. This fifteen-year-old specimen of* Wisteria sinensis *at Foggy Bottom regularly performs each year in late spring* (left)

CAPTIVES IN CONTAINERS

Wouldn't you be frightened of growing in your garden plants that behave like invasive weeds? There are several plants with attractive foliage which I would hesitate to let loose in the garden but the answer is to grow them in pots, tubs or other containers, keeping them captive by restricting their root run. Simply plant them in container compost, keep them fed and watered like any other plant and they will remain decorative all summer long. Since most of them are vigorous, I would suggest splitting and replanting them at least every other year. Some suggestions are:

Aegopodium podogaria 'Variegata' – a less aggressive form of ground elder which has brightly variegated leaves and will grow in quite deep shade.

Houttuynia cordata 'Chameleon' – a late-shooting plant which is stunning in a herb pot or container; its multi-coloured foliage has a pungent smell. Though a relatively new plant to western gardeners, this was in cultivation in Japan before 1850.

Trifolium repens 'Purpurascens' – a purple-leaved clover which spreads rapidly in a garden situation but makes an attractive mat of purple leaves in a container.

Disporum sessile 'Variegatum' – a choice plant for shade or semi-shade where it will run happily; it is equally satisfied in confinement in a pot to brighten up a dull corner.

Arundinaria viridistriata – a golden-leaved dwarf bamboo which is quite content in captivity.

Phalaria arundinacea var. picta 'Feesey' – this is a brightly variegated selection of gardener's garters, normally extremely invasive, especially in moist soil.

Kalimeris yomena 'Shogun' – another brightly variegated plant which spreads, though not particularly invasively. Related to the aster, it has stiff upright stems and small leaves edged creamy-white, followed by insignificant lilac flowers.

Aegopodium podogaria *'Variegata'*

Disporum sessile *'Variegatum'*

Houttuynia cordata *'Chameleon'*

'Shade Fanfare' – are recommended, but top of my list, both for the garden and for containers, is a selection of a Japanese native, *Hosta fluctuans* 'Variegated', whose leaves present a sculptural quality. Unfortunately it is still rare and highly priced as well as prized – but probably the technique of micropropagation will alter that in time. On this page are but a few examples of plants used in containers at Foggy Bottom to provide summer colour or form.

MIXED PLANTING FOR YEAR-ROUND COLOUR
THE PUTTS' GARDEN FROM LATE SPRING TO LATE SUMMER

By almost any standard, 6m x 6m (20ft x 20ft) is a small front garden. Yet how many people make the most of their front gardens, which, although they are generally not places to sit or relax in, are walked past by the home owner at least a thousand times a year!

Of course the situation of a garden, its type of soil and aspect, whether it is in a city or a more open location, will all have an effect on what can be grown. Personal preference also plays a significant role – some may prefer a landscaped garden, with very few types of plants – but in both the Putts' and the Johnsons' gardens (see page 210), I was able to concentrate on a wide selection of plants. I used about 80 different varieties in each garden, in fact. In my opinion, plants can provide interest and excitement all year round, and with careful initial selection and a degree of control, can last for years without a great amount of work.

Although the Putts' garden was planned particularly for autumn and winter interest, it has colour in spring and summer too, though it is less spectacular than the next-door Johnsons' garden during these seasons of the year. Foliage plays an important part too, and bulbs, alpines, perennials and shrubs all contribute something during their flowering period. There is a feeling of informality in the design of this garden, which looks almost like a scaled-down part of Foggy Bottom! And where in my

THIS SCREE BED HAS been planted with dwarf conifers for year-round colour (some of which will need thinning out in due course) and interplanted with dwarf perennials or alpines. Spots of colour can be provided by dwarf bulbs in spring and early summer but in mid-summer when this photograph was taken, Geranium cinereum *'Laurence Flatman', dianthus and thymes provide flower, the bronze* Ajuga reptans *'Braunherz' strongly contrasting with* Juniperus × media *'Gold Sovereign'. Including the bed behind, this front garden measures only 6m x 6m (20ft x 20ft) and contains 80 different species and cultivars* (below)

own garden I would have used groups of between five and twenty of certain plants, here it is primarily singles or threes, and the effect is similar, though on a considerably smaller scale. We have had to make good use of the secateurs to prune the few faster-growing shrubs, but that is good and necessary husbandry in such a small garden and allows a wide variety of interest to be added by smaller plants such as bulbs and some perennials which still have room to put on a flowering display in between the woodier plants.

After five years the Putts' garden has matured, without looking overgrown, though before too long one or two conifers will need to be removed from the scree bed to somewhere in the larger back garden.

This garden is certainly as maintenance-free as was the original lawn: Maggie Putt estimates that she spends barely half an hour a week on it, even during the spring and summer, though no doubt more time could be spent if desired. And there is always something happening or about to happen from January to December, which can be enjoyed either by looking out of the window or by walking past each day — each season being fully appreciated as plants grow, flower and fade and as foliage changes its hues and colour through the spring, summer, autumn and winter.

THE ORIGINAL Campanula carpatica *has seeded itself to make this pleasing combination on the scree bed in mid-summer, contrasting with the conifers and purple-leaved* Berberis thunbergii *'Bagatelle' (below)*

WINTER STEMMED DOGWOODS are pushed out of the limelight by Lavandula *'Hidcote' and* Coreopsis verticillata *'Golden Gain', soon to flower, both lasting several weeks.* Microbiota decussata *in the foreground will turn purple-bronze in winter (below)*

A Garden Without a Lawn
The Johnsons' Drought-resistant Garden

Planted in spring 1991, Judy and Roy Johnson's garden was designed to be quite different from the average suburban front garden. A front garden without a lawn was to be planted somewhat Mediterranean-style with a shingle and pebble covering. Like the Putts' garden next door, it was all planted in one day, but as there are considerably more hours of daylight in May than there are in November, this gave us longer to apply the finer touches.

The front lawn disappeared, carefully cut away to reveal free-draining, sandy soil. Although the flat area was too small to create much in the way of undulations, we dug an impression curving from the centre of a dried-up "river bed" throughout which, after planting, I placed some larger stones or pebbles to create interest and a natural feel.

The plants were once again the main ingredient. Few shrubs were chosen, except one or two towards the back to soften the lines of the brick wall of the house, and a small shrubby specimen of *Acer negundo* 'Flamingo' in the front to give summer-long colour. Though termed a "drought-resistant" garden, not all the plants I selected would in fact take happily to prolonged drought with intense heat. Droughts in Britain tend to be somewhat gentler affairs than where hot summers are the norm, but with water restrictions from local councils coming in quite early, this is still a concern to many gardeners.

Ornamental grasses, perennials and alpines were the main ingredients in the Johnsons' garden and here the choice was fairly critical in order to select plants to give a long period of summer interest. Bulbs were also used to give spring colour. Apart from their diversity, the perennials and grasses quickly mature to give colour in the first year and to look totally at home by the second. Some of course can be quite vigorous and those types need to be watched, particularly if rapid top growth starts to smother other smaller or slower-growing plants surrounding them. Even such a small garden can give the opportunity to create some attractive plant combinations and associations. Although 80 varieties of plants might seem like an extravagance which would lead to a rather congested mess, this does not have to be the case – as hopefully some of the plant groups on these pages show.

The shingle or gravel mulch works very well at helping to retain moisture and ideally it should be kept in a layer as thick as 5cm (2in) to control weeds. The larger the grade of shingle the fewer weeds will prosper, but too large a grade may look heavy in a small garden. Seedlings from weeds and plants alike will enjoy the benefits of protection offered by the shingle while germination takes place. It is best to look for annual weeds regularly and ensure that they are not allowed to seed, and to check that plants which seed freely, like the *Carex comans, Campanula carpatica* and origanum, are not allowed to grow in all the wrong places. But despite the potential drawbacks, this garden has been a success and is greatly enjoyed by the Johnsons, who can certainly claim to have their own summer garden glory right outside their front door!

ANOTHER EXAMPLE of a successful partnership is the white-flowered Dicentra *'Snowflakes' intermingling with* Geranium × cantabrigiense *'Cambridge'* (far left)

THE IMPRESSION IS of a much larger garden with this vista across from the neighbouring garden. Acer negundo *'Flamingo' is this side of the boundary.* Diascia elegans *contrasts with the grey foliage of* Artemisia nutans, *while* Campanula carpatica *'Forester's Blue' is sandwiched between* Geranium *'Ann Folkard' in the distance and* Geranium × riversleaianum *'Russell Prichard' in the centre* (left)

PLANTING ASSOCIATIONS FOR SUMMER COLOUR

Planting to create interesting, even exciting plant combinations is, to my mind, the most rewarding of all gardening challenges – and success in this area can often be elusive. There are many factors to bear in mind before you start, in relation to your site – whether you have a clear "green field" site or whether you are planting against a fence, wall or hedge, or underneath existing trees and shrubs. You need to decide whether it is desirable or necessary to build a plant association into an existing framework, or whether it is better to try and start from scratch.

Starting from scratch, as I have assumed for many of the following association ideas, is, at least in theory, much easier. The soil can be prepared to suit the plants chosen and there is no competition from existing structures or plantings. Planting around existing specimens can not only create immediate microclimates of sun or shade, but the developed root systems demand water and space, so that new plantings may need considerable assistance in establishing their own root systems.

You must then think about the effects you would like to achieve, and decide on the best plants to create that effect, given the aspect and soil conditions of your site. Are you looking for spring, summer, autumn or winter appeal or hoping to achieve a combination of interest in all seasons?

Taking advice from a garden designer or following suggested plans in books will give you a guide and a starting point, but in a way it is more fun working out ideas for yourself after doing some basic reading and research. Just as with cookery recipes, the information you glean can give you ideas which will enable you to change some of the ingredients to create your own association or design.

The illustrations and outline plans on the following pages come mostly from associations and plants which I have used at Foggy Bottom. Some 'artist's licence' has been used in conveying compatible flowering periods in the illustrations but none will vary by more than a few weeks. Remember that if suggested plants are unavailable in your area, others may well fit the bill.

SUMMER BRILLIANCE IS PROVIDED in this mixed planting of perennials in front of the steel-blue foliage of the Juniperus chinensis *'Blue Alps'.* Agapanthus *'Bressingham Blue', interplanted with* Crocosmia *'Lucifer', contrasts strongly with the clump of* Rudbeckia fulgida *var.* sullivantii *'Goldsturm' behind.*

A SMALL ISLAND BED FOR CONTINUAL COLOUR

The fairly dwarf plants in this narrow bed, shown here in mid-summer, are colourful during all other seasons too. The purple-leaved shrub *Berberis thunbergii* 'Dart's Red Lady' is the only shrub, though several of the other plants will offer autumn, winter and early spring interest before the berberis even comes into leaf. The *Stipa calamagrostis* will reach a height of 120cm (4ft) or so, the plumes remaining attractive well into winter, when the steely-blue leaves of *Euphorbia myrsinites* will contrast vividly with *Bergenia* 'Bressingham Ruby', whose leaves turn from summer green to ruby red. The grass *Festuca glauca* 'Blueglow', dotted around the bed to contrast with the surrounding plants, forms a strong juxtaposition with the summer purple of the berberis. Summer-long interest at this end of the bed is offered by the silver leaves and white flowers of *Lamium maculatum* 'White Nancy', the white, pink and red flowers on *Persicaria affinis* 'Dimity', and *Geranium* × *riversleanum* 'Mavis Simpson' which, with its grey leaves and soft pink flowers, knits in with its neighbours and offsets the strong colour of the berberis. *Iris pallida* 'Argentea', with erect, sword-like leaves, remains a bright focal point, enhanced in mid-summer by pale blue flowers. The diascia, with its creeping habit and striking flowers, will flower all summer long to contrast in late summer with one of the best, yet most underrated perennials, *Aster thompsonii* 'Nana'. This in turn makes the classic yellow and blue combination with the dwarf daylily, *Hemerocallis* 'Stella d'Oro'.

This bed should be in full sun, most of the plants requiring reasonable drainage.

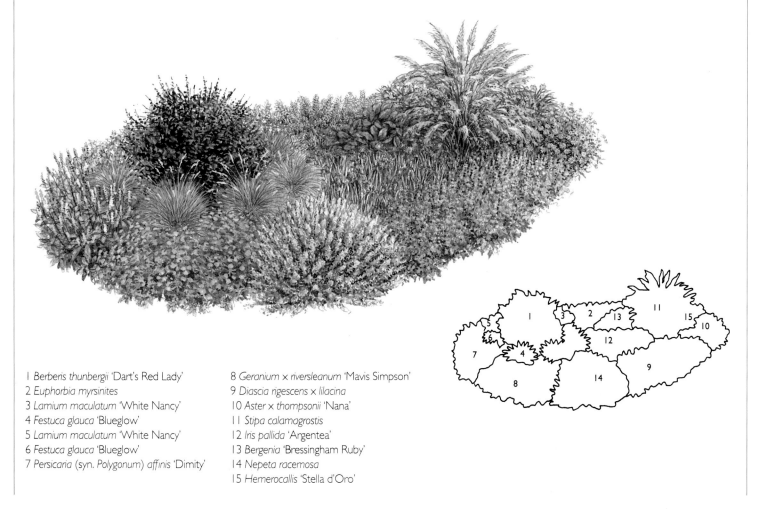

1 *Berberis thunbergii* 'Dart's Red Lady'
2 *Euphorbia myrsinites*
3 *Lamium maculatum* 'White Nancy'
4 *Festuca glauca* 'Blueglow'
5 *Lamium maculatum* 'White Nancy'
6 *Festuca glauca* 'Blueglow'
7 *Persicaria* (syn. *Polygonum*) *affinis* 'Dimity'
8 *Geranium* × *riversleanum* 'Mavis Simpson'
9 *Diascia rigescens* × *lilacina*
10 *Aster* × *thompsonii* 'Nana'
11 *Stipa calamagrostis*
12 *Iris pallida* 'Argentea'
13 *Bergenia* 'Bressingham Ruby'
14 *Nepeta racemosa*
15 *Hemerocallis* 'Stella d'Oro'

AN ASSOCIATION FOR LIGHT SHADE WITH SOME MOISTURE

While the background to this association is provided by trees here, sites and situations will vary, and the shade could be afforded by a high canopy of trees some distance from the bed or even by the high boundary wall of the garden or the wall of the house. With younger trees of lower height, the roots may be a problem, taking the moisture from the soil. It is always difficult to achieve a balance of shade and the right amounts of moisture. But root pruning of trees by digging a trench every two or three years, besides digging in well-rotted compost and mulching the whole bed, plus irrigation if available, will all help to maintain the ideal conditions.

A great many shade-loving woodland plants flower in spring, including trilliums, uvullaria, epimediums and the startling blue *Corydalis flexuosa* cultivars. Other bulbs can be added here, including hardy cyclamen, erythronium, woodland anemones, snowdrops and aconites. But in this association most plants provide foliage or flower interest for a long period in summer. Plants such as hostas, *Rodgersia pinnata* and

Dryopteris erythrosora create a background against which other foreground plants can be shown off to advantage. The blue flowers on the spreading *Geranium himalayense* form a natural contrast to the white and green leaves of *Hosta* 'Francee' and the soft pink spikes of × *Heucherella* 'Bridget Bloom'. The flowers of the latter remain in bloom for many weeks but these will be fading before the pretty pink plumes of *Astilbe* 'Sprite' make a show. The deschampsia will tolerate sun or shade and its grassy green leaves will create an effective backcloth to the attractive variegated Jacob's ladder (*Polemonium caeruleum* 'Brise d'Anjou').

Contrast exists too between *Lysimachia nummularia* 'Aurea', the golden-leaved creeping Jenny and the powder-blue foliage of *Hosta* 'Krossa Regal', long-flowering *Dicentra* 'Snowflakes' and *Persicaria* (formerly *Polygonum*) *milletii*. By summer the bronze fronds of *Dryopteris erythrosora* will give a foliage contrast to the silver-spotted leaves of *Pulmonaria* 'Roy Davidson', whose light blue spring flowers have long finished.

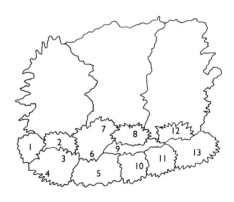

1 *Geranium himalayense*
2 *Hosta* 'Francee'
3 × *Heucherella* 'Bridget Bloom'
4 *Astilbe* 'Sprite'
5 *Polemonium caeruleum* 'Brise d'Anjou'
6 *Deschampsia caespitosa* 'Golden Dew'
7 *Rodgersia pinnata* 'Elegans'
8 *Hosta* 'Krossa Regal'
9 *Lysimachia nummularia* 'Aurea'
10 *Dicentra* 'Snowflakes'
11 *Persicaria* (syn. *Polygonum*) *milletii*
12 *Dryopteris erythrosora*
13 *Pulmonaria* 'Roy Davidson'

A Mediterranean-style Garden in Full Sun

Much publicity has been given in recent years to the potential effects of global warming, and a succession of milder winters in northern Europe, parts of North America and Britain. At the same time, more people visiting countries with a Mediterranean climate has led to the increasing popularity of plants formerly considered appropriate only for coastal and warmer districts. "Mediterranean" plants may come from any part of the world with a similar climate, be it South Africa, Australasia or California but the many new introductions may include an even wider range of plants that like the same conditions of sun and good drainage.

This bed, shown here in late summer, could be freestanding or backed by a hedge. Height is provided by the *Eucalyptus niphophila*, the Mount Etna broom (*Genista aetnensis*) and eventually by *Arbutus unedo*, the adaptable strawberry tree. A mixture of shrubs and perennials make up the rest of an interesting association of flowering and foliage plants. *Lavatera* 'Barnsley' will rapidly grow to about 2.4m(8ft) but will eventually be surpassed by the genista, which may reach a height of 3m(10ft) or more. By summer, spent flowers should be cut off the euphorbia, leaving grey-green foliage. The compact *Scabiosa graminifolia* has shiny silvery leaves and a succession of powder-blue flowers, while *Cosmos atrosanguinea*, though not reliably hardy, will provide a dark contrast to both the scabious and the grey-leaved non-flowering *Artemisia* 'Powis Castle'. The flat heads of the sedum are an ideal counterpoint to the spiky, erect, sword-like yucca and the rounded, deep blue umbels of the hardy *Agapanthus* 'Bressingham Blue'. Along the front of the bed, the rich pink *Geranium* 'Alan Bloom' vividly offsets the soft yellow of *Molinia caerulea* 'Variegata' and *Coreopsis verticillata* 'Moonbeam'. Coupled with both the azure blue of the spiky perovskia and the soft pink of the penstemon, this should provide more than enough colour for most people. There is also sufficient structure to keep this bed looking interesting into autumn and even winter.

The bed needs to be mulched with a mixture of fine and coarser gravel to help retain moisture but allow free drainage on the surface as well as offering some degree of weed control.

1 *Eucalyptus niphophila*
2 *Euphorbia characias* ssp. *wulfenii*
3 *Yucca gloriosa* 'Variegata'
4 *Scabiosa graminifolia*
5 *Cosmos atrosanguinea*
6 *Sedum* 'Autumn Joy' (syn. *Herbstfreude*)
7 *Artemisia* 'Powis Castle'
8 *Agapanthus* 'Bressingham Blue'
9 *Geranium sanguineum* 'Alan Bloom'
10 *Genista aetnensis*
11 *Lavatera thuringiaca* 'Barnsley'
12 *Molinia caerulea* 'Variegata'
13 *Arbutus unedo*
14 *Gaura lindheimeri*
15 *Perovskia* 'Blue Spire'
16 *Coreopsis verticillata* 'Moonbeam'
17 *Penstemon* 'Hidcote Pink'
18 *Phlomis fruticosa*

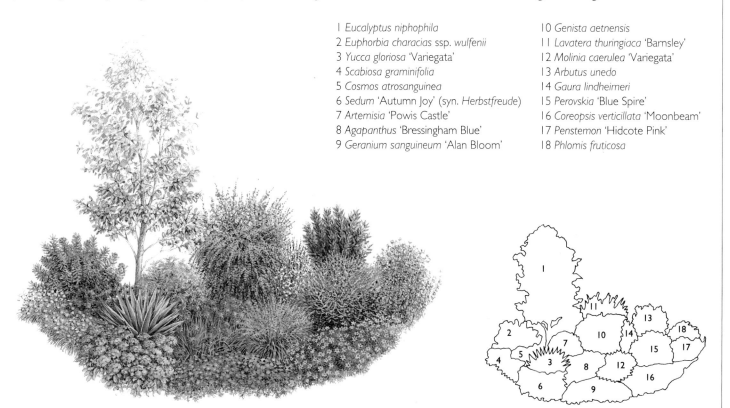

Perennials with Ornamental Grasses

In recent years hardy perennials have made a tremendous comeback and are now probably the most popular group of garden plants. The popularity of ornamental grasses is even more recent and owes much to the efforts of German and American nurserymen, garden designers and plantspeople. Initially, grasses tended to be used on their own but their real value lies in the contrast in form, foliage, light and movement that they offer to more brilliant flowering and non-flowering plants. The wide variety of ornamental grasses now available has given even greater opportunities to create pleasing combinations. The period of interest of ornamental grasses extends well beyond summer, and most continue to look attractive through autumn and winter, before they are cut back to encourage them to rejuvenate.

There are no invasive grasses in this bed, which could be an island bed or a bed against a wall, hedge or shrubs. However this plant association idea is adapted, always remember the importance of allowing light to pass round it all year. In the reflected view, with light flashing through stems or plumes, you will derive much enjoyment. A position in full sun is recommended and a fertile, but reasonably well-drained soil will suit most plants.

Three different miscanthus provide the most height, along with *Stipa gigantea*, and although the wispy plumes of the latter will reach 1.8m(6ft) or more by mid-summer, the full height of miscanthus foliage and flower will not be achieved until a month or more later. Spots of colour and bright contrast will be provided by this bed throughout summer, though late summer will be its peak season, as shown here. The late flowers of rudbeckia, *Aster × frikartii*, persicaria, kniphofia, scabious, diascia and anthemis continue well into autumn – particularly if earlier flowers are cut back after their first main flush of flowering in mid-summer.

This bed could be mulched with gravel.

1 *Stipa gigantea*
2 *Miscanthus sinensis* 'Flamingo'
3 *Aster × frikartii*
4 *Persicaria* (syn. *Polygonum*) 'Taurus'
5 *Pennisetum alopecuroides* 'Hameln'
6 *Diascia vigilis*
7 *Kniphofia* 'Bressingham Comet'
8 *Miscanthus sinensis* 'Variegatus'
9 *Carex comans* 'Bronze'
10 *Agapanthus* 'Isis'
11 *Miscanthus sinensis* 'Klein Silberspinne'
12 *Crocosmia* 'Bressingham Beacon'
13 *Anthemis tinctoria* 'E.C. Buxton'
14 *Scabiosa caucasica* 'Clive Greaves'
15 *Festuca glauca* 'Blueglow'
16 *Rudbeckia fulgida* var. *sullivantii* 'Goldsturm'
17 *Agapanthus* 'Bressingham White'
18 *Salvia × sylvestris* 'Blauhugel'
19 *Calamagrostis* 'Overdam'
20 *Phlox paniculata* 'Franz Schubert'

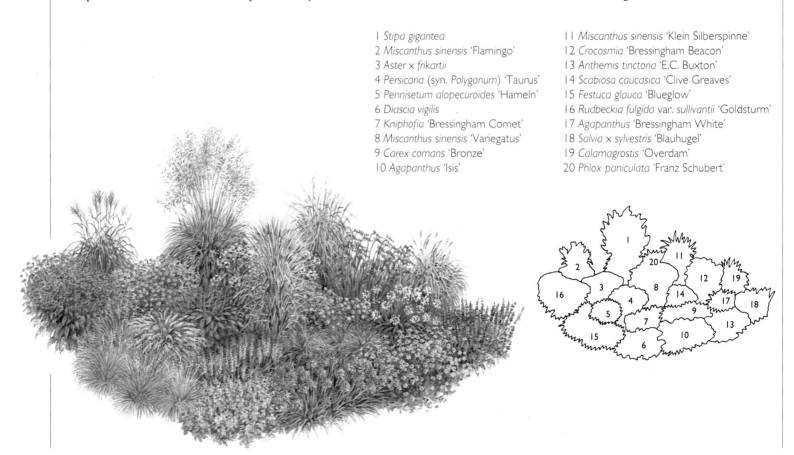

A MIXED BORDER OF SUMMER-LONG COLOUR

From my experience at Foggy Bottom, I believe that some structure is important in a garden – and for most gardeners it already exists when they move into another property. This illustration, which shows the bed in mid- to late summer, shows some striking associations including small trees, shrubs and conifers, as well as ornamental grasses and perennials. Even if some of these plants are not available to you, similar forms and colours may be sought. Always think of the year-round aspect, the foliage colours as well as those of the flowers and – as mentioned time and again – consider what is likely to succeed in your own conditions, soil and climate.

Spring-flowering bulbs can be added for an earlier effect, and if I was planning with year-round colour in mind, I might wish to add a red- or orange-stemmed dogwood against the blue spruce. Highlights in this border will certainly include the bright reddish-pink *Geranium sanguineum* 'John Elsley' against the three golden spires of *Thuja orientalis* 'Golden Sceptre' –

but do not plant them too close together or it will spoil the conifer foliage. The silver-leaved pear, *Pyrus salicifolia* 'Pendula', will make a pleasing backdrop to the bed. Though *Acer negundo* 'Flamingo' can be grown as a tree on a stem, it is far better to keep it as a shrub at less than 3m(10ft), by pruning regularly. This multi-coloured, easily grown maple will offer good contrasts to both the pear and to the *Picea pungens* 'Hoopsii' behind, a striking silver-blue spruce.

Completing the shrubs is one I rate highly for its broad purple leaves, *Cercis canadensis* 'Forest Pansy'. If this is not available, a purple smokebush (*Cotinus coggygria* 'Purpureus') would be a good substitute. Various long-flowering perennials complete the colourful picture in the front of the bed, with the golden-yellow *Coreopsis verticillata* 'Golden Gain' and *Lavandula* 'Blue Cushion' creating a splash in mid- to late summer. This combination of shrubs and perennials would suit a sunny bed or border for most soils.

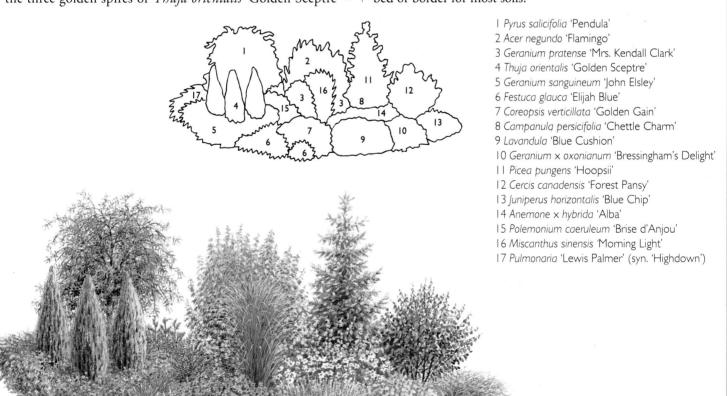

1 *Pyrus salicifolia* 'Pendula'
2 *Acer negundo* 'Flamingo'
3 *Geranium pratense* 'Mrs. Kendall Clark'
4 *Thuja orientalis* 'Golden Sceptre'
5 *Geranium sanguineum* 'John Elsley'
6 *Festuca glauca* 'Elijah Blue'
7 *Coreopsis verticillata* 'Golden Gain'
8 *Campanula persicifolia* 'Chettle Charm'
9 *Lavandula* 'Blue Cushion'
10 *Geranium* x *oxonianum* 'Bressingham's Delight'
11 *Picea pungens* 'Hoopsii'
12 *Cercis canadensis* 'Forest Pansy'
13 *Juniperus horizontalis* 'Blue Chip'
14 *Anemone* x *hybrida* 'Alba'
15 *Polemonium caeruleum* 'Brise d'Anjou'
16 *Miscanthus sinensis* 'Morning Light'
17 *Pulmonaria* 'Lewis Palmer' (syn. 'Highdown')

DIRECTORY OF PLANTS

FOR LATE SPRING AND SUMMER

ZONES AND PLANTING

This directory is a personal selection of hundreds of plants recommended to provide colour and interest in the garden from late spring through to late summer. While it includes both popular and unusual plants, and species for all situations in the garden, it is necessarily selective rather than comprehensive – there are just too many plants from which to choose.

CULTURAL REQUIREMENTS

Most of the plants listed are "hardy" in Europe and the British Isles (Zones 7-9 in the USA hardiness zones – see below) and will adapt to most garden soils except where a specific need is stated. A soil testing kit enables you to determine whether your soil is acid or alkaline.

Soil Unless you already have good, friable, fertile soil, you will probably need to dig thoroughly to a depth of 35-45cm (14-18in). Mix in some organic material, such as well-rotted garden compost or manure. This will help to retain moisture in light soils and to aerate heavier soil types.

Planting Before planting, soak plants in their containers – for an hour or two if the compost is dry or a few minutes if it is moist. Dig the hole deep enough for the level of the soil in the container to come just below the surface of the soil. Add some fertilizer: select a slow-release type for conifers, shrubs or trees, but use a faster-acting, balanced one if you are planting perennials.

After planting, fill the hole in with soil, firming gently on heavy soils but more firmly on lighter soils. Do not compact the soil too much. Water in the plant, then mulch to retain moisture, protect new roots from frost and keep down weeds. Water regularly until the plant is established; for a tree that means for at least a year.

SIZE AND RATE OF GROWTH

The approximate size of each tree, shrub and conifer after ten years is given at the end of its description. Always remember that geographical situation, climate, soil conditions and pruning will affect a plant's size as well as its precise flowering times and sometimes even a plant's appearance.

HARDINESS ZONES

Though hardiness zones are generally used little in Europe and the British Isles, they are commonplace in horticultural reference works, catalogues and labels in North America. The plant hardiness zones given in the chart below are determined by the United States Department of Agriculture and are based on the average annual minimum winter temperatures for each zone. Hardiness zones are of particular relevance in the USA, where considerable variation in climate occurs across the country. In the British Isles, such variation is much less: Zone 7 covers the eastern Scottish Highlands; Zone 8 includes most of inland and eastern Britain and Ireland; and Zone 9 covers the western coastal areas of Britain and Ireland.

Each plant in the directories has been allocated a zonal range (for example, Z7-9) within which it is most likely to thrive. However, these zones can give only an approximate indication of appropriate climate for the plants listed. Within any one zone several local microclimates can occur, and other factors, such as site, aspect and soil, may also affect a plant's growth. Heat and humidity are other factors affecting a plant's performance, and the protection afforded by, for example, sunny walls, provides an exception to every rule. Please use the hardiness zones as a guideline only.

HARDINESS ZONES

Zone	Range of temperatures
1	Below -45°C/-50°F
2	-45° to -39°C/-50° to -40°
3	-39° to -35°C/-40° to -30°F
4	-35° to -29°C/-30° to -20°F
5	-29° to -23°C/-20° to -10°F
6	-23° to -18°C/-10° to 0°F
7	-18° to -12°C/0° to 10°F
8	-12° to -6°C/10° to 20°F
9	-6° to -1°C/20° to 30°F
10	-1° to 4°C/30° to 40°F
11	Above 4°C/40°F

KEY TO SYMBOLS

☀	full sun
❂	semi-shade
✳	shade
□	dry soil
◪	moist soil
■	well-drained soil
⊙	alkaline soil
⊕	acid soil
☆	most soils
✩	fertile soil
★	humus-rich soil

TREES DIRECTORY

MANY GARDENERS ARE HESITANT TO PLANT TREES, particularly if their garden is small – but there are many small trees which can provide foliage, flower, bark or catkins to enhance rather than take over the garden. In warmer climates trees provide some shade in summer. In spacious plots trees help to provide the garden's structure and framework, furnishing a backcloth to other plants. Many trees can be pruned to keep them within the limits required – but this is a subject for another book! The selection made here is primarily for late spring and summer colour.

Planting trees
Make the planting hole two or three times the width and depth of the rootball; on heavy soils break up the clay at the bottom to avoid possible waterlogging. Provide a sturdy stake for anything over 90cm/3ft and use proper tree ties. Leave a circular ridge of soil just beyond the circumference of the rootball and fill with a good mulch.

H: Approximate height after 10 years
W: Approximate width after 10 years
F: Months usually in flower
Z: Relevant suggested hardiness zone(s) – see page 220

ACER Maple

Deciduous. For further selections and more detail, see Shrubs Directory, page 224.

A. griseum Paperbark maple. Year-round interest. With age, slowly flaking bark reveals orange-brown beneath. Trifoliate green leaves, often colouring well in late autumn. H3-4m/10-13ft, W1.5-2m/5-6ft. Z5. ☼ ❋ ✫

A. hersii (syn. *A. grosseri hersii*) Snake-bark maple. Small, shapely tree for autumn colour. Smooth, grey-green, silver-streaked or marbled bark. Broadly ovate leaves. On mature specimens, pendulous greenish flowers in spring and greenish-yellow fruits in autumn. ☼ ❋ ☆ (where not too dry).

A. negundo Box elder (though not an elder). Fast growing, adaptable tree with light green, pinnate leaves. More garden worthy and slower in growth are the cultivars 'Elegans', green with irregular bright yellow margins, 'Flamingo' whose leaves are multi-coloured pink, cream and green, and 'Kelly's Gold', with bright yellow foliage. All can be pruned as shrubs and grown as patio

Acer platanoides 'Princeton Gold'

specimens. All (unpruned) H5-7m/16-23ft, W4-6m/13-20ft. Z3-9. ☼ ☆
A. platanoides 'Crimson Sentry'. A selection of the Norway maple. Narrow, columnar habit, rich crimson-purple leaves, a striking form. H5m/16ft, W75cm-1m/30in-3ft. 'Princeton Gold', broader habit, bright yellow leaves in spring and early summer, yellow-green later. Both H6-7m/20-23ft, W4-5m/13-16ft; both Z3-8. ☼ ☆

Cornus controversa 'Variegata'

A. pseudoplatanus 'Brilliantissimum'. An ornamental, slow-growing sycamore whose spring buds unfurl to reveal shrimp-pink leaves paling to cream then deepening with age to green in summer. Usually good autumn colour. H4m/13ft, W2-2.5m/6-8ft. Z4-8. ☼ ❋(in hot climates), ☆

CORNUS CONTROVERSA 'VARIEGATA' A choice plant which slowly makes a magnificent wide, spreading tree with layered branches bearing creamy-white and green leaves. H3m/10ft, W2-3m/7-10ft. Z5-8. ☼ ❋ ✫

EUCALYPTUS Gum tree Evergreen trees with aromatic foliage. ☼ ✫ ★
E. niphophila Snow gum. One of the hardiest and most ornamental, and one of the few eucalyptus that can be classed as a small tree. Leathery, oval, grey-green juvenile leaves become grey, narrow and lance-shaped as plant matures. Main stem usually develops a "lean", the smooth, grey-green bark flaking to reveal creamy-white, green and brown. Grown from seed, like all the gums, it is best planted as a young pot-grown plant so that early roots

establish quickly to support the rapid growth. The foliage is excellent for flower arranging and, if cut back by hand or frost, vigorous new shoots will emerge from the base. H10m/33ft, W5-6m/16-20ft. Z7-9.

FAGUS SYLVATICA Beech Among the many forms of the common beech are some suitable for the smaller garden. They are very adaptable trees for acid or alkaline soils and some are extremely ornamental in habit and foliage. Z4-8 (dislikes extreme heat). ☼ ❋ ☆

Eucalyptus niphophila

Gleditsia triacanthos 'Sunburst'

'Aurea Pendula'. Though rare, this is worth looking out for, for its pendulous habit, slow early growth and golden leaves. Best in half shade when young. Train up a cane in early years. H3-4m/10-13ft, W1.5-2m/5-6ft. **'Dawyck Gold'**, attractive, narrow column, leaves light yellow in spring, greeny-yellow in summer; **'Dawyck Purple'** is similar but broader in habit with dark purple foliage, making a striking accent plant. Both approx. H5-6m/16-20ft, W1-1.5m/3-5ft. **'Purpurea Pendula'**, the weeping purple beech, makes a strong accent plant for a small garden. Top-grafted on a stem, it cascades downwards; its leaves fade in late summer. H usually 2-3m/6-10ft, W2m/6ft.

GLEDITSIA TRIACANTHOS 'SUNBURST'
Golden honey locust
Small to medium tree with thornless branches. Bright yellow, finely cut new leaves, older leaves green then brighter yellow again in autumn. Light, airy appearance. H5-6m/16-20ft, W3-4m/10-13ft. Z3-9. ☼ ☆

MALUS **Crab apple**
Some of the most ornamental flowering and fruiting deciduous

Malus 'Liset'

trees, including many suitable for the small garden. Flowers appear in mid- to late spring, often creating clouds of blossom and later colourful fruits. All Z5-8. ☆ (neither very dry nor very wet).
M. **'Evereste'**. Good-value small tree with large white flowers, red in bud, deep green foliage and a profusion of orange-yellow fruits in autumn.
M. floribunda. The Japanese crab makes a broad-headed small tree, its arching branches carrying red buds which open pink, fading to white, and small yellow fruits. H5-6m/16-20ft, W3-4m/10-13ft. F4-5.
M. hupehensis. Erect branching habit. Pink buds open to smother the tree in fragrant white blossom. Yellow fruits tinted red. H5-6m/16-20ft, W2-3m/6-10ft.
M. **'Liset'**. Striking small tree. Deep crimson buds open to rosy-red flowers; purple young foliage; small red fruits. H4-5m/13-16ft, W2-3m/6-10ft. F4-5.
M. **'Maypole'**. An ornamental crab for the smaller garden forming a narrow column; carmine-pink flowers, bronze foliage tints; reddish-purple crab apples, good for jelly. H5-6m/16-10ft, W30-45cm/12-18in.
M. **'Royalty'**. Wine-red flowers and

shining dark red-purple leaves make this a tree of long-term appeal, the leaves turning red in autumn. Deep red fruits. H4-5m/13-16ft, W2-3m/6-10ft. F4-5.
M. **'Van Eseltine'**. Flowering crab apple forming an excellent columnar tree. Large semi-double flowers, rose-red in bud opening pale pink; yellow fruits. H5-6m/16-20ft, W2-3m/6-10ft. F4-5.

POPULUS ALBA 'RICHARDII'
Slower growing form of the white poplar. Maple-like leaves with white undersides and bright golden-yellow upper sides – a brilliant combination, especially where wind can ruffle the foliage, giving flashes of silver and gold; green winter stems; eventually a suckering habit. Can be pruned as a shrub or small tree. H8m/26ft, W4m/13ft. Z5.

PRUNUS
Many of the cherries make excellent trees both for flower and autumn colour, though some become large in time. Plums, almonds, peaches and laurels as well as "flowering cherries" all come under this genus. Most are adaptable to a wide range of soils, including alkaline and chalk soils. The few forms listed here have been selected for flower and foliage. ☼ (preferred), ✳
P. **'Accolade'**. Though eventually too large for the smaller garden, this is a graceful, wide spreading tree with arching branchlets. Clusters of pendulous rich pink flowers, fading gradually to almost white.

Prunus 'Accolade'

Outstanding. H5-6m/16-20ft, W4-5m/13-16ft. F3-4. Z5-8.

P. 'Amanogawa'. Considered one of the most suitable for smaller gardens with its narrow columnar habit, but on heavier soils attains some size. Fragrant, semi-double, light pink flowers, good autumn colour. H5-6m/16-20ft, W1-2m/3-6ft. F4-5. Z5-8.

P. cerasifera 'Pissardii'. Purple-leaved plum. White, pink-budded flowers wreathe the branches in spring; red young shoots and leaves turn deep purple in summer. Good for hedging too. H3-4m/10-13ft, W2.4-3m/8-10ft. F3-4. Z2-8.

P. 'Cheal's Weeping'. One of the most popular of weeping Japanese cherries, also known as 'Kiku-shidare Sakura'. Deep pink double flowers adorn the branches. Bronze-tinted shoots, glossy green leaves in summer. H2.4-3m/8-10ft, W2-3m/6-10ft. F4-5. Z5-8.

P. 'Mount Fuji'. Formerly known as *P.* 'Shirotae', a famous Japanese cherry with horizontal, slightly pendulous branches which in spring are clustered in large, fragrant snow-

Pyrus salicifolia 'Pendula'

white flowers. Distinctive. H6-7m/20-23ft, W4-5m/13-16ft. F4-5, Z4-8.

P. padus 'Colorata'. This form of the bird cherry has bronze-purple shoots and purplish-green leaves, contrasting elegantly with pendulous racemes of fragrant lilac-pink flowers. Leaves in summer deep green. H6-8m/20-26ft, W3-4m/10-13ft. F4-5. Z3-8.

P. 'Spire' (*P.* × *hillieri* 'Spire'). First-class hybrid between *P. sargentii* and *P. incisa*. Erect, vase-shaped branching habit, light pink flowers and good autumn colour. H5-6m/16-20ft, W2-3m/6-10ft. F3-4. Z4-8.

PYRUS SALICIFOLIA 'PENDULA'
Weeping form of the willow-leaf pear makes a striking accent plant, with branches sweeping to the ground, creamy-white flowers in spring and silvery-grey leaves all summer. Prunes well. H3-4m/10-13ft, W2-3m/6-10ft. F4. Z4-8. ☼ ❉ ☆

ROBINIA PSEUDOACACIA 'FRISIA'
A selected form of the false acacia with bright golden-yellow pinnate leaves all summer and into autumn. Grow as a tree or shrub; the latter will need annual pruning in spring. Prefers well drained soil. H6-7m/20-23ft, W3-4m/10-13ft. Z4-8. ☼ ■

SALIX Willow
S. alba 'Sericea'. Though quite a large tree if unpruned, this selection of the white willow can be kept as a small tree by annual pruning. Bright, silvery leaves shimmer in the wind. A striking foliage background plant. H7-8m/23-26ft, W3-4m/10-13ft. Z2-8. ☼ ❉ ☆

S. exigua Coyote willow. Graceful shrub or small tree. Long slender stems, somewhat suckering habit, narrow silvery-grey leaves. H3-4m/10-13ft, W2.1-3m/7-10ft. Z6-8.

From left to right: *Eucalyptus niphophila* x *canadensis, Populus* 'Aurea', *Fagus sylvatica* 'Dawyck Purple', *Robinia pseudoacacia* 'Frisia'.

SORBUS
Popular trees for the smaller garden. Two distinct types: the whitebeams, grown primarily for their broad green or grey leaves, and mountain ashes, grown for their fruits and

Salix alba 'Sericea'

finely cut, often showy foliage.. ☼ ■

S. aria 'Lutescens'. Selected form of the round-headed common whitebeam, with brighter, creamy-white upper oval leaves in spring, becoming green with white beneath. White flowers in spring, bunches of crimson fruits in late summer. Withstands wind even in coastal areas. H6-7m/20-23ft, W3-4m/10-13ft. Z5-8.

S. aucuparia. Mountain ash or rowan. Relatively small trees whose pinnate leaves turn tints of orange-red and yellow in autumn. White, early summer flowers are quickly followed by often heavy bunches of orange or red fruits. Many selections exist with somewhat different habits and fruits from crimson and red to orange and yellow. H5m/16ft, W2-3m/6-10ft. F5. Z3-9.

S. thibetica 'John Mitchell' (syn. *S. mitchellii*). One of the most striking foliage trees; strong growing, large, silver-backed leaves, a broad head, few fruits. H7-8m/23-26ft, W3-4m/10-13ft. Z5-8.

SHRUBS DIRECTORY

SHRUBS INCLUDE BOTH DECIDUOUS AND EVERGREEN woody plants and climbers. Like trees, they provide structure in the garden and it is important to aim for a balance of shrubs in order to provide year-round interest. Luckily, many of the dwarfer shrubs provide long flowering periods or attractive foliage, so even for the smaller garden there is ample choice. Apart from their structural role, flower and foliage need to be assessed in choosing shrubs and climbers that will create late spring and summer-long appeal. The selection offered here includes some of the lesser known as well as the more popular shrubs.

Planting shrubs

Always assess the requirements of a particular plant with regard to soil and aspect prior to planting (see page 220 for cultural requirements and hardiness zones). After planting it is a good idea to mulch around newly planted shrubs, particularly shallow- or fibrous-rooted ones, and then mulch annually or every two years. Apply a general, slow-release fertilizer in spring if shrubs lack colour or vigour. Protect susceptible new shrubs from wind or frosts with close-woven or shade netting.

H: Approximate height after 10 years
W: Approximate width after 10 years
F: Months in flower
Z: Relevant hardiness zone(s)

ABELIA

Bright-foliaged evergreen or deciduous shrubs, late flowers. Best grown in a warm, sheltered position. Trim or prune as required in spring. ☼ ■ ✭
A. × *grandiflora*. This glossy shrub has oval, shiny green leaves and pale pink, softly fragrant flowers for many months. **'Francis Mason'** offers yellow variegated leaves and **'Gold Sport'** brighter golden-yellow foliage, the colour of both brightest in full sun. All H1.2-1.5m/4-5ft, W1.2-1.5m/4-5ft, F7-10, Z7-9. A recent introduction, **'Confetti'** promises equally striking foliage, but is a more compact plant, the leaves prettily edged cream and pink. H90-120cm/3-4ft, W90-120cm/3-4ft. F7-10. Z7-9.

ACER Maple

Most maples are trees (see page 221) but some can be considered shrubs, mostly the Japanese maples, which are outstanding for their attractive and colourful foliage and autumn

colour. They are happiest on moist, neutral to acid soil though will succeed, given shelter from cold winds, if non-acid soils are thoroughly prepared with humus or leafmould. ☼ ✽ ■ ✭ ⊙
A. japonicum 'Aureum' – see *A. shirasawanum* **'Aureum'**.
A. palmatum Japanese Maple. A very wide selection is available from specialists including:
'Atropurpureum', with rounded head and purple leaves, colouring red in autumn; **'Aureum'**, light yellow; **'Bloodgood'**, striking reddish-purple; **'Butterfly'**, erect branches, green leaves edged pink and cream; **'Trompenburg'**, purple-red, deeply lobed leaves, rounded at the margins, turn greener in summer, red in autumn. Average H1.8-3m/6-10ft, W1.5-1.8m/5-6ft. F4-5. Z5-8.
Dissectum group. Shrubby, spreading pendulous branches, fern-like leaves. **'Atropurpureum'**, **'Garnet'** and **'Inaba Shidare'** all strong purple, red in autumn;

Berberis temolaica

'Viridis', fresh green leaves. Average H1.2-1.5m/4-5ft, W1.5-2.1m/5-7ft. Z5-8. **'Linearilobum'**, green-leaved, and **'Linearilobum Atropurpureum'**, purple-leaved, form broad-headed shrubs with leaves that have widely spaced, finger-like lobes. Both H1.5-1.8m/5-6ft, W.1.5-1.8m/5-6ft. Z5-8. **'Ribesifolium'** (syn. 'Shishigashira'), very slow growing, with greenish stems and deep green, finely cut leaves, golden in autumn.
A. shirasawanum **'Aureum'** (syn. *A.*

japonicum 'Aureum'). Very slow growing, with bright yellow leaves all summer, which can scorch in full sun. H1.2-1.5m/4-5ft, W90-120cm/3-4ft. F4-5. Z6-8.

ACTINIDIA KOLOMIKTA

Striking foliage climber for walls, pergolas or through shrubs, its oval leaves are irregularly splashed with white and pink. Small, white, scented flowers. Deciduous. H3-4m/10-13ft, W3-4m/10-13ft. F6. Z5-9. ☼ ✽

AESCULUS PARVIFLORA

Bottlebrush buckeye
Spreading deciduous shrub, whose erect stems make a rounded dome. It has light green leaves and candle-like heads of white flowers in summer. H2.4-3m/8-10ft, W2.4-3m/8-10ft. F7-8. Z5-9. ☼ ✽ ☆

AKEBIA QUINATA

Vigorous semi-evergreen twining climber. Five-fingered leaves, clusters of scented chocolate-purple flowers in spring; after hot summers, sausage-shaped purplish fruits appear in autumn. H.6-7m/20-23ft, W6-7m/20-23ft. F3-5. Z5-9. ☼ ✽ ☆

Acer palmatum 'Aureum'

Berberis thunbergii 'Bagatelle'

ARTEMESIA

Silver- or grey-leaved shrubs revel in full sun with good drainage. *A.* 'Powis Castle' is particularly recommended, with its non-flowering mound of finely cut silver-grey foliage, semi-evergreen in mild localities. H90-120cm/3-4ft, W90-120cm/3-4ft. Z5-8. ✿ ☆

BERBERIS

A wide range of deciduous and evergreen adaptable shrubs, many with coloured foliage as well as showy flowers and fruits; some very thorny. Most withstand pruning. ✿ ☆

B. darwinii. Popular evergreen shrub with arching branches, dark green leaves, racemes of orange-yellow flowers in late spring, sometimes again in autumn, and plum-coloured fruits. Prune if required after early flowering. H1.5-2.1m/5-7ft, W1.2-1.5m/4-5ft. F4-5. Z7-9.

B. × *stenophylla*. Three distinct selections are all excellent: 'Corallina Compacta', an underrated dwarf shrub with coral-red buds, deep orange flowers. H30-45cm/12-18in, W60-75cm/24-30in. F4-5. 'Cream Showers', vigorous, arching branches, dark green leaves, creamy-white bell-like flowers. Prune after flowering. H1.5-1.8m/5-6ft, W1.5-1.8m/5-6ft. F4-5. Z6-9. 'Etna', dense, medium-sized shrub with green-bronze leaves, red buds, orange flowers. H90-120cm/3-4ft, W90cm/3ft. F4-5. Z6-9.

B. temolaica. A superb flowering and foliage plant with large, striking blue-grey leaves and vigorous growth. Difficult to find and to propagate. Keep compact by pruning away one-third of stems in spring. H2.4-3m/8-10ft, W1.5-2.1m/5-7ft. F5. Z7-9.

B. thunbergii. The biggest group of cultivars come from this hardy Chinese deciduous species, all thorny; foliage colours of purple, red, green, yellow, some variegated. Except where indicated, all H1.5-1.8m/5-6ft, W1.2-1.5m/4-5ft. F4-5. Z5-8. Purple-leaved forms need sun to colour well but not too much. 'Atropurpurea', arching branches, red-purple leaves, free fruiting, with good autumn colour. 'Atropurpurea Nana' (syn. 'Crimson Pygmy', 'Little Favourite'), with congested branches, compact habit, dark purple leaves. H45cm/18in, W45cm/18in. 'Aurea', a first-class contrast plant, with bright yellow leaves in spring and summer, yellow-green in shade; can scorch by late summer. H60-75cm/2-3ft, W60-75cm/2-3ft. 'Bagatelle', dense dwarf bush with small purple leaves, copper-red new shoots, rounded habit; ideal with dwarf shrubs or alpines. H30cm/12in, W30-45cm/12-18in. 'Bonanza Gold', dwarf golden-leaved selection to match 'Atropurpurea Nana', yellow leaves, tinged red in summer. H30-45cm/12-18in, W45-60cm/18-24in. 'Dart's Red Lady', excellent contrast shrub with dark, glossy purple leaves, broad habit, good autumn colour. H60-75cm/24-30in, W75-90cm/30-36in. 'Helmond Pillar', an erect form, narrow when young, vase-shaped when older, with deep purple leaves. H1.2-1.5m/4-5ft, W30-45cm/12-18in. 'Rose Glow', similar to 'Atropurpurea' but new summer growth attractively mottled and splashed with cream and pink; 'Harlequin' is similar.

BUDDLEJA Butterfly bush

Free-flowering shrubs, mostly deciduous in cool, temperate climates. Many hybrids are renowned for their summer colour and attractiveness to bees and butterflies. Prune annually in early spring to 30cm/12in from the ground to produce strong flowering shoots. Wide variety, some growing quite large. ☆ where not too wet.

B. davidii. Cultivars have fragrant flowers. All F7-9. Z5-9. 'Black Knight', erect habit, with deep violet-blue trusses. H2.4m/8ft, W2.4m/8ft. 'Dartmoor', striking form with arching branches, large panicles of magenta flowers. H2.4m/8ft, W2.4m/8ft. 'Harlequin', creamy variegated leaves contrast with purple-red flowers. H1.2-1.5m/4-5ft, W1.2-1.5m/4-5ft. Var. *nanhoensis alba*, 'Nanho Blue' and 'Nanho Purple' are all small-leaved, dwarfer in habit with arching branches and give a succession of flowers. All H1.2-

Buddleja globosa

1.5m/4-5ft, W1.2-1.5m/4-5ft. 'Pink Delight', excellent compact selection with large lilac-pink flowers. H1.8-2.1m/6-7ft, W1.8-2.1m/6-7ft. 'Royal Red', compact habit, purple-red flowers. H1.8m/6ft, W1.8m/6ft. *B. globosa*. Unusual early-summer-flowering species with rounded heads of orange-yellow flowers. Prune after flowering. H2.4-3m/8-10ft, W2.4-3m/8-10ft.

BUXUS

Adaptable slow-growing, small-leaved evergreen shrubs, often used for topiary. All withstand clipping well. Many introductions, some dwarf and compact, others upright, some pendulous. Ideal for containers and formal dwarf hedges. Some have colourful variegated leaves. ✿ ✹ ☆ *B. sempervirens* 'Elegantissima'. A selection with green and creamy-white variegated leaves, fits well with other plants. H45-60cm/18-24in, W45-60cm/18-24in (eventually much more). Z7-8.

CALLUNA – see HEATHS AND HEATHERS

CARPENTERIA Tree anemone
C. californica. A delightful evergreen shrub for milder climates, often

Caryopteris × *clandonensis* 'Heavenly Blue'

grown as a wall shrub. Pure white, saucer-shaped flowers with yellow anthers produced in summer on old wood. H2.1m/7ft, W1.8m/6ft. F7-8. Z8-9. ☼ ■ ☆

CARYOPTERIS Bluebeard, blue spiraea

Aromatic, deciduous, mostly dwarf or low-growing shrubs. Bright blue flowers produced in late summer. Prune each spring to 10-15cm/4-6in from the ground. In cold climates, grow against a wall facing the sun. Plant in spring. ☼ ■

C. × *clandonensis.* 'Arthur Simmonds', hybrid with grey-green leaves, profuse bright blue flowers. 'Heavenly Blue', more compact, with deep blue flowers. 'Worcester

Gold', greenish-gold leaves, bright blue flowers, less hardy. All H60-75cm/24-30in, W60-75cm/24-30in. F8-9. Z6-9.

CEANOTHUS

Popular evergreen and deciduous shrubs, some quite tender, often used as wall shrubs. Good seaside plants but need shelter from cold winds and frost. The evergreens are mostly spring-flowering and less hardy than the deciduous summer-flowering forms. Best planted in spring. Prune larger spring-flowering evergreens after flowering but not into old wood. ☼ ■

C. 'Autumnal Blue'. Glossy evergreen leaves, deep blue flowers, quite hardy. H1.5-1.8m/5-6ft, W1.5-1.8m/5-6ft. F8-9. Z8-10.

C. 'Blue Mound', evergreen mound of small, shiny leaves, light blue flowers. H60-75cm/24-30in, W60-90cm/2-3ft. F5. Z8-10.

C. delinianus. Deciduous French hybrids, flowering on wood made in the same year; prune in late spring. 'Gloire de Versailles', powder-blue panicles; 'Henri Desfosse', deep blue; 'Marie Simon', rose-pink heads; all H1.5-1.8m/5-6ft, W1.2-1.5m/4-5ft. F8-9. Z8-10. There are innumerable other selections, including white-flowered forms.

Cercis canadensis

CERATOSTIGMA Hardy plumbago

The two species listed behave like perennials in cool, temperate climates. Both late-flowering, bright blue, periwinkle-like flowers. ☼ ■

C. plumbaginoides. Dwarf, spreading, with leaves that turn reddish in autumn, contrasting with blue flowers. H15-20cm/6-8in, W30cm/1ft. F7-9. Z5-8.

C. willmottianum. Twiggy, upright stems, bright deep blue flowers; prune to the ground in late spring. 'Forest Blue' is a more compact, very free-flowering selection. H60-75cm/24-30in, W60-75cm/24-30in. F8-10. Z5-9.

CERCIS

Slow-growing shrubs or small trees. ☼ ■

C. canadensis 'Forest Pansy'. Striking, purple-leaved form of the north American redbud. Small pink flowers on mature plants appear before the broad purple leaves, softer purple beneath. Good autumn colour. Prune lightly in early spring if necessary to keep shape. H1.5-2.4m/5-8ft, W1.8-2.4m/6-8ft. F4-5. Z4-9.

CHOISYA

Evergreen shrubs with glossy leaves. ☼ ❀ ☆

C. 'Aztec Pearl'. Free-flowering evergreen hybrid with narrow aromatic leaves; pink buds open to

appealing display of fragrant white flowers late spring/early summer, sometimes again in late summer. H1.5-1.8m/5-6ft, W1.2-1.5m/4-5ft. F5-6. Z7-9.

C. ternata Mexican orange blossom. Popular evergreen shrub, bright green leaves, makes a rounded bush. White fragrant flowers. Prune lightly after flowering, though will take harder pruning in early spring. H1.5-1.8m/5-6ft, W1.2-1.5m/4-5ft. F5-6. Z7-9. 'Sundance', a popular selection with bold yellow leaves, ideal for patio containers. Slightly less hardy; foliage not so bright in less sun. H1.2-1.5m/4-5ft, W1.2-1.5m/4-5ft. F5-6. Z7-9.

CISTUS

A group of evergreens from the Mediterranean regions, splashy in flower and needing sun and good drainage for longevity. Many are tender, but provide bright, colourful single rose-type flowers in summer. These are mostly white, pink or purple, often with contrasting patches on the inside of the papery petals, and yellow stamens. Grey or green leaves. Sometimes short-lived, not breaking easily from old wood. Many species and varieties available, including two closely related genera, *Halimium* and *Halimiocistus*. Plant

Ceanothus 'Blue Mound'

Choisya 'Aztec Pearl'

Clematis 'Jackmanii Superba'

in late spring or early summer. F6-7. Z7-9. ✿ ■

CLEMATIS

Indispensable climbers for spring and summer colour for use on pergolas, walls, fences, up into trees, over shrubs or as container plants. Best if roots are shaded, and planted with well rotted compost. ✿ ★

C. alpina. Perfect for walls and fences, masses of pendent flowers in early summer, followed by silky seedheads. Little or no pruning needed. Named forms include 'Columbine', pale blue, 'Pamela Jackman', mid-blue, 'Ruby', purple-pink, 'White Moth', double white. All H2.4m/8ft, W1.8-2.4m/6-8ft. F4-5. Z5-9.

C. macropetala. Related, but more vigorous than *C. alpina*. Light green divided leaves, nodding lavender-blue flowers, attractive seedheads. ✿ ★. 'Markham's Pink', rose-pink and 'White Swan', white, widen the choice. All H3m/10ft, W3m/10ft. F5-6. Z5-9.

C. montana. Vigorous species for climbing up walls or trees, flowers white to deep pink, ✿ ★ roots preferring moisture. 'Alexander', fragrant white flowers, yellow stamens; 'Elizabeth', pale pink, heady fragrance; 'Marjorie', creamy-pink, semi-double flowers; 'Tetrarose', bronze foliage, large

rose-pink flowers. No pruning needed except to control size. H10m/33ft, W10m/33ft. F5-6. Z6-9.

C. orientalis. Vigorous scrambler or climber with finely dissected leaves, fragrant yellow pendent flowers for weeks, fluffy seedheads. Larger-flowered selection, 'Bill Mackenzie', is outstanding. Almost identical is the species *C. tangutica*. All if required can be pruned back in early spring, but not necessary for flowering. All H5-6m/16-20ft, W5-6m/16-20ft. F7-9. Z6-9.

C. viticella. Species variable but excellent for scrambling over fences, through shrubs and up trees. Prune in early spring only if required. Abundance of nodding wine-red, dark-veined flowers. 'Alba Luxurians', white, flushed mauve, green markings; 'Etoile Violette', violet with yellow anthers; 'Kermesina', deep red-purple; 'Polish Spirit', velvety purple-violet; 'Purpurea Plena Elegans', nodding double violet flowers. All H3m/10ft, W3m/10ft. F7-9. Z5-9.

Large-flowered hybrids. In general the spread is roughly the same as the height. A great choice exists but ten recommendations follow. All Z4-9. 'Ascotiensis', bright blue, green stamens, H3m/10ft. F7-9. 'Daniel Deronda', free-flowering with large, purple-blue semi-double and single

flowers, good seedheads. H2.4m/8ft. F6. 'Dr. Ruppel', deep rose-pink flowers, darker bar. H2.4m/8ft. F6. 'Duchess of Edinburgh', large double white, scented flowers. H2.4m/8ft. F6-7. 'Jackmanii Superba', rich purple flowers, reliable performer. H3m/10ft. F8. 'Marie Boisselot', excellent large white flowers, long season. H3m/ 10ft. F6-7. 'Mrs Cholmondeley', free-flowering, with lavender-blue flowers, good seedheads. H2.4m/8ft. F6-8. 'Mrs. N. Thompson', blue with red bar, striking. H2.4m/8ft. F6-7. 'Niobe', ruby-red, velvety flowers, long season. H3m/10ft. F6-8. 'Will Goodwin', attractive pale blue flowers, long season. H3m/10ft. F6-8.

CLETHRA

Acid-loving, mostly deciduous shrubs bearing fragrant flowers in late summer. Best in hot summers. ✿ ❋ ☆

C. alnifolia Sweet pepper bush. Erect branches, bottlebrush heads of fragrant white flowers. 'Paniculata' has larger panicles, 'Pink Spire' and 'Rosea' both pink fading to white. All H1.5-1.8m/5-6ft, W90-120cm/3-4ft. F8-9. Z4-9.

COLUTEA ARBORESCENS Bladder senna

Underrated shrub, member of the

Clematis tangutica

pea family, ✿ ❋ ■ Small yellow flowers all summer continue as green bladder-like pods develop.

C. × media 'Copper Beauty'. Bluish-green leaves, copper-orange flowers. Both H1.8-2.4m/6-8ft, W1.8-2.4m/6-8ft. F7-9. Z6-8.

CORNUS Dogwood

Deciduous shrubs attractive for their summer foliage, flowers and winter stems.

C. alba Red-barked dogwood. These plants have year-round appeal. All have white flowers and bluish-white fruits on the second-year wood. 'Aurea' is first-class, with golden leaves all summer, good red twigs in

Cornus alba 'Aurea'

winter; '**Elegantissima**', grey-green leaves splashed with silvery-white and maroon stems; '**Kesselringii**', dark purple-green shoots, deep green leaves, purple-black winter stems; '**Sibirica Variegata**', small, dark green leaves, cream margins, deep red stems. '**Spaethii**', golden variegated leaves. Prune all for best stem colour in early spring. H1.5-2.4m/5-8ft, W1.5-2.4m/5-8ft (without pruning). F5-6. Z3-9.

C. alternifolia '**Argentea**'. A choice shrub or small tree. Layered purplish, twiggy branches covered in small, white-variegated, light green leaves. Needs shelter. H1.5-2.4m/5-8ft, W1.5-2.4m/5-8ft. F5-6. Z5-8. ✿ ◪

C. florida Flowering dogwood. Slow-growing shrubs and small trees. Seldom performs as well in Europe as in its native North America where flowers or bracts of white, pink and red make a spectacular show in late spring or early summer. '**Rainbow**' has bright golden-yellow and green variegated leaves, which have longer appeal. H1.8-2.4m/6-8ft, W1.8-2.4m/6-8ft. F5. Z5-9. ✿ ✿ ⊙

C. mas '**Variegata**' Cornelian cherry. This selection is an excellent, though little-known, slow-growing shrub with striking white and green summer foliage. Bare stems covered with tiny yellow flowers in early spring, red fruits in autumn. H1.5-1.8m/5-6ft, W1.2-1.5m/4-5ft. F2. Z6-9. ✿ ✿ ☆

C. stolonifera (syn. *C. sericea*). Closely related to *C. alba*, with similar habit and requirements. Two good selections offer colourful summer foliage: '**Kelsey Gold**', a sport on the green-leaved '**Kelsey's Dwarf**', has bright yellow leaves, dwarf habit. H45-60cm/18-24in, W60-90cm/2-3ft. Z3-8. '**White Gold**' has yellow winter stems, green and golden-yellow leaves which turn

Cytisus battandieri

creamy-white. H1.5-1.8m/5-6ft, W1.5m/5ft. F5-6. Z3-8.

CORYLUS Hazel

Large deciduous shrubs or small trees, easy to grow in most soils. Two or three are worth growing for their striking colourful foliage.

C. avellana '**Aurea**'. Dense bush with large round or oval leaves, bright yellow throughout the summer. Long yellow male catkins on older plants in late winter. H3-4.5m/10-15ft, W3-4.5m/10-15ft. F2-3. Z5-9.

C. maxima '**Purpurea**'. Bold, deep purple leaves on vigorous, erectly branching bush; colour fades to green in hot climates. Purplish catkins. H3-4.5m/10-15ft, W3-4.5m/10-15ft, F2-3. Z5-8. '**Te Terra Red**' is a more dwarf form with smaller reddish-purple leaves. H1.5-1.8m/5-6ft, W1.2-1.5m/4-5ft. Z5-8. ✿

COTINUS Smoke bush, Venetian sumach

Several selections of these deciduous shrubs are outstanding for summer foliage as well as for fluffy, plumed, beige-pink panicles which turn smokey-grey in late summer. Prune lightly in late spring; severe pruning will lose the season's flowers. ✿ ☆ ■

Cotinus 'Grace'

C. coggygria. '**Foliis Purpureis**', '**Notcutt's Variety**' and '**Royal Purple**' are all purple-leaved selections providing summer-long colour, though the purple effect diminishes in hot summers. Reddish-purple and crimson autumn tints. All H2.4-3m/8-10ft, W2.4-3m/8-10ft. F7-8. Z5-9.

C. '**Grace**'. Strong-growing hybrid with large purple-red leaves, good autumn colour, imposing pinkish inflorescences. H3-5m/10-16ft, W3m/10ft. F7-8. Z5-9.

COTONEASTER

Large group of deciduous and evergreen shrubs and small trees. While attractive in summer for their small white flowers, most are grown for their late summer and autumn displays of fruits varying from crimson to scarlet-orange and yellow, even to pink. Some have attractive silver-backed leaves. One of the best is *C. horizontalis* '**Variegata**' which seldom fruits, but makes up for it with small green cream-edged leaves with pink tinges in autumn. Good for a wall or a bank. H60-75cm/24-30in, W1.2-1.5m/4-5ft. F6-7. Z5-8.

CYTISUS Broom

Easily grown, sun-loving members of

the pea family with narrow, evergreen stems and leaves. Most species are yellow-flowered, in late spring and early summer, but there is a wide range of colours in selected cultivars. Prune with a sharp knife if necessary immediately after flowering, but not into old wood. ✿ ■

C. ardoinii. Showy dwarf, smothered in creamy-white flowers. H30cm/12in, W60-90cm/2-3ft. F5-6. Z6-8.

C. battandieri. Morocco Broom is quite distinct, with silvery-grey oval leaves and bottlebrush heads of golden-yellow, pineapple-scented flowers. Train against a wall or as a freestanding shrub. Trim regularly after flowering. Needs a warm, sheltered position. H3-5m/10-16ft, W2.4-3m/8-10ft. F7. Z8-9.

C. praecox Warminster broom. Compact, free-flowering species, with creamy-yellow flowers. '**Albus**', taller, white; '**Frisia**', striking, with white-pink, lilac, yellow and brown flowers; '**Hollandia**', showy cream and cerise blooms. All H1.2-1.8m/4-6ft, W1.2-1.5m/4-5ft. F4-5. Z6-9.

C. scoparius Common broom. Though it looks evergreen from the appearance of its green stems, this yellow-flowered species is deciduous.

Daphne burkwoodii 'Somerset Gold Edge'

Deutzia x *hybrida* 'Strawberry Fields'

Many selections include: 'Andreanus', large yellow and brown pea flowers; '**Burkwoodii**', red, brown and yellow; '**Goldfinch**', crimson, pink and yellow; '**Killiney Red**', brightest red; '**Windlesham Ruby**', popular carmine-red. All H1.5-1.8m/5-6ft, W1.2-1.5m/4-5ft. F6. Z7-9.

Hybrids. Some of the best for the smaller garden include: '**Compact Crimson**', broadly spreading, with rich crimson flowers, H90-120cm/3-4ft, W90-120cm/3-4ft. F5-6. Z7-9; '**Dukaat**', bushy, upright habit, bicolor gold and creamy-white, H45-60cm/18-24in, W30-45cm/12-18in. F5-6. Z7-9; '**Lena**', spectacular crimson and yellow, contrasting with dark green foliage, H90-120cm/3-4ft, W60-90cm/2-3ft. F5-6. Z7-9.

DAPHNE

Choice fragrant shrubs, deciduous and evergreen. Contains both dwarf, prostrate and taller growing shrubs, some flowering in late winter/early spring, most in late spring/early summer. Berries are poisonous. Most prefer good drainage but not extremes of wet or dry. Of many choice species the easiest are: *D.* x *burkwoodii* 'Carol Mackie', 'Somerset Variegated', '**Somerset Gold Edge**' and '**Astrid**', all with

variegated leaves which follow the fragrant white, suffused pink, flowers. All H90-120cm/3-4ft, W90-120cm/3-4ft. F5-6. Z5-9.

☼ ◪ ◼ ◾

DEUTZIA

Deciduous shrubs, showy in flower but mostly dull for the rest of the summer. Easy to grow. Prune immediately after flowering if necessary, thin out old stems in winter. ☼ ☀ ☆ ◼

D. crenata '**Nikko**'. Pleasing dwarf shrub, with clusters of white flowers. H45-60cm/18-24in, W60-90cm/2-3ft. F5-6. Z5-8.

D. x *elegantissima* '**Rosealind**' (syn. *D.* x *hybrida* 'Rosea Plena'). Excellent broadly spreading shrub, with arching branches laden with carmine-red and pink scented flowers. H90-120cm/3-4ft, W1.2-1.5m/4-5ft. F6-7. Z6-8.

D. x *hybrida*. '**Magicien**', vigorous, erect shrub with purple-red buds opening to carmine-pink flowers with white-edged petals. '**Mont Rose**', clear pink, starry flowers; '**Pink Pompon**', with arching branches, rounded clusters of double pink flowers, fading to white. '**Strawberry Fields**', large flowers, with crimson outside petals, white, suffused pink, inside. All H1.8-

2.4m/6-8ft, W1.5-1.8m/5-6ft. F6-7. Z6-9.

D. scabra. Vigorous upright species with erect white flower clusters on narrow spikes, peeling bark on old plants. '**Candidissima**', double white, '**Pride of Rochester**', rosy-pink outer petals, white inside. All H1.8-2.4m/6-8ft, W1.5-1.8m/5-6ft. F6-7. Z5-8.

ERICA – see HEATHS AND HEATHERS

ESCALLONIA

Colourful shrubs originating from South America. Evergreen in warmer coastal or mild localities, deciduous in colder areas. Excellent near coasts. Glossy green leaves, usually masses of small tubular flowers lasting for weeks from early summer. Many selections, most flowering on previous year's wood. Most F6-8. All Z8-9. ☼ ☀ ☆

E. '**Apple Blossom**'. Free-flowering,

Escallonia 'Apple Blossom'

Exochorda macrantha 'The Bride'

with glossy leaves, mostly single pink, white-eyed flowers. H1.5-1.8m/5-6ft, W1.2-1.5m/4-5ft. F7-9. **'Donard Brilliance'**, large-leaved, vigorous shrub with profuse, rich crimson flowers. H1.5-1.8m/5-6ft, W1.2-1.5m/4-5ft. **'Donard Radiance'**, bushy habit, rosy-pink flowers. H1.2-1.5m/4-5ft, W1.5-1.8m/5-6ft. **'Gwendolyn Anley'**, hardier variety with small leaves, masses of small, shell-pink flowers and a spreading habit. H60-90cm/2-3ft, W60-90cm/2-3ft. *E. laevis.* **'Gold Brian'**, large, golden

Fremontodendron californicum

leaves draw the eye, making a dramatic background to rosy-red flowers. H60-75cm/2ft 6in, W60-90cm/2-3ft. **'Red Elf'**, a compact, upright shrub with glossy green leaves and crimson flowers. H90-120cm/3-4ft, W90-120cm/3-4ft. F6-9.

EUONYMUS
Some evergreen selections of these hardy shrubs, particularly those with variegated leaves, offer year-round colour. Very adaptable as to soils, including chalk. Some are grown as ground cover and climbers. ✿ ❈ ❈☆ *E. fortunei.* Many selections and species have green foliage, but the year-round colour of **'Emerald Gaiety'** cannot be bettered, with green and white margined leaves, and of **'Emerald 'n Gold'**, with green and gold leaves, pinkish-tinged in winter, and bright gold new shoots. Both will climb into other plants or up trees and walls, given a little encouragement. Prune in late spring if required. H60-75cm/2ft-2ft 6in, W90-120cm/3-4ft. Z5-9.

EXOCHORDA Pearlbush
Deciduous shrubs, striking in flower. *E. macrantha.* **The Bride'** is the outstanding selection, a broad, spreading pendulous bush covered in pure white flowers in late spring/early summer. H1.2-1.5m/4-5ft, W1.5-1.8m/5-6ft. F5. Z5-8. ✿ ❈ ☆

FOTHERGILLA
Early-flowering, acid-loving shrubs worth including for their autumn colour too. Honey-scented bottlebrush flowers are borne on bare branches in late spring and early summer. *F. gardenii* (syn. *F. alnifolia*). Dwarf, twiggy stems and small, fragrant, white bottlebrush flowers. Dull green, oval summer leaves turn yellow, orange and fiery red in

autumn. H45-60cm/18-24in, W45-60cm/18-24in. F5. Z5-9. *F. major* (syn. *F. monticola*). Erect, picturesque shrub, variable in habit, which can reach 3m/10ft. Congested branches, small, white scented, cylindrical flowers. Most have yellow, orange and crimson autumn colour, sometimes on the same leaf. H90-120cm/3-4ft, W75-90cm/30-36in. F5. Z5-9.

FREMONTODENDRON CALIFORNICUM
Often listed as a climber, this spectacular Californian evergreen or semi-evergreen shrub needs a sunny south or west wall, sheltered from cold winds. Vigorous growth, with light brown, woolly branches and shiny green, lobed leaves, their undersides covered in hairs. Large, golden-yellow, saucer-shaped flowers continue for months. Tie or train against a wall and prune regularly to shorten outward growth. Selections to look for are **'California Glory'** and **'Pacific Sunset'**. H3-5m/10-16ft, W2.1-3m/7-10ft. F6-9. Z8-10. ✿ ■

FUCHSIA
Of this vast group of shrubs, small trees and climbers, only "hardy fuchsias" are listed below. The long-flowering shrubs, some with colourful gold or variegated leaves, all give a display of pendulous flowers for several months and are ideal for containers as well as in the garden. Deciduous, except in mild localities, they make excellent seaside plants. Cut old wood to the ground in spring. All Z8-10. ✿ ◪ ■ *F. magellanica.* Dwarfer selections, most having arching stems and long, narrow flowers, with scarlet sepals and purple petals. **'Aurea'**, bushy and spreading, has deep yellow leaves and red flowers. H90-120cm/3-4ft, W90-120cm/3-4ft. F6-10. **'Pumila'**, dainty dwarf, with crimson and purple flowers.

Genista pilosa 'Lemon Spreader'

H30cm/1ft, W30cm/1ft. F6-10. **'Versicolor'**, grey-green leaves, flushed pink, and creamy-white, purple and red flowers. H90-120cm/3-4ft, W90-120cm/3-4ft. F6-10.

Hybrids. There are innumerable hardy hybrids. Recommendations include: **'Alice Hoffman'**, bushy, purple-tinged foliage, white petals, rosy-red calyx. H90-120cm/3-4ft, W90-120cm/3-4ft. F6-10. **'Chillerton Beauty'**, pale pink and purple. H1.2-1.5m/4-5ft, W90-120cm/3-4ft. F6-10. **'Dollar Princess'**, free-flowering, double purple and cerise. H75-90cm/30-36in, W60-75cm/24-30in. F5-10. **'Genii'**, golden-yellow leaves in sun, small red and purple flowers. H90-120cm/3-4ft, W90-120cm/3-4ft. F6-10. **'Madame Cornelissen'**, bushy, semi-double white and scarlet. H1.2-1.5m/4-5ft, W1.2-1.5m/4-5ft. F6-10. **'Mrs. Popple'**, one of the hardiest, masses of crimson and violet blooms. H1.2-1.5m/4-5ft, W1.2-1.5m/4-5ft. F6-10. **'Tom Thumb'**, a true dwarf, bushy, with crimson and purple flowers. H30-45cm/12-18in, W30-45cm/12-18in. F6-10.

Calluna vulgaris 'Dark Beauty'

Daboecia cantabrica

GENISTA Broom

Sharing the same common name as *Cytisus*, to which they are closely related. All have yellow blooms and can be very showy. Tolerate a wide range of soils, preferring ☼ ■
G. aetnensis Mount Etna broom. Eventually a large shrub or small tree, with wispy, pendulous branches. A good background shrub with golden-yellow flowers for many weeks in summer. Prune, only if necessary, after flowering but not into old wood. H3m/10ft, W3m/10ft. F7-8. Z9-10.
G. lydia. Dense, twiggy bush with slender green stems swathed in small, bright yellow flowers in early summer. H45-60cm/18-24in, W90-120cm/3-4ft. F6. Z7-9.
G. pilosa. Prostrate, deciduous bush which looks evergreen. Best selections are '**Lemon Spreader**' and the more compact and ground-hugging '**Vancouver Gold**', covered in sheets of golden-yellow flowers in early summer. Excellent on banks or over walls. Both H15-30cm/6-12in, W1.2-1.5m/4-5ft. F6. Z6-8.

HALIMIOCISTUS and HALIMIUM – see CISTUS

HEATHS and HEATHERS

I have put both these groups of shrubs together for easy reference and because they associate so well together. Where they can be grown successfully they offer year-round colour from both flower and foliage. Acid soil is required for the majority of summer-flowering types, but there are many lime-tolerant winter-flowering ones that also have colourful foliage in summer. Heaths (*Erica*) and heathers (*Calluna vulgaris*) grow well in cooler temperate or alpine regions, but resent cold, drying winter winds as well as high heat and humidity. Best planted in groups, but a wide range can offer flower almost every month of the year. They can be used on their own, in foreground groups to shrubs or conifers, or with ornamental grasses. Well over 500 cultivars are currently in cultivation, and wider selections can be obtained from specialists. Those recommended below are primarily for summer colour. As a guide to planting densities, the approximate width or spread of heathers after only 3-4 years' growth is given, after which time the plants will have carpeted together. All do best on well-drained but moisture-retentive soil, responding well to a surface mulch of composted bark.

CALLUNA Common heather, ling
C. vulgaris. Hundreds of cultivars of this heathland plant offer an amazing range of colours, shapes and sizes. Prune all except the dwarfest and very prostrate types in early to mid-spring, before growth really begins. All flowers are single unless otherwise stated. All Z5-7. ☼ ⊖
'**Allegro**', a profusion of deep red flowers, with dark green foliage. H45-60cm/18-24in, W45cm/18in. F8-10. '**Anne Marie**', bushy habit, dark green foliage; flowers open bright pink, gradually deepening to brilliant carmine-rose. H23-30cm/9-12in, W45cm/18in. F8-11. '**Beoley Gold**', one of the best yellow-foliaged cultivars, with bushy year-round foliage, contrasting with white flowers. H30-45cm/12-18in, W45cm/18in. F8-9. '**Boskoop**', superb, dense, feathery foliage, golden-orange in summer, bronze-red in winter; light mauve-purple flowers. H30-45cm/12-18in, W45cm/18in. F8-9. '**Dark Beauty**', compact, bushy plant with dark green foliage, bright crimson flowers over a long period in autumn. H30cm/12in, W30-45cm/12-18in. F8-10. '**H.E. Beale**', vigorous, with strong, erect spikes of soft, double silver-pink flowers lasting for weeks. H30-45cm/12-18in, W50cm/20in. F9-11. '**Robert Chapman**', foliage changes from gold to yellow, orange to bronze and red; lower winter temperatures enhance the colour intensity; purple flowers. H30-45cm/12-18in, W45cm/18in. F8-9. '**Sir John Charrington**', arguably the best foliage cultivar, compact and bushy, with golden-yellow summer foliage, orange with bright red and crimson tips in winter; excellent in bloom, with short spikes of crimson flowers. H30-45cm/12-18in, W40cm/16in. F8-9.

DABOECIA Irish bell heather
Summer-flowering, needs acid soil. ☼ ❋ ◿ ⊖
D. cantabrica. Long flowering period, glossy green leaves and bell-shaped flowers. Resent drought almost as much as severe frost, but where they can be grown offer a contrast to other heathers. Many cultivars available from specialists; stronger-growing ones can get straggly with age and should be pruned each year, either lightly once the flowers have finished in late autumn, then more severely in spring, or all in spring. All Z7-9.
'**Atropurpurea**', one of the hardiest and most reliable, with bronze-green leaves, rich purple flowers. H60cm/2ft, W50cm/20in. F6-10. '**Snowdrift**', bright green foliage, masses of white bell flowers; '**Alba**' is similar. Both H45cm/18in, W45cm/18in. F6-10.
D. × *scotica* '**William Buchanan**'. One of several dwarf hybrids between *D. azorica* and *D. cantabrica*. Glossy green leaves, masses of crimson flowers. One of

Erica cinerea 'Rock Pool'

the hardiest cultivars. H30cm/1ft, W30cm/1ft. F5-10. Z7.

ERICA Heath

E. carnea (syn. *E. herbacea*). Winter heaths are among the most valuable garden plants. Most cultivars are low-growing with a bushy or spreading habit, and flower from late autumn to late spring, some lasting several months. Very few need pruning, except to prevent spreading into other plants or to tidy them occasionally. Those listed below have colourful summer foliage. All Z5-8. Acid soil, some alkaline soil. **'Ann Sparkes'** slowly makes a compact bush of deep orange-yellow foliage, tipped bronze-red; deep carmine-red flowers. H15cm/6in, W25cm/10in. F2-4. **'Foxhollow'**, low-growing, spreading habit, brilliant golden-yellow foliage in late spring and summer, deep gold in winter, often flecked with red; in low-lying areas, new growth can be caught by late spring frost; pale pink flowers, rarely borne. H15-25cm/6-10in, W45cm/18in. F2-4. **'Vivellii'** (syn. 'Urville'), dark, bronze-green attractive foliage, ideal against gold, silver or blue evergreen plants; deep carmine-red flowers. H10cm/4in, W35cm/14in. F2-3. **'Westwood**

Yellow', similar to 'Foxhollow' but more compact, flowering more freely. H15cm/6in, W40cm/16in. F2-4.

E. cinerea Bell heather. Grows on cliffs by the sea and on moorlands, surviving with less moisture than most species. Wide range of cultivars, some with golden foliage, others with startling flowers and a long flowering period. Prune in spring, just as new growth begins. ☼ ⊖. All Z7-9. **'Alba Minor'**, compact, with bright green foliage and short spikes of white bell flowers. H15cm/6in, W25cm/10in. F6-10. **'Atrosanguinea Smith's Variety'**, excellent, free-flowering, with dark green leaves, intense scarlet blooms. H15-20cm/6-8in, W25cm/10in. F6-9. **'C.D. Eason'**, reliable old cultivar, with darker green foliage glowing red-pink. H23-30cm/9-12in, W30cm/1ft. F7-9. **'C.G. Best'**, tall, with erect, clear salmon-pink flower spikes. H30cm/1ft, W40cm/16in. F7-8. **'Eden Valley'**, compact and bushy, with soft lavender and white bicolored flowers. H15-20cm/6-8in, W25cm/10in. F7-10. **'Foxhollow Mahogany'**, deep green foliage, rich mahogany-red flowers. H25-30cm/10-12in, W35-40cm/14-16in. F7-9. **'Hookstone White'**, vigorous, long-lived, slightly loose in habit, with a profusion of white flowers.**'Hookstone Lavender'**, similar, with pale lavender flowers. Both H30-45cm/12-18in, W40cm/16in. F7-10. **'My Love'**, striking luminous blue-mauve flowers, dark foliage. H23-30cm/9-12in, W30cm/1ft. F6-9. **'Pink Ice'**, outstanding, compact mound, masses of bright pink flowers. H23-30cm/9-12in, W23-30cm/9-12in. F6-9. **'Purple Beauty'**, reliable and showy, spreading, with dark green leaves, large, bright purple flowers. H30cm/1ft, W40cm/16in. F6-10. **'Rock Pool'**, low spreading habit,

Erica erigena 'Irish Dusk'

deep golden-yellow in summer, copper-bronze in winter, occasional purple-red flowers. H15cm/6in, W25cm/10in. F6-9. **'Velvet Night'**, one of the darkest-flowered bell heathers, with dark green foliage, deep maroon-purple flowers. H30cm/1ft, W30cm/1ft. F6-9. **'Windlebrooke'**, excellent foliage plant, with yellow foliage in summer, orange-yellow in winter, purple flowers. H25-30cm/10-12in, W30cm/1ft. F7-9.

E. × darleyensis. Easily grown, long-flowering hybrids which flower from late autumn to late spring; lime-tolerant. Though new growth on many cultivars is quite colourful, only one, **'J.H. Brummage'**, an attractive and reliable cultivar, has yellow year-round foliage. **'J.W. Porter'** has cream and red shoots. All need full sun for best flowering. Prune if necessary to tidy plants just as flowering finishes in spring and new growth begins. Most H30-45cm/12-18in, W45-60cm/18-24in. F11-4. Z7-8.

E. erigena. The Irish heath is lime-tolerant, flowering in late spring and early summer, but is less hardy than other winter-flowering heaths. Both the variable species and the many selected cultivars are honey-scented.

All Z8. **'Golden Lady'**, dense bush of bright yellow foliage, with white flowers; can scorch, so best in slight shade. H45-60cm/18-24in, W35cm/14in. F4-5. **'Irish Dusk'**, compact and bushy, erect habit, deep green foliage, intense salmon-pink flowers. H45-60cm/18-24in, W40cm/16in. F12-5. **'W.T. Rackliff'**, dense, rounded, deep green bush, white flowers. H60-75cm/24-30in, W40cm/16in. F3-5.

E. tetralix Cross-leaved heath. Acid loving, best where some moisture exists. Flowers held in terminal clusters on erect shoots. Prune in spring, by cutting back old flowerheads and a third of the stem. All Z6-8. **'Alba Mollis'**, silver-grey, downy foliage and white flowers. H20-25cm/8-10in, W35cm/14in. F6-9. **'Con Underwood'**, grey-green hummocks, large crimson flowers. H20-25cm/8-10in, W30cm/1ft. F6-10. **'Pink Star'**, soft pink, star-like flowers on compact, silver-grey bushes. H20-25cm/8-10in, W25cm/10in. F6-9.

E. vagans Cornish heath. Valuable group for year-round interest. Will tolerate some lime; grow in full sun or light shade. Old flower spikes attractive through the winter; prune away in mid-spring. All Z7-8. **'Lyonesse'**, light green leaves, white flowers with golden anthers. H30-45cm/12-18in, W45cm/18in. F8-10. **'Mrs. D.F. Maxwell'**, neat habit, with attractive spikes of deep cerise flowers. H45-60cm/18-24in, W45-60cm/18-24in. F8-10. **'Valerie Proudley'**, bright yellow leaves, few white flowers; can scorch in exposed positions, try in light shade. H15-20cm/6-8in, W35cm/14in. F8-9.

TREE HEATHERS

Taller species which mostly flower in late spring or early summer. Some, like *E. australis*, *E. lusitanica* and *E. × veitchii*, are not completely hardy

Erica arborea 'Alpina'

but all are reasonably lime-tolerant. *E. arborea* is best represented by the selection **'Alpina'** which makes a tall evergreen shrub with green foliage and masses of fragrant white flowers in late spring. H1.5-2.4m/5-8ft, W60-75cm/24-30in. F4-5. **'Albert's Gold'** is an excellent, quite hardy selection with bright yellow year-round foliage and white flowers on older plants. H60-75cm/24-30in, W45-60cm/18-24in. F3-5.

HEBE

A wide range of evergreen shrubs originating from the southern hemisphere. The more dwarf, smaller-leaved varieties tend to be hardier than taller, large-leaved types. Tolerant of seaside conditions and cool, temperate climates but not extremes of cold, heat or humidity. Prune as required to keep shape or cut away old or dead wood; plants will mostly break from the base. ✿ ✺ ☆

H. albicans. Attractive bush with glaucous, oblong leaves, white flowers. H45cm/18in, W60cm/2ft. F6-8. Z8-11.

H. 'Autumn Glory'. Purple-tinged foliage, short spikes of bluish-purple flowers. H60cm/2ft, W90cm/3ft. F8-9. Z8-11.

H. cupressoides. 'Boughton Dome' is the best form of this species with grey-green, scale-like foliage making a compact bush, bright green in summer; seldom flowers. H45-60cm/18-24in, W45-60cm/18-24in. Z8-10.
H. Emerald Green' (syn. 'Emerald Gem'). Few richer greens exist than this dense compact bush; white flowers; ideal for a container. H30cm/1ft, W45cm/18in. F6-8. Z8-10.
H. × *franciscana.* 'Blue Gem' is small and dome-shaped, with green leaves, bright blue flowers. Hardier than the brighter-foliaged 'Variegata', whose leaves are margined creamy-white. H1.2m/4ft, W1.2m/4ft. F6-8. Z8-10.
H. 'Glaucophylla Variegata', slender shoots, small grey-green leaves, prettily edged with creamy-white, white flowers. H60-75cm/24-30in, W60cm/2ft. F7-8. Z8-10.
H. 'Great Orme'. Lance-shaped leaves, tapering racemes of deep pink flowers. H90cm/3ft, W90cm/3ft. F6-9. Z8-10.
H. 'Margret', hardy dwarf, with deep green leaves, bright blue flowers fading to white. H30cm/1ft, W30-45cm/18-24in. F6-9. Z8-10.
H. 'Midsummer Beauty'. Large leaves, red beneath, and profuse lavender-purple flowers. H1.2m/4ft, W1.5m/5ft. F7-10. Z8-10.
H. pinguifolia. 'Pagei', compact, glaucous-leaved cultivar, with small, round leaves, white flowers. H15cm/6in, W30-45cm/12-18in. F6-7. Z8-10. 'Red Edge', good year-round foliage, grey green, red-tipped through winter to late spring; lilac flowers fade to white. H45cm/18in, W45cm/18in. F6-8. Z8-11. 'Rosie', free-flowering selection, rosy-pink flowers fading to white. H30-45cm/12-18in, W60cm/2ft. F6-8. Z8-10.

HEDERA Ivy

Adaptable evergreen shrubs, grown as ground cover or climbers, many

Hibiscus syriacus 'Pink Giant'

with variegated leaves. Ideal for hanging baskets and containers, especially in autumn and winter when less colour is available. For larger-leaved types, *H. colchica* 'Dentata Variegata' and *H. c.* 'Sulphur Heart' (syn. 'Paddy's Pride'), both selections of the Persian ivy, would be good choices, the former with broad green leaves margined creamy-yellow, the latter with an irregular golden splash in the centre of the leaf. Both H30cm/1ft, W1.8-3m/6-10ft. Z6-9.
H. helix Common ivy. There are innumerable selections of this species with variegated foliage, and other attractive green-leaved forms with deeply cut or lobed leaves. Excellent as ground cover in sun or shade, or grown as climbers. Green forms mostly Z4-9, variegated forms Z6-9.

HIBISCUS Mallow

H. syriacus Tree hollyhock. From eastern Asia, these medium-sized deciduous shrubs are showy in flower during late summer in hot weather, with a succession of exotic trumpet-shaped blooms. Seldom need pruning. ✿ ☆ ■ 'Admiral Dewey', double white; 'Bluebird' (syn. 'Oiseau Bleu'), deep violet-

blue, with darker centres; 'Diane', single white; 'Duc de Brabant', reddish-purple, double; 'Hamabo', white or pink flushed white, crimson eye, single; 'Pink Giant', bright rose-pink, dark centre, single; 'Red Heart', white, red-centred, single; 'Russian Violet', vigorous leafy habit, violet, single; 'Woodbridge', pink, red-centred, single. All H1.5-1.8m/5-6ft, W1.2-1.5m/4-5ft. F7-10. Z6-9.

HUMULUS

H. lupulus 'Aureus'. The golden hop is a hardy herbaceous climber, useful for climbing up trees or over a roof, wall or fence – wherever its clinging tendrils can reach. Coarse, bright yellow leaves in full sun, flowers insignificant; attractive autumn hops can be used for making beer. Cut away old foliage after winter dieback. H5-6m/16-20ft, W5-6m/16-20ft. F7-8. Z6-9.

HYDRANGEA

Indispensable deciduous shrubs for summer flowers – unless you happen to live in a frost pocket like Foggy Bottom! Frosts can damage some flowering shoots enough to prevent them flowering the same year, but other forms which flower on the

Hydrangea arborescens 'Annabelle'

Hydrangea paniculata 'Pink Diamond'

same year's growth will escape. Selections range from dwarf to large, some with spectacular flowerheads; the "mopheads", with large, rounded heads, and the lacecaps come in a considerable range of colours. ☼ ☀ ◪ ⊖

H. arborescens. Easy in full sun or light shade, any soil, flowering on same year's growth; prune by half or to the ground in early spring. **'Grandiflora'**, large round heads of creamy-white, sterile flowers, attractive in winter. H1.2-1.5m/4-5ft, W1.5-1.8m/5-6ft. F7-9. Z3-9. **'Annabelle'** has even larger heads, sometimes as much as 30cm/1ft across, but on shorter stems; especially striking when early green florets turn to brilliant white. H90-120cm/3-4ft, W1.2-1.5m/4-5ft. F7-9. Z3-9.

H. aspera. The species is variable but **'Villosa'** is a good selection. Shade-loving, slow-growing, erect woody shrub, sometimes tender when young. Soft, dark green felted leaves, flat flowerheads of tiny bluish-purple flowers with lilac florets; attractive bark on older plants. ◪. Prune to tidy or remove dieback. H1.5-1.8m/5-6ft, W1.5-1.8m/5-6ft. F8-9. Z7-9.

H. macrophylla. This Japanese species includes the mopheads and lacecaps, both dense bushes with erect branches, often weighed down by flowers. ☼ ☀ ★. Buds can be damaged by winter or spring frost; mature plants are more resistant but an autumn mulch of composted bark, leafmould or rotted manure helps. Prune in spring, removing only the previous year's dead flowerheads and, on older plants, a few woody stems from the base if congested. Both mopheads and lacecaps make good container plants. Some *H. macrophylla* types can change colour; very acid soils produce real blue, neutral or alkaline soils pink or red. To achieve blue flowers on neutral or alkaline soils, add aluminium sulphate.

Lacecaps have small flowers surrounded by large, showy, flat ray florets. Most H1.2-1.5m/4-5ft, W1.2-1.5m/4-5ft. F6-9. Z6-9. **'Blue Wave'** needs shade; blue fertile flowers, pink ray florets on alkaline soils, blue on acid soils. **'Geoffrey Chadbund'**, deep crimson, purple on acid soils. **'Lanarth White'** and **'Mariesii'**, dwarf (H90cm/3ft), the former pink or blue with white ray florets; the latter, rose-pink ray florets, blue on acid soils. **'Tricolor'** has flowers like **'Mariesii'**, leaves splashed green, grey and pale yellow. **'White Wave'** (syn. 'Mariesii Alba'), large heads, pink on limey soils, blue on acid soils, with white ray florets.

Mopheads or **Hortensias** have round heads of sterile florets in various colours, some changing according to soil. Dried flowerheads attractive when cut. Most H1.2-1.5m/4-5ft, W1.2-1.5/4.5ft. F6-9. Z7-9. ☼ ☀ **'Altonia'**, rose-pink, deep blue on acid soils. **'Ami Pasquier'**, dwarf, crimson turning purple. **'Europe'**, vigorous, deep pink, changing to mid-blue. **'Generale Vicomtesse de Vibraye'**, pink, clear blue on acid soil; needs shade. **'Madame Emile Mouillere'**, slightly tender, serrated white florets with a pink or blue central spot according to soil. **'Masja'** has deep crimson heads. For containers or sheltered gardens, **'Pia'**, pink, and **'Tovelit'**, bright pink (both H30-45cm/12-18in).

H. paniculata. Easily grown shrubs flowering on new season's growth. White flowers rounded or pyramidal, some quickly fading to pink. ☼ ☀ ◪ Prune in spring if required to restrict growth or initiate stronger flowering shoots, by as much as half the shrub's height. **'Grandiflora'**, sometimes pruned to a standard with few flowers to achieve grotesquely huge pyramidal flowers. **'Kyushu'**, more compact, has glossy leaves and profuse long panicles of creamy-white florets. **'Pink Diamond'**, large, creamy-white heads, turning pink, finally red-brown. **'Unique'**, with large, erect heads, turns rosy-pink in autumn. All H2.4-3m/8-10ft, W2.4-3m/8-10ft. F7-10. Z4-8.

H. 'Preziosa' (syn. *H. serrata* 'Preziosa'), one of the best raised; deep green, later bronze, foliage and domed pink flowerheads, turning crimson. ☼ ☀. H75cm/30in, W60-90cm/2.3ft. F6-9. Z6-8.

H. quercifolia Oak leaf hydrangea. Responds best to hot summers. Large, dark green oak-type leaves turn bronze to purple in autumn. Small, erect, long-lasting greeny-white flower panicles flop with age. **'Snowflake'**, double flowered, with a spreading habit. Both require a warm, sheltered position for best flowering. H90-150cm/3-5ft, W1.2-1.5m/4-5ft. F6-8. Z5-9. **'Snow Queen'**, erect habit, large leaves, free-flowering in hotter climates. Large panicles of white florets, later tinged pink; bronze-purple leaves in autumn. A good container plant. H1.2-1.5m/4-5ft, W1.2-1.5m/4-5ft. F6-8. Z5-9.

H. serrata. Variable species rarely exceeding 90cm/3ft high; allied to *H. macrophylla* and needing similar conditions. '**Bluebird**', dense, erect habit, deep blue flowers, large ray florets, crimson-purple on alkaline soils, deep blue on acid ones. '**Blue Deckle**', '**Blue Diadem**', both dwarf forms, pink on alkaline soils, blue on acid ones. All H60-90cm/2-3ft, W60-90cm/2-3ft. F6-9. Z6-8.

HYPERICUM

A family containing woody shrubs and semi-woody alpines; most deciduous but some evergreen in mild winters, all with yellow flowers. Long flowering period, some with attractive red or black fruits. Prune back by a third of the previous season's growth in spring, occasionally on older plants more severely, to rejuvenate. Some are prone to rust which can be difficult to eradicate. ☼ ❀

H. androsaemum Tutsan hypericum. Adaptable species used for ground cover. Dark green leaves, small yellow flowers with prominent stamens; red-brown fruits turn black in autumn. '**Gladys Brabazon**', attractive selection with new leaves splashed with cream-yellow flowers, bright red fruits; seeds quite freely. '**Hidcote**', dense, free-flowering bush with profusion of large, saucer-shaped yellow flowers; non-fruiting. H1.2-1.5m/4-5ft, W1.5-1.8m/5-6ft. F7-10. Z6-9.

H. prolificum. Showy species, densely branched, with slender upright stems and a profuse show of small, tufted, bright yellow flowers; adaptable and very hardy. H60-75cm/2ft-2ft 6in, W60-90cm/2-3ft. F7-9. Z5-8.

Indigofera heterantha

INDIGOFERA

Includes some valuable summer- and autumn-flowering plants, with pinnate leaves and racemes of pink, white or purple long-lasting flowers. Except in mild climates, most die back to the ground in winter, the new shoots emerging in late spring or early summer. Prune semi-evergreen shoots back in spring. ☼ ❀ ■

I. decora (syn. I. incarnata). Rare Chinese and Japanese species makes a beautiful dwarf shrub with low, arching stems and large pink flowers. '**Alba**', also impressive, with white flowers. Both H45-60cm/18-24in, W45-60cm/18-24in. F7. Z7-9.

I. heterantha (syn. I. gerardiana). The most popular indigo makes a twiggy, upright bush with small green leaves and purple-pink flowers. H1.8-2.4m/6-8ft, W1.2-1.5m/4-5ft. F7-9. Z7-9.

JASMINUM Jasmine

Popular as wall plants and climbers, many species also make adaptable freestanding or sprawling shrubs, ideal to cover a fence, wall or a stump. Most are deciduous but their

green stems create an evergreen effect. The trumpet-like flowers are sweetly fragrant. Those grown as climbers or wall shrubs require careful tying in and training against firm supports. ☼ ❀ ■

J. officinale. Summer jasmine, with fragrant white flowers. Mostly used as a wall climber where it can reach 10m/33ft in mild areas. '**Aureum**', with gold-splashed leaves, is slower: left to its own devices it will sprawl, but as a wall shrub it can reach 1.8-2.4m/6-8ft, W1.8-2.4m/6-8ft. '**Fiona Sunrise**', a recent introduction with golden-yellow leaves makes quite an impact; will reach a height and spread of 6m/20ft against a wall. Of similar growth rate is '**Grandiflorum**' which has larger flowers than the species. All F7-9. Z8-11.

KALMIA

Spring- and summer-flowering, mainly evergreen shrubs requiring acid soil and similar conditions to rhododendrons.

K. angustifolia. The sheep laurel forms a thicket of small, bright green leaves, grey-green when mature, with dense clusters of deep rose-red flowers. '**Rubra**' is more compact and showy; '**Candida**' has white flowers. All H60-75cm/24-30in. F5-6. Z2-7.

K. latifolia Calico bush. The species grows wild in central and north-eastern U.S.A. but recent hybridizing has produced some spectacular flowers which in summer make up for the shrub's woody, untidy appearance. Named cultivars include '**Bullseye**', with white, purple-banded flowers and reddish foliage; '**Candy**', with white flowers striped pink and red; '**Carousel**', pink in bud opening white with vivid purple-cinnamon banding; '**Olympic Fire**', with deep crimson buds and light pink, white-centred flowers; '**Ostbo Red**', red buds and

Kalmia latifolia 'Ostbo Red'

deep pink blooms; '**Silver Dollar**', with profuse, large white flowers. H1.2-1.5m/4-5ft, W90-120cm/3-4ft. F5-6. Z5-9.

KERRIA JAPONICA

Deciduous shrub with upright, graceful, arching branches, light green serrated leaves and yellow, saucer-shaped spring flowers. Use freestanding, massed or against a wall. The green-leaved forms are suckering. All have distinctive green stems, attractive in winter, but these become congested; prune older branches from the base immediately after flowering. '**Golden Guinea**', similar to the species but with larger, single, golden-yellow flowers. Both H1.5-1.8m/5-6ft, W1.5-1.8m/5-6ft. F3-5. Z5-9. '**Pleniflora**', showy, taller form, with more upright stems and double yellow flowers; needs regular pruning. H1.8-2.4m/6-8ft, W1.8-2.4m/6-8ft. F3-5. Z5-9. '**Variegata**' (syn. '**Picta**') is slower-growing and more spreading, with its green leaves irregularly edged creamy-white and with single yellow flowers. H1.2-1.5m/4-5ft, W1.5-1.8m/5-6ft. F3-5. Z5-9.

Kolkwitzia amabilis

KOLKWITZIA

K. amabilis. The deciduous beauty bush is a hardy, trouble-free, flowering shrub from China. It has densely erect, later arching, branches, light green leaves and freely borne clusters of trumpet-shaped, pale pink flowers with yellow throats. It makes a good specimen or background plant where space permits. Very little pruning needed, but remove some older stems of specimen shrubs to the base, thinning out congested branches, immediately after flowering. '**Pink Cloud**' has deeper pink flowers. Both H1.8-2.4m/6-8ft, W1.8-2.4m/6-8ft. F5-6. Z5-8. ✿ ❋ ☆

LAVANDULA Lavender

Indispensable summer-flowering shrubs. Can be used for groups, edging or low hedges, renowned for its flowers and fragrance. Silver-grey, mostly aromatic foliage, blue or violet flowers. A wide choice but some species much hardier than others; many selected cultivars. Unless tender, most species are long lived, their longevity improved by pruning by half each spring or every two or three years. ✿ ❋ ■ ⊖ ⊕.

L. angustifolia. The old English or common lavender from which most garden lavenders derive. Narrow grey leaves, spikes of deep purple flowers. Excellent for seaside, herb, silver or grey gardens and mixed planting. H60-75cm/24-30in, W60-75cm/24-30in. The following selections all F6-8, Z6-9. '**Alba**' is a robust, white-flowered form. '**Grappenhall**', equally robust, is lavender-blue. Both H90-120cm/3-4ft, W90-120cm/3-4ft. The best and most popular, '**Hidcote**', is compact, with violet-blue spikes. H60-75cm/24-30in, W60-75cm/24-30in. '**Hidcote Pink**', '**Loddon Pink**' and '**Rosea**' are tinged pink, quickly fading. All H60-75cm/24-30in, W60-75cm/2ft-2ft 6in. The more compact '**Munstead**' has grey-green foliage and blue flowers. H60-75cm/24-30in, W60-75cm/24-30in. '**Nana Alba**' makes a compact bush of grey leaves and white flowers. H30cm/1ft, W30-45cm/12-18in. '**Vera**', the Dutch lavender, has large grey leaves and long spikes of lavender-blue flowers. H90-120cm/3-4ft, W90-120cm/3-4ft.

Lavandula 'Blue Cushion'

Lavatera 'Candy Floss'

L. 'Blue Cushion'. A compact, mound-forming hybrid with grey-green leaves, free flowering, deep blue. H30-40cm/12-15in, W45-60cm/18-24in.

L. 'Fragrant Memories'. Considered an old hybrid. Robust habit, large silvery-grey, strongly aromatic leaves, a long succession rather than a mass of tall spikes bearing lavender-blue flowers. H60-75cm/24-30in, W75cm/30in. F7-10.

L. stoechas. French lavender. Native of south-west Europe, Greece and North Africa. Not reliably hardy, requiring warm, well-drained positions. Flowers appear in early summer on short spikes, their ovoid heads surmounted by purple bracts. Several selections now available: '**Album**' has white flowers; '**Helmsdale**', compact habit, bronze tinges to deep mauve-purple flowers; '**Marshwood**', large flowers, purple-pink bracts with a distinctive twirl. All 30-45cm/12-18in, W45cm/18in. F6-7. Z8-9. '**Pedunculata**', a showy lavender which seems hardier than the species, has grey-green aromatic foliage and usually a striking show of flowers topped by wispy lilac-blue bracts. H45-60cm/18-24in, W45-60cm/18-24in. F6-7. Z7-9.

LAVATERA Mallow

Whatever the botanical classification there are some fine flowering plants among these deciduous, semi-woody plants providing colour throughout the summer and into autumn. Leafy foliage provides a backcloth to a succession of cup-shaped flowers. Plants may die back in winter or even be killed in hard winters, but even if grown as annuals they give a long period of colour. Prune back to 30-45cm/12-18in in late spring. Good near the sea. All below F6-10. Z8-10. ✿ ☆ ■

L. 'Barnsley'. Vigorous, a sport of '**Rosea**', with white, red-centred flowers fading to a delicate pink. Sometimes flowers revert to pink and these should be cut out. '**Burgundy Wine**', wine-red flowers, compact habit, free flowering. H1.8m/6ft, W1.5-1.8m/5-6ft. '**Candy Floss**', pale pink saucer-shaped flowers, open habit. H1.8-2.1m/6-7ft, W1.5-1.8m/5-6ft. '**Pink Frills**', dense upright habit, pretty pale pink frilled flowers over a relatively short period. H1.5m/5ft, W1.2m/4ft. F7-8.

LIGUSTRUM Privet

Common and often condemned, but some selections of this family are quite showy and highly adaptable. Some have colourful variegated or golden foliage and most if unpruned produce heads of white tubular flowers followed by black fruits. Many are used for hedging but are quite hungry feeders so site with care. Prune as necessary, but for hedges two or three times in the growing season. ✿ ✻ ☆

L. lucidum. The Chinese privet is relatively tender but vigorous and large leaved. The species has glossy leaves and erect panicles of white scented flowers. '**Excelsum Superbum**' has variegated white and yellow leaves, '**Tricolor**' has leaves margined white flushed pink when young. All H3m/10ft, W3m/10ft. F8. Z8-11.

L. vicaryi. I rate this semi-evergreen privet for its striking yellow foliage, white flowers and in autumn a good display of black fruits, the leaves then purplish. H2.1-3m/7-10ft, W2.1-3m/7-10ft. F7-8. Z6-8. ✿

L. vulgare Common privet. A hardy adaptable shrub growing in poor, dry soil. Deciduous, loose habit with dullish white flower plumes, black fruits. '**Aureum**' has dull yellow leaves. Both H3m/10ft, W3m/10ft. F7-8. Z5-7.

Lonicera periclymenum

LONICERA **Honeysuckle**
This family includes both free standing deciduous and evergreen shrubs grown for foliage and winter flowers as well as the more usual climbers or scramblers. The climbers are renowned for their fragrance, but not all are scented. They are tolerant of a wide range of soils, but usually prefer their roots in shade. Prune climbers after flowering to remove old wood if necessary and reduce growth.

L. × americana. Glossy green leaves, showy clusters of erect, sweetly fragrant flowers, purple in bud opening to yellow, then fading to cream. Red fruits. Train and prune in early spring. H5m/16ft, W5m/16ft. F7-9. Z5-9.

L. korolkowii. The blue leaf honeysuckle is an excellent, easily grown foliage shrub with intensely blue leaves in summer. Pretty small pink flowers on the shoot tips are followed by red fruits. A good background shrub. Trim after flowering to keep compact. H3m/10ft, W2.4-3m/8-10ft. F6-7. Z5-8.

L. periclymenum Common honeysuckle or woodbine. Grows wild in British hedgerows. A deciduous, scrambling, twining climber, happy in most soils where not too dry. Fragrant yellow or purplish flowers with a mostly white centre in early summer followed by red fruits. '**Belgica**', the early Dutch honeysuckle, has purple-red buds, opening yellow in late spring for several weeks. '**Graham Thomas**', found in a Warwickshire hedgerow by the distinguished English plantsman, has large yellow flowers, a wonderful plant. '**Harlequin**' adds a new note with long-season interest from cream- and pink-variegated leaves. Although there may be several forms of '**Serotina**', the late Dutch honeysuckle is the best, with purple-tinged leaves, deep purple,

Magnolia × liliflora × stellata 'Jane'

red-budded flowers opening creamy-white and is deliciously fragrant; worth searching for. All H3-4m/10-13ft, W3-4m/10-13ft. F5-9. Z5-9.

MAGNOLIA
Aristocratic trees and shrubs, both deciduous and evergreen, and mostly spring flowering. Magnolias are relatively trouble-free on suitable soils. Ideally they like any good, moist but well drained loam including those containing lime, but not thin, dry or chalky soils. They will benefit from the annual addition of a mulch of composted bark, acid leafmould or well rotted compost. Most spring shoots and flowers are susceptible to damage from spring frosts, so if possible site near a tree or a wall to protect plants from the early morning sun. Little or no pruning required. Some worthwhile later-flowering varieties are described below.

M. grandiflora. This handsome evergreen species makes a large tree in warmer climates but in cooler temperate zones is often used as a wall plant where it will get more heat and protection to induce it to flower. Dark green, glossy leathery leaves have cinnamon-brown felt beneath. Large, fragrant cup-shaped

creamy-white flowers in summer are an inspiring sight. Plants from seed will take several years to flower, but many selections have been made which are propagated by cuttings and these will flower much earlier, so go for named cultivars. '**Exmouth**' and '**Goliath**' are but two but many new selections are being introduced from the United States. Average ten year growth rate of the species and two cultivars above: H2.4-3m/8-10ft, W1.5-1.8m/5-6ft. F7-9. Z7-9. ✿ ◢

M. × kewensis '**Wada's Memory**'. An erect bush with fragrant white, somewhat drooping white flowers which appear before the leaves. Good for a small garden. H3m/10ft, W1.5-1.8m/5-6ft. F7-9. F4-5. Z4-8.

M. × liliflora (syn. *M. discolor*). The lily magnolia is ideal if untidy for a small garden, its tulip-like flowers appearing with the leaves, so mostly avoiding frost damage; it continues in flower for several months. Flower petals wine-purple outside, white inside. '**Nigra**' has larger, darker flowers, flushed rose-purple inside. H1.5-1.8m/5-6ft, W1.5-1.8m/5-6ft. F5-7. Z6-8.

M. × liliflora × stellata. Although many are similar, the hybrids made from various crosses between these two species have proved valuable garden plants. All have girls' names; most resemble *M. liliflora* in flower, some are fragrant but are generally bushier and freer flowering. These include '**Ann**', '**Betty**', '**Jane**' (my favourite), '**Judy**', '**Pinkie**', '**Randy**', '**Ricki**' and '**Susan**'. All H1.5-1.8m/5-6ft, W90-120cm/3-4ft. F5-6. Z5-8.

OLEARIA **Daisy bush**
A large family of Australasian evergreen shrubs and small trees, known as tree asters or tree daisies, but they seldom make trees in cooler temperate climates. Useful summer-

Olearia 'Waikariensis'

flowering shrubs even if their panicles or clusters of daisy-like flowers are mostly white or cream. Most are tender but thrive in mild coastal districts, withstanding gales and salt spray. In cold inland regions grow against a sunny south-facing wall. Best on well-drained soils including chalk. Cut back hard old, untidy or frost-damaged bushes in spring as new growth begins, since they break freely from old wood. Two of the hardiest are described but wider ranges can be obtained from specialists.

O. × *haastii*. Rounded bush with sage green, leathery leaves, silver-grey beneath and clusters of fragrant white flowers in summer. Good hedging shrub in milder areas. H1.2-1.5m/4-5ft, W1.2-1.5m/4-5ft. F7-9. Z8-10.

O. 'Waikariensis'. Compact evergreen, leaves glossy green above with silver-grey undersides. Clusters of white daisy flowers, a good plant for the sunny "Mediterranean" garden. H90-120cm/3-4ft, W120-150cm/4-5ft. F7-8. Z8-10.

OSMANTHUS
Related to the olive, though some of these evergreens look more akin to hollies. Grown for their foliage and

small fragrant flowers, those listed below make attractive summer foliage plants for sheltered positions or patios.

O. heterophyllus (syn. *O. ilicifolius*). Large, round, dense shrub or small tree in mild climates. Shining, holly-like leaves, some spined, but mature leaves smooth-edged and oval. Small clusters of fragrant white flowers in hot climates, followed by blue berries. All selections can be tender, especially when young. H1.8-2.4m/6-8ft, W1.8-2.4m/6-8ft. F9-11. Z7-9. '**Aureomarginatus**', leaves edged in yellow. '**Aureus**', bright gold summer leaves, greeny-yellow in winter. '**Latifolius Variegatus**', wide leaves edged silvery-white. '**Purpureus**', striking, purple young shoots and leaves in spring. '**Tricolor**' (syn. 'Goshiki'), dark green, white and pink leaves. '**Variegatus**', creamy-white margins. Average H1.2-1.8m/4-6ft, W1.2-1.8m/4-6ft. F9-11. Z8-9.

OXYDENDRUM
O. arboreum. Deciduous. May reach 15m/50ft in its native eastern U.S.A. but seldom more than a large shrub in climates with cool summers. Open, erect branches with long, narrow, graceful leaves, turning yellow or crimson in autumn, given

Paeonia delavayi

Osmanthus heterophyllus 'Tricolor'

an open situation. Long, pendulous racemes of white, fragrant flowers. H1.5-2.4m/5-8ft, W1.2-1.5m/4-5ft. F7-8. Z5-9.

PAEONIA Tree peony
The woody plants of this genus seldom reach tree size, mostly forming irregular, gaunt, often untidy deciduous shrubs but they can be attractive in leaf and spectacular in flower. All are frost-hardy in winter but can be susceptible to damage from spring frosts, so avoid planting in frost pockets and protect from early morning sun. Best if given fertile but well drained loam that stays moist in summer. Add well rotted compost to the soil and mulch in spring. ☼ ☀

P. delavayi. A variable, Chinese species, mostly red-tinged, deeply divided new leaves and deep crimson cup-shaped flowers with golden anthers. H1.2-1.5m/4-5ft, W90-120cm/3-4ft. F5-6. Z5-8.

P. lutea. Variable from seed and similar in leaf to *P. delavayi* though generally a lighter green. Small saucer-shaped, often semi-double, canary yellow flowers partly hidden by foliage. *P.l. ludlowii* is a superior, more vigorous form with larger, slightly earlier flowers. Both

somewhat shy to flower but foliage is effective. Both 1.5-1.8m/5-6ft, W1.2-1.5m/4-5ft.

P. suffruticosa. The Japanese or Chinese "moutans" have a fascinating history going back to the 6th century. Spectacular single and double flowers both have attractive stamens and can be up to 30cm/1ft across; 15cm/6in is more usual and even these can weigh the branches down when wet. Colours range from white through pink, carmine red, purple, orange and yellow. Most that are sold now will be grafted, so plant with the visible graft union 10cm/4in below ground level and cover with soil – the plant should in time then make its own roots. Expect flowers on named varieties within two years of planting. Little or no pruning required, except to cut out any dead wood, best done after flowering. Average H1.2-1.5m/4-5ft, W90-120cm/3-4ft. F5-6. Z5-8.

PASSIFLORA Passion flower
This Brazilian species is the hardiest and most popular of the genus of woody and herbaceous climbers native to South America. Evergreen and woody in mild localities, elsewhere herbaceous. Extremely

Philadelphus 'Beauclerk'

vigorous, clinging by means of tendrils. Unusually striking white or pink flowers are flattened and star-shaped with a raised circular crown of blue or purple and white filaments, followed in hot summers by orange-yellow fruits. Protect from cold winds. '**Constance Elliott**', an equally vigorous grower, has white flowers. Both H5m/16ft. F7-8. Z8-9. ✿ ❊ ◼

PEROVSKIA Russian sage

Indispensable deciduous sub-shrubs. Long, late display of shimmering blue flower spikes. Quite hardy, but young stems can die back in cold winters, new shoots appearing from the base. Prune to 15-30cm/6-12in from the ground in spring to promote new flowering growth.

P. atriplicifolia. Aromatic, downy, grey-green, serrated leaves, white stems and hazy panicles of lavender-blue flowers. '**Blue Spire**', more deeply cut leaves and larger flowerheads. H90-120cm/3-4ft, W90-120cm/3-4ft. F8-10. Z6-8.

PHILADELPHUS Mock orange

Popular, deciduous hardy shrubs though, except for foliage forms, a short flowering season and not much to recommend them for the rest of the year. Small, medium and large types, generally densely branched. Light green leaves darken in summer; white, fragrant single or double flowers with yellow stamens, the centres sometimes stained purple. On older plants, old branches can be thinned out after flowering, others shortened if required. ✿ ❊ ☆

P. coronarius. Sweet mock orange denotes the heavy fragrance of this species which is seldom offered in its green-leaved form, being surpassed by modern hybrids. Coloured foliage forms are well worth growing for their longer period of interest. They include '**Aureus**' with bright yellow leaves turning yellow-green and even green in hotter climates, and '**Variegatus**', with grey-green leaves irregularly edged creamy-white and single or semi-double, scented flowers. Both best in part shade and less vigorous than the species. H1.8-2.4m/6-8ft, W1.8-2.4m/6-8ft. F6. Z5-8.

Hybrids. All F6-7, Z5-8 unless otherwise indicated. '**Avalanche**', profuse small, single, heavily fragrant white flowers on arching branches. H1.5m/5ft, W1.5m/5ft. '**Beauclerk**', creamy-white single, saucer-shaped, fragrant rose-stained flowers. H1.8m/6ft, W1.8m/6ft. '**Enchantment**', arching branches, fully double, richly fragrant white flowers. H2.4m/8ft, W2-4m/8ft. '**Manteau d'Hermine**' dwarf shrub, small leaves, masses of double or semi-double fragrant white flowers. H90-120cm/3-4ft, W90-120cm/3-4ft. '**Minnesota Snowflake**', vigorous with fully double, sweetly scented white flowers in clusters. H2.4m/8ft, W2.4m/8ft. Z4-8.

PHLOMIS

Large genus of shrubs and sub-shrubs with woody, grey or grey-green leaves and lax spikes with tiers of flowers in whorls or circles around

Phlomis fruticosa 'Edward Bowles'

the stem. They prefer sun and good drainage, thriving against hot dry walls or banks. Prune back a third or a half of the old woody stems as needed in spring as new growth starts.

P. chrysophylla. Attractive compact shrub with grey-green sage-like leaves and golden-yellow flowers. H90-120cm/3-4ft, W1.2m/4ft. F7-8. Z8-10.

P. fruticosa Jerusalem sage. Perhaps the hardiest species, with grey-green woolly leaves and spikes of bright yellow whorled flowers. H90-120cm/3-4ft, W120cm/4ft. F7-8. Z8-11. '**Edward Bowles**', large woolly silver-grey leaves and impressive sulphur-yellow flowers, semi-shrubby. H1.2-1.5m/4-5ft, W1.2-1.5m/4-5ft. F7-9. Z8-11.

PHORMIUM New Zealand flax

Distinctive and colourful foliage plants, classed as shrubs but hardly woody. Sword-shaped leaves are flexible and pithy. Selections are available from 30cm/1ft to 3m/10ft in height. The species and some cultivars produce quite spectacular flowers in hotter climates. Phormiums grow well in most soils where not too dry but vary in hardiness and adaptability. Excellent for coastal areas. Some make striking accent plants and are ideal for pots and patios, though pot-grown plants will need taking under cover in frosty weather.

P. cookianum (syn. *P. colensoi*) Mountain flax. Variable species with shining green arching leaves. Older plants bear exotic yellow and red flowers on spikes which vary from 90cm/3ft to 1.8m/6ft in height. Foliage H60-90cm/2-3ft, W90-120cm/3-4ft. F7-8. Z9-11. '**Tricolor**', bright green strap-like leaves striped white, margined red. H45-75cm/18-30in, W75-90cm/30-36in. F7-8. Z8-11.

P. tenax. Imposing architectural clump-forming plant, eventually large. Broad, erect sword-like leaves. Flower spikes to 4.5m/15ft with panicles of bronze-red flowers, then reddish seedheads. H1.8-3m/6-10ft, W1.5-3m/5-10ft. F7-8. Z8-11. '**Purpureum**', similar to the species with broad blades of bronze-purple leaves. H1.5-1.8m/5-6ft, W1.2-1.5m/4-5ft. '**Sundowner**', outstanding with leaves striped grey, coppery red and pink. '**Variegatum**', broad green leaves edged creamy-white. Both H1.5-1.8m/5-6ft, W1.2-1.5m/4-5ft.

Hybrids. Parentage between the two species and cultivars. Many cultivars cannot be relied upon to flower but, if they do, F7-8. All Z8-11. '**Bronze Baby**', narrow, bronze-purple leaves. H60-90cm/2-3ft, W45-60cm/18-24in. '**Cream Delight**', sometimes listed under *P. cookianum*, has broad green arching leaves with a central band of creamy-yellow. H60-90cm/2-3ft, W90-120cm/3-4ft. '**Dark Delight**', broad, erect, glossy red-purple leaves, pendulous tips. H90-120cm/3-4ft, W90-120cm/3-4ft. '**Maori Chief**', robust, clump-forming, erect leaves striped bright red, with maroon and bronze drooping tips. H90-120cm/3-4ft, W60-90cm/2-3ft. '**Tom Thumb**',

Physocarpus opulifolius 'Dart's Gold'

dwarf with narrow green leaves margined bronze. H30-45cm/12-18in, W30-45cm/12-18in. **'Yellow Wave'**, striking, bright yellow arched leaves, some edged green. H75-90cm/30-36in, W90-120cm/3-4ft.

PHOTINIA
Mostly south-east Asian in origin, these make large shrubs or trees, depending on climate. Deciduous types dislike lime but the evergreens thrive in it, even on chalky soil. Both types prefer reasonably moist but free-draining, warm soil. ✿ ❋. In cool summers, the evergreens are shy to flower, but still make excellent foliage plants. The flowers are white, hawthorn-like and borne in clusters or panicles, followed by red fruits. In cold regions the evergreens need shelter from freezing winds and severe frost. If leaf drop occurs they normally shoot again in spring. For compact, dense growth and ample new colourful shoots, prune leading shoots back by 30-60cm/1-2ft in spring, as new growth commences; hedges or screens might also need a summer trim.

P. davidiana 'Palette' (syn. *Stransvaesia davidiana* 'Palette'). Foliage shrub, variable, but relatively bushy, leaves irregularly splashed and variegated white, pink and green,

new shoots flushed reddish-pink. White flowers do not always develop into impressive red fruit. H1.5-1.8m/5-6ft, W1.2-1.5m/4-5ft. F6-7. Z7-9.

P. × fraseri **'Birmingham'**. Robust evergreen, glossy dark green leaves, copper-red when young. Denser and hardier than the closely related, more colourful **'Red Robin'**, with an almost continuous show of brilliant red new growth all summer. Both make outstanding focal points. H2.4-3m/8-10ft, W1.8-2.4m/6-8ft. F6. Z8-9.

× PHYLLIOPSIS
× *P. hillieri*. **'Pinocchio'**, a first class hybrid, a compact rounded bush with green leaves and a long display of deep pink bell flowers. **'Coppelia'**, slightly more vigorous with profuse lavender-pink flowers. Ideal for rock gardens or peat beds. Both H30-45cm/12-18in, W38-45cm/15-18in. F5-6. Z5-8. ✿ ❋ ⊖

PHYSOCARPUS Ninebark
P. opulifolius 'Dart's Gold'. Striking deciduous foliage shrub, brighter and more compact than a similar form **'Luteus'**, which will reach 3m/10ft or more. Erect branching habit, the stems attractively peeling with age; bright yellow new shoots

in spring might be mistaken at a distance for a forsythia. Broad lobed, serrated leaves are bright yellow all summer and into autumn. Species and cultivars carry round clusters of pink-tinged white flowers on second-year wood so pruning to keep it compact in spring will remove the chance of flowers, though this is no great loss. Prune in late winter or early spring. **'Diabolo'** is a selection with bronze-purple leaves, and equally striking foliage plant against the right background. Yellow leaves can scorch in full sun or from spring frost, but soon recover. Both 1.5-1.8m/5-6ft, W1.5-1.8m/5-6ft. F6. Z3-7. ✿ ❋ ☆

PIERIS
Evergreen, attractive in flower and foliage and early summer growth often spectacular. Most make slow-growing, mounded bushes, with lance-shaped, glossy leaves. Racemes often develop in autumn, opening in spring, with mostly pendulous, fragrant, bell-shaped white flowers. New growth can be vulnerable to spring frosts. Prune only to tidy up bushes or remove old flowerheads as the new growth begins. Mulch with leafmould or composted bark every two or three years. Needs a peaty soil.

P. **'Flaming Silver'**. One of several selections with variegated foliage and new growth of scarlet or crimson in late spring. Leaves edged silvery-white. H1.2m/4ft, W1.2-1.5m/4-5ft. F3-5. Z5-8.

P. **'Forest Flame'**. One of the best hybrids. Dense flower sprays; scarlet young growth turns pink and white, then green. H1.5m/5ft, W1.5m/5ft. F4-5. Z6-8.

P. japonica. Source of most new European and North American cultivars. Usually glossy leaves, pendulous flower racemes, with waxy, often fragrant, bell-like flowers, showy even in winter as

Pieris 'Forest Flame'

flowering racemes develop. Most prefer an open, sheltered spot. All F3-5. Most Z6-8. **'Debutante'**, dense trusses of white flowers. H75cm/30in, W75-90cm/30-36in. **'Little Heath'**, dwarf, compact, variegated form, seldom flowers; small white, pink and copper leaves. H60cm/2ft, W60cm/2ft. **'Mountain Fire'**, coppery-red new leaves, sparse white flowers. H90cm/3ft, W90-120cm/3-4ft. **'Red Mill'**, glossy wine-red leaves, white flowers. H1.2m/4ft, W1.2m/4ft. **'Variegata'**, covers a fast-growing form with white margins, also called **'White Rim'** (H90cm/3ft, W90cm/3ft), and a compact form, with creamy-yellow variegations, which needs shelter. H45-60cm/18-24in. W45-60cm/18-24in.

PIPTANTHUS
P. nepalensis. A Himalayan semi-evergreen with trifoliate leaves and golden-yellow pea flowers. It forms an open bush of flexible stems bearing dark green leaves, with flowers appearing throughout the plant. It makes a good wall plant, but can also be used in the same situations as brooms, enjoying sun and good drainage. There is a form from Bhutan, *P. tomentosus*, with silvery leaves, which promises to be

Potentilla 'Goldfinger'

even more showy. If bushes get untidy, prune stems back after flowering. H3-4m/10-13ft, W2.1-3m/7-10ft. F5-6. Z9-10.

PITTOSPORUM

Evergreen shrubs or small trees grown for foliage, useful for cutting. Few are hardy in cool temperate zones, but for mild and seaside areas there are good species and cultivars, the latter mostly belonging to *P. tenuifolium*. Leaves are rounded and undulating, pale or olive green with more recent variations purple, silver, gold or variegated. Purple or brown flowers, often small and fragrant, on mature plants in warmer climates. In cold, inland areas, grow against a sunny wall. Wet soil and cold, desiccating winds are fatal. If cut back by frost, most make new growth from old wood. Overwinter containerized plants in a greenhouse or conservatory. Plant in late spring. All below F4-5. Z9-11.
P. 'Garnettii'. Hybrid. Grey-green leaves, edged white and tinged pink. H3m/10ft, W1.5m/5ft.
P. tenuifolium. Bushy tree, columnar when young. Glossy, pale, wavy-edged leaves, black stems. Good for hedging. Innumerable cultivars. H3m/10ft, W1.5m/5ft.
'Purpureum', red-purple leaves.

'Silver Queen', white-edged leaves. Both H1.8-2.1m/6-7ft, W1.5-1.8m/5-6ft. 'Tom Thumb', dwarf, purple-leaved form. H1m/39in, W1m/39in.

POTENTILLA Cinquefoil

A valuable range of long-flowering, colourful and adaptable deciduous shrubs for even the smaller garden. Also good for autumn flowers, wide range of colours, some best in cooler weather. Prune established plants annually as new shoots appear. Cut back by a third each year to improve vigour and flowering. Coloured forms may retain deeper hues in shade.
The following are hybrids, mostly listed at one time under *P. fruticosa*, which is the parent of many. All F4-10. Most Z3-8. 'Abbotswood', the best white, profuse-flowering, blue-green leaves. H1.2m/4ft, W1.5m/5ft. 'Elizabeth', bushy, grey-green leaves, golden-yellow flowers, long-flowering. H90cm/3ft, W1.2m/4ft. 'Goldfinger', bright green leaves, golden flowers. H90cm/3ft, W1.2m/4ft. 'Goldstar', erect, open habit, huge yellow flowers. H90cm/3ft, W1.2m/4ft. 'Hopleys Orange', orange flowers. H75cm/30in, W1m/39in. 'Kobold', dense, dwarf, small yellow flowers.

H30-45cm/12-18in, W40-60cm/16-24in. 'Pretty Polly', dwarf, low-growing, light rose-pink flowers. H35-50cm/14-20in, W45-65cm/18-26in. 'Princess', long-flowering, pale pink, then paler, fading to white in heat. H75cm/30in, W1m/39in. 'Red Ace', bright vermilion-flame at best, fading to yellow in heat. 'Red Robin', similar but deeper red. Both H60cm/2ft, W80cm/32in. 'Tilford Cream', low habit, rigid branches, white flowers, can look scruffy. H60cm/2ft, W60cm/2ft.

PRUNUS

Large family of trees and shrubs (see also Trees Directory), most of the latter flowering in early to mid-spring. Some useful for coloured foliage in summer. Deciduous ✿ Evergreens ✿ ❋ All ☆ ■.
P. × *cistena* (syn. 'Crimson Dwarf'). Deciduous. White flowers, reddish purple foliage. As a hedge, prune after flowering, then regularly through summer. H1.5-1.8m/5-6ft, W1.2-1.5m/4-5ft. F3-4. Z2-8.
P. glandulosa. The Chinese bush cherry, or, in the USA, Chinese dwarf flowering almond, has erect, branched stems with single white or pink flowers, which appear before and with the leaves. Best in warm sun; hard prune the previous year's growth immediately after flowering. There are several ornamental, double-flowered forms, including 'Alba Plena', white, and the densely petalled pink 'Sinensis' (syn. 'Flore Roseoplena'). All H1.2-1.5m/4-5ft, W1.2m/4ft. F4-5. Z5-8.
P. laurocerasus Cherry laurel. Evergreen adaptable shrubs with glossy, leathery leaves. Taller, erect forms are good for screening, hedging and windbreaks, prostrate types for ground cover. Bottlebrush white flowers held above the branches do not last long but are quite showy. Sun or shade on all but thin chalk; take well to pruning after

flowering. All F4-5. Most Z6-8.
'Low and Green', low, free-flowering, glossy green leaves. H90cm/3ft, W2.1-3m/7-10ft. 'Marbled White', broad, spreading; leaves green, grey and cream. H2.4m/8ft, W2.4m/8ft. 'Otto Luyken', broad, semi-prostrate; narrow, shiny leaves, white flowers, often again in autumn, good for hedging. H1.5m/5ft, W1.5m/5ft. 'Renault Ace', erect branching habit, dark green leaves, good flowering performance, excellent for hedges. H1.8-2.4m/6-8ft, W1.8-2.4m/6-8ft. 'Zabeliana', low, spreading ground cover, narrow leaves. H1.2m/4ft, W1.8m/6ft.

RHODODENDRON

Vast range of deciduous and evergreen flowering shrubs requiring (with one or two exceptions) an acid soil. Dwarf and large forms with flowering periods from late winter to mid-summer; a good range of colours, some with striking and exotic blooms. If you are lucky enough to have an acid or even neutral pH soil, the rhododendrons and azaleas will give vibrant spring colours which can fit with other plants. But beware – frost can also damage winter and even late spring

Prunus laurocerasus 'Otto Luyken'

Rhododendron yakushimanum hybrid

Rosa moyesii 'Geranium'

flowers; site plants facing away from early morning sun, under the shade of tall trees and out of a frost pocket. Severe winters or frosts can damage swelling buds. All, except those classed as tender, can be planted throughout the year as long as soil conditions are suitable, early autumn better than late spring for those less hardy for your area.

So large and varied is the selection of rhododendrons that only a brief guide to the types can be given. Consult a book or specialist supplier, or even your nearest garden centre who should be able to advise on the most suitable selections for your area. Rhododendrons tend to be grouped by species, both large and small, and evergreen hybrids, which again can be large or small. The hardy evergreen azaleas and deciduous azaleas are also rhododendrons and among my favourites, since they seem to fit better among other plants. The deciduous azaleas flower later, often avoiding spring frost damage, and provide good autumn colour too. In recent years breeding work has introduced some excellent varieties of rhododendron for the smaller garden, including hybrids of *Rhododendron yakushimanum*, attractive not only

for flower but for foliage. Almost wherever you live, there will be rhododendrons to suit your climate.

ROSA Rose

No directory of summer plants could be complete without the inclusion of roses, but with limited space only general guidelines can be given and some arbitrary selections made in each main group listed. While shrub, ground cover, climbing and rambling roses are included below, detailed advice and lists of bush roses (hybrid teas and floribundas) patio roses (dwarf cluster roses) and miniature types must be sought elsewhere. All roses are shrubs and although they are often used on their own in rose gardens, today's gardener expects them to mix in with other plants, shrubs and herbaceous in particular. They should also be relatively trouble free from pests and diseases and provide a long period of interest. While gardeners are becoming more demanding, rose breeders are rising to the challenge, with exciting developments coming through. There are roses for climbing walls and fences, others for rambling over banks and other shrubs; for ground cover or use

among other low growing plants; for hedges, window boxes and tubs. Roses succeed best in sun on rich, loamy soil, and dislike extremes of wet or dry. For best results, add well-rotted compost when planting, and give an annual dressing of fertilizer. Most roses also benefit from mulching with well-rotted compost. Prune as new buds swell in early spring, firstly any thin or dead stems, then to balance the shape; prune just above the bud at an angle of 45 degrees away from it. Brief individual pruning notes are given with each group. Roses are bred, too, for adaptability to different climates, but quite often those which thrive in southern France may not be as happy in northern Europe or cooler areas of the USA, and vice versa. Local experts know what succeeds best in their region.

Shrub roses

Shrub roses can be species or cultivars, tall specimen plants or low, ground-covering types, recent introductions of which provide colour from summer until well into autumn. Prune only to shape or to control size. If the stems of ground-cover types become old or untidy they can be pruned hard to

15cm/6in above the ground every two or three years.

R. 'Ballerina'. Outstanding, with the bold trusses of recurrent, soft pink, white-centred, weather-resistant flowers. Bushy, spreading habit and glossy green leaves. Good ground cover. H1.2m/4ft, W1.2m/4ft. F7-10. Z6-8.

R. 'Bonica'. Popular and versatile, with arching branches and masses of small pink flowers for months. Good ground cover. H90cm/3ft, W90cm/3ft. F7-10. Z4-9.

R. californica 'Plena'. Imposing specimen shrub rose with tall arching branches and a profusion of semi-double, deep pink flowers fading to rose-pink. H3m/10ft, W2.4-3m/8-10ft. F6-7. Z6-8.

R. 'Canary Bird'. An early-flowering, modern shrub rose, which mixes well with shrubs or perennials. Long, arching stems clothed with daintily cut leaves, and freely borne, single, canary-yellow scented flowers. H1.8-2.1m/6-7ft, W1.5-2.1m/5-7ft. F5-6. Z5-9.

R. 'Heritage'. Similar to the above and equally attractive, with blush-pink flowers. H1.2m/4ft, W1.2m/4ft. F6-10. Z4-9.

R. 'Kent'. An award-winning, repeat-blooming, ground-cover shrub with pure white, semi-double flowers. Weathers well. H45cm/8in, W60-90cm/2-3ft. F7-10. Z5-8.

R. moyesii 'Geranium'. At its peak a glorious sight, the tall, arching, thorny branches ablaze with single, bright scarlet flowers and yellow stamens. Flask-shaped, orange-red hips in autumn. H2.4-3m/8-10ft, W2.4m/8ft. F6-7. Z6-8.

R. 'Surrey'. Outstanding ground-cover rose with beautiful, soft, double, pink flowers. H90cm/3ft, W1.2m/4ft. F7-10. Z6-8.

Climbing and rambling roses

Use climbing and rambling roses for walls, over fences, pergolas, trellises and arches, or up trees. Most need tying in and training. Plant as for other climbers, ideally at least 45cm/18in away from a wall, so they can more easily obtain moisture. To prune, reduce side shoots by two-thirds in autumn, but only reduce main leading stems if they are too tall. If plants become bare at the base, severely prune one main stem to 30-60cm/1-2ft above ground to encourage new growth. Ramblers can have old stems cut away in late summer as soon as flowering has finished.

R. 'Albéric Barbier'. An old favourite rambler with vigorous, semi-evergreen, glossy dark green foliage and fragrant, creamy-white, double flowers opening from creamy-yellow buds. Good for a tree or an arch. H3-5m/10-16ft. F6-8. Z5-8.

R. 'Dublin Bay'. Long-flowering climber with clusters of slightly fragrant, crimson flowers and glossy, dark green leaves. H1.8-2.4m/6-8ft, W1.8-2.4m/6-8ft. F7-10. Z6-8.

R. 'Felicia'. A hybrid musk rose of considerable merit. Salmon-pink, semi-double, fragrant. H1.5-1.8m /5-6ft, W1.2-1.5m/4-5ft. F6-9. Z6-8.

R. 'Golden Showers'. Modern shrub

Rosa 'Felicia'

climber with glossy, dark green foliage, clusters of recurrent, large, fragrant, single bright yellow flowers, fading to cream. Upright grower, good for pillars. H2.4-3m/8-10ft, W2.4m/8ft. F6-9. Z5-8.

R. 'Handel'. Climber, with deep green, bronze-tinted leaves, distinctive semi-double, recurrent cream flowers edged rosy-red, slightly fragrant. H3m/10ft, W3m/10ft. F7-9. Z5-8.

R. 'Iceberg' Climbing. A climbing Floribunda sport with profuse, semi-double, sweetly scented white flowers, sometimes tinged with pale pink. A repeat-bloomer. H3-4m/10-13ft, W3-4m/10-13ft. F7-10. Z4-8.

R. 'Madame Grégoire Staechelin'. Outstanding, vigorous climber with richly fragrant, large, semi-double, coral-pink blooms, the outer petals splashed with carmine. H5-6m/16-20ft, W3.6-5m/12-16ft. F6-7. Z4-8.

R. 'Mermaid'. At its best a superb old climber, producing a succession of soft, primrose-yellow, single flowers with amber stamens. Can be difficult to establish, and best against a warm, sunny wall, but worth the effort. H5-6m/16-20ft, W5-6m/16-20ft. F6-11. Z6-8.

ROSMARINUS **Rosemary**

R. officinalis. Aromatic evergreen with narrow, dark green leaves, silver beneath, used extensively in cooking, but excellent foliage and flowering shrubs. A Mediterranean native, it revels in hot sun, but adapts surprisingly well. Light blue flowers appear on growth made the previous year, so unless plants are severely damaged, prune after flowering, usually in mid-summer. It makes an irregular, spreading bush, providing good contrast to silver, sun-loving shrubs. H90-150cm/3-5ft, W1.2-1.8m/4-6ft. F4-6. Z7-9. 'Alba' is tender, with white flowers. H90-120cm/3-4ft, W90-120cm/3-4ft. F4-6. Z8-9. 'McConnell's Blue' makes a prostrate mound, useful for tumbling over a path or sunny wall, and hardier than the similar 'Prostratus' (syn. *R. lavandulaceus*). H45cm/18in, W1.2m/4ft. F4-6. Z7-9. The most popular and hardiest cultivar 'Miss Jessopps's Upright' (syn. 'Fastigiatus') makes good hedging, with an erect but informal habit. H1.2-1.5m/4-5ft, W90-120cm/3-4ft. F4-6. Z7-9. 'Sissinghurst Blue', a chance seedling raised at Sissinghurst Castle, Kent, England, has an erect habit and rich blue flowers. H90-120cm/3-4ft, W90-120cm/3-4ft. F5-6. Z7-8.

RUBUS **Bramble**

Many useful for winter stems, two of those below also have attractive summer foliage. These are best cut to the ground in late spring.

R. cockburnianus 'Golden Vale'. Spreading habit, year-round interest, golden-yellow leaves, silver-white arching branches in winter. H90-120cm/3-4ft, W1.2-1.5m/4-5ft. F6-7. Z5-9.

R. odoratus. Suckering, spreading shrub, erect, thornless stems, large lobed leaves and purple-pink, fragrant flowers, followed by edible

Rubus cockburnianus 'Golden Vale'

red berries. Good in shade. H1.8-2.4m/6-8ft, W1.2-1.8m/4-8ft. F6-8. Z4-9.

R. thibetanus 'Silver Fern'. Suckering shrub, grey-green, finely cut leaves, arching bright white stems in winter. Unpruned H1.8-2.4m/6-8ft, W1.5-1.8m/5-6ft. F6-7. Z6-9.

SALIX **Willow**

Enormous range of trees (see Trees Directory, page 221) and shrubs, attractive for leaves, catkins and winter stems. Most are easy to grow in any but poor dry soil. The few described below are mentioned for foliage effect in the garden.

S. 'Boydii'. Chance hybrid, a gem for troughs and alpine gardens, with stubby, erect branches forming a miniature tree. Limited grey woolly catkins, silver-grey new leaves. H30cm/1ft, W20-30cm/8-12in. F5. Z4-7.

S. helvetica Swiss willow. Bright dwarf, multi-branched silver-leaved shrub, greyish-white catkins. H60-75cm/24-30in, W60-90cm/2-3ft. F4-5. Z6-7.

S. integra 'Hakuro Nishiki' (syn. 'Albomaculata'). Twiggy shrub, open habit, renowned for bright shrimp-pink shoots opening to mottled, variegated cream and white leaves. Most effective pruned back annually in early spring and kept dwarf. ☼ ❋ where not too dry. H1.8m/6ft, W1.2-1.5m/4-5ft. F4. Z6-8.

S. lanata. Woolly willow. Low spreading habit, rigid branches, silver-yellow catkins, soft, grey-green downy leaves. H60-90cm/2-3ft, W60-90cm/2-3ft. F4-5. Z4-6.

SALVIA Sage

S. officinalis Common sage. Indispensable evergreen. Plants are best kept young; prune back if required in spring every two or three years. Various coloured-foliage forms, but shy to flower in cool climates. **'Berggarten'**, hardy, felted grey leaves. **'Icterina'** (syn. 'Variegata'), leaves splashed and variegated with creamy-yellow, golden-yellow and light green. **'Purpurascens'**, purple younger shoots, older leaves turning soft grey-green. **'Tricolor'**, the most tender but colourful, grey-green leaves boldly marked white and pink, new shoots purple, tinged red. H45-60cm/18-24in, W75-90cm/ 30-36in. F6-7. Z7-9. ☼ ❋ ■

SAMBUCUS Elder

Some attractive foliage forms among these common deciduous shrubs. Adaptable, growing in acid or alkaline soils both wet and dry. Coloured foliage forms need sun but all tolerate shade. To tidy bushes or to create new growth for foliage colour prune in early spring, perhaps by a third but if necessary to within 30cm/1ft of the ground.

S. nigra. Common or European elder. There are several interesting foliage forms. All respond well to regular annual pruning. **'Albovariegata'**, with dark green, white-edged leaves. **'Aurea'**, the golden elder, with bright yellow foliage, dulling with age. 'Aureo-

Salix integra 'Hakuro Nishiki'

marginata', with gold-edged leaves. **'Guincho Purple'** (syn. 'Purpurea'), with black-purple leaves, in vivid contrast to its white flowers. **'Laciniata'**, with graceful, deeply cut green leaves. **'Pulverulenta'**, less vigorous, with leaves striped and splashed white. All tend to dislike high humidity. Average H2.4-3m/8-10ft, W2.4-3m/8-10ft. F6-7. Z5-7.

S. racemosa. The red-berried elder, an erect shrub with arching branches and clusters or panicles of relatively small, creamy-white flowers. Red fruits appear in favourable climates in mid-to late summer. Attractive garden forms with striking, golden-yellow foliage include **'Plumosa Aurea'** and **'Sutherland'** (syn. 'Sutherland Gold'), with finely cut, coppery-yellow leaves, bright yellow in summer. Primrose-yellow flowers are sometimes followed by red fruit, but neither appear if plants are severely pruned. 'Plumosa Aurea' leaves can scorch, less likely with 'Sutherland'. All H3m/10ft, W2.4-3m/8-10ft. F3. Z3-6.

SANTOLINA Cotton lavender

Sun-loving, dwarf evergreen shrubs have cypress-like, grey or green foliage on soft, semi-woody stems and make low, spreading mounds. Most have profuse, yellow button flowers. ☼ ■ They grow quickly and

Sambucus racemosa 'Plumosa Aurea'

can soon look untidy unless pruned annually or every other year in mid-spring. Prune all branches away to just above newly developing shoots.

S. chamaecyparissus (syn. *S. incana*). Popular species, reliably hardy and vigorous, with bright silver-grey, woolly foliage in summer, dull grey in winter, and yellow flowers which last for several weeks. H45-60cm/18-24in, W60-90cm/2-3ft. F7. Z6-9. **'Nana'**, a compact, dense bush with smaller leaves and flowers than the species but similarly attractive. H30-45cm/12-18in, W45-60cm/18-24in. F6-8. Z6-9.

S. incana See *S. chamaecyparissus.*

S. virens. This distinct alternative to the grey-leaved forms has bright green foliage, in vivid contrast to its deep yellow flowers. H45-60cm/

18-24in, W45-60cm/18-24in. F7-8. Z7-9.

SENECIO

S. 'Sunshine'. Often listed as *S. greyi* or *S. laxifolius*. The true *S. greyi* is tender, with soft grey, felted leaves. 'Sunshine' is hardier, making a compact, later spreading, bush, its white, woolly stems clothed with grey-green, leathery leaves, white beneath. In a warm, sunny position it has masses of golden-yellow, daisy-like flowers. In spring, lightly prune established shrubs annually and older, woody plants to 10cm/4in of the ground every few years for rejuvenation. H90-120cm/3-4ft, W1.2-1.5m/4-5ft. F6-8. Z9-11.

SPARTIUM Spanish broom

S. junceum. The only species in the genus is closely related to *Cytisus* and *Genista*, with similar requirements. Makes a tall, upright shrub, with young, slender stems a deep green. Thrives on chalk and in coastal areas, with large, deep yellow, pea-like flowers. Prune green shoots when quite young to prevent plants becoming leggy, gathering several stems together and cutting with a sharp knife. Flowers on growth made in the same year, so prune to within 2.5cm/1in of the previous year's growth, just as shoots begin to appear in spring. Never prune into

Spiraea japonica 'Golden Princess'

old wood. New shoots will form rapidly, giving a bright display within a few weeks. H2.4-3m/8-10ft, W1.8-2.4m/6-8ft. F7-8. Z7-11. ☼ ■

SPIRAEA

Useful and ornamental hardy deciduous shrubs, particularly for a small garden. ☼ ❀ ☆

S. x arguta (syn. *S.* 'Arguta'). Popular hybrid, commonly known as bridal wreath, its arching branches carry a mass of dazzling white flowers. Vigorous and tall, it makes an effective hedge. Prune some old stems to the base and shorten others, if required, immediately after flowering. H1.8-2.4m/6-8ft, W1.8-2.4m/6-8ft. F4-5. Z5-8.

S. japonica. The Japanese spiraea cultivars are some of the best garden shrubs, easy to grow, generally dwarf and with flowers that continue for many weeks. The recent addition of many coloured-foliage forms provides added interest, from early spring until autumn leaf-fall. All benefit from annual pruning in late winter, at least by half the length of the previous year's growth. ☼ ❀ New shoots, especially golden-leaved forms, may be damaged by spring frost but soon recover. Can be prone to mildew. All Z4-8. '**Anthony Waterer**'(syn. *S.* x *bumalda* 'Anthony Waterer') is vigorous, strong and bushy. Its dark green leaves are sometimes yellow or variegated and its large, flat heads of bright carmine flowers are borne over a long period. H90-120cm/3-4ft, W90-120cm/3-4ft. F7-9. '**Gold Mound**' and '**Golden Princess**' are considerably more colourful than the previously popular '**Goldflame**'; their early shoots are more yellow and bronze respectively, their summer leaves brighter, with no hint of reversion. '**Golden Princess**' is round and compact, with golden-yellow leaves and pink flowers. H60-90cm/2-3ft, W60-75cm/24-30in. F7-8. '**Gold Mound**' is low and more spreading, its leaves brighter yellow and its flowers a brighter pink. H60-90cm/2-3ft, W75-90cm/30-36in. F6-8. '**Goldflame**' (syn. *S.* x *bumalda* 'Goldflame') coppery-crimson young shoots and deep golden-yellow leaves in early summer, fading by the time rose-pink flowers appear; prone to reversion to green. H60-90cm/2-3ft, W60-90cm/2-3ft. F6-7. Look for new selections '**Magic Carpet**', '**Firelight**' and '**Candlelight**', all striking yellow or gold foliage forms. The green-leaved '**Little Princess**' forms a broad dome of densely congested stems with free-flowering, pretty pink flowers. H45-60cm/18-24in,W60-75cm/24-30in. F6-7. '**Shirobana**' (syn. 'Shibori'), popular, green-leaved Japanese introduction, carries both white and red flowers on the same plant. H90-120cm/3-4ft, W90-120cm/3-4ft. F7-8.

S. nipponica '**Snowmound**'. Erect shrub, arching branches festooned with small white flowers in early summer. H1.8-2.4m/6-8ft. F5-6. Z4-8.

S. x *vanhouttei* '**Pink Ice**'. Compact foliage shrub, broad leaves splashed with white and pink. White flowers in mid-summer. H90-120cm/3-4ft, W60-90cm/2-3ft. F6-7. Z3-8.

SYRINGA Lilac

Common spring and early summer flowering deciduous shrubs, known for their fragrance. The common lilac, *S. vulgaris* and its cultivars are the best known, but all have in common a relatively short period of flower, and unless grown on their own roots, are prone to sucker. ☼ Grow on most soils though preferring heavier alkaline types to acid or peaty soils. They benefit from heavy feeding, and regular topdressing with compost or manure.

Syringa patula 'Miss Kim'

S. x *hyacinthiflora*. From this hybrid have come many early-flowering selections, mostly upright, with lightly fragrant flowers. '**Alice Eastwood**' has double flowers, deep wine-purple in bud, opening pale blue. The popular, vigorous '**Esther Staley**' has carmine-red buds, opening pink. All H1.8-2.4m/6-8ft, W1.5-1.8m/5-6ft. F4-5. Z4-7.

S. meyeri '**Palibin**' (syn. *S. palibiniana*). Densely branched shrub, smothered in small panicles of very fragrant, pale pink flowers, even when young. It remains reasonably attractive all year. H1.2-1.5m/4-5ft, W90-120cm/3-4ft. F6. Z4-8.

S. microphylla '**Superba**'. Attractive, with deep rose-pink flowers continuing on and off for weeks. H90-120cm/3-4ft, W90-120cm/3-4ft. F7-9. Z4-8.

S. patula '**Miss Kim**'. Slow-growing lilac. Freely branching and upright in habit, its pink flower buds open deep lilac, fading to blue. Both floriferous and fragrant. H1.5-1.8m/5-6ft, W90-120cm/3-4ft. F5-6. Z3-8.

S. x *prestoniae*. The Canadian hybrids are noted for their hardiness and abundant flowers. The large, open panicles are only slightly less fragrant than those of the common lilac. '**Audrey**', an older cultivar, has deep pink flowers. '**Elinor**', deep wine-red in bud, opens to pale lavender-pink. '**Isabella**' has large panicles of lilac-pink. A wider range of vigorous cultivars is now available in Canada and the USA. All H2.4-3m/8-10ft, W2.4-3m/8-10ft. F5-6. Z3-7.

S. vulgaris. Species seldom offered but there are numerous cultivars. Lilacs are often unhappy in a container, so these may not look their best at garden centres. They make erect, eventually bushy shrubs, but young plants may not flower for a few years. The single or double flowers are borne in dense panicles in white, violet, blue, lilac, pink, purple and yellow. All cultivars listed below are scented. '**Charles Joly**', deep purple, double. '**Congo**', lilac-red, small heads. '**Firmament**', free-flowering, blue. '**Katherine Havemeyer**', dense trusses of deep lavender-purple, fading to lilac-pink. '**Madame Lemoine**', popular double, white, cream in bud. '**Maud Notcutt**', large, white panicles. '**Michel Buchner**', lilac-blue, double. '**Primrose**', small, pale primrose heads. '**Sensation**', purpled-red flowers, margined white. '**Souvenir de Louis Spath**', an old cultivar, deep wine-red. All H2.4-3m/8-10ft, W1.5-1.8m/5-6ft. F6. Z4-7/8.

Viburnum × burkwoodii

TAMARIX Tamarisk

Distinctive shrubs often seen in coastal areas, most with narrow, upright, later arching branches, feathery, scale-like leaves and plumes of wispy pink flowers. Plants can become unkempt and straggly, so trim every year or two. Prune late-summer and autumn-flowering species to within 2.5cm/1in of old wood in spring before new growth begins; prune spring-flowering species just after flowering. ☼ ❊ ■

T. parviflora (syn. *T. tetrandra purpurea*). This hardy species has purplish stems, bright green leaves and rose-pink flowers. H1.8-2.4m/ 6-8ft, W1.8-2.4m/6-8ft. F5/6. Z5-8.

T. ramosissima (syn. *T. pentandra*). This has red-brown branches, bluish-green foliage and clouds of rose-pink flowers. 'Pink Cascade', shell-pink. 'Rosea', rosy pink, very hardy. 'Rubra', deeper pink. All H2.4-3m/8-10ft, W2.4-3m/8-10ft. F8-9. Z3-8.

T. tetrandra. Hardy, early-flowering and rather open and straggly in habit, with arching branches and light pink flowers. H2.4-3m/8-10ft, W2.4-3m/8-10ft. F5-6. Z6-8.

VIBURNUM

Evergreen and deciduous shrubs and small trees, some winter-flowering, most in spring or early summer, early types often fragrant. Generally easy, most grow in any soil, including chalk. Some need moist soil; others, especially evergreens, may need shelter from cold desiccating winds.

V. × burkwoodii. Fragrant, spring-flowering hybrid is now only one of many similar forms, most upright, eventually round, semi-evergreen, often with good autumn colour, the original hybrid nearly deciduous. In winter, round heads of tight, pink buds form, opening white and continuing for many weeks, their fragrance spreading some distance on warm days. Good for cutting. H1.5-1.8m/5-6ft, W1.5-1.8m/5-6ft. F3. Z5-8. 'Chenaultii', pale pink flowers, fading white. 'Fulbrook' and 'Park Farm' are more evergreen, spreading and slightly later flowering.

V. × carcephalum. Similar to *V. carlesii*, one of its parents, but has larger, fragrant flower clusters, pink in bud, opening white. H1.5-1.8m/5-6ft, W1.5-1.8m/5-6ft. F5-6. Z6-8.

V. carlesii. Fragrant, deciduous shrub forms tight clusters of flower buds in autumn, becoming pink before opening to white in spring. Cultivars include 'Aurora', red flower buds, opening pink, slow-growing. 'Charis', more vigorous, with flowers fading to white. 'Diana', compact, with red buds which open to pink. All H1.2-1.5m/4-5ft, W1.2-1.5m/4-5ft. F5-6. Z4-8.

V. davidii. Evergreen, low, spreading shrub, with leathery, narrow, corrugated leaves, dull flowers, but bright metallic-blue fruit in autumn and winter, not always freely produced. Plant several to ensure cross-pollination – many nurserymen offer fruiting female plants with an identifiable male. ❊ ◪ H60-75cm/24-30in, W90-120cm/3-4ft. F6-7. Z8-9.

V. 'Eskimo'. Deciduous or semi-evergreen dwarf shrub, with glossy, dark green leaves and a succession of snowball-white flowers from late spring. Prune after the main flowering to keep density. H1.2-1.5m/4-5ft, W1.2-1.5m/4-5ft. F4-6. Z6-8.

V. opulus. European native, called guelder rose in Britain, and the European cranberry-bush viburnum in the USA. An easy, deciduous shrub, often found in country hedgerows, outstanding in late summer when hung with clusters of succulent, bright red fruit. It prefers moist soil but adapts to drier ones. All selections have maple-like leaves and flat, white, lacecap flowers in early summer. Some have good autumn leaf colour, but fruit appears when leaves are green. 'Aureum' has bright yellow leaves which can scorch in full sun, but which stay yellow through summer. Red fruit and reddish-brown autumn tints. H1.5-1.8m/5-6ft, W1.2-1.5m/4-5ft. F6-7. Z3-8. 'Roseum' (syn. 'Sterile'), the snowball tree, has light green leaves and masses of round, green flowerheads, opening white. Non-fruiting. H2.4-3m/8-10ft, W1.8-2.4m/6-8ft. F6. Z4-8.

V. plicatum. These include snowball and lacecap types, the latter with central flowers surrounded by larger, sterile florets; both often with fruit following. Undeniably showy. The species is now rare, but many fine cultivars are sold. Most Z6-8. ☼ ❊ ◪ 'Cascade', dense, bushy habit; large, lacecap flowers, often abundant red fruit. H1.5m/5ft, W1.8m/6ft. F5-6. The choice 'Grandiflorum' needs shade and moist soil, forming an erect shrub with large, pale green, sterile, snowball heads, turning white. H1.5-1.8m/5-6ft, W1.2-1.5m/4-5ft. F5-6. 'Lanarth' and 'Mariesii', wide-spreading, horizontally tiered branches with rows of flat, white florets raised above the branches. Both H1.8m/6ft, W2.4m/8ft. F5-6. 'Watanabe' (syn. 'Nanum Semperflorens'), from Japan, is narrow and upright, its small, lacecap flowers appearing on young plants, and continuing, in a small way, to bloom throughout the summer. Advisable to provide shelter; excellent for small gardens. 'Summer Snowflake' is similar. Both H1.2-1.5m/4-5ft, W60-90cm/ 2-3ft. F5-8.

V. sargentii 'Onondaga'. Narrow and upright, its bronze shoots open

Weigela praecox 'Variegata'

to maroon-purple leaves, the flower buds purple, surrounded by white florets. Shoots break freely from the base, given hard pruning in early spring, but flowers will be lost. H1.5-1.8m/5-6ft, W90-120cm/3-4ft. F6-7. Z4-7.

WEIGELA

Ornamental group of easily grown flowering shrubs, include dwarf, coloured-foliage and long-flowering types. Once listed under *Diervilla*, weigelas flower only on last year's stems, the former genus flowering on new season's growth. The trumpet-like flowers, often with prominent stamens, are sometimes so profuse that they weigh down the outer branches. Prune after flowering, thinning congested, old stems to the base and shortening untidy shoots by half, keeping the general habit of the plant. Most are very hardy, though some can be tender and vulnerable to spring frosts. Those offering a longer season of interest than the flowers alone are best value for space.
☼ ❄ ■

W. florida. Parent to many hybrids but rarely grown, it and most hybrids have an upright, arching habit, dark green leaves and rosy-pink flowers, paler inside. H1.5-1.8m/5-6ft, W1.2-1.5m/4-5ft. F5-6. Z5-8. 'Foliis Purpureis' has purple-green leaves and purplish-pink flowers. The Canadian 'Minuet', similar in habit and leaf, has clusters of rosy-purple flowers, with prominent, creamy-white stamens. 'Rumba' is similar again, but with red flowers. 'Tango' has purplish foliage and red flowers. All H75-90cm/30-36in, W90cm/3ft. F5-6. Z5-8. 'Variegata', similar to the species, has coarse leaves with creamy-yellow margins, pinkish in autumn, and pink flowers; more erect, with coarser, yellower leaves than *W. praecox* 'Variegata'. H1.5-

Wisteria sinensis

1.8m/5-6ft, W1.2-1.5m/4-5ft. F5-6. Z5-8.
W. praecox 'Variegata'. White-edged, wavy leaves in sun, golden-yellow in shade, and fragrant, rose-pink flowers with a yellow throat. Can suffer from spring frost; best in shelter. ☼ ❄ H1.2-1.5m/4-5ft, W1.2-1.5m/4-5ft. F5-6. Z6-8.
Hybrids. Most flower from mid-summer. Unless otherwise indicated, all H1.5-2.4m/5-8ft, W1.5-1.8m/5-6ft. F5-6. Z5-8. 'Abel Carrière', over 100 years old, is still one of the best; red buds opening carmine-rose, large and free-flowering. 'Boskoop Glory', large, satin-pink flowers. 'Bristol Ruby', large, deep red flowers, good foliage. 'Candida', white-flowered. The French 'Carnival', salmon-pink, white and dark pink. 'Dropmore Pink', deep pink, very hardy. 'Eva Supreme', vigorous, profuse, deep red flowers. 'Looymansii Aurea', open and graceful, golden-yellow leaves and pink flowers all summer; lovely in part shade. 'Mont Blanc', fragrant, white flowers. 'Rubigold' (syn. 'Briant Rubidor'), French sport of 'Bristol Ruby', golden-yellow leaves prone to sunscorch, occasional green variegations, deep red flowers. 'Snowflake', pale foliage, robust

white flowers. 'Victoria', dwarf, black-purple leaves, rose-pink flowers, often recurring. H90-120cm/3-4ft, W90-120cm/3-4ft. F5-8. Z6-8.

WISTERIA

Small group of ornamental twiners, with pinnate leaves and often spectacular, pendulous racemes of white, blue, purple or pink flowers. Most named forms are grafted and usually flower within two or three years of purchase, but cheaper, seed-raised plants can take several years to flower. Wisterias can be trained and tied against walls and fences and over pergolas. They can also be trained up stakes and carefully pruned to form small trees, or grown as patio specimens in containers, as long as they are regularly fertilized. Plant in a sunny, sheltered spot and well-drained, fertile soil.

In climates with late spring frosts, grow against a west-facing wall, to protect the flower buds. Prune to control size and improve flowering. Train new growth to form a framework for two or three years, longer if necessary. On established plants, prune long shoots in late summer back to about 15cm/6in of the season's new growth, and in mid-winter, prune a few more

centimetres/inches back to two or three flowering buds which should have formed. Once out of reach, wisterias can be allowed to go their own way.
W. floribunda. The Japanese wisteria has stems which twine in a clockwise direction, while the Chinese wisteria, *W. sinensis,* goes anti-clockwise – one of the small wonders of nature! The Japanese wisteria has dark green leaves which unfurl as the 15-25cm/6-10in pendulous racemes of fragrant, bluish-purple flowers appear in succession. Pale yellow autumn leaf colour. 'Alba' has 60cm/2ft long racemes on established specimens, the white flowers often tinged lilac. 'Macrobotrys' (syn. 'Multijuga'), impressive, with racemes sometimes reaching 90cm/3ft or more in length; a specimen draped with numerous flowers is quite breathtaking. 'Rosea', pale rose-pink and purple. 'Violacea', violet-blue. 'Violacea Plena', unusual double, violet-blue. All H5-6m/16-20ft, W5-6m/16-20ft. F5-6. Z4-9.
W. sinensis. The Chinese wisteria is the most widely grown form. It is often sold as a seed-raised plant, liable to have inferior flowers and take up to ten years to flower, so be sure to look for grafted plants. The species has mauve-lilac, fading to pale lilac, fragrant flowers on pendulous racemes to 30cm/1ft long, all opening at once and before the leaves appear. 'Alba' has white flowers. 'Black Dragon', double, dark purple, long trusses. 'Peaches and Cream' (syn. 'Kuchibeni'), pink buds opening creamy- white. 'Pink Ice' (syn. 'Hond Beni'), rose-pink, long racemes. 'Plena', lilac double flowers. 'Purple Patches' (syn. 'Murasaki Naga Fuji'), long trusses, deep violet-purple flowers. 'Snow Showers' (syn. 'Shiro Naga Fuji'), pure white. All H6-8m/20-26ft, W6-8m/20-26ft. F5. Z5-9.

CONIFERS

Juniperus communis 'Suecica Nana'

Flowers on *Pinus heldreichii*

Although a full conifer directory cannot be included here for reasons of space, conifers have a definite part to play in creating summer colour in the garden. Contrary to some views, conifers can and do change quite dramatically with the seasons, as is illustrated in earlier chapters of this book.

Though conifers tend to have a more supporting role in summer, when there is so much of interest in the garden, their colours and effects can be breathtaking, particularly during the period of new growth in early to mid-summer. The foliage varies according to type, with firs (*Abies*), spruce (*Picea*) and pines (*Pinus*) having needles or leaves which are completely different from those of the junipers (*Juniperus*) or the chamaecyparis. Some, like the larch (*Larix*) or swamp cypress (*Taxodium*), are deciduous.

Conifers come in all shapes and sizes and can be fast- or slow-growing. They may be low, bushy or bun-shaped, narrow, upright, prostrate or semi-prostrate, wide-spreading – or, indeed, any shape in between.

Foliage colours vary from silver-blue, deep blue, gold, yellow and, of course, all shades of green as well as variegated. Their colours have the most intensity during the periods of active growth in spring and summer, though the winter colours on some plants are even brighter than in summer.

Most conifers actually have flowers – some a dramatic red – and many have attractive cones. Some, for example the pines, put on only one

Pinus mugo 'Jeddeloh' making new growth in early summer

burst of growth each year, while chamaecyparis will continue to make growth throughout the summer.

As the illustrations from Foggy Bottom earlier in the book will show, conifers act as important background plants, offering colour contrasts to shrubs, perennials, alpines and grasses. They do not have to be grown on their own or with plants like heathers but can be an integral part of garden planting, either as hedges or specimens. What must be remembered is that conifers will not only provide valuable year-round colour but, in the larger types, will also give structure to the garden.

This part of the book can present only a general view of conifers and their role in the spring and summer garden, but hopefully this should be sufficient to promote wider interest.

New growth on *Abies lasiocarpa* 'Compacta'

An association of conifers at Foggy Bottom

PERENNIALS DIRECTORY

PERENNIALS ARE THE PERFECT INGREDIENT to create spring and summer colour in the garden, however large or small. Enormously diverse and adaptable, perennials can be found to fit almost all garden sites and situations. This, the largest single directory in the book, includes a few bulbs as well as my selection of the most worthwhile of all perennials. Remember that if a particular recommended selection is not available to you, good alternatives can usually be found at either local specialist growers or at garden centres. Local and regional climates will of course hav e a bearing on what can be grown successfully, flowering times and longevity also varying according to seasonal variations.

H:	Approximate height
W:	Approximate width
F :	Months in flower
Z:	Relevant hardiness zone(s)

Mid-summer grouping: *Acanthus spinosus, Geranium* 'Mavis Simpson'

ACANTHUS Bear's breeches
Stately plants with handsome, divided leaves and striking flower spikes of overlapping bracts, good for drying. Protect young plants with a mulch where winters are cold. The deep, fleshy roots are difficult to eradicate once established. ✢ ■
A. spinosus. Large, glossy, divided leaves, tipped with spines, form handsome mounds of deep green foliage. Tall spikes bearing hooded purplish flowers are dramatic and imposing. H1.2m/4ft, W60cm/2ft. F7-9. Z7-10.

ACHILLEA Yarrow, milfoil
Most achilleas have ferny leaves and small, tight clusters of flowers, some excellent for cutting or drying. ✢ ■
A. 'Anthea'. A first-class hybrid, with soft and silvery foliage. The flower heads, 8-10cm/3-4in across, are primrose-yellow and fade to creamy-yellow. Cut out faded stems to prolong flowering. H60cm/2ft, W30cm/1ft. F6-8. Z4-8.
'Galaxy Hybrids'. A range of hybrids between *A. millefolium* and *A. sibirica* 'Taygetea'. Colourful, easy to grow, good for cutting. All

W60cm/2ft. F6-9. Z4-8. 'Apple Blossom' (syn. 'Apfelblüte') light lilac-pink. H40cm/16in. 'Great Expectations' (syn. 'Hoffnung') buff-primrose flowers. H60cm/2ft. 'Salmon Beauty' (syn. 'Lachsscönheit') light salmon-pink. H60cm/2ft. 'The Beacon' (syn. 'Fanal') bright red flowers, with yellow centres. H60cm/2ft.
A. 'Moonshine'. Showy, flat heads of lemon-yellow above silvery foliage. H60cm/2ft, W45cm/18in. F6-9. Z4-8.

ACONITUM Aconite, monkshood
Distinctive but underrated garden plants. Divide congested clumps every 2 or 3 years. Roots are poisonous if eaten. ✢ ✳ ☆ ✭
A. 'Blue Sceptre'. A striking cultivar with erect spikes of violet-blue and white flowers. H75cm/30in, W45cm/18in. F7-9. Z4-8.
A. 'Bressingham Spire' makes a strong-stemmed, perfect narrow pyramid with deeply cut green leaves. Flowers violet-blue. H90-100cm/36-39in, W45cm/18in. F7-9. Z4-8.
A. 'Ivorine'. Distinctive bushy habit with good foliage; ivory-white flowers on branching spikes. H up to 90cm/3ft, W75cm/30in. F6-8. Z5-8.

AGAPANTHUS African lily
Popular perennials originally from South Africa, some hardier than imagined. Strap-like leaves and rounded stems bearing heads of blue or white flowers. Ideal for containers. In colder areas mulch in late autumn with straw or bracken. All below Z8-10. ✭ ☆
A. 'Bressingham Blue'. Amethyst-blue, free-flowering. *A.* 'Bressingham White'. Pure white blooms. Both H90cm/3ft, W45cm/18in. F7-9.
A. companulatus 'Isis'. A sturdy cultivar with a bright display of deep blue flowers. H60cm/2ft, W45cm/18in. F7-9.
A. 'Lilliput'. Quite dwarf with small,

Allium schoenoprasum 'Forescate'

rich blue flowers on slender stems. H10cm/12in, W10cm/4in. F7-8.

ALCHEMILLA MOLLIS Lady's mantle
Indispensable, adaptable perennial. Large, grey-green, rounded leaves are slightly hairy and hold raindrops. Good for cutting, sprays of tiny, yellow-green flowers are attractive. Self-seeding so remove heads after flowering if required. H45cm/18in, W60cm/2ft. F6-8. Z4-8. ✢ ✳

ALLIUM Ornamental onion
Strictly bulbs but often grown as perennials. A very wide range of generally easy-to-grow plants. ✢ ■
A. afflatuense. The Persian Onion fits well with other perennials, pushing up stump-like leaves which soon disappear as large purple flower heads appear in late spring. H60-90cm/ 2-3ft, W45cm/18in. F5-6. Z4-8.
A. schoenoprasum 'Forescate' has bright purple-crimson blooms. H30cm/1ft, W23 cm/9in. F6-8. Z3-9.
A. senescens. Late-flowering display of flesh-pink flowers from neat-growing, grey-green clumps. H30cm/12in, W15cm/6in. F8-9. Z4-8.

AMSONIA
A. tabernaemontana. Pretty species forms clump with narrow willow-like leaves on arching stems tipped with

small, light blue flowers for many weeks. Graceful, long-lived. H75cm/30in, W45cm/18in. F6-9. Z4-9. ☼ ☀ ☆

ANAPHALIS Pearl everlasting
A. triplinervis 'Summer Snow'. Perhaps the most effective of these grey- and silver-leaved plants. Easy to grow. Flowers white with yellow centres, excellent for cutting, makes a good foil. H30cm/12in, W60cm/2ft. F7-9. Z4-9. ☼ ◣ ☀

ANCHUSA
A group of fleshy-rooted perennials. From coarse, hairy leaves emerge branched spikes carrying striking blue flowers in early summer. Cut stems back after flowering. May need staking. ☼ ■
A. 'Royalist'. Perhaps the most reliable, with gentian-blue flowers. H1.5m/5ft, W60cm/2ft. F5-7. 'Opal', light blue. H1.1m/43in, W60cm/2ft. F5-7.

ANEMONE
There are some excellent perennials in this genus, few more so than the **Japanese anemones** (*A. × hybrida*) flowering in late summer/autumn.
A. × hybrida. Classic perennials with leafy foliage, wiry stems and single and double yellow-stamened flowers. ☼ ☀ ☆ (including lime).
'Alba', strong grower, pure white flowers, golden-yellow stamens. H75cm/30in, W45cm/18in. F8-10. Z5-8. 'Bressingham Glow', rich, deep pink, semi-double flowers. H60cm/ 2ft, W45cm/18in. F8-10. Z5-8. 'Hadspen Abundance', deep rose-pink, almost semi-double flowers. H60cm/2ft, W30cm/1ft. F8-10. Z5-9. 'Lady Gilmour', large, double clear pink flowers. H60cm/2ft, W45cm/ 18in. F7-10. Z5-8.

ANTHEMIS
Easy-to-grow sun lovers for open positions. ☼ ■

Anemone 'Hadspen Abundance'

A. cupaniana. Greyish, aromatic leaves and a spectacular show of white, yellow-centred daisies. H25cm/ 10in, W75cm/30in. F5-8. Z5-8.
A. tinctoria 'E C Buxton'. Free-flowering daisy, ideal for hot, dry positions. Spreading habit, rich green foliage and a succession of lemon-yellow petalled flowers with a gold centre; provides weeks of summer colour. Cut back hard after flowering to create basal growth which will help over-wintering. H75cm/2ft 6in, W75cm/2ft 6in. F6-8. Z 4-8.

AQUILEGIA Columbine
Popular plants, though few are long-lived and, while freely seeding, they are inclined to cross-breed. Space each group some distance apart. ☼
A. vulgaris. Clustered flowers come in a profusion of white, pink, indigo, violet and crimson. H60cm/2ft, W45cm/18in, F5-7. Z5-9. There are several selections with yellow leaves: 'Granny's Gold' is distinctive but can have white or lilac-purple flowers; 'Mellow Yellow' similar, with white flowers. 'Nora Barlow' is an interesting variation with double rose-pink and cream flowers. H60cm/2ft, W30cm/1ft. F6-7. Z5-9.
McKana Hybrids. Mixed colours with extra-long spurs. H75cm/30in, W30cm/1ft. F5-7. Z3-9.

ARTEMISIA
Primarily used as foliage plants, with flowers of little significance. Woodier types need pruning in spring if becoming unshapely. ☼ ■
A. lactiflora. Fine green, deeply cut leaves and stiff stems carrying creamy-white plumes in late summer. 'Guizhou', with bronze-purple leaves, is even more effective. H1.5-1.8m/ 5-6ft, W60cm/2ft. F8-10. Z4-9. ◣
A. ludoviciana 'Silver Queen'. Rapid-spreader with willow-like silvery leaves and leafy stems. 'Valerie Finnis' has broader leaves and is more vigorous. Both H80cm/32in, W60cm/2ft. Z4-9.
A. stelleriana. Vigorous, spreading habit, deeply cut silver leaves carried on ground-hugging stems. Good evergreen ground cover. 'Mori' (sometimes called 'Silver Brocade'), is similar but more compact. H30cm/1ft, W60cm/2ft. Z4-8.

ARUNCUS Goat's beard
Showy plants, closely related to *Spiraea*, are adaptable to moist or dry soils. ☀ ◣
A. dioicus (syn. *A. sylvester*). Imposing, creamy-white plumes are carried above a mass of fern-like foliage. H1.5-2.1m/5-7ft, W1.2m/ 4ft. F6-7. Z3-8. 'Kneiffii' is dwarfer, with dark green, deeply cut leaves,

wiry stems and flower plumes. 'Dublin' has finer creamy-white plumes. H90cm/3ft, W45cm/18in. F6-7. Z3-8.
A. sylvester. See A. *dioicus*.

ASCLEPIAS Butterfly weed, milkweed
A. luberosa. Butterfly weed is the best-known species but is not always easy to grow. It prefers a warm, sandy loam to produce its bright heads of burnished deep orange and needs summer warmth to succeed. H45cm/18in, W30cm/1ft. F7-9. Z4-9.

ASPHODELINE
A. lutea. King's spear, or asphodel, forms clumps of narrow, glaucous leaves and strong spikes of bright yellow starry flowers, followed by attractive seedheads. The German cultivar 'Gelbkerze' has larger, slightly brighter flowers. Both H1m/39in, W30cm/1ft. F6-8. Z6-8.

ASTER
This vast and varied genus has many species of great garden value, varying in height from 10cm/4in to 2.1m/7ft and flowering from mid-spring to late autumn. Most are easy to grow and popular for cutting. ☼ ■
A. amellus. Trouble-free perennials, all single rayed, yellow-centred flowers with no faults or diseases. All

Aruncus dioicus (syn. *A. sylvester*)

Astilbe simplicifolia 'Sprite'

long-lived and long-flowering. For autumn planting, pot-grown plants are best. All F8-10. Z5-8. ☼ ✹

'King George', an old, violet-blue favourite. H60cm/2ft, W45cm/18in. 'Nocturne', rich lilac-lavender. H75cm/30in, W45cm/18in. 'Pink Zenith', the most prolific pink variety. H60cm/2ft, W45cm/18in. 'Violet Queen', masses of deep violet-blue flowers. H60cm/2ft, W45cm/18in. *A.* × *frikartii* 'Flora's Delight'. Dwarf, free-flowering, disease-free. Raised by my father Alan Bloom and named for my stepmother, first-class with bluish-lilac flowers for months. H45cm/18in, W40cm/16in. F7-10. Z4-9. 'Mönch' and 'Wunder von Stäfa' are outstanding perennials, long-flowering with soft lavender-blue petals, yellow daisy centres. Both H1m/39in. F7-9. Z5-8. ☼ ■
A. lateriflorus 'Prince'. Really a foliage plant of stiff, upright habit, bronze-purple from spring onwards. Flowers pink, small. H60cm/2ft, W45cm/18in. F9-11. Z4-8.
A. novae-angliae. The New England asters offer some bright colour late in summer. All trouble-free and easy to grow; some are quite tall. 'Alma Pötschke', striking, warm salmon-rose. H1.5m/5ft, W60cm/2ft. 'Autumn Snow' (syn. 'Herbst-

Astrantia carniolica rubra

schnee'), large white flowers in bushy heads. H1.5m/5ft, W50cm/20in. 'Harrington's Pink', clear pink. 'Rosa Sieger' is similar. H1.5m/5ft, W60cm/2ft. F8-10. Z4-8.
A. thomsonii 'Nanus'. A first-class perennial of bushy habit, set with grey-green foliage and rayed, light blue flowers for weeks on end. H40cm/16in, W25cm/10in. F7-10. Z4-9.

ASTILBE
Popular hardy perennials ranging in size from a few centimetres to over a metre, some with attractive foliage. Good for cutting and excellent as container plants given adequate moisture. Divide and replant every few years from late autumn to early spring. The very dwarf ones are shade lovers. All benefit from a spring mulch of enriched peat or leafmould. ☼ ✹ ◿
A. chinensis 'Pumila'. Low spreading foliage and short lilac-pink flower spikes. Good ground cover. H30cm/1ft, W25cm/10in. F7-9. Z4-8.
A. chinensis tacquetii 'Superba'. Tall spikes of purple-magenta flowers.

'Purpurlanze' ('Purple Lance') is brighter. Both H1.2-1.5m/4-5ft, W45cm/18in. F8-9. Z4-8.
A. simplicifolia. Parent of several good dwarf hybrids. Small leaves, pink flowers. H30cm/1ft, W20cm/8in. F6-8. All Z4-8.
'Bronze Elegans', arching stems, pink flowers, pretty bronze-tinged leaves, compact habit. 'Sprite', dark bronze-green, deeply cut foliage and late display of arching sprays of pink flowers, fading to white. Both H25-30cm/10-12in, W30cm/1ft. F8-9.
Hybrids. The following are sometimes classified as *A.* × *arendsii* or *A. japonica*. All Z4-8. 'Amethyst', full, lilac-rose spikes. H90cm/3ft, W60cm/2ft. F6-7. 'Bressingham Beauty', fine pink spikes on strong stems above attractive foliage. H1m/39in, W60cm/2ft. F6-8. 'Catherine Deneuve', deep rose-pink spikes, dark foliage. 'Elizabeth Bloom', free-flowering, rich pink spikes, abundant dark green foliage. Both H60cm/2ft, W60cm/2ft. F6-8. 'Fanal', long-flowering, with short, red, dense spikes, striking foliage.

H50cm/20in, W45cm/18in. F6-8. 'Federsee', sturdy, full rosy red plumes. H60cm/2ft, W60cm/2ft. F6-8. 'Ostrich Plume', distinctive, arching, salmon-pink plumes. H80cm/32in, W60cm/2ft. F7-8. 'Sheila Haxton', outstanding, compact, pink with a hint of lilac. H40cm/16in, W30cm/1ft. F6-8. 'Snowdrift', bright green mounds of cut foliage, clear white plumes. H60cm/2ft, W45cm/18in. F6-8.

ASTRANTIA Masterwort
Popular for garden and cut flowers, their curiously shaped blooms each have a dome of tiny florets backed by a collar-like bract. Clump-forming and easy to grow. Some seed freely and can soon become mixed. All Z4-8. ☼ ✹ ◿
A. carniolica rubra. Deep crimson-green flowers above mounds of divided foliage. H45cm/18in, W30cm/1ft. F6-8. ◿ ✴
A. major involucrata 'Shaggy' (syn. 'Margery Fish') has larger bracts and is quite showy. H75cm/2ft 6in, W45cm/18in. F6-8. 'Rosea' has deep rose-red flowers. H75cm/30in, W45cm/18in. F6-8. 'Ruby Wedding', outstanding, glowing ruby-red flowers. H75cm/2ft 6in, W45cm/18in. F6-8. 'Sunningdale Variegated', bright foliage in spring and early summer, the leaves edged white then cream, but fading when greenish-white flowers appear. H75cm/2ft 6in, W45cm/18in. F6-8.

BAPTISIA Wild indigo
B. australis. Long-lived, bushy perennial with abundant blue-green foliage topped by short spikes of indigo-blue, lupin-like flowers, followed by attractive seed pods. Non-invasive. H90-120cm/3-4ft, W60cm/2ft. F6-8. Z3-9. ☼ ◿

BERGENIA
Good foliage in summer, some colouring up well in winter. Flowers

attractive in spring but can get spoilt by frost. Mainly evergreen, shiny leaves up to 25cm/10in across. Spreading habit, good ground cover. ✿ ✱ ✽

Hybrids. Crosses between various species have produced some excellent forms. '**Abendglut**' (syn. 'Evening Glow'), small, almost prostrate, with short spikes of crimson flowers and purplish leaves in winter. H25cm/10in, W30cm/1ft. F3-5. Z3-8. '**Baby Doll**', compact spikes of sugar-pink flowers. H20cm/8in, W30cm/1ft. F3-5. Z4-8. '**Bressingham Ruby**', intense, deep red flowers and almost beetroot-red leaves in winter. H30cm/1ft, W30cm/1ft. F3-5. Z3-8. '**Bressingham White**', clean white flowers, handsome rounded leaves. H30cm/1ft, W30cm/1ft. F3-5. Z4-8. '**Morgenröte**', dwarf, bright carmine-pink flowers, often flowering a second time in summer. H30cm/1ft, W30cm/1ft. F3-5. Z3-8.

BRUNNERA
B. macrophylla. Adaptable perennial with large, heart-shaped, deep green leaves, sprays of bright blue forget-me-not flowers in spring. Good ground cover for all but hot, dry

Brunnera macrophylla 'Variegata'

positions. H40cm/16in, W60cm/2ft. F4-6. All Z4-8. '**Hadspen Cream**', vigorous, with wide, creamy-buff-edged leaves. H35cm/14in, W60cm/2ft. F5-6. '**Langtrees**' has small, silvery-white blotches on the leaves. H40cm/16in, W60cm/2ft. F4-6. '**Variegata**' has bright leaf variegation, but needs shelter from sun and some moisture. H40cm/16in, W60cm/2ft. F4-6.

CAMPANULA **Bellflower**
A varied and invaluable genus, from dwarf alpine to tall perennials, which is easy to grow. ✿ ■ ✫ (*See also* Alpines Directory).
C. '**Burghaltii**'. Distinctive for its large, dangling bells of smokey lavender-blue, hanging from short, leafy stems. H60cm/2ft, W30cm/1ft. F6-8. Z4-8.
C. glomerata. Species with violet-blue flowers, variable and inclined to be invasive. Selections recommended: '**Schneekrone**' ('Crown of Snow'), sturdy spikes of white bells. '**Purple Pixie**', late, with dark foliage and deep blue flowers on stiff spikes. Both H45cm/18in, W30cm/1ft. F7-9. '**Superba**', large, rich purple-violet flowers, but can be invasive. H80cm/32in, W60cm/2ft. F6-8.
C. '**Kent Belle**'. A striking hybrid with arching stems carrying rich violet-blue bells. H120-150cm/4-5ft, W45cm/18in. F6-8. Z4-8.
C. lactiflora. The milky bellflowers add a considerable presence in the summer garden with their willowy stems and heads of massed flowers. Adaptable to sun or shade; some taller forms may need staking. All Z4-8. '**Alba**' has milky-white flowers. '**Loddon Anna**' is equally imposing, with flesh-pink flowers. Both H1.8m/6ft, W60cm/2ft. F6-8. '**Pouffe**', forms dense mounds of light green foliage, with light lavender-blue flowers. H25cm/10in, W25cm/10in. F6-9. '**Prichard's Variety**', outstanding show of lavender-blue

flowers. H1.2m/4ft, W60cm/2ft. F6-8. '**White Pouffe**', similar to 'Pouffe'; both flower best in sun. H25cm/10in, W25cm/10in. F6-9.
C. persicifolia. Popular bellflower with nodding, cup-shaped flowers varying from white to pale and deep blue. Good for cutting. H70-80cm/28-32in, W30cm/1ft. All F6-8. Z4-8. '**Alba Coronata**', with semi-double pale white flowers. H90-120cm/3-4ft, W30cm/1ft. '**Chettle Charm**', a pretty selection with off-white, blue-tinged cup-shaped bells on wiry stems. Excellent for cutting. H90-120cm/3-4ft, W30cm/1ft.

CATANANCHE CAERULEA
Sun-loving perennial with lavender-blue flowers surrounded by papery bracts, grassy foliage. The white form '**Alba**' is an interesting variation. Good for cutting and drying. H60cm/2ft, W30cm/12in. F7-8. Z3-9.

CENTAUREA **Knapweed**
The perennial cornflowers include some good species, usually with purple, thistle-like flowers, easy to grow in open, sunny positions.
C. hypoleuca '**John Coutts**' has bright, glistening pink flowers above

Campanula 'Kent Belle'

ample grey foliage. H60cm/2ft, W45cm/18in. F5-7. Z4-8.
C. macrocephala. The globe centre has large mid-green leaves and stout stems topped by large yellow thistles, good for drying. H1.2-1.5m/4-5ft, W60cm/2ft. F6-8. Z3-8.
C. montana. Mountain knapweed has a spreading habit. The lance-shaped leaves are grey and slightly hairy; flowers on single stalks have one row of toothed or lacy petals around a central cone. Colours vary from white to pink, light blue, lilac and violet-blue. A few cultivars are offered. '**Gold Bullion**' is worth special mention for its yellow-gold foliage and blue flowers, giving summer-long appeal. Excellent on chalk and poor soil. All H30cm/1ft, W30cm/1ft. F5-6. Z3-8.
C. '**Pulchra Major**'. Outstandingly handsome, deeply cut, arching grey leaves and rigid stems topped by large, deep pink thistles. H90cm/3ft, W30cm/1ft. F6-8. Z7-8.

CENTRANTHUS **Valerian**
C. ruber. This easily grown plant will colonize almost anywhere from self-sown seed, even in the poorest soil, on walls and rocky banks, especially

Centaurea montana 'Gold Bullion'

Chrysanthemum weyrichii

on limestone. The colours are mostly pink to brick-red but **'Albus'** is a good white form. All have fleshy leaves. H80cm/32in, W45cm/18in. F6-9. Z5-8. ✿ ✾

CHELONE Turtle head
C. obliqua. An underrated perennial with erect, leafy stems tipped with a good display of ruby-pink flowers. A reliable plant for sun. The white form **'Alba'** is also worth growing. Both H80cm/32in, W45cm/18in. F7-9. Z4-9.

CHRYSANTHEMUM
There have been so many name changes in this popular genus in recent years that even the genus name itself, *Chrysanthemum,* has disappeared!
C. weyrichii (syn. *Dendranthema weyrichii*). Early summer-flowering species with low, spreading habit and large, brilliant white yellow-centred flowers, on stems only 10cm/4in high, fading to pink. Flowers again in autumn. H10-15cm/4-6in, W15cm/6in. F6-7. Z4-9.

CIMICIFUGA Bugbane
C. cordifolia. Broad, deep green leaves and tapering spikes of creamy-white on wiry, purplish stems.

H90-120cm/3-4ft, W60cm/2ft. F8-9. Z4-8.
C. ramosa. Large, divided leaves and lofty, tapering, branched spikes, creamy-white, late in the season. H2.1m/7ft, W60cm/2ft. F8-9. Z4-8. **'Atropurpurea'**, outstanding for its purplish leaves and stems, contrasting effectively with the white flowers. H2.1m/7ft, W60cm/2ft. F8-9. Z4-8. **'Brunette'** has even more striking black-purple foliage. H1.8m/6ft, W60cm/2ft. F8-10. Z4-8.

CLEMATIS
This genus includes perennial, non-climbing species of real garden value, reliably hardy and long-lived, needing minimal attention. ✿ ✾ ☆
C. davidiana See *C. heracleifolia*.
C. × *eriostemon* **'Hendersonii'**. Nodding flowers with deep blue, reflexed petals from late spring to mid-summer, followed by attractive seedheads. This, and the similar *C. integrifolia* are inclined to flop. Both H60-70cm/24-28in if supported, otherwise 40cm/16in, W60cm/2ft. F5-7. Z4-9.
C. heracleifolia (syn. *C. davidiana*). Makes a woody-based, leafy bush with hyacinth-like clusters of scented blue flowers for many weeks, followed by attractive seedheads. Though dying down over winter, its lush summer growth needs ample space. **'Alan Bloom'**, a new selection, has an upstanding habit, dark green leaves and deep blue fragrant flowers. **'Crepuscule'**, **'Cote D'Azur'** and **'Wyevale'** are all slightly different shades of blue, all worthwhile. All H90cm/3ft, W60cm/2ft. F7-9. Z4-9.

COREOPSIS Tickseed
Yellow daisies, with yellow or orange central discs. ✿ ☆
C. auriculata **'Nana'**. A splendid dwarf perennial whose deep green mounds produce a summer-long succession of bright yellow flowers. H30cm/1ft, W30cm/1ft. F5-10. Z4-9.

Coreopsis verticillata 'Moonbeam'

C. rosea. Unique for its small, pale pink flowers on narrow-leaved stems. Spreads below ground. A selected form, **'American Dream'**, has deeper pink flowers. Both H30cm/1ft, W30cm/1ft. F8-9. Z3-9.
C. verticillata **'Golden Gain'**. Makes a compact bush with finely divided leaves and bright yellow flowers for weeks. H60cm/2ft, W38cm/15in. F7-9. Z4-9. **'Grandiflora'** has larger, deeper yellow flowers. H50cm/20in, W45cm/18in. F7-9. Z4-9. **'Moonbeam'**, light lemon-yellow flowers, scented foliage and spreading growth. H40cm/16in, W30cm/1ft. F7-9. Z3-9. **'Zagreb'** has clear yellow flowers, dwarf bushy growth. H35cm/14in, W30cm/1ft. F7-9. Z3-7.

COSMOS
C. atrosanguineus (syn. *Bidens atrosanguinea*). Long succession of chocolate-scented, rich deep crimson, single dahlia-like flowers above bushy, dark green, divided foliage. Tuberous root. Survives outdoors only if covered to prevent frost penetration; roots may be lifted and stored as for dahlias. H80cm/32in, W38cm/15in. F7-10. Z8-9. ✿ ◢ ■

CORDYALIS FLEXUOSA
A species only recently discovered in China, with finely cut leaves through late winter and into summer and azur-blue flowers for many weeks in spring and early summer. Foliage dies back in summer, shows again in autumn or early spring. ✾ ◢
Several selections, including **'Père David'**, **'China Blue'**, **'Purple Leaf'** and **'Blue Panda'** are all good. Some variations, but generally H30-45cm/12-18in, W20cm/8in. F4-6. Z7-8.

CROCOSMIA
Some of these South African plants create vivid splashes of colour in late summer and autumn. Parentage very mixed: montbretia types (M) are less hardy. Plant in spring and protect by leaves or dig up for winter. ✿ ■
C. **'Bressingham Beacon'**. Vigorous flame-orange cultivar, dark stems, good cut flower. H75cm/2ft 6in, W15cm/6in. F7-8. Z5-9.
C. **'Emberglow'**. A glowing, burnt red shade with abundant, rush-like foliage. H1.2m/4ft, W15cm/6in. F7-9. Z5-9.
C. **'Jenny Bloom'**. This has soft butter-yellow flowers and is strong-growing and prolific. H75cm/2ft 6in, W15cm/6in. F7-9. Z5-9.

Crocosmia 'Spitfire'

C. 'Lucifer'. The flowers on wiry, upstanding spikes are deep flame-red. H1.2-1.5m/4-5ft. F6-8. Z5-9.
C. masonorum. The parent of many hybrids, selected for its hardiness and arching stems revealing wide-petalled, upward-facing, vermilion-orange flowers. Handsome broad foliage. H80cm/32in, W15cm/6in. F7-9. Z7-9. 'Firebird', an improved Bressingham selection, is quite outstanding for its large, flame-orange flowers on arching stems. H80cm/32in, W15cm/6in. F7-9.

Delphinium × *belladonna* 'Peace'

Z6-9. 'Rowallane Yellow', similar, with large, pure-yellow flowerheads making a striking variation. H90cm/3ft, W15cm/6in. F6-9. Z7-9.
C. 'Spitfire'. Dense foliage, brilliant fiery orange flowers on strong stems. H75cm/2ft 6in, W15cm/6in. F7-9. Z5-9.
C. 'Vulcan'. Bright flame-red flowers with a yellow throat. Compact habit. H60cm/2ft, W15cm/6in. F7-9. Z5-9.

CYNARA Cardoon
C. cardunculus. Closely related to the globe artichoke, *C. scolymus,* and, like it, a very ornamental species for the decorative garden. Tall, strong stems carry terminal thistle flowers, with scaly bracts enclosing a large, purple-mauve tuft. The basal foliage has large, silvery, deeply jagged leaves up to 60cm/2ft long. Handsome all summer, attractive to bees. H1.8-2.1m/6-7ft, W60cm/2ft. F7-8. Z7-9. ☼ ■

DELPHINIUM
Magnificent perennials at their best, many grown from seed, the more choice cultivars by cuttings or division. Taller forms will need to have their spikes supported by canes. In warmer climates few will be long-lived. ☼ ☀
D. × belladonna. Perhaps the best perennial delphinium. This type is single-flowered, producing an abundance of graceful, loose racemes of flowers and deeply cut leaves. If cut back after flowering, most flower again. All Z3-8. 'Blue Bees', a favourite, with sky-blue flowers. H1m/39in, W60cm/2ft. F6-7. 'Casa Blanca', a white which comes true from seed. H90cm/3ft, W60cm/2ft. F6-7. 'Lamartine', shapely Oxford-blue spikes. H1.2m/4ft, W60cm/2ft. F6-7. 'Peace' (syn. 'Volkerfrieden'*)* the finest, brightest mid-blue. H1.2m/4ft, W60cm/2ft. F6-7.
D. grandiflorum (syn. *D. chinensis).* A short-lived dwarf species. 'Blue Butterfly' is especially popular for its

Dianthus 'Pretty'

brilliant cobalt-blue flowers and finely cut leaves. Good drainage needed. H25-30cm/10-12in, W25cm/10in. F6-8. Z4-9.

DENDRANTHEMA See CHRYSANTHEMUM

DIANTHUS Pink
The dianthus are a large and highly interbred family for the front of the perennial border or on a scree or rock garden. Most garden favourites, but not all, are grey-leaved; many are fragrant. ☼ ■
The border pinks cover taller varieties – single- or double-flowered, mostly highly fragrant – and dwarfer forms, with often spreading habits; the latter fall under alpine or rock garden types but vary greatly. Most flower late spring to summer. Z3-8.

DIASCIA
These free-flowering South African plants are very popular, with new introductions each year. Though not fully hardy they are easy to grow, creating low-growing mats from which a continual display of blooms emerge. Take cuttings in late summer to ensure continuity in the event of cold winters. Most F6-9. Z7-8. ☼ ◢

'Blackthorn Apricot'. Just a suggestion of apricot in the warm pink of this low, floriferous variety. H15cm/6in, W30cm/1ft.
D. rigesens × lilacina. Richer, almost magenta-pink, vigorous spreading habit. H20-25cm/8-10in, W30cm/1ft.
D. barberiae. Deep pink, free-flowering spurred shell-like blooms. H30cm/1ft, W45cm/18in.
D. vigilis (syn. *D. elegans).* Slender spikes bear clear pink flowers all summer. H30cm/1ft, W30cm/1ft.

DICENTRA Bleeding heart
A group of popular and garden-worthy perennials with flowers like hanging lockets. Finely cut foliage and fleshy roots. ☼ ☀ ☀ ◢
D. eximia. From the eastern USA, grey-green fine-cut leaves, dangling pink flowers and spreading habit. 'Alba' is an attractive variation with white flowers.
D. formosa. The 'Pacific bleeding heart' is very similar to *D. eximia.* Rose pink flowers. Both H45cm/18in, W45cm/18in. F5-7. Z4-8.
Hybrids between the above. All Z4-8. 'Adrian Bloom', profuse crimson-rose flowers, glaucous green leaves. H25cm/10in, W20cm/8in. F5-8. 'Luxuriant', deep green leaves,

Digitalis purpurea 'Alba'

crimson flowers. H25cm/10in, W20cm/8in. F5-8. **'Pearl Drops'**, white flowers on arching tips above a mass of bluish-green foliage. H30cm/1ft, W45cm/18in. F5-8. **'Snowflakes'**, long succession of pure white flowers from early spring. H25cm/10in, W25cm/10in. F4-9. *D. macrocapnos* and the similar *D. scandens* are vigorous climbing perennials with yellow flowers and glaucous foliage. H1.8-2.4m/6-8ft, W150cm/5ft. F7-9. Z8-9. *D. spectabilis.* The true bleeding heart, with deep pink and white lockets dangling above light green, delicately cut foliage. The ivory-white **'Alba'** is also charming, with lighter green foliage. Both H60cm/2ft, W45cm/18in. F5-7. Z3-8.

DICTAMNUS Burning bush
Named for its volatility when ignited on a hot summer's day as the seedpods ripen. Best raised from seed and must be planted young. ✳ ■ ✲
D. albus (syn. *D. faxinella albus*). Also called dittany or fraxinella, it has strongly aromatic, light green pinnate leaves and stiff spikes of white flowers with prominent stamens. The more commonly seen form, **D. a. purpureus**

has reddish-lilac flowers. H80cm/32in, W60cm/2ft. F6-8. Z3-8.

DIGITALIS Foxglove
Many foxgloves are biennial and even the perennials are short-lived, but they are excellent for naturalizing and will colonize shady places. ✳ ✺ ☆
D. grandiflora (syn. *D. ambigua*). Most live for three or four years, with spikes of primrose-yellow flowers on compact plants. H60cm/2ft, W30cm/1ft. F6-8. Z4-8.
D. purpurea. Biennial but some forms are ideal to naturalize in garden. Good in half shade, allow to seed. **D. p. 'Alba'** (syn. *D. albiflora*), attractive white flowers all held on one side of the stem. Bees continue to hybridize, so remove coloured selection near white early to avoid degeneration to other colours. F5-7. Z4-9.

DISPORUM Fairy bell
D. sessile 'Variegatum'. Prettily variegated woodland plant which spreads just below the soil surface, producing creamy-white striped foliage and greenish flowers. Most effective grown in a container where it looks good all summer. H30cm/1ft, W30cm/1ft. F5-6.

DORONICUM Leopard bane
These easy-to-grow, yellow-flowered daisies herald spring. Their toothed, heart-shaped leaves usually die down in hot summers. Clumps need replanting every three years to renew vigour. Good for cutting. ✳ ✺ ◢
D. 'Miss Mason'. A hybrid, making a fine show for weeks with persistent, clump-forming leaves. H50cm/20in, W60cm/2ft. F4-6. Z4-8.
D. orientale (syn. *D. caucasicum*). Bright green leaves, cheerful yellow daisies 8cm/3in across. Dies down quickly in summer heat. H45cm/18in, W30cm/1ft. F4-5. Z5-8. 'Goldzwerg' is the best dwarf form. H25cm/10in, W30cm/1ft. F4-6. Z4-8.

Doronicum caucasicum 'Goldzwerg'

Echinacea purpurea 'Magnus'

D. 'Spring Beauty'. Showy with fully double flowers, but can be unreliable. H30cm/1ft, W30cm/1ft. F4-6. Z4-8.

ECHINACEA Coneflower
First-class perennials for summer colour, being reliable and easy to grow. Daisy-like flowers with prominent dark centres and radiating, crimson-magenta petals, often with lighter tips. Much loved by bees. ✳ ✲
E. purpurea. The purple coneflower is mostly represented by named cultivars. All Z4-9. **Bressingham**

Hybrids have stout stems and cerise-purple shades. H1m/39in, W45cm/18in. F7-9. **'Magnus'**, outstanding large-flowered selection, the flowers almost 10cm/4in across, a warm purplish-rose, and borne on sturdy stems for a long period. H90cm/3ft, W38cm/15in. F7-10. **'Robert Bloom'**, rich, glowing rose-red flowers and sturdy stems. **'White Lustre'**, a striking variation. Both H90cm/3ft, W38cm/15in. F7-9.

ECHINOPS Globe thistle
Distinctive perennials with jagged, mostly greyish, prickly foliage and spherical, metallic blue flowerheads on branching stems. Taller species may need staking. All attractive to bees and butterflies. Drought-resistant. Excellent for cutting and drying. ✳ ☆
E. ritro. The best garden species. Compact with abundant, mid-blue flowers above greyish, thistle-like foliage. **'Veitch's Blue'** is a good selection with smaller, lighter blue heads. Both H1.2m/4ft, W60cm/2ft. F7-8. Z3-9.

EPIMEDIUM Barrenwort
Valuable evergreen and deciduous perennials, good foliage effects on new

Erigeron 'Dimity'

growth. Many new species being introduced from Asia. ☼ ✳ (in cooler climates) ☆

E. grandiflorum. 'Album', pretty white starry flowers on long stems. 'Crimson Beauty', outstanding deep crimson red flowers. 'Lilafee', free-flowering, deep lilac purple, dark new leaves. All H20cm/8in, W20cm/8in. F3-5. Z5-8.

E . × perralchicum. 'Fröhnleiten', a neat evergreen form, with yellow flowers and marbled new foliage. H25cm/10in, W25cm/10in. F4-5. Z5-9.

E. × rubrum. Compact clumps of rounded foliage, attractively coloured when young, and deep pink, white-spurred, starry flowers. H20cm/8in, W20cm/8in. F3-5. Z4-9.

ERIGERON Fleabane

A useful genus with daisy-like flowers and lance-shaped leaves. Most are hybrids with bright colours and semi-double flowers, easy to grow and tolerant of maritime conditions. Almost all are good for cutting. Best divided in spring. ☼ ■

Hybrids. A selection of some of the best: '**Amity**', single, lilac-pink flowers. H70cm/28in, W45cm/18in.

F6-8. Z5-8. '**Dimity**', light green leaves, obliquely held sprays of pink flowers, orange-tinted buds. H25cm/10in, W25cm/10in. F6-8. Z4-8. '**Foerster's Liebling**', still popular for its deep pink, semi-double flowers. H40cm/16in, W45cm/18in. F6-8. Z5-8. '**Prosperity**', dwarf and spreading, near double, light blue flowers. H35cm/14in, W45cm/18in. F6-8. Z5-8. '**Rotes Meer**', near red, finely rayed petals. '**Schwarzes Meer**', deep violet with prominent yellow disc. Both H60cm/2ft, W45cm/18in. F6-8. Z5-8.

Eryngium alpinum 'Superbum'

ERYNGIUM Sea holly

These distinctive thistle-like sun lovers have attractive foliage as well as long-lasting, rounded, teazle-like flowers, or bracts, excellent for cutting and drying. Bees love them. ☼ ■

E. alpinum. This has rounded green basal leaves and smooth, branching, blue stems with large steely-blue bracts, each with a decorative calyx 'ruff'. There are several named selections. H75cm/2ft 6in, W45cm/18in. F6-8. Z5-8.

E. bourgati. Striking silver, jagged basal leaves veined white; wiry, much branched stems carry blue ruffled flowers with the upper stems also blue. H60cm/2ft, W30cm/1ft. F6-9. Z5-9.

E. giganteum. Though a biennial, included for its large showy flowers which are surrounded by silvery ruffled bracts. Free-seeding on well-drained soil. H60-75cm/2ft-2ft 6in, W45cm/18in. F6-8. Z4-8.

E. '**Jos Eijking**'. Striking hybrid with upright stems, the cones of blue flowers surrounded by silver-blue bracts; as flowering develops, stems turn a deep blue. H70cm/28in, W45cm/18in. F6-8. Z5-8.

EUPATORIUM

Easily grown perennials, some tall with large flower heads, becoming fluffy in autumn. ◢

E. purpureum. American Joe Pye weed. Stately, late-flowering background plant. Stiff stems with whorls of pointed leaves carry wide, flat, rose-purple flower heads. '**Atropurpureum**', deep purple heads. '**Album**', white flowers. H1.8-2.1m/6-7ft, W90cm/3ft. F8-10. Z3-9. Some new selections of dwarfer habit are worth noting, particularly '**Glutball**', large heads of intense purple-red. H1.5m/5ft, W60cm/2ft. F8-10. Z3-9.

EUPHORBIA Spurge

Popular deciduous and evergreen plants for foliage and flower, mostly

Euphorbia amygdaloides 'Rubra'

spring- and summer-flowering in the form of bracts, generally in shades of yellow. When trimming or taking cuttings, use gloves as the milky sap can irritate skin. Many types.

E. amygdaloides '**Rubra**'. Excellent foliage plant with purple, semi-evergreen leaves, contrasting with yellow flowers. Will seed itself. H30cm/1ft, W45cm/18in. F4-5. Z7-9. ☼ ✳ ■

E. characias. There is much confusion between this and the sub-species *wulfenii*, especially as there now exist innumerable selections. Both have evergreen, glaucous leaves, except in the variegated forms. *E. characias* has dark brown centres to greenish-yellow flowers while *E.* **subsp.** *wulfenii* and hybrids have yellow-centred flowers. From the western Mediterranean, all prefer sun and good drainage. Flower heads begin to form in late winter, opening into full flower in mid- to late spring. In summer, cut back dying flower heads to allow new foliage to develop. Free-seeding. *E.c.* '**Humpty Dumpty**', compact bushy form. H75cm/2ft 6in, W90cm/3ft. F3-5. Z8-9. *E.c.* '**Burrow's Silver**' has brightly variegated leaves but lacks

Euphorbia characias 'Burrow's Silver'

vigour. H60cm/2ft, W45cm/18in. F3-5. Z8-9. *E.c.* subsp. *wulfenii* 'Lambrook Gold' and 'Spring Splendour', large heads on tall stems. H1.5m/5ft, W1.2m/4ft. F3-5. Z7-10. *E. griffithii* 'Fireglow'. This striking, slow-spreading plant emerges in spring with reddish-purple shoots that develop into a bushy mass of greenery, carrying fiery orange flowers. 'Dixter' has a slightly darker hue. Revels in moisture. H1m/39in,

W60cm/2ft. F4-6. Z4-9. ✿ ☆
E. myrsinites. Attractive, blue-grey fleshy leaves closely set along the trailing stems which carry heads of sulphur-yellow flowers. Evergreen. H15cm/6in, W30cm/1ft. E5-7. Z5-8.
E. palustris. Vigorous, clump-forming and deep-rooted species, its huge, greenish-yellow flowerheads make a spectacular late spring display, the foliage orange and yellow in autumn. H1m/39in, W1m/39in. F5-6. Z5-8. ◢
E. polychroma (syn. *E. epithymoides*). Compact and clump-forming, its outstanding yellowish flowers appear before the foliage. As the flowers fade to green, the whole plant becomes a neat, leafy bush. 'Purpurea' has purple-tinged foliage. 'Sonnengold' has showy yellow bracts. All H50cm/20in, W50cm/20in. F4-5. Z4-9.
E. schillingii. Soft green leaves, bushy habit and yellow-green flowers make this a useful late-flowering spurge. H90cm/3ft, W60cm/2ft. F7-9. Z6-9. *E. longifolia* and *E. wallichii* have similar foliage attractions and yellow summer flowers.

FILIPENDULA Meadowsweet

Closely related and often confused with the astilbes, the meadowsweets used to be called *Spiraea*. ✿ ❀ ☆
F. kakome. A cultivar from Japan of great garden merit. Compact habit and a succession of miniature rosy red plumes over green leaves. H30cm/1ft, W30cm/1ft. F7-9. Z3-9.
F. ulmaria. Queen of the Meadows. The species is seldom grown except as a wildflower, with its creamy white fragrant flowers held above the leaves. 'Aurea' is first-class as a foliage plant for shade, with golden-yellow cut leaves which can scorch. 'Variegata', brightly variegated leaves, dark green splashed with yellow. Cut away flowers as soon as finished on larger two varieties as any seedlings will come up green. All H60-120cm/2-4ft, W45cm/18in. F6-8. Z3-9.
F. purpurea. Outstanding for its display of cerise-red flowers over leafy, bushy foliage. H90cm/3ft, W60cm/ 2ft. F6-7. Z4-9. ❀ ◢

FRAGARIA Strawberry

F. 'Pink Panda'. A large pink-flowered hybrid crossing *Potentilla palustris*, the marsh cinquefoil, with the domestic fruiting strawberry. Excellent for ground cover, containers and hanging baskets, it flowers from early summer to late autumn, less in extreme heat. Fruits occur in hotter climates. 'Red Ruby' and 'Serenata' are other selections with deeper coloured flowers. H30cm/1ft, W45cm/18in. F5-10. Z5-9.

GAILLARDIA Blanket flower

Colourful perennials and annuals, the former mostly represented by selected cultivars. Daisy-like flowers have a reddish brown or burgundy centre and yellow or red petals, sometimes both, creating colour at the expense of subtlety! Some strains come from seed; selected cultivars are propagated by root cuttings. ✿ ■
G x *grandiflora* 'Goblin', an eye-

Galega officinalis 'His Majesty'

catching dwarf form, petals deep crimson, tipped yellow. H30cm/1ft, W30cm/1ft. F6-8. Z2-10. 'Croftway Yellow', pure yellow. 'Mandarin', deep flame orange, mahogany centre. Both H60cm/2ft, W30cm/1ft. F6-8. Z2-10.

GALEGA Goat's rue

Vigorous members of the pea family, useful for their long-flowering period and abundant fresh green foliage. ✿ ■
G. officinalis 'Alba'. The species can be variable, with light blue or white flowers, but this selection holds its own in any garden, with showy white-flowered racemes over a long period. A closely related hybrid 'His Majesty', often misnamed 'Her Majesty', is of a similar status, with blue and white flowers. May need staking. H1.5m/5ft, W60cm/2ft. F6-8. Z3-8.

GAURA

G. lindheimeri. A free-flowering perennial with insignificant foliage but the small flowers which cling to willowy stems provide a mass of white-petalled blooms all summer. 'Whirling Butterflies' is a well-named selected form. 'Corrie's Gold' offers golden variegated leaves as an added attraction. All 75-90cm/2ft 6in-3ft, W45cm/18in. F6-10. Z5-9. ✿ ■

Fragaria 'Pink Panda'

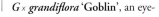

GERANIUM **Cranesbill**

One of the indispensable perennials, now available in an increasingly wide range. Species exist for sun or shade, with selected varieties useful to cover the flowering period from late spring to late autumn. Dwarfer types are listed in the Alpines Directory (see page 280). The forms listed below represent a limited selection. ☼ ✹ ☆

G. '**Ann Folkard**'. Wide-spreading, with magenta-purple, saucer-shaped flowers. Yellow-tinged leaves early in the year. Excellent if allowed to scramble among other plants. H30cm/1ft, W30cm/1ft. F6-9. Z5-8.

G. × cantabrigiense. Two outstanding forms of this hybrid, like a dwarf *G. macrorrhizum*, are the semi-evergreen '**Cambridge**', with glossy leaves and rose-pink flowers, and '**Biokovo**', which makes a spreading carpet topped by white flowers with pink centres. Both 20-30cm/8-12in, W30cm/1ft. F6-8. Z3-8.

G. himalayense. Good ground cover forming low, leafy carpets, with finely cut leaves and blue flowers with a fine red veining and reddish-purple centre. '**Gravetye**' (formerly *G. h. alpinium*) is

slightly more reddish-veined and centred. '**Plenum**' is vigorous and quite distinct, with masses of fully double purplish-blue flowers. All easy and trouble-free. H30cm/1ft, W60cm/2ft. F6-7. Z4-8. ☼ ✹

G. '**Johnson's Blue**'. Perhaps the most popular hardy geranium ever. Finely cut leaves and a glorious display of clear blue, darker-veined flowers in mid-summer, with some re-blooming. H30cm/1ft, W60cm/2ft. F6-7. Z4-8.

G. macrorrhizum. Semi-evergreen sweet briar-scented leaves, colouring well in autumn, somewhat woody stems and short sprays of magenta flowers, 4cm/1.5in across. The form *album* is white, '**Ingwersen's Variety**' is soft pink, '**Bevan's Variety**' deep rose-pink. Good, quick-spreading, weed-proof ground cover for sun or shade. All H25cm/10in, W60cm/2ft. F6-7, Z4-8.

G. × magnificum. Striking deep violet-blue flowers held above hairy leaves. Vigorous and upright but can flop. ☼ ■

G. × oxonianum. Under this hybrid come many first-class free-flowering

Geranium pratense 'Mrs Kendall Clark'

selections; all have light green, semi-evergreen leaves and make leafy mounds of foliage, varying in vigour and colour. All Z4-8. '**A.T. Johnson**' is one of the oldest selections, good ground cover with silvery pink flowers. H40cm/16in, W60cm/2ft. F6-8. Z4-8. '**Bressingham's Delight**' was selected for its light pink veined flowers which continue for months.

G. phaeum. The mourning widow. Named for its small, nodding purple-black flowers, excellent for shade, but a trifle dull. '**Album**' is brighter, with an erect habit and masses of white flowers. Both H60cm/2ft, W45cm/18in. F5-7. Z4-8.

G. pratense. The meadow cranesbill. Finely cut leaves, good autumn tints. Somewhat floppy stems bear sprays with flowers in shades of violet-blue, freely seeding as do most of the singles. '**Album**' is good but the erect-flowered white '**Galactic**' is outstanding. '**Mrs Kendall Clark**' is an old favourite with pale blue flowers marked with lilac. Doubles include white '**Plenum Album**', light blue '**Plenum Caeruleum**' and deep violet-blue '**Plenum Violaceum**'. '**Summer Skies**' has masses of small double flowers with shades of blue, pink and white all on the same plants. All 60-75cm/2-2ft 6in, W60cm/2ft. F6-7. Z5-8.

G. psilostemon (syn. *G. armenum*). Large, deeply cut leaves make this an attractive foliage form above which bright magenta flowers with black centres make an arresting display. '**Bressingham Flair**', slightly lower-growing, flowers more carmine. Full sun; some seeding may occur. Both H90cm/3ft, W90cm/3ft. F6-8. Z4-8.

G. × riversleianum '**Mavis Simpson**'. A superb long-flowering plant with grey-green leaves and wide-spreading foliage, giving a succession of pale pink flowers from mid-summer until autumn. Equally garden-worthy is '**Russell Prichard**', an older variety with vivid magenta-rose flowers for a similar period. Both H30cm/12in, W60cm/2ft. F6-9. Z6-8. ☼ ■

G. sanguineum. The bloody cranesbill. Most forms have sharply divided leaves, forming mounds studded with flowers from mid-summer for several weeks. '**Alan Bloom**' makes low hummocks with bright magenta-pink flowers, *G. s. album*, a taller white, '**John Elsley**' deep magenta pink, '**Shepherd's Warning**', lower-spreading, lighter pink, *G. s. striatum* '**Splendens**' (syn. *G. lancastrense* '**Splendens**'), outstanding and distinct, pale pink flowers veined crimson. All approx. H30cm/12in, W45cm/18in. F6-8. Z4-8.

G. sylvaticum. Early-flowering European species, forming clumps of green-fingered leaves and mostly blue or lilac-white centres. Seeds freely. ☼ ✹ '**Album**' lights up a shady corner. '**Mayflower**' is a fine deep blue selection. All 60cm/2ft, W45cm/18in. F5-7. Z4-8.

G. wallichianum '**Buxton's Variety**'. Splendid spreading leafy plant with dark green foliage and a succession of light blue saucer-shaped flowers with white centres, the blue turning to lilac in heat. Ideal for a frontal position in a border or on a bank or a wall. H30cm/1ft, W75cm/2ft 6in. F6-10. Z4-8.

Geranium phaeum 'Album'

Gypsophila repens 'Rosa Schonheit'

GEUM Avens

Colourful clump-forming perennials, best if divided every few years. ✿ ❀
G. 'Borisii'. Popular and reliable, the low clumps of green leaves bear bright orange or scarlet flowers in late spring and occasionally, later coppertone sprays of coppery orange flowers. 'Georgenberg', dwarfer, with pale yellow flowers. All approx. H30cm/ 1ft, W30cm/1ft. F5-7. Z5-8.

GYPSOPHILA Baby's breath

Sun-loving, drought-resistant perennials. They resent disturbance once established. Good for cut flowers. ✿ ☆ ☉ ■
G. paniculata. The single-flowered perennial baby's breath has deep, fleshy roots, much branched, airy stems, small greyish leaves and masses of tiny white flowers. This and its cultivars are much used for cutting and flower arranging. H90cm/3ft, W90cm/3ft. F6-8. All Z4-9. The double white 'Bristol Fairy' is a little less robust but the flowers are larger. H90cm/3ft, W90cm/3ft. F6-8. 'Compacta Plena' is a very reliable double white. H50cm/20in, W45cm/18in. F6-9. 'Rosenschleier' ('Rosy Veil'), taller with airy stems and clear pink flowers. H30cm/1ft, W45cm/18in. F5-7. Z3-8.

G. repens 'Rosa Schonheit'.

Outstanding for its free-flowering pink flowers and mounded grey-green foliage. H15cm/6in, W30cm/1ft. F5-7. Z3-8.

HELENIUM Sneezewort

Most of these well-loved plants bloom in late summer, producing daisy flowers in bright shades of yellow, orange and brownish-crimson with a central conical disc. Lift and divide regularly. All Z4-8. ✿ ☆
'Bressingham Gold', deep yellow, crimson-streaked flowers, long, spear-shaped stem leaves. H1.1m/43in, W45cm/18in. F7-8. 'Bruno', late-flowering crimson-mahogany. H1.2m/4ft, W45cm/18in. F8-9. 'Butterpat', pure yellow, late-flowering. H1.1m/43in, W45cm/ 18in. F8-9. 'Coppelia', warm coppery orange, sturdy growth. H1m/39in, W45cm/18in. F8-9. 'Morheim Beauty', bronze-red flowers and a sturdy habit. H1.1m/ 43in, W45cm/18in. F7-8. 'Wyndley', compact, leafy, orange-brown flecked flowers for a long period. H70cm/28in, W45cm/18in. F6-8.

HELIANTHELLA

H. quinquinervis. A pleasing plant for the back of the border. Leafy clumps produce a mass of small, lemon-yellow flowers. H1.5-1.8m/ 5-6ft, W90cm/3ft. F8-9. Z4-8.

HELIANTHUS Perennial sunflower

Though some species are invasive, those below make compact clumps and strong stems topped by single, double or semi-double yellow flowers in late summer: a good, trouble-free display.
H. decapetalus (syn. *H. multiflorus*). 'Capenoch Star' has single lemon-yellow flowers; 'Lemon Queen' is similar and both fit better into colour schemes than brighter yellows. Both H1.5-1.8m/5-6ft, W60cm/2ft. F8-9. Z4-8. 'Loddon Gold', a sturdy plant

Helenium 'Butterpat'

with fully double bright yellow flowers in late summer. H1.5-1.8m/5-6ft, W60cm/2ft. F8-9. Z4-8.

HELIOPSIS

H. scabra. Related to the sunflowers, these are brash, colourful perennials for sunny spots which thrive in any reasonable soil. All F6-9. Z4-9. 'Ballerina', very free-flowering, single yellow. H1m/39in, W60cm/2ft. 'Gold Green Heart', semi-double, lemon-yellow flowers with greenish centre. H1.1m/43in, W60cm/2ft. 'Golden Plume', almost double, bushy habit. H1.1m/43in, W60cm/2ft. 'Bressingham Doubloon' large, semi-double blooms make an impressive display. H1.2m/4ft, W40cm/18in.

HEMEROCALLIS Daylily

These tough perennials with fresh green, arching leaves and lily-like, often fragrant, flowers, are immensely popular. The blooms last for only one day but open in succession. All are reliable and adaptable and, though preferring good soil, will do well on most. ✿ ❀ ✫
H. dumortieri. This has early, deep yellow, fragrant flowers, dark brown in bud. H70cm/28in, W45cm/18in. F5-7. Z3-9.

Hybrids. Recent hybridizing, particularly in the USA, has created innumerable hybrids, including some with large flowers, ruffled flowers, brightly and subtly coloured, miniatures and re-blooming types. The selections made below have all succeeded well at Bressingham. All Z4-9. 'Anzac' is as near to true red as you are likely to find. H75cm/30in, W45cm/18in. F6-8. 'Children's Festival', compact habit, ruffled peach, apricot-throated trumpets. H60cm/2ft, W45cm/18in. F6-7. 'Burning Daylight', deep glowing orange. H90cm/3ft, W60cm/2ft. F7-

Hemerocallis 'Children's Festival'

9. 'Catherine Woodbury', deep pink flowers. H80cm/32in, W60cm/2ft. F6-8. 'Cherry Cheeks' has extra-large, cherry-pink flowers. H80cm/ 32in, W60cm/2ft. F6-8. 'Corky', free-flowering pale yellow, backed brown-gold, dark brown stems, grassy foliage. H75cm/ 2ft 6in, W45cm/ 18in. F6-8. 'Golden Chimes', fairly dwarf and very free to flower. H70cm/28in, W45cm/18in. F6-8. 'Hyperion', long a favourite, with scented, pure yellow flowers. H90cm/3ft, W45cm/18in. F6-8. 'Lark Song', light canary-yellow. H90cm/3ft, W45cm/18 in. F6-8. 'Luxury Lace', light satiny pink, with ruffled edges to the petals. H80cm/32in, W60cm/2ft. F6-8. 'Cream Drop', scented miniature creamy yellow blooms held above the foliage. H45cm/18in, W45cm/18in. F6-7. 'Stafford', rich red with a deep yellow throat. H90cm/3ft, W90cm/ 3ft. F7-9. 'Stella d'Oro', distinctive for its dwarf, dense clumps of leaves and long season of pale gold flowers. Divide regularly. H50cm/20in, W45cm/18in. F6-10. 'Varsity', large peach flowers, maroon in the centre. H75cm/30in, W45cm/18in. F6-8.

HEUCHERA Coral bells

This distinctive plant group has had much attention from hybridists in recent years, particularly in the development of coloured or marbled foliage leading to a longer appeal than the flowering season alone. Older plants become woody and younger side shoots should be used for replanting. ✳ ■

H. × *brizoides*. Hybrids with large leaves and large sprays of flowers good for cutting. 'Charles Bloom' has large purplish, crinkled leaves and sprays of light pink flowers; 'Pearl Drops' is white. Both H60-70cm/24-28in, W30cm/1ft. F6-8. Z3-8.

H. cyclindrica. A species with greenish-white bells and clumps of deep green silver-marbled leaves.

Heuchera micrantha 'Bressingham Bronze'

'Green Ivory' and 'Greenfinch' are distinct improvements, much used by flower arrangers. All H60-70cm/24-18in, W30cm/1ft. F6-8. Z4-8.

H. micrantha 'Palace Purple' is variable from seed but at its best an excellent garden-worthy form whose leaves are large, glossy and richly coloured, almost beetroot-red. 'Bressingham Bronze' is an outstanding selection with large, crinkled bronze leaves, bright purple beneath. The tiny flowers have a hint of white. Both H70cm/28in, W30cm/1ft. F6-8. Z4-8.

H. 'Pewter Moon'. Forms a low hummock of silver-marbled leaves on a deep maroon reverse. Pretty, light pink flowers. H30cm/1ft, W30cm/ 1ft. F6-8. Z4-8.

Hybrids. As a mixed strain Bressingham hybrids have an international reputation. Those below are named cultivars which have *H. sanguinea* 'Coral Bells' as their dominant parent, a great many introduced by my father Alan Bloom over the years. All approximately W30cm/1ft, F5-7 or F5-8 where suited in fertile soil. 'Bressingham Blaze', bright coral-red bells. H50cm/20in. Z3-8. 'Pretty Polly', compact but with large, pure pink

flowers. H35cm/14in. Z4-8. 'Red Spangles', intensely blood-red flowers. H50cm/20in. Z3-8. 'Rosemary Bloom', bright coral pink bells, with light pink centre, for many weeks. H45-60cm/18-24in. F6-8. Z4-8. 'Scintillation', red-tipped, deep pink flowers. H50cm/20in. Z3-8. 'Snowstorm', notable for its white and green leaves, which contrast with the cerise flowers. H40cm/16in. Z4-8.

× HEUCHERELLA

Hybrids between *Heuchera* and *Tiarella*.

× *H.* 'Bridget Bloom'. The first inter-generic hybrid raised by Alan Bloom in 1950 and named after my sister. It makes compact mounds of pretty evergreen foliage and stems of starry pink flowers which will often bloom a second time in late summer. H35cm/ 14in, W30cm/1ft. F5-7. Z4-8. ✳ □

HOSTA Plantain lily

Deservedly popular plants for their hardiness, adaptability and, in the best foliage types, long period of interest. Since the first species arrived from Asia, much breeding and selection has given us a bewildering choice, from miniatures to giants, some with astonishing blue or variegated leaves and many with fragrant flowers. Their only drawback is that slugs like them too! All Z3-9. ✳ ✳ ◢

H. 'August Moon'. This has bright golden-green leaves in summer and pale mauve flowers. H60cm/2ft, W45cm/18in. F8-9.

H. 'Big Daddy'. Large, puckered leaves, decidedly bluish, make a fine specimen plant in semi or full shade. H90cm/3ft, W60cm/2ft. F8-9.

H. 'Blue Moon'. Small round, intensely blue ribbed leaves and profuse light mauve flowers. H30cm/12in, W30cm/12in. F7-8.

H. fortunei 'Albo-marginata'. Striking, with large leaves margined creamy white. H80cm/32in, W60cm/2ft. F6-8. 'Aureo-marginata',

Hosta fluctuans 'Variegated'

similar, but with a yellow leaf margin. The vigorous 'Francee' is outstanding with wide, oval, white-edged leaves making a splendid clump. H60cm/2ft, W50cm/20in. F8-9.

H. 'Frances Williams'. Deservedly popular with its huge, glaucous ribbed leaves and buff variegations. H1m/39in, W60cm/2ft. F6-8.

H. fluctuans 'Variegated'. A most impressive variegated Japanese hosta whose large, wavy green leaves, edged creamy yellow, and open habit give it a sculptural quality. H75cm/2ft 6in, W75cm/2ft 6in. F6-8.

H. 'Gold Standard'. This strong-growing, free-flowering form has leaves with green outer edges and colourful golden centres. H60cm/2ft, W50cm/20in. F7-8.

H. 'Ground Master'. Dense spread of green and white variegated foliage for sun or shade, giving a good display of purple flowers. H30cm/1ft, W45cm/18in. F6-7.

H. 'Halcyon'. Very glaucous blue foliage and a good show of mauve flowers make this English variety especially garden-worthy. H45cm/ 18in, W45cm/18in. F7-8.

H. 'Krossa Regal'. Strong-growing, erect and glaucous-leaved, with purple flowers. H80cm/32in, W60cm/2ft. F6-8.

H. 'Montana Aurea Margianata'. The large soft-textured leaves are bright green, edged golden yellow, and very striking. H60cm/2ft, W60cm/2ft. F6-7.

H. 'Sum and Substance'. Considered to have the largest leaves of any hosta, and slug resistant. Impressive ribbed leaves light green to soft green, golden green in summer. Lavender flowers. H60cm/2ft, W60cm/2ft. F7-8.

H. 'Shade Fanfare'. Light green leaves with broad, creamy margins, mauve flowers and a rapid spread. H40cm/16in, W45cm/18in. F7-8.

H. sieboldiana. Large glaucous leaves with mauve flowers. H80cm/32in; 'Elegans', even larger, with grey-blue ribbed leaves up to 50cm/20in across and 1m/39in high flower spikes. 'Bressingham Blue', equally robust but the leaves have a distinctive bluish tinge. All H90cm/3ft. W60cm/2ft. F7-8.

H. ventricosa. The species has deep green leaves and upstanding deep lavender-blue flowers. 'Aureo-maculata' has glossy leaves with a central greenish-gold splash. 'Variegata' (syn. *H.v.* 'Aureo Marginata') whose ribbed foliage is

margined creamy yellow. All are free-flowering. H75cm/2ft 6in, W60cm/2ft. F7-8.

H. 'Wide Brim'. Dense overlapping leaves are green, broadly edged cream to golden yellow, and finely ribbed. Lavender flowers. H40cm/16in, W60cm/2ft. F7-8.

HOUTTUYNIA

H. cordata 'Chameleon'. A spreading plant, particularly in moist soils and hot climates, but undoubtedly colourful. Leaves appear late in the season and vary in intensity and colour, usually mixing green, yellow, cream and red. The small flowers are white and the plant has a distinctive aroma. Striking and safe in a container! H15cm/6in, W30cm/1ft. F6-8. Z5-9.

INCARVILLEA

Tap-rooted plants which appear above ground in mid-spring and within a few weeks show their quite large, trumpet-shaped flowers, followed by deeply cut leaves. ☼ ■ ☀
I. delavayi. Rosy-red trumpets borne on spikes which expand from a few centimetres (inches) to nearly

60cm/2ft, by the time flowering ends. 'Alba', a recent selection of merit, with striking white trumpets. Both H60cm/2ft, W30cm/1ft. F5-7. Z6-8.

IRIS

The iris are a large and varied family, mostly easy to grow and often providing spectacular flowers. Though there are several notable exceptions, most flower in spring or summer.

I. ensata (syn. *I. kaempferi*). Large-flowered and popular, but not always easy, the Japanese iris dislikes lime, heavy clay and excessive winter wet, but needs moisture in summer. Its single or double, often velvety flowers, up to 20cm/8in across, can be quite spectacular. A huge variety of shapes, colours and sizes is now available, in seed mixtures and named varieties.

I. germanica. Flag, bearded or June-flowering iris are colourful, often spectacular perennials which are not fussy about soil, but need good drainage and like lime. The following are good colour representatives. They need to be placed carefully in the garden since, once flowers are finished, there is little to recommend them. Grow among or through low-spreading plants. 'Berkeley Gold', deep yellow. 'Black Swan', nearly black. 'Braithwaite', lavender and purple. 'Edward Windsor', pastel pink. 'Frost and Flame', snow-white with tangerine beard. 'Jane Phillips', light blue. 'Kent Pride', chestnut-brown, with yellow and white markings. 'Party Dress', peach-pink and tangerine-yellow. 'Tall Chief', purple and maroon. 'Wabash', white and violet. All H60-90cm/2-3ft, W30cm/1ft. F6. Z4-9. ☼

I. kaempferi. See *I. ensata.*
I. pallida 'Argentea' (formerly *I.p.* 'Variegata'), with white and grey striped leaves, and 'Variegata' (formerly *I.p.* 'Aurea Variegata'), with golden-yellow stripes, deserve a place

in any garden. Both have clear blue flowers. All H60-75cm/2ft-2ft 6in, W30cm/1ft. F6-7. Z4-8. ☼ ☀

I. sibirica. These are easy to grow in sun and moist soil, especially as waterside subjects. They form clumps of upright, grassy foliage. Erect stems carry graceful flowers. 'Butter and Sugar', large flowers, deep yellow outer petals, creamy white inner. H60cm/2ft, W30cm/1ft. F6-7. 'Ego', bright blue, deepening towards the centre. H80cm/32in, W25cm/10in. 'Flight of Butterflies', relatively small flowers, blue with white veining. H90cm/3ft, W30cm/1ft. 'Persimmon', mid-blue. H90cm/3ft, W25cm/10in. 'Silver Edge', outstanding: large flowers, lilac-blue with yellow markings and a clear silver edge to the petals. H75cm/2ft 6in, W45cm/18in. 'White Swirl', pure white. H90cm/3ft, W25cm/ 10in. All F6-7. Z3-9.

KNIPHOFIA Red hot poker

A wide range is now available of these plants indispensable for summer colour, some flowering well into autumn. They vary from 35cm/14in

Iris sibirica 'Silver Edge'

Kniphofia 'Percy's Pride'

Lamium maculatum 'Pink Pewter'

to over 1.8m/6ft in height, some needing considerable space. Best planted in spring, though pot-grown plants can be planted in early autumn if protected in their first winter. Generally easy. ☼ ■

K. 'Atlanta' (syn. *K. tuckii*). Early-flowering, with heavy spikes of yellow and red above broad glaucous foliage. H90cm/3ft, W60cm/2ft. F5-7. Z6-9. 'Bressingham Comet', bright orange, red-tipped spikes and grassy leaves. H60cm/2ft, W45cm/18in. F8-10. Z6-9. 'Fiery Fred', striking orange-red flowers and green leaves. H90cm/3ft, W60cm/2ft. F6-8. Z6-9. 'Little Maid', a charmer with narrow leaves and profuse, ivory-white spikes. H60cm/2ft, W45cm/18in. F7-9. Z5-9. 'Percy's Pride', robust, with sulphur-yellow flowers. H1.1m/43in, W60cm/2ft. F8-10. Z6-9. 'Shining Sceptre', glowing, orange-gold spikes. H90cm/3ft, W60cm/2ft. F7-9. Z6-9. 'Samuel's Sensation', truly red hot with fiery orange-flame heads. H1.2m/4ft, W45cm/18in. F7-9. Z6-9.

LAMIUM Deadnettle

This genus includes useful ground-cover plants for shade and a few of greater garden value both as foliage and flowering plants.

Leucanthemum maximum 'Snowcap'

L. galeobdolon 'Hermann's Pride', with silvery leaves; compact, with free-flowering yellow blooms. H15cm/6in, W20cm/8in. F4-7. Z4-8.

L. maculatum. There are some attractive and garden-worthy selections of this species, ideal to create eye-catching plant associations. 'Aureum', bright golden-yellow leaves and pink flowers. 'Beacon Silver', one of the best for leaf colour, with leaves silvered with green margins, and 15cm/6in high red-to-pink flowers in early summer. 'Beedham's White', flowers freely, from golden carpets. 'Pink Pewter',

silver leaves and soft pink flowers. 'White Nancy', silvered foliage with green margins and pure white flowers. All H30cm/1ft, W60cm/2ft. F4-7. Z4-8.

LAVANDULA. See under Shrubs (p.224)

LEUCANTHEMUM

(syn. *Chrysanthemum leucanthemum*, *L. vulgare*). H50-70cm/20-28in, W30cm/1ft. F5-7. Z4-9.

L. maximum. The shasta daisy includes single and double flowers, such as the well-known doubles, 'Esther Read' and 'Wirral Supreme'. Both H50-75cm/20-30in, W30cm/1ft. Forms with lacy-edged petals include 'Aglaia' and 'Thomas Killin'. H75cm/30in, W30cm/1ft. 'Snowcap', single white flowers massed on stems only 35cm/14in tall, W30cm/1ft. 'Summer Snowball', outstanding pure white, fully double. H75cm/30in, W30cm/1ft. Support may be needed. All F6-8. Z4-8.

LIATRIS Gayfeather, Blazing star

These spike-forming plants are unusual in opening from the tip down, and make a bright display with narrow leaves and mostly light purple, fluffy pokers. The plants are

Ligularia przewalskii 'Sungold'

fleshy but not deep-rooted and any reasonable soil in sun suits them.

L. spicata (syn. *L. callilepis*). This has stiff spikes of bright lilac-purple flowers. H60cm/2ft, W25cm/10in. F6-8. Z4-9. 'Floristan White' is an attractive variation. H60cm/2ft, W25cm/10in. F6-8. Z4-9. 'Kobold' (syn. 'Gnome'). Lilac mauve with shorter, sturdy spikes. H45cm/18in, W23cm/9in. F6-8. Z4-9.

LIGULARIA

All the species below are partial to moisture but most thrive in any good soil and sun. Almost all have yellow, daisy-type flowers.

L. dentata (syn. *L. clivorum*) 'Desdemona'. This striking plant has very large, leathery, heart-shaped, brownish-green leaves, purple when young and later purplish beneath, and branching stems of orange daisy flowers. H1.2m/4ft, W60cm/2ft. F7-8. Z4-8.

L. przewalskii. Outstanding for its deeply cut, elegant foliage, black slender stems and small yellow flowers. H1.8m/6ft, W45cm/18in. F7-8. Z4-8. 'The Rocket' is a striking variation, showier and with leaves more rounded and toothed. H2.1m/7ft, W60cm/2ft. F7-8. Z4-8.

L. 'Sungold'. A first-class plant, adaptable, bushy and with a fine display of deep golden-yellow flowers on branching stems. H1.5m/5ft, W60cm/2ft. F7-8. Z4-8.

LIMONIUM

L. platyphyllum (syn. *L. latifolium*). This needs a warm, dry place to produce its sprays of tiny blue flowers in late summer. These are a deeper shade in 'Violetta'. Both H80cm/32in, W60cm/2ft. F7-9. Z4-9.

LOBELIA

Somewhat flashy perennials with bright colours in foliage and flower. Well worth growing as border plants. Cultivars are best covered by litter over winter if left *in situ*.
L. fulgens. The main parent of many hybrids, this has downy purple stems, purple leaves and bright red flowers. H75cm/2ft 6in, W30cm/1ft. F8-10. Z8-9. The following are some of the hybrids: 'Bees Flame', large, very bright scarlet flowers and beetroot-red foliage. H80cm/32in, W30cm/1ft. F7-10. Z4-8. 'Dark Crusader', similar leaves and deep crimson-purple flowers. H80cm/32in, W30cm/1ft. F7-10. Z4-8. 'Eulalia Berridge', a tall cerise pink. H1.2m/4ft, W30cm/1ft. F7-10. Z4-8. 'Queen Victoria', an old favourite, with purple foliage and bright red flowers. H80cm/32in, W30cm/1ft. F7-10. Z4-8. 'Will Scarlet', green-leaved with red flowers. H80cm/32in, W30cm/1ft. F7-10. Z4-8.

LUPINUS Lupin

Popular and colourful perennials which are now mostly represented by seed strains originating from *L. polyphyllus* which come true to colour. They are relatively short-lived but add much vibrancy to the early summer garden, coming in a wide range of colours, single as well as bicoloured on the same plant, from white, pink, yellow, red, blue, purple

Lychnis flos-jovis 'Hort's Variety'

and orange. Seed strains and selected varieties come in varying heights from 45cm/18in to 1.2m/4ft, their spikes carrying multitudes of small flowers which open from the base to the top. Cut the spikes back immediately after flowering to prevent unwanted seedlings. H(see above), W30-45cm/12-18in. F6-7. Z3-6. ✿ ⊝

LYCHNIS

Brightly flowered perennials which are easy to grow. ✿ ■
L. × arkwrightii. Intense vermilion-scarlet open flowers, 2.5cm/1in or more across, above purple-bronze foliage; can be short-lived. H30cm/1ft, W25cm/10in. F6-8. Z6-8.
L. chalcedonica. The Maltese cross, or Jerusalem cross, has green leaves and stems crowned by cross-shaped scarlet-vermilion flowers, 1.5cm/½in across, in heads up to 13cm/5in wide. H1.1m/43in, W30cm/1ft. F6-8. Z4-8. ◪
L. coronaria. The rose campion or mullein pink has rosettes of hairy, silver leaves and branching stems carrying many open-petalled, magenta flowers for several weeks. A colour difficult to fit with other plants. 'Abbotswood Rose' (syn. *L. ×*

walkeri 'Abbotswood Rose'), intensely bright carmine; 'Alba' is white; 'Atrosanguinea' is purple-red. 'Gardeners World' covers a purple-red double-flowered form. 'Oculata' has red-eyed, white flowers. All H60-80cm/24-32in, W45cm/18in. F6-8. Z4-8.
L. flos-jovis. The flower of Jove has felty grey foliage, a dense, tufty habit, and sprays of purple-red flowers for several weeks. 'Hort's Variety' has clear bright pink flowers. Both H45cm/18in, W30cm/1ft. F6-8. Z5-9.
L. viscaria. 'Plena' is a rare double red form. H90cm/3ft, W30cm/1ft. F6-8. Z4-8.

LYSIMACHIA

This genus includes such diverse species as yellow loosestrife and creeping Jenny. Some are inclined to become invasive. ✿ ✤ ◪
L. ciliata 'Firecracker'. Has reddish-purple leaves which offer a striking foliage contrast to yellow flowers. H90cm/3ft, W60cm/2ft. F6-8. Z3-9.
L. punctata. The vigorous yellow loosestrife is showy but invasive, making a splendid display of yellow flowers on leafy stems. H90cm/3ft, W60cm/2ft. F6-8. Z4-8.

LYTHRUM Purple loosestrife

Adaptable and long-lived perennials. Though happiest in moist soil, tolerating even boggy conditions, they still flower where quite dry. Dead-head to prevent self-seeding. Hybrids of both species below are the only ones in circulation, with richer colours than the species. ✿ ✱ ◪
L. salicaria 'Blush'. A colour breakthrough in soft blush-pink. H75cm/2ft 6in, W45cm/18in. Z4-9. 'Firecandle' has graceful, tapering spikes of small but intense rosy-red flowers. H1.2m/4ft, W45cm/18in. F7-9. Z4-9. 'Robert' has a bushier, leafier habit and clear pink flowers. H60cm/2ft, W45cm/18in. F7-9. Z4-9. 'The Beacon' is also bushy, with strong stems and full spikes of rosy red. H1.2m/4ft, W45cm/18in. F7-9. Z4-9.

MERTENSIA

These are valued for their clear blue flowers in spring and early summer. ✱ ■ ✤
M. asiatica. Prostrate, brilliant silver-blue, striking foliage with small, sky-blue flowers. H15in/6in, W30cm/1ft. F6-9. Z4-9. ✿ ✱ ★
M. pulmonarioides (syn. *M. virginica*). A shade lover for cool woodland conditions, fleshy roots produce purplish-blue shoots in spring, unfurling to fragile branching stems from which dangle sky-blue, bell-shaped flowers. The plant dies down in mid-summer. H45cm/18in, W30cm/1ft. F4-5. Z4-9

MIMULUS Monkey flower

Colourful lipped flowers, often blotched or spotted with contrasting colours. Most are not fussy, though mat-forming kinds need replanting every year or two. ✿ ◪
M. cardinalis. The scarlet monkey flower has greener stems and leaves, and orange-scarlet to cerise flowers. H70cm/28in, W45cm/18in. F6-9. Z7-10.

M. guttatus and *M. luteus*, together with *M. cupreus*, have produced several sturdy hybrids and cultivars, listed below, with fascinating bright colours. All F6-8. Z8-10. '**A. T. Johnson**' has large yellow flowers with brown blotches. H30cm/1ft, W30cm/1ft. '**Firedragon**' has flame-orange, dark-spotted flowers. H25cm/10in, W30cm/1ft. '**Puck**' is a vigorous, mound-forming hybrid, covered in butter-yellow flowers, tinged orange. H15cm/6in, W25cm/10in.

MONARDA Bee balm, Sweet bergamot

These showy perennials are back in fashion, with many new selections available. Erect, square stems have aromatic leaves and are topped by brightly coloured heads of hooded flowers. Their mat-like roots are best if divided every year or two. All W45cm/18in. F6-8. Z4-9. ☼ ◢ **Hybrids. 'Adam'**, bright red, H1.2m/4ft. '**Aquarius**', violet, H1.35cm/4ft 6in. '**Balance**', pink, H1.2m/4ft. '**Blue Stocking**', lavender-blue, H1.2m/4ft. '**Cambridge Scarlet**', an old favourite introduced prior to 1914, H1.2m/4ft. '**Croftway Pink**', pure rose-pink, H1.2m/4ft. '**Fishes**',

Mimulus guttatus 'Puck'

light pink, H1m/39in. '**Gardenview Scarlet**', bright green leaves, brilliant, scarlet flowers. H1.35cm/4ft 6in. '**Marshalls Delight**', shining pink, H1.2m/4ft. '**Prairie Night**', close to purple, H1.2m/4ft. '**Scorpion**', deep violet, H1.35cm/4ft 6in. '**Snow Queen**', one of several whites, H1.35m/ 4ft 6in. All W45cm/18in. F6-8. Z4-9.

MYOSOTIS Forget-me-not

M. scorpioides (syn. *M. palustris)*. '**Maytime**' is an eye-catching forget-me-not with a vigorous habit and leaves brightly margined with white. Flowers bright blue but relatively sparse. H20cm/8in, W45cm/18in. F6-8. Z4-10. ☼ ✹ ◢ '**Mermaid**' makes green mats of foliage and sprays of sky-blue flowers. Hardy, best divided regularly. H15cm/6in, W30cm/1ft. F6-8. Z4-10.

NEPETA Catmint

Mostly good garden plants, easy to grow and with a long season of small-flowered spikes and aromatic leaves. ☼ ■

N. racemosa (syn. *N. mussinii)*. This is the favourite catmint for bedding and edging, with a succession of bright blue flowers all summer.

Oenothera 'Sonnenwende'

H30cm/1ft, W30cm/1ft. F6-9. Z3-8. *N. nervosa*. A neat-growing, showy species, with long display of short, violet-blue spikes. Distinct and worthwhile. H25cm/10in, W30cm/ 1ft. F6-8. Z5-8.

OENOTHERA Evening primrose

Several perennials in this family are garden-worthy, with large, saucer-shaped flowers for a long period. ☼ ■ *O. fruticosa* (syn. *O. tetragona)*. Under this species belong some of the brightest and most reliable of all perennials. '**Fireworks**' (syn. '**Fyrverkeri**'). Rosette-forming hybrid with multi-coloured leaves in spring, followed by sprays of sizeable yellow flowers. H35cm/14in, W30cm/1ft. F6-8. Z5-9. *O*. '**Macrocarpa**' (syn. *O. missouriensis)*. Large, light yellow flowers last for weeks on end, followed by huge seedpods, useful in dried flower displays. Its sprawling habit lends itself to sloping ground, but as a deep-rooting hardy plant it is invaluable. H23cm/9in, W60cm/2ft. F6-9. Z5-8. *O*. '**Sonnenwende**' (syn. '**Solstice**'*)*. Neat and free-flowering with maroon young leaves and flower buds. H60cm/2ft. W30cm/1ft. F6-8. Z5-9.

OMPHALODES Navelwort

These pretty, long-lived plants have forget-me-not-type flowers and lush, oval-shaped foliage. *O. cappadocica*. In cool shade this slowly makes a clump of near-evergreen leaves and short sprays of bright blue flowers. '**Starry Eyes**' is a pretty variant with blue flowers edged mauve-white. H13cm/5in, W30cm/1ft. F4-5. Z6-9. *O. luciliae*. A choice species for a rock crevice or alpine house, this has blue-grey leaves and sprays of sky-blue flowers. H15cm/6in, W45cm/18in. F4-5. Z6-7. ☼

OPHIOPOGON

O. planiscapus nigrescens. Also known as '**Black Dragon**', this is one of the most striking plants for year-round colour. A member of the lily family, it makes a low-spreading, striking hummock of arching black leaves. Slender spikes bear lilac flowers, later black fruits. Best where not too dry; add a mulch. H20cm/ 8in, W20cm/8in. F7-8. Z6-10. ☼ ✹

ORIGANUM Marjoram

Sun-loving herbs, which make first-class flowering and foliage plants.

O. 'Herrenhausen'. This hybrid is mauve-pink, flowering continuously all summer. 'Rosenkuppel' is even brighter. Both H60cm/2ft, W30cm/1ft. F7-10. Z5-8.

O. laevigatum. Dense, twiggy sprays of tiny, deep purple-violet flowers in late summer, with small, rounded, glaucous leaves. 'Hopleys' has brighter, deep mauve blue flowers. H45cm/18in, W30cm/1ft. F8-10. Z5-9.

O. vulgare. The culinary marjoram has a more or less evergreen, golden-leaved form, 'Aureum'. The flowers are insignificant but plants make good ground cover. 'Thumble's Variety' has larger, deeper golden-yellow leaves. Both H15cm/6in, W30cm/1ft. Z4-8.

PAEONIA Peony

These long-lived perennials are a favourite among many gardeners, loved for their often exotic, richly coloured flowers and their foliage. Flowering of some species begins in late spring, but large-flowered types are at their best in early summer. Plant in autumn in well-prepared, enriched, deep soil with buds about 2.5cm/1in below the surface: deeper planting inhibits flowering. Allow ample spacing. Tree peonies (*P. suffruticosa*) are covered under Shrubs.

P. lactiflora. The majority of the early-summer flowering varieties originate from this Chinese species. A small selection is listed below but a wider range can be sought from specialists. All H75-100cm/30-39in, W60cm/2ft. F6. Z3-9. 'Bowl of Beauty', large semi-double flowers of glowing deep pink with a cream centre. 'Duchesse de Nemours', a favourite double white. 'Edulis Superba', fully double soft pink and scented. 'Felix Crousse', free-flowering, carmine-red double. 'Festiva Maxima', large double white, flecked crimson. 'Le Cygne', purest

Origanum 'Rosenkuppel'

white, large-flowered double. 'Sarah Bernhardt', still the most popular double, soft pink. 'Shirley Temple', large, deep rose double. 'Solange', pale salmon double, with a hint of orange. 'Coral Supreme', salmon-coral cup-shaped blooms. 'Miss America', semi-double, snow white, yellow anthers.

P. mlokosewitschii. A superb early-flowering species with light green foliage and soft yellow cups.

P. officinalis. The old-fashioned peony rose flowers a little earlier than *P.lactiflora* varieties. All are strong-growing, usually H80-90cm/32-36in, W60cm/2ft. F5-6. Z3-9. 'Alba Plena', a large double-white; 'Lize van Veen', a double blush-pink; 'Rosea Superba' a bright pink, large double; 'Rubra Plena' deep crimson-red double.

PAPAVER Poppy

These showy, sun-loving plants prefer ordinary or poor, deep soil, dryish rather than moist.

P. 'Fireball'. This resembles a miniature *P. orientale,* except for its spreading habit and shallow roots. The flowers, 5cm/2in across, are early and fully double orange-scarlet. H30cm/1ft, W30cm/1ft. F5-7. Z4-9.

Papaver orientale 'Glowing Embers'

P. orientale. Oriental poppies are quite outstanding for size and brilliance, though some flowers are so huge that they are top-heavy and difficult to support. Cut back after flowering. All F5-7. Z4-9. ☼ ■ 'Beauty of Livermere' (syn. 'Goliath'), one of the most reliable poppies, a fine, upright blood-red single. H1.1m/43in, W60cm/2ft. 'Black and White', striking with its white petals and black centre. H75cm/30in, W60cm/2ft. 'Glowing Embers', fairly erect with glowing orange-red ruffled petals, H1m/39in, W60cm/2ft. 'Harvest Moon', deep orange, semi-double flowers, effective until they begin to fade. H1m/39in,

W60cm/2ft. 'Picotée', frilly white petals suffused scarlet. H70cm/ 28in, W60cm/2ft. 'Turkish Delight', glowing flesh-pink. H75cm/30in, W60cm/2ft.

PENSTEMON

A large and diverse genus which includes some species with vivid colours, and low-growing, semi-shrubby alpines. Though some are only reliably hardy in milder climates, the hybrid garden cultivars are showy, flowering for months in summer and early autumn if cut back. Most hybrids need winter protection in cold regions. Take cuttings in early autumn and overwinter them under glass, to replace possible losses. ☼ ☀ ◢ ■

P. digitalis. Erect stems bear pale lilac foxglove-like flowers, with plenty of basal foliage. 'Huskers Red' is similar in flower but has striking red-purple leaves and stems. Both H60cm/2ft, W38cm/15in. F6-8. Z3-9.

Hybrids. These floriferous semi-shrubby perennials have occurred through crossing of *P. hartwegii*, *P. companulatus* and *P. gloxinioides*. The selections arising have then been crossed and selected again. All fill the need for summer colour for the

Penstemon 'King George'

garden or for pots and containers. All
F6-10 unless otherwise noted. All Z9-
10. **'Apple Blossom'**, blush-pink
trumpet flowers. H45cm/18in,
W30cm/1ft. **'Blackbird'**, deep
purple. H60cm/2ft, W45cm/18in.
'Evelyn', pale pink. H45cm/18in,
W30cm/1ft. **'Garnet'**, wine-red.
H50cm/20in, W45cm/18in.
'Hidcote Pink', outstandingly free-
flowering. H60cm/2ft, W45cm/18in.
'King George', salmon-red with a
white throat. H60cm/2ft, W45cm/
18in. **'Purple Passion'**, deep glowing
purple, white throat. H60cm/2ft,
W45cm/18in. **'Rubicunda'**, large,
warm red. H60cm/2ft, W45cm/18in.
'Sour Grapes', large, pale purple
flowers, strong-growing. H70cm/
28in, W45cm/18in. F6-9.
'Snowstorm', distinctive white
flowers. H70cm/28in, W45cm/18in.

PERSICARIA Knotweed
Formerly listed under *Polygonum*, all
below now fall under *Persicaria*, a
genus which includes some first-rate
and choice plants as well as easier and
spreading types. Most have a long
season of flowering. ✻ ◪

P. affine. Long-flowering species for
ground cover. Narrow leaves and
poker-flowers. H15-23cm/6-9in,
W38cm/15in. F6-7. Z3-9. **'Dimity'**
has fuller, long-lasting pink spikes
and is more reliable, with good
autumn colour. Excellent for
containers. H15cm/6in, W45cm/
18in. F6-7. Z3-9.

P. amplexicaule. An abundant, leafy
perennial with a long succession of
red flowers. H1.2m/4ft, W75cm/2ft
6in. F6-9. Z5-9. **'Atrosanguineum'** is
a deep crimson; **'Firetail'** is an
outstanding bright red. Both H1.2m/
4ft, W1.2m/4ft. F6-10. Z5-9.
'Taurus', perhaps the best to date:
bright green leaves set off the
succession of crimson bottlebrush
flowers from mid-summer to autumn
frosts. H75cm/2ft 6in, W1.2m/4ft.
F6-10. Z5-9.

Persicaria amplexicaule 'Taurus'

P. bistorta **'Superbum'**. Handsome,
finger-sized, light pink pokers on
erect stems. Vigorous. H80cm/32in,
W60cm/2ft. F5-7 but may repeat.
Z4-8. ◪

P. macrophyllum. Deep green leaves
and distinct, clear, light pink pokers
on erect stems. A choice and beautiful
plant. H45cm/18in, W45cm/18in.
F7-9. Z4-9.

P. milletii. Choice for good, moist,
deep soil, this has clumps of narrow
leaves and crimson-red pokers on and
off all summer. H30cm/1ft, W30cm/
1ft. Mainly F6-8. Z5-9. ✿ ❋

PHLOMIS
See also under Shrubs
P. russeliana (syn. *P. samia*). A sturdy
plant with large, basal woolly ever-
green leaves and whorls of hooded
yellow flowers on strong stems.
H90cm/3ft, W60cm/2ft. F6-8.
Z4-9. ✿ ◪

P. tuberosa **'Amazone'**. An imposing
plant with deep green foliage and
spikes with rose-pink hooded flowers.
H1.5m/5ft, W45cm/18in. F6-8. Z6-8.

PHLOX
Included in this family of spring- and
summer-flowering perennials are the
indispensable border phlox, mostly

listed under *P. paniculata.* They come
in a wide range of colours, the
majority being scented.

P. carolina **'Bill Baker'**. Trouble-free
selection with a long display of bright
pink flowers. H45cm/18in,
W30cm/1ft. F6-7. Z5-8. ✿ ❋

P. divaricata. Attractive heads of
fragrant blue flowers from creeping
basal growth. H25cm/10in,
W25cm/10in. F5-6. Z3-9. Two
excellent selections include **'Blue
Dreams'**, mid-blue, and **'May
Breeze'**, lilac-white. Both
H40cm/16in. ✿ ❋

P. maculata. Narrow-leaved, slender
stems, crowned with cylindrical
flower trusses. Grown in light soil,
they make a fine show and, like most
larger hybrids, are pleasantly fragrant.
'Alpha' is pink, **'Delta'** is white with
a lilac centre and **'Omega'** is white
with a red eye. All H90cm/3ft,
W30cm/1ft. F7-9. Z4-8.

P. paniculata. Some well-tried
selections are listed. All H75-
90cm/2ft 6in-3ft, W30cm/1ft. F7-9.
Z4-8. **'Bright Eyes'**, neat clusters,
pink with crimson centre. **'Caroline
van den Berg'**, as near a blue as can
be. **'Eva Cullum'**, strong and leafy,
warm pink, red eye. **'Franz
Schubert'**, lilac, long-flowering and

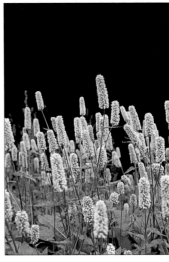
Persicaria bistorta 'Superbum'

reliable. **'Harlequin'**, golden-yellow
variegated leaves and violet-purple
flowers. H80cm/32in, W30cm/1ft.
'Marlborough', violet-purple with
dark foliage. H90cm/3ft, W30cm/
1ft. **'Mother of Pearl'**, white suffused
pink. **'Norah Leigh'**, bright, creamy
variegated leaves with pale lilac-purple
flowers. **'Prince of Orange'**,
outstanding salmon-orange.
'Prospero', strong-growing light lilac.
'Sandringham', cyclamen-pink, with
a darker centre; an old but still
worthwhile cultivar. **'Skylight'**,
lavender-blue, with dark foliage.
'Starfire', unsurpassed bright, deep
red. **'Windsor'**, deep carmine with a
magenta eye.

Phlox paniculata 'Franz Schubert'

PHYSOSTEGIA **Obedient plant**
Easy plants of spreading habit, which need to be divided and replanted regularly. ✳ ☆ ◢
P. virginiana. Produces an abundance of erect spikes of mauve-pink, snapdragon-like flowers. H1.1m/43in, W60cm/2ft. F7-9. Z4-8. Cultivars include: '**Rose Bouquet**', rosy lilac. H80cm/32in, W60cm/2ft. F7-9. '**Summer Snow**', white. H70cm/28in, W60cm/2ft. F7-9. '**Variegata**', lilac-pink flowers and striking, variegated leaves. H50cm/20in, W45cm/18in. F8-10. '**Vivid**', much dwarfer and later, deep pink. H50cm/20in, W45cm/18in. F8-10.

PLATYCODON **Balloon flower**
Buds that swell into little 'balloons' before they fully open into saucer-shaped flowers have given this plant its common name. Easily grown, long-lived plants, preferring sun but adaptable to partial shade. ✳ ◢ ✦
P. grandiflorus. The parent species of several forms, including the white *alba*, the dwarf, deep blue *apoyama*, *mariesii* in shades of light blue, and the pale pink '**Mother of Pearl**'. All H40-50cm/16-20in, W45cm/18in.

POLEMONIUM **Jacob's ladder**
Popular perennials, mostly with blue or white flowers with rich yellow stamens and basal clumps of ferny foliage. They are easy to grow, preferring a sunny position.
P. caeruleum. The best-known, but not the most reliable, and apt to seed itself. It has heads of lavender-blue, saucer-shaped flowers. H60cm/2ft, W60cm/2ft. F5-7. Z4-8. '**Brise d'Anjou**', an attractive form which makes a mound of finely cut variegated leaves, hardly needing the addition of its blue flowers. Good in a container. H60cm/2ft, W45cm/18in. F6-7. Z4-8. '**Dawn Flight**' is reliably perennial, with light green, ferny foliage and a fine display of white flowers. H70cm/28in,

Polemonium caeruleum 'Brise d'Anjou'

W60cm/2ft. F5-7. Z4-8.
P. carneum. Lilac-pink flowers dangle above low, clumpy growth. H25cm/10in, W30cm/1ft. F6-7. Z4-9.

POLYGONATUM **Solomon's seal**
Early summer-flowering shade lovers with spreading, fleshy roots. Most have attractive foliage with little white bell-shaped flowers, which dangle from strong, leafy stems, arching in the taller species. ✳ ✦
P. falcatum (syn. *P. japonicum).* A dwarf species with dense, leafy, arching stems and tiny, dangling white flowers. '**Variegatum**' has white-edged leaves. H60cm/2ft, W30cm/1ft. F5-6. Z4-9.
P. biflorum (syn. *P. giganteum).* The tallest, strong-growing species, the giant Solomon's seal. H1m/39in (or more in good soil), W60cm/2ft. F5-7. Z4-9.
P. × hybridum (syn. *P. multiflorum).* A somewhat variable species. It has a striking variegated form '**Striatum**' (syn. '**Variegatum**'). H50-60cm/20-24in, W30cm/1ft. F5-7. Z3-9.

POLYGONUM See PERSICARIA

POTENTILLA **Cinquefoil**
Sun lovers for well-drained soil, with strawberry-like leaves and brightly coloured, saucer-shaped flowers.

P. atrosanguinea. Clumps of silvery lobed leaves and dark red flowers. *P. a. argyrophylla,* similar foliage but sprays of clear yellow flowers. Both H40cm/16in, W60cm/2ft. F-7. Z6-9.
P. argyrophylla hybrids. '**Blazeaway**', suffused orange-red, with greyish leaves. H30cm/1ft, W45cm/18in. F6-8. '**Flamenco**', robust, early, blood-red. H50cm/20in, W60cm/2ft. F5-7. '**Gibson's Scarlet**', popular, glowing red, long season. H60cm/2ft, W60cm/2ft. F6-9. '**William Rollison**', intensely bright flame-orange, semi-double. H40cm/16in, W45cm/18in. F6-8. '**Yellow Queen**', silvery leaves, shining yellow flowers. H25cm/10in, W45cm/18in. F5-7.
P. nepalensis. '**Helen Jane**', bright pink flowers on branching stems. '**Miss Willmott**', a favourite, with strawberry flowers of warm carmine pink. Both H45cm/18in, W40cm/16in. F6-9. Z5-8.
P. recta '**Warrenii**'. Erect-growing, showy, with branching heads of small yellow flowers above dissected greenery. H70cm/28in, W30cm/1ft. F6-8. Z4-8.

PRIMULA
This large and varied genus has many beautiful forms for summer colour, many quite easy to grow. Others require moist soil and some shade to

succeed, according to climate. Those below are described under distinct categories.

Candelabra primulas
These include most tall kinds and moisture lovers for sun or part shade. Flowers are carried in whorls up tall stems. Heights vary according to soil fertility and moisture content. Some may be short-lived, others will self-seed in suitable conditions. Besides those listed below, there are several mixed, mostly long-lived candelabra strains, such as '**Bressingham Strain**' and '**Inshriach Hybrids**'.
P. × bulleesiana. A strain of mixed colours, in shades of cream, yellow, apricot, pink, orange, red and purple. Also known as '**Asthore Hybrids**'. H50-60cm/20-24in, W30cm/1ft. F5-7. Z5-8.
P. bulleyana. A popular plant, with dark green leaves and warm, deep orange flowers. H60-80cm/24-32in, W45cm/18in. F5-7. Z6-8.
P. burmanica. Purple-red, yellow-eyed flowers and long, whitish, dusty leaves. H60-70cm/24-28in, W45cm/18in. F5-7. Z5-8.
P. japonica. The Japanese primrose has leafy growth resembling young cabbages, and pink flowers, near red

Primula 'Bressingham Strain'

with a black eye in **'Miller's Crimson'** and white with a yellow eye in **'Postford White'**. All H60-80cm/24-32in, W45cm/18in. F5-7. Z6-8.

P. pulverulenta. Brilliant rosy-red flowers are carried profusely above crinkled leaves. H40-50cm/16-20in, W45cm/18in. F5-6. Z6-8.

***P. sieboldii* group**
This charming group produces loose umbels of white-eyed flowers above soft green, lobed and toothed foliage. Hardy, easy and not invasive. Often sold as mixtures but good named selections include: **'Cherubim'**, light lavender-blue, **'Geisha Girl'**, clear light pink, **'Mikado'**, reddish-pink, **'Seraphim'**, deep pink, **'Snowflake'**, pure white. All H15-25cm/6-10in, W10-20cm/4-8in. F4-5. Z4-8.
✹ ■ ◪ ★

P. vialii. A distinct species with red hot poker-type, lavender-blue flower spikes on smooth stalks above a small and rather sparsely leaved rootstock. Spectacular in some shade in well-drained but moist, humus-rich soil, flowering later than most primulas. Short-lived but worth the effort. H30-50cm/12-20in, W23cm/9in. F6-8. Z6-8.

PRUNELLA **Self-heal**
These easily grown, mat-forming plants, closely related to *Stachys,* are useful for front-of-the-border groups.

P. grandiflora. This has dense spikes of tubular, purple-violet flowers. It is best in **'Blue Loveliness'**, **'Pink Loveliness'** and **'White Loveliness'**. All H20cm/8in, W45cm/18in. F6-8. Z5-8. **'Little Red Riding Hood'** makes a fine show of rosy red. H15cm/6in, W25cm/10in. F6-8. Z5-8.

PULMONARIA **Lungwort**
Though these are invaluable early spring flowering plants, some flowers last into late spring. The selections listed here offer attractive summer foliage to equal that of any hosta. ☼
✹ ◪

P. longifolia. Conspicuously spotted leaves, 15cm/6in long, blue flowers on terminal sprays; white in the form ***alba.*** **'Bertram Anderson'**, deep violet-blue flowers. **'Roy Davidson'**, lighter blue flowers. All H25cm/10in, W45cm/18in. F4-5/. Z5-8.

P. officinalis **'Sissinghurst White'**. White sprays, white-spotted leaves. H25cm/10in, W60cm/2ft. F3-5.

P. rubra **'David Ward'**. A selection with light green leaves and broad white

Ranunculus gramineus

markings, coral-red blooms. H3cm/1ft, W60cm/2ft. F3-4. Z5-8. ✹

P. saccharata. Bethlehem sage. Widest range of choice, with overlapping evergreen leaves. Almost all have pink flowers which fade to blue on short sprays. All Z4-8. **'Argentea'**, almost entirely silver-leaved. **'Highdown'** (syn. 'Lewis Palmer'), outstanding for its deep blue flowers, vigour and attractive foliage. **'Leopard'**, spotted silver leaves, deep rose-pink spring flowers. All H25cm/10in, W60cm/2ft. F3-5.

PYRETHRUM See *TANACETUM*

RANUNCULUS **Buttercup**
Though generally moisture-loving, any good, well-drained soil and a sunny spot will suit those below.

R. aconitifolius **'Flore Pleno'**. A choice and lovely form with dazzling, fully double white flowers.H40-70cm/16-28in, W60cm/2ft. F5-6. Z5-9. ■

R. gramineus. A first-class perennial with glaucous grassy leaves and sprays of clear yellow flowers. H60cm/2ft, W45cm/18in. F5-7. Z4-8. ☆

RODGERSIA
Long-lived perennials with handsome leaves and imposing flower spikes in summer. Most species have creamy-white plumes, similar to astilbes. Though adaptable for sun or shade, or as marginal plants, they are not suitable for places where it is both dry and sunny. Early growth can be hit by spring frosts.

R. aesculifolia. 'Chestnut-leaved' describes the crinkled bronzed foliage, and it has conical creamy-white flower spikes. **'Irish Bronze'** has purple-tinted leaves and stems, and white flowers. Both H1.2m/4ft, W60cm/2ft. F6-8. Z5-8.

R. pinnata. This has paired, fingered, deeply divided leaves, pink or white flowers. The form **'Elegans'** is freer to flower with imposing creamy spikes. H1.2m/4ft, W60cm/2ft. F6-8. Z5-8. **'Superba'** lives up to its name; not only is the foliage tinted purple, but the flowers are a glistening rose-pink. H1.2m/4ft, W50cm/20in. F6-7. Z5-8.

ROMNEYA **California tree poppy**
Glaucous-leaved and semi-shrubby, these perennials have white, scented, poppy-like flowers carried over a long period. Although the roots have a tendency to spread, their beauty outweighs such a disadvantage. They are difficult to divide, so pot-grown plants are best. ☼ ■

R. coulteri. This has large, yellow-centred white flowers and is the species most likely to be available. H2.1m/7ft, W90cm/3ft. F7-10. Z8-10.

ROSCOEA
Fleshy-rooted, distinctive perennials, easy to grow. They are late to break the surface in spring but soon produce light green, sheath-like leaves and spikes of orchid-like flowers on erect stems. ☼ ✹

R. cautleoides. Early and of an open, slender habit, the flowers are soft primrose-yellow. **'Kew Beauty'**, later to flower than the species, its leafy stalks sheathe large, primrose-yellow

Primula vialii

flowers. Both H35cm/14in, W15cm/6in. F6-8. Z7-9.

R. procera. The finest blue-flowered species, this has large, deep violet-blue flowers above abundant greenery. H35cm/14in, W15cm/6in. F6-8. Z6-9.

R. purpurea. Also violet-blue, this has smaller flowers and leaves. H35cm/14in, W15cm/6in. F6-8. Z6-9.

RUDBECKIA Coneflower, Black-eyed Susan

These are some of the showiest and easiest of late-flowering perennials. All come from North America and have daisy-like flowers. ☀ ☆

R. fulgida. There are several selections of this species, somewhat similar to each other, all with a central black cone and golden-yellow rayed petals. They prefer moist to dry soils but are generally quite adaptable. All tend to seed freely. F7-10, Z4-9. *R. f.* var. *deamii* has light green leaves, tall at 90cm/3ft, W45cm/18in. *R. f.* var. *sullivantii* **'Goldsturm'**, one of the best plants ever raised, with shining dark green foliage, black-centred gold flowers. H45-60cm/18-24in, W45cm/18in. *R. f.* **Viette's Little Suzy'.** Diminutive selection, smaller flowers and leaves. H30cm/1ft, W30cm/1ft.

Rudbeckia 'Goldquelle'

Salvia × *superba*

R. **'Herbstsonne'** (syn. 'Autumn Sun'). Garden-worthy, though tall, with long stems of bright green leaves topped with greenish-yellow cone. H2.1m/7ft, W60cm/2ft. F7-9. Z5-9.

R. **'Goldquelle'.** A distinctive, very beautiful plant with leafy, deep green bushy growth covered in fully double, chrome-yellow flowers, 8cm/3in across. H1m/39in, W60cm/2ft. F7-9. Z3-9.

SALVIA

A vast genus which includes some good garden plants, though some of the brightest colours are not hardy. Many are aromatic and most have hairy leaves; colourful bracts are also common. They enjoy sun and well-drained soil.

S. nemerosa **'Ost Friesland'** (syn. 'East Friesland'). Outstanding free-flowering cultivar, bushy habit, numerous spikes bearing violet-blue flowers. **'Lubecca'** is similar but twice the height. H45cm/18in, W45cm/18in. F6-8. Z5-9.

S. pratensis **'Rosea'.** A pretty form with long branched spikes of pale lilac-pink flowers. H60cm/2ft, W45cm/18in. F6-8. Z5-9.

S. × *superba*. A popular hybrid with fine violet-blue upstanding spikes with crimson-purple bracts, making

an excellent contrast to yellow, daisy-flowered subjects. H1.2m/4ft, W60cm/2ft. F6-8. Z5-9.

S. × *sylvestris* **'Blauhügel'** ('Blue Hills'). Closest to blue of any of this type, providing a succession of flowers on compact bushes throughout the summer. There is also a white form **'Weisshügel'** ('White Hills'). Both 45cm/18in, W30cm/1ft. F6-9. Z5-9. **'Mainacht'** ('May Night'), earliest to flower with striking violet-blue flowers on erect spikes. H45cm/18in, W30cm/1ft. F5-7. Z5-9.

S. verticillata **'Purple Rain'.** Leafy, hairy foliage and spikes with whorls of rich purple flowers for weeks on end. H45cm/18in, W45cm/18 in. F7-9. Z5-9.

SANGUISORBA Burnet

Strong-growing leafy perennials with elegant, pinnate foliage and bottlebrush flowers. Hardy and long-lived. ☀ ☆

S. magnifica alba. A robust plant with nodding white pokers above abundant foliage. H80cm/32in, W60cm/2ft. F6-8. Z4-8.

SCABIOSA Scabious, pincushion flower

Popular perennials with a long flowering season. ☀ ■

S. **'Butterfly Blue'.** Lavender-blue flowers all summer. Similar in habit but with lilac-pink flowers is **'Pink Mist'.** Both H30cm/1ft, W30cm/1ft. F5-9. Z5-8.

S. caucasica. Valuable perennials for garden and cutting, these prefer sun and well-drained soil, ideally with lime. Deadhead to prolong flowering. All H60-80cm/24-32in, W45-60cm/18-24in. F6-9. Z4-9. **'Blausiegel'** ('Blue Seal'), a strong constitution and a succession of rich blue flowers. **'Bressingham White'** and **'Miss Willmott'** are both good whites, the latter more ivory. **'Clive Greaves'**, is a prolific mid-blue and **'Moonlight'** a fairly tall light blue.

S. graminifolia. One of the finest plants for frontal groups, it makes dense mats of narrow, silver-grey leaves with a long show of light blue flowers. H30cm/1ft, W30cm/1ft. F6-9. Z7-9. **'Pink Cushion'**, from Bressingham, is light pink and less robust. H25cm/10in, W25cm/10in. F6-9. Z7-9. ☀ Light soil

SEDUM Stonecrop

Indispensable and easy perennials whose flat or domed heads of starry flowers also attract butterflies. ☀ ■ ☆

S. aizoon **'Aurantiacum'.** Striking for its bronzy stems and leaves and its deep yellow, almost orange, flowers. H30cm/1ft, W30cm/1ft. F6-8. Z4-9.

S. **'Autumn Joy'** ('Herbstfreude'). Spring growth of glaucous, fleshy stem and leaves remaining attractive all summer. Glistening pink flowerheads widen to 25cm/10in across, turning a deep bronze, then coppery red. Divide and replant regularly. H50cm/20in, W50cm/20in. F8-10. Z3-10.

S. **'Mörchen'.** Erect habit and deep purple-bronze leaves, smallish yellow flowers but foliage effect impressive. H45cm/18in, W30cm/1ft. F8-9. Z4-9.

S. floriferum **'Weihenstephaner Gold'.** For the front of a border, this makes spreading, dark green mats and a long succession of orange-gold heads. H15-18cm/6-7in, W45cm/18in. F6-9. Z4-8.

S. 'Ruby Glow'. Hybrid with greyish-purple foliage and a good display of ruby-red flowers. H20cm/8in, W20cm/8in. F7-9. Z4-8.

S. spectabile. Sometimes called ice plants, their fleshy glaucous foliage is effective infill all summer before the wide heads of chalky pink flowers appear. Not much variation in the varieties offered. 'Brilliant', 'Indian Chief', 'Meteor' and 'September Glow' all have more vivid flowers. H30-40cm/12-16in, W30-40cm/12-16in. F8-10. Z4-9.

S. telephium maximum. 'Atropurpureum' has handsome purple-red leaves and heads of glistening rosy-red flowers. H50cm/20in, W30cm/1ft. F7-8. Z5-9.

S. 'Vera Jameson'. Dwarf form with bluish-purple leaves and loose heads of warm pink flowers. H25cm/10in, W25cm/10in. F7-9. Z4-9.

SIDALCEA

Useful for their spiky habit and mallow flowers which add to the structure of the perennial bed or

Sidalcea candida 'Elsie Heugh'

border. All are easy to grow and have silky, hollyhock-like flowers, graceful divided foliage and a clumpy, ground-covering base.

S. candida. Small pretty white flowers on narrow spikes make an attractive variation. Some may need staking. H90cm/3ft, W30cm/1ft. All F6-9. Z5-8. 'Croftway Red', deep rose. H1m/39in, W45cm/18in. 'Elsie Heugh', upstanding clear pink, fringed petals. H1.2m/4ft, W45cm/18in. 'Loveliness', warm pink, compact. H80cm/32in, W45cm/18in. 'Mrs Alderson', deep pink, heavy foliage. H1.2m/4ft, W45cm/18in. 'Oberon', shell-pink, erect, self-supporting. H80cm/32in, W45cm/18in. 'William Smith', salmon-pink, H1.2m/4ft, W45cm/18in.

SISYRINCHIUM

Resembling the iris, most are classed as alpines. ☼ ■

S. striatum. Broad, light green evergreen leaves and light yellow flowers. Tolerates light shade. Not long-lived but self-seeding. Of considerable merit is the creamy-yellow variegated form 'Aunt May', which has summer-long interest. H60cm/2ft, W23cm/9in. F6-8. Z7-8.

SOLIDAGO Goldenrod

Considered weeds by some and certainly a few of the taller self-seeding or spreading species fit that description. However there are many hybrids which offer attractive foliage and flower to add to the summer palette, all variations of yellow. All Z4-9. ☼ ✳ ☆

'Cloth of Gold', dwarf, abundant foliage, wide heads. H40cm/16in, W30cm/1ft. F6-8. 'Crown of Rays' ('Strahlenkrone'), similar, but a little taller. H45cm/18in, W30cm/1ft. F7-8. 'Golden Shower', attractive splayed plumes. H70cm/28in, W45cm/18in. F7-8. 'Lemore', soft primrose-yellow. H70cm/28in, W45cm/18in. F7-8.

Solidago 'Queenie'

'Mimosa', the best tall form, golden-yellow. H1.2m/ 4ft, W60cm/2ft. F8-9. 'Queenie' (syn. 'Golden Thumb'), neat, small, light-leaved bush, short yellow flower spikes. H25cm/10in, W25cm/10in. F8-9.

STACHYS

These woolly-leaved plants are all easy to grow. ☼ ■

S. byzantina (syn. *S. lanata* and *S. olympica*). Lamb's tongue, or lamb's ear, is vigorous but shallow-rooting, with lilac flowers above mats of downy leaves. H45cm/18in, W30cm/1ft. F5-6. Z4-9. 'Primrose Heron', new felted leaves emerge golden in spring and last for many weeks. H45cm/18in, W30cm/1ft. F5-6. Z4-9. 'Silver Carpet' is a non-flowering, excellent carpeter. H20cm/8in, W30cm/1ft. Z4-9

S. macrantha. A showy plant with dark green, downy foliage and spikes of deep lilac. 'Robusta', the best form, has stiff growth, crinkly, bright green leaves and deep pink spikes. Both H40cm/16in, W23cm/9in. F6-8. Z4-8.

STOKESIA Stoke's aster, cornflower aster

S. laevis. Formerly *S. cyanea,* this has leathery, broad, strap-like basal leaves

and large, solitary, cornflower-like flowers on short stems for many weeks. These are wide-petalled, in shades of blue and, less commonly, white, with fluffy centres. Ideal for the front of a sunny border. 'Blue Star' has light blue flowers, 'Wyoming', a deeper purple-blue. Both H25-30cm/10-12in, W30cm/1ft. F6-9. Z5-8. ■

SYMPHYTUM Comfrey

Most comfreys have coarse, hairy leaves and drooping, tubular flowers. Place with care in the garden due to their invasive nature. Adaptable and not fussy about soil, though cool, moist soil is ideal. ☼ ✳ ✳ ◣ ☆

S. 'Hidcote Blue'. Strong-growing ground cover with red buds turning to blue and white bells, making often dark green leafy carpets. 'Hidcote Pink' has deep rose-pink and white flowers. Pretty in flower, useful under trees but both need controlling. Both H45cm/18in, W60cm/2ft. F4-6. Z5-9.

S. ibericum (syn. *S. grandiflorum)*. A vigorous, low-growing spreader with mid-green leaves and creamy-yellow flowers. 'Goldsmith' (syn. 'Variegata'), makes a bright show with green leaves, irregularly edged gold.

Can revert if roots are damaged. Both species and this H20cm/8in, W45cm/18in. F4-6. Z5-9.

TANACETUM
T. coccineum (syn. *Pyrethrum coccineum, Chrysanthemum pyrethrum*). The pyrethrums are showy perennials with carrot-like foliage and early summer daisy-like flowers of red, pink and white, some double, excellent for cutting. Cut back after flowering. Best planted in spring, pot-grown plants only in autumn. All F5-7. Z5-9. ✲ ■ ⊙
'Avalanche', robust, single white. 'Brenda', strong-growing deep pink, single. Both H80cm/32in, W45cm/18in. 'Bressingham Red', blood-red, single-rayed flowers. 'Eileen May Robinson', still supreme as a single clear pink. Both H70cm/28in, W45cm/18in. 'Philippa', double, glowing deep carmine. The following dwarf cultivars are all vigorous: 'Laurin', single pink. H38cm/15in, W30cm/1ft. 'Peter Pan', almost double carmine-red. H30cm/1ft, W20cm/8in. 'Pink Petite', clear pink. H38cm/15in, W25cm/10in. 'Red Dwarf' (syn. 'Rote Zwerg'), compact with yellow centres and bright crimson petals. H30cm/1ft, W20cm/8in.
T. parthenium (syn. *Pyrethrum parthenium, Chrysanthemum parthenium*) 'Aureum'. Feverfew, a free-seeding perennial of great charm. Bright golden-leaved bushes are covered with tiny single daisy flowers in mid-summer. H45cm/18in, W45cm/18in. F6-7. Z4-8.

TELLIMA Fringecup
T. grandiflora This relative of *Heuchera* has the same mounded, evergreen foliage, but the flowers, on hairy-stemmed sprays, are creamy-green. The purplish-leaved 'Rubra' (syn. 'Purpurea') is more effective. Both H50cm/20in, W50cm/20in. F5-6. Z4-9. ✲ ✱ □

THALICTRUM Meadow rue
Tall and robust, small and delicate, both are represented in this variable genus. ✲ ✱ ✰
T. aquilegiifolium. A clump-forming species making an early display of columbine-like leaves and small, fluffy flowers in terminal clusters. The rounded flowers are purplish, except in 'Album' where they are white. H1m/39in, W30cm/1ft. F5-7. Z5-9. 'Purpureum' is purple-lilac, but shades and heights vary greatly since they are often offered from seed-raised plants. H80-120cm/32-48in, W30cm/1ft. F5-7. Z5-9.
T. delavayi (syn. *T. dipterocarpum*). Small mauve-blue flowers with yellow centres appear in great profusion on widely branching stems, apt to tangle. H1.2m/4ft, W45cm/18in. F7-9. Z5-9. 'Hewitt's Double' is a choice and beautiful plant. H90cm/3ft, W30cm/1ft. F7-9. Z5-9. ✱ ◪
T. flavum. Yellow meadow rue is green-leaved, with yellow flowers in terminal clusters on strong stems. H1.5m/5ft, W45cm/18in. F6-8. Z6-9.

THERMOPSIS False lupin
Lupin-like in appearance, with palmate leaves and racemes of yellow

Thalictrum flavum

Tiarella polyphylla 'Moorgrün'

flowers in early summer. All are easy, given sun and well-drained soil. ■
T. angustifolia, T. caroliniana and **T. mollis** are clump-forming, sun-loving plants, giving a good display from leafy bushes. All H80-100cm/32-39in, W60cm/2ft. F5-7. Z3-9.
T. montana. Bright yellow, pea-like flower spikes on smooth stems. H75cm/2ft 6in, W60cm/2ft. F6-7. Z3-8.

TIARELLA Foam flower
Dwarf, shade-loving plants allied to *Heuchera,* these are shallow-rooting and like sandy, cool, moist soil. New breeding work is bringing forward some valuable new forms. ✱ ■ ✰
T. cordifolia. This carpets shady places with pretty evergreen leaves, bronzy in winter, and gives a charming summer display with racemes of starry small white flowers. Spreads by runners. H15cm/6in, W45cm/18in. F5-6. Z3-8.
T. polyphylla. This forms low green hummocks of lobed, toothed leaves and tiny, pearl-like, white or pink-tinged flowers. 'Moorgrün' makes effective ground cover, with a mass of pure white flowers. Both H20cm/8in, W30cm/1ft. F5-7. Z5-8.
T. wherryi (syn. *T. collina*). This species varies in the wild, but all the selections are clump-forming, not

spreading or invasive, many with attractive bronze foliage and spikes of dainty star-like flowers, white or pink. 'Bronze Beauty' is outstanding, with maple-like leaves with bronze markings and narrow spikes, whose pink buds open to delicate blush-pink flowers. 'Green Velvet' has white flowers. Both H25cm/10in, W30cm/1ft. F5-6. Z-8.

TRADESCANTIA
Free-flowering hardy perennials, mostly represented in cultivation by hybrids. Easy to grow and long-flowering. Bright, three-petalled flowers are carried amid copious narrow foliage. Apt to become untidy with lolling stalks, but worthwhile. ✲
T. × andersoniana 'Carmine Glow' (syn. 'Karminglut'). Crimson flowers, neat habit. 'Iris Prichard', white flowers stained azure-blue. 'Innocence', large-flowered white. 'Isis', warm Oxford blue. 'Osprey', white, lilac-centred flowers. 'Pauline', light lilac-pink flowers. 'Purple Dome' rich velvety purple flowers. 'Zwanenburg Blue'. Another good deep blue. All approx. H50cm/20in, W50cm/20in. F6-9. Z5-9.

TRICYRTIS Toad lily
A wider range now exists of these charming and distinctive plants. Most have spotted, bell-shaped flowers and grow reliably in good, deep soil. Besides those listed, there are several other more recently introduced species. ✲ ✱ ✰
T. formosana. This makes a clumpy plant, best in sun, with erect leafy stems carrying open heads of mauve, yellow-throated flowers with a hint of brown. H75cm/2ft 6in, W45cm/18in. F8-10. Z5-9.
T. hirta. The flowers along the stems are near-white, heavily spotted lilac; the leaves are hairy. H90cm/3ft, W60cm/2ft. F8-10. Z4-9. 'Miyazaki', arching stems have leaves edged with yellow, flowers white with prominent

lilac spots. H75cm/2ft 6in, W45cm/18in. F8-10. Z6-9.

TRILLIUM **Wood lily, Wake robin**
Bulbous perennials for a late spring display. The flowers have three petals and three calyces; three leaves form a ruff-like whorl beneath each flower. All are woodland subjects and respond to humus-rich, moist, but well-drained soil and light shade. Slow-growing, and once they settle satisfactorily they can be left alone for years, expanding into clumps producing more and more flowers.
☼ ☆ ■
T. erectum. This has rich maroon nodding flowers with recurving petals, among large deep green leaves. The white form, *T. e. albiflorum*, with yellow anthers and reddish centres, is even more striking. Both H30cm/1ft, W30cm/1ft. F4-6. Z4-9.
T. grandiflorum. The wake robin has large, beautiful, pure white flowers, but most prized of all is the sumptuous double white, '**Flore Pleno**' which remains lovely for a long time. So does the rare, single, clear pink '**Roseum**'. All H30cm/1ft, W30cm/1ft. F4-6. Z4-9.
T. sessile. The maroon flowers have

narrow, slightly twisted petals and stand erectly above the beautifully marbled, grey and dark green leaves. Forms with yellow and white flowers exist. H45cm/18in, W30cm/1ft. F4-6. Z5-9.

TROLLIUS **Globe flower**
These make a fine display in early summer of mainly globe- or bowl-shaped, buttercup-like flowers. They thrive in deep soil which does not dry out. Flowers vary from pale primrose to yellow and orange and are carried above deeply divided leaves. ☼ ■
T. chinensis (syn. *T. ledebourii*). '**Golden Queen**' and '**Imperial Orange**' are distinctive in having open, deep yellow flowers with a central tuft of fiery orange, petal-like stamens. Later than most to flower. H90cm/3ft, W45cm/18in. F6-7. Z4-8.
T. × cultorum. These hybrids between *T. chinensis, T. europaeus* and *T. asiaticus* provide a good colour range. All F5-7. Z4-8. '**Bressingham Sunshine**', pure, glistening yellow, vigorous. H75cm/2ft 6in, W45cm/18in. '**Commander in Chief**', extra-large flowers, warm orange-gold. H70cm/28in, W45cm/18in. '**Cressida**', a more vigorous creamy-

Trollius europaeus 'Superbus'

yellow. H60cm/2ft, W45cm/18in. '**Orange Princess**', deep yellow. H75cm/2ft 6in, W45cm/18in.
T. europaeus. Compact habit, making clumps of bright green leaves and a fine show of lemon-yellow globe flowers. '**Superbus**' is a select form worth looking for. H60cm/2ft, W45cm/18in. F5-7. Z4-8.

TROPAEOLUM
T. speciosum. From Chile, this climber thrives in cool, moist climates. Its fast-growing, slender stems grow up and into plants to surprise in late summer with small, bright scarlet trumpet flowers, making a striking contrast to almost any tree, conifer or shrub to which it attaches itself. H1.5-3m/5-10ft, W60cm/2ft. F7-9. Z8-9.

VERBASCUM **Mullein**
Spiky perennials with fleshy roots thrive in quite poor soil. All Z5-9. ☼ ■
V. chaixii. This has imposing, very erect spikes of rather small flowers, yellow with mauve eyes, rising from a leafy base. '**Album**' has mauve-centred white flowers; both forms are inclined to self-seed. Both H1.1m/43in, W45cm/18in. F6-8.
Hybrids. Three are very similar – '**Cotswold Beauty**', '**Gem**' and

'**Queen**' – all with branching stems and flowers of varying buff-yellow shades with purple or mauve centres. All H1m/39in, W45cm/18in. F6-8.
'**Gainsborough**', woolly grey foliage, light yellow spikes. H1.1m/43in, W45cm/18in. F6-8. '**Helen Johnson**', a unique and striking plant with well-branched spikes with grey felted stems and leaves, the flowers a warm coppery beige. H60-75cm/2ft-2ft 6in, W45cm/18in. F6-9. '**Mont Blanc**', the finest white, felty grey leaves, short-lived. H1.1m/43in, W45cm/18in. F6-8. '**Pink Domino**',

Trillium grandiflorum

Verbascum 'Helen Johnson'

deep green leaves, full, deep rosy pink flowers. H1 1m/39in, W45cm/18in. F6-8.

VERBENA

A genus of colourful plants which includes several non-hardy species, suitable for bedding. ☼ ■

V. bonariensis. This has little heads of lavender-blue, fragrant flowers above slender, sparsely leaved, branching stems. Long-flowering and pretty as a group. Excellent for late flower. Not very long-lived, but self-seeds freely. H1.5m/5ft, W60cm/2ft. F6-9. Z7-10.

V. 'Homestead Purple'. A vigorous spreading selection found in a homestead garden in Georgia, U.S.A. Bright purple flowers last all summer. Hardy at least to minus 10°C (12°F). H30cm/1ft, W60cm/2ft. F6-10. Z8-10.

VERONICA Speedwell

This widely varying genus provides some good, reliable perennials as well as alpines. The spike-forming kinds are especially useful and almost all are hardy and easy to grow in mainly sunny positions.

V. austriaca teucrium (syn. *V. teucrium*). Reliable, clump-forming plants with fresh green, deciduous foliage and profuse spikes of tiny flowers. All have bright mid- to deep blue flowers, but vary in height. All Z5-8. **'Blue Fountain'**, rich blue. H50cm/20in, W30cm/1ft. F6-8. **'Crater Lake Blue'**, dark blue. H30cm/1ft, W30cm/1ft. F6-8. **'Kapitan'**, light blue. H25cm/10in, W30cm/1ft. F5-7.

V. gentianoides. This forms basal, light green, rosette-type foliage with ample spread and pleasing early spikes of light blue. **'Variegata'** has creamy variegated leaves. All 35cm/14in, W35cm/14in. F5-6. Z5-8.

V. longifolia **'Blauriesin'** (syn. 'Foerster's Blue') and **'Schneeriesin'** are outstanding forms with abundant spikes bearing deep blue and white

Veronica peduncularis 'Georgia Blue'

flowers respectively. Moist soils will produce taller plants. Both H50-90cm/20-36in, W38cm/15in. F7-9. Z4-8.

V. peduncularis **'Georgia Blue'**. Dark green hummocks of foliage covered with masses of deep blue flowers. H15cm/6in, W30cm/1ft. F4-6. Z6-8.

V. spicata. Mat-forming, deciduous perennials, many with greyish foliage. All Z4-8. ☼ ■ **'Barcarolle'**, deep rosy-pink spikes, green foliage. H30cm/1ft, W45cm/18in. F7-9. **'Blue Fox'**, lavender-blue spikes, green-leaved. H30cm/1ft, W45cm/18in. F7-9. **'Heidekind'**, short, rosy red, not vigorous. H20cm/8in, W30cm/1ft. F4-5.

VIOLA

Popular plants which add early colour in the garden. Those mentioned are hardy and should be cut back after spring flowering. ☼ ✳ ☀

V. cornuta. Masses of small, violet-purple flowers for many weeks, and clumps of rich green leaves, making effective ground cover. H15-25cm/6-10in, W30cm/1ft. F5-7. Z5-8. **'Alba'** has white flowers. H15cm/6in, W3cm/1ft. F4-7. Z5-8.

V. cucullata. The marsh violet has white flowers on erect stems and tolerates damp soil. H8-15cm/3-6in,

W15cm/6in. F4-5. Z4-9. **'Freckles'** has palest blue flowers with purple spots. H15cm/6in, W15cm/6in. F4-5. Z4-9.

Hybrids. All Z5-7. **'Ardross Gem'**, light blue flowers, flushed with gold. H13cm/5in, W30cm/1ft. F4-7. **'Boughton Blue'**, charming ethereal blue. H15cm/6in, W30cm/1ft. F4-7. **'Bullion'**, the most reliable pure yellow. H15cm/6in, W30cm/1ft. F5-8. **'Clementina'**, large violet flowers, vigorous. H15cm/6in, W30cm/1ft. F4-9. **'Columbine'**, lilac-white petals streaked with blue. H15cm/6in, W30cm/1ft. F4-9. **'Irish Molly'** softly suffused colours. H15cm/6in,

Viola 'Columbine'

W30cm/1ft. F5-8. **'Maggie Mott'**, light blue and scented. H13cm/5in, W30cm/1ft. F5-8. **'Norah Leigh'**, mid-blue. H13cm/5in, W30cm/1ft. F4-7. **'Molly Sanderson'**, nearly black. H8-15cm/3-6in, W15-25cm/6-10in. F4-7. Z5-7.

YUCCA

These evergreen plants, often classed as shrubs, display sword-like foliage throughout the year and, though long-lived, some flower irregularly. It is worth the wait for the spectacular ivory-white or pink-tinged, lily-like flowers on stiff spikes. ☼ ■

Y. filamentosa. Adam's needle is almost stemless and has greyish foliage with hair-like fibres along the edges and ivory-white, bell-shaped flowers most years. H1. 5m/5ft, W1.5m/5ft. F7-8. Z5-10. **'Bright Edge'**, gold, and **'Variegata'** have brightly variegated leaves. Both H90cm/3ft, W60cm/2ft. F7-8. Z5-9.

Y. flaccida. Notable for flowering most seasons, it is similar to the above, but with narrower, less rigid leaves. **'Golden Sword'** has irregular central golden stripes on the leaves. H1.5m/5ft, W1.5m/5ft. F7-8. Z5-10.

Y. gloriosa. The Spanish dagger grows large and is spectacular in flower. **'Variegata'** has brightly striped leaves. H2.1-3m/7-10ft, W1.5m/5ft. F8-9. Z7-10.

ZANTEDESCHIA Arum lily, Calla lily

Z. aethiopica. Hardy given ample covering from mid-autumn to mid-spring in cold districts. **'Crowborough'**, widely accepted as the most reliable form, with handsome white spathes above large, shiny green leaves. Although moisture-loving and able to grow in mud in 15-30cm/6-12in deep water, it is surprisingly adaptable to any fertile soil. **'Green Goddess'**, with greenish flower spathes, scarcely different in colour from the lush foliage. H1.2m/4ft, W60cm/2ft. F7-9. Z8-10.

FERNS DIRECTORY

HARDY FERNS ARE A GROUP OF PLANTS which have many uses in the summer garden, their bright green foliage a wonderful foil to summer-flowering subjects. But they are still under-used. Their names are confusing, and their parentage too. Not all ferns need shade and damp soil but those that do fit in well with moisture-loving plants, such as hostas or astilbes, or will thrive in woodland conditions.

H: Approximate height after 2 years
W: Approximate width after 2 years
Z: Relevant hardiness zone(s)

ADIANTUM Maidenhair fern

Deciduous, delicate-looking ferns with new growth appearing in spring and lasting until winter. ✳ ★
A. pedatum. The American or northern maidenhair has branching fronds made up of many toothed lobes on slender black stems. H45cm/18in, W30cm/1ft. Z3-8.

ASPLENIUM

This genus of evergreen lime lovers now includes what were formerly *Phyllitis* and *Scolopendrium*.
A. scolopendrium. The hart's tongue, a British native, is well known for its long, leathery leaves. Given shade it is easy to grow, in crevices or on walls. H up to 35cm/14in, W40cm/16in. Z4-8. 'Cristatum' has curiously dissected crests on the light green fronds. H35cm/14in, W40cm/16in. Z4-8. 'Undulatum' has narrow fronds with attractive wavy edges. H30-40cm/12-16in, W30-45cm/12-18in. Z4-8.

ATHYRIUM

A. filix-femina. The lady fern has lacy, light green, deciduous fronds. Damp shade is best. H60-100cm/24-39in, W60cm/2ft. Z4-9. There are many variations. 'Plumosum'. Plumosum Group covers variations with elegant, leathery, golden-green fronds. H90cm/3ft, W60cm/2ft. Z4-9.
A. nipponicum 'Pictum' (syn. 'Metallicum'). The Japanese painted fern is low-spreading, with dark red,

arching stems and silvery fronds. It needs shelter. H30-60cm/1-2ft, W45cm/18in. Z3-8.
A. otophorum var. **okanum.** Outstanding foliage form whose spring fronds emerge daubed with silver-white, remaining silvery all summer. H30cm/1ft, W30cm/1ft. Z5-9.

BLECHNUM Hard fern

Most have a moderately spreading habit and deep green, fairly narrow, leathery evergreen fronds. They dislike lime, but tolerate a dry atmosphere.
B. spicant. The common hard fern, or deer fern, is clump-forming and produces two types of pinnate frond: arching, spreading, sterile ones and erect, spore-bearing, deciduous ones. H30-60cm/1-2ft, W45cm/18in. Z4-8. ★

Athyrium filix-femina

Polystichum setiferum 'Plumosum'

DRYOPTERIS Buckler fern

This genus is widely variable but most species are long-lived, vigorous, hardy and deciduous and form stout clumps which rise above soil level.
D. affinis (syn. *D. borreri* and *D. pseudomas*). 'Crispa', a group form with usually arching, deep green, crisped fronds. The form 'Cristata The King', a selection of the golden-scaled male fern, has evenly crested, arching fronds from a symmetrical central crown. Tolerates dry soil. Both H80-90cm/32-36in, W80-90cm/32-36in. Z4-8.
D. erythrosora. The Japanese shield fern has unusual pink or bronze-tinged young fronds that mature to light green. Deciduous, but the leaves remain until mid-winter. H60cm/2ft, W30cm/1ft. Z5-9. ✳ ★
D. filix-mas. The common male fern is adaptable to almost any but parched places. H90cm/3ft, W90cm/3ft. Z4-8. There are many varieties.
D. wallichiana. A beautiful fern whose unfolding golden-green shoots in spring deepen to rich green fronds, erectly held, in summer. H1.2m/4ft, W90cm/3ft. Z7-9.

MATTEUCCIA Ostrich fern, Shuttlecock fern

M. struthiopteris. This is quite spectacular, with large, shapely fronds forming shuttlecock-like rosettes from stout stocks and spreading runners which are likely to

colonize in rich, moist soil. H1m/39in, W60-90cm/2-3ft. Z2-8.

OSMUNDA Royal fern

O. regalis. A majestic specimen, forming a massive crown above ground from which sprout deciduous fronds, coppery when young, then fresh green and, finally, yellow-brown in autumn. H up to 1.8m/6ft, W1.8m/6ft. Z3-9. ✿ ✳ ★
◪ ⊙

POLYSTICHUM Shield fern, holly fern

These attractive evergreen ferns have large, broad fronds. Most are fully hardy and adaptable even where soil is poor, dry or limy if they are given a good start. ✳
P. setiferum. The soft shield fern. The several forms differ in the pattern of the broad, deeply cleft fronds, arching from a stout central crown. H up to 90cm/3ft, W90-120cm/3-4ft. Z5-8. **Divisilobum Group** has finely divided fronds and tolerates fairly dry conditions. 'Herrenhausen', dense clumps of spreading fronds of finely feathered, mid-green foliage. H45cm/18in, W75cm/2ft 6in. Z5-8. 'Plumosum' has soft, semi-prostrate, densely clothed, evergreen fronds. H30cm/1ft, W50cm/20in. Z5-8.

Matteuccia struthiopteris

GRASSES DIRECTORY

ORNAMENTAL GRASSES ARE FINALLY BEING RECOGNIZED for the colour, grace and movement they can bring to the garden. More than that, they have a long period of interest which, for many, lasts throughout autumn and winter. They can be planted with many different groups of plants, but they associate particularly well with perennials, conifers, heathers and shrubs, softening harsh or bright colours and adding their own in summer, in both foliage and flowers. Grasses provide the perfect plant associations to colourful perennials such as crocosmias, kniphofias and phlox . Many are effective used in pots and other containers for patios and terraces. Container-grown plants can be planted out at any time of year in free-draining soil, but most field-grown plants, and those divided from garden clumps, are best planted in mid-spring. Because of their winter interest, it is best to leave most grasses until early or mid-spring to be cut back, just before the new growth starts. Though there are variations according to species, most ornamental grasses prefer well-drained, if not dry, soil.

H:	Approximate height
W:	Approximate width
F :	Months in flower
Z:	Relevant hardiness zone(s)

Stipa tenuissima in the volcano bed at Foggy Bottom

Carex hachijoensis

ACORUS
A. gramineus 'Ogon'. Not strictly a grass but looks like one with rush-like foliage. Narrow, gold and green leaves arching in fan-like sprays are almost brighter in winter than summer. 'Variegatus', less showy with white-edged leaves. ☼ ❋ ◢

ARUNDO Giant reed
A. donax. This is a giant among grasses, having strong stems with floppy, wide, somewhat sheathed glaucous leaves. It does not flower in cool temperate climates but is still worthwhile where space allows, in any reasonable or moist soil and sun. H3m/10ft, W1.2m/4ft. Z7-10. 'Versicolor' (syn. 'Variegata') is less vigorous but has very effective brightly variegated leaves, and is particularly suited to patio containers. Hardier than often supposed. H1.8-2.4m/6-8ft, W90cm/3ft. Z7-10.

BOUTELOUA Mosquito grass
B. gracilis (syn. *B. oligostachya).* Short sprays of curious, brownish flower spikes, at right angles to the stems, resemble hovering mosquitoes, above a tufty, semi-evergreen, deep green base. Attractive in winter frost. H25cm/10in, W20cm/8in. F6-8. Z5-9.

CALAMAGROSTIS
C. × acutiflora 'Karl Foerster'. This is an attractive hybrid with an erect habit, its foliage a rich green followed by plum-brown spikes which remain until spring growth is renewed. 'Overdam', a striking plant whose early growth is striped with white-flushed pink, then forming erect green stems prior to a late summer display of feathery plumes. Both H1.5m/5ft, W60cm/2ft. F7-8. Z5-9.

CAREX Sedge
Though members of the *Cyperaceae* family, these are grass-like in appearance and are identifiable by their stems, triangular in section. *C. buchananii.* Leatherleaf sedge. Evergreen, erect tufts of unusual coppery-brown, thin, needle-like blades, reddish towards the base. H60cm/2ft, W20cm/8in. Z6-9. *C. comans.* More mounded, wide-spreading habit. The thin, dense growth has a decidedly light brownish hue, held all year round. Flowers are not conspicuous. There are various forms of the species. 'Bronze', deep bronze-green foliage. Very similar in form but classed as a hybrid is 'Frosted Curls' which looks, even in summer, as though its

narrow foliage is frosted with creamy white. All H45cm/18in, W60cm/2ft. F6-8. Z6-9.

C. elata (syn. *C. stricta*) **'Aurea'**. Bright golden-yellow leaves during spring and summer and deep brown flowers in mid-summer. H50cm/20in, W45cm/18in. F6-8. Z5-9. ✿ ◢

C. hachijoensis **'Evergold'** (syn. *C. morrowii* 'Evergold'*)* is one of the brightest year-round plants, forming large clumps with narrow, shiny, dark green leaves, striped golden-yellow. H25cm/10in, W60cm/2ft. Z7-9.

C. morrowii (syn. *C. oshimensis*). The Japanese sedge has dark evergreen foliage in long-lived clumps, but rarely flowers. **'Fisher's Form'** and **'Variegata'** are both good foliage plants with golden-edged leaves. Both 30cm/1ft, W30cm/1ft. Z7-9.

C. pendula. A plant for woodland or wild garden. Clumps of broad green leaves and long arching stems terminate in long grass tassels. H1.2m/4ft, W1.2m/4ft. F6-7. Z7-9.

CHIONOCHLOA
C. rubra. Finely spaced, arching leaves rounded and graceful in habit, olive-green in summer, bronzed in winter. H60cm/2ft, W60cm/2ft. F7-8. Z7-9.

CORTADERIA Pampas grass
Often spectacular flowering grasses, most of which are not suitable for the smaller garden. The variegated forms offer year-round interest in milder climates, but foliage dies back in colder ones.

C. selloana. Several variations, from 1.5m/5ft to 3m/10ft high, making large clumps and silvery white plumes in autumn. In **'Pumila'** and others in sheltered situations, these last until spring. **'Gold Band'**, narrow, golden-green striped leaves and silvery plumes. H1.8m/6ft, W1.2m/4ft. F9-10. Z8-10. **'Silver Comet'**, leaves margined white and a good display of flowers but needs a

warm, sheltered spot. H1.5m/5ft, W90cm/3ft. F9-10. Z8-10.

DESCHAMPSIA Tufted hair grass
D. caespitosa. Large tufts of narrow, deep green leaves and sheaves of very graceful spikes, valuable for autumn and winter interest. Self-seeds freely. **'Bronze Veil'** (syn. 'Bronzeschleier'), effective bronze plumes. **'Gold Veil'** (syn. 'Goldschleier'), strong, clumpy evergreen with plumes of green stems and flowers which turn a warm golden-yellow. H90cm/3ft, W90cm/3ft. F6-8. Z4-9. **'Golden Dew'** (syn. 'Goldtau'), similar growth with fountains of green stems and flowers which mature to a rich golden-brown. Good, compact form. H70cm/28in, W50cm/20in. F6-9. Z4-9.

ELYMUS
E. magellanicus (syn. *E. pubiflorum*). One of the brightest blue grasses with narrow sword-like leaves of silvered blue. H60cm/2ft, W45cm/18in. Z5-8.

FESTUCA Fescue
F. glauca. Blue fescue. Neat, bluish evergreen tufts, useful as edging,

Festuca glauca 'Blue Glow'

ground cover or frontal groups. Several selections worth looking for: **'Blue Glow'** (syn. 'Blauglut'), striking silver-blue leaves and a good show of flowers; **'Elijah Blue'**, compact, silver-blue. Colour good into winter. Best divided every two or three years. Average H25cm/10in, W25cm/10in. F6-7. Z4-8. **'Golden Toupee'**, an unflattering name for a pleasing, brightly coloured grass. It makes hummocks of silver-gold, light brown plumes in summer.

Imperata cylindrica 'Rubra'

Hakonechloa macra 'Alboaurea'

HAKONECHLOA
H. macra. Seldom offered species with wavy bright green leaves and slowly spreading habit. **'Alboaurea'** is one of the best of all ornamental grasses, with bright green and yellow striped leaves in spring and summer, ageing to reddish brown then light brown into late autumn. Appreciates friable, well-drained but not too dry soil. In a container it is magnificent. H25cm/10in, W39cm/15in. F8-9. Z7-9. ✿ ✺ ◼

IMPERATA CYLINDRICA 'Rubra'
Known as **'Japanese Blood Grass'** for good reason: the soft erect leaves become ruby crimson from base to tip, stunning when light shines through. H45cm/18in, W30cm/1ft. ✿ ◼

MILIUM
M.effusum **'Aureum'**. Bowles Golden Grass. A self-seeding plant with soft, bright golden, arching leaves. A cheery sight in light shade, the golden flower plumes are an added bonus. H45cm/18in, W30cm/1ft. Z5-8.

MISCANTHUS Silver grass
This genus includes some very good grasses, mostly fairly tall and clump-

forming, with an annual crop of strong stems with bladed leaves. Taller forms are good as windbreaks and for specimen planting. Though none is evergreen, the foliage remains attractive over winter, and is then cut down in spring. They flower best in hot summers. Some selections have been introduced which flower regularly in cooler, northerly climates. A number are quite dwarf and many variegated, so excellent for the smaller garden.
M. sacchariflorus. Much like a bamboo in appearance with a wealth of long blades, Amur silver grass makes an effective screen from early summer until the following early spring. Does not flower in cooler climates. H3m/10ft, W90cm/3ft. F9-10. Z5-10.
M. sinensis. Chinese silver grass. Ample green and silver-striped foliage but seldom planted. H1.8m/6ft, W90cm/3ft. F7-9. Z5-10. Its many erect-growing and non-invasive cultivars are more garden-worthy. All Z5-10. 'Cascade' (syn. 'Kaskade'), pendulous, silvery white flowers. H1.2-1.5m/4-5ft, W60cm/12ft. F8-10. 'Flamingo', deep crimson flowers fading to white. H1.2-1.5m/4-5ft, W60cm/2ft. F8-10. 'Gracillimus', elegant narrow leaves and a shapely habit; seldom flowers in cooler climates. H1.5m/5ft, W45cm/18in. 'Purpureus', bronze-purple leaves in late summer. 1.2m/4ft, W90cm/3ft. F8-9. 'Strictus', a stiff columnar habit and green leaves, horizontally striped yellow, brighter than 'Zebrinus'. H90cm/3ft, W50-60cm/20-24in. 'Variegatus' is stately and brightly variegated with vertical white stripes. H1.5m/5ft, W90cm/3ft. 'Zebrinus', or zebra grass, is distinctive for having lateral bands of gold across green leaves. H1.5m/5ft, W90cm/3ft. 'Kleine Fontane', tall, free-flowering with pendulous silver heads. H1.5cm/5ft,

W90cm/3ft. F7-10. 'Malepartus', vigorous, broad, silver-striped leaves, crimson flowers fading pink then light brown. H1.8m/6ft, W90cm/3ft. F8-10. 'Morning Light' outstanding variegated Japanese selection: compact, densely foliaged, silver and white. Needs heat to flower. H1.2m/4ft, W60cm/2ft. F9-10.

MOLINIA Moor grass
M. caerulea subsp. *altissima* (syn. *M. litoralis).* Strong-growing, free-flowering, good autumn colour as stems fade. The terminal flower sprays are greenish purple, turning brown in autumn. Some good selections: 'Fontane', pendulous heads; 'Transparent', slender stems, wispy flower heads; 'Windspiel', smaller heads, all turning to golden-brown autumn colours. All 1.5-1.8m/5-6ft, W45cm/18in. F8-10. Z5-9.
M. caerulea subsp. *caerulea.* Purple moor grass. British native for damp, acid soils. 'Moorehexe' a good green-leaved selection with purplish flower heads, brown in autumn. H40cm/16in, W40cm/16in. F8-9. Z5-9. 'Variegata', stout clumps of soft, deciduous, creamy yellow-green leaves and long-lasting, small, purplish buff flowers. Prefers a light, deep soil and sun. H60cm/2ft, W60cm/2ft. F7-10. Z5-9.

PANICUM Switch grass
P. virgatum 'Rubrum'. A pretty grass with red-tinted leaves in summer, crimson in autumn. A haze of brown seedheads complement the airy feel. H90-120cm/3-4ft, W60cm/2ft. F8-9. Z5-9.

PENNISETUM
Large, deciduous tussocks, but not all produce their bottlebrush flowers freely. Long, arching and narrow grey-green leaves.
P. alopecuroides (syn. *P. compressum).* Shy to flower in cool temperate zones but 'Hameln' and 'Woodside' are

Miscanthus sinensis 'Variegatus'

much freer, their flowers attractive well into winter. All H60-90cm/2-3ft, W60cm/2ft. F8-10. Z5-10.
P. orientale. Hairy leaves, tufty growth. Its bottlebrush, silvery pink flowers are long-lasting and reliable, fading to grey. H45cm/18in, W30cm/1ft. F7-9. Z6-9.

PHALARIS Gardener's garters
P. arundinacea var. *picta.* This variegated leaved grass, its creamy green and white stripes brightest in spring, should be planted only where its invasive habit can do no harm. Less invasive and more striking in its white intensity is *P.a.* var. *picta* 'Feesey'. Both H90cm/3ft, W60cm/2ft. Z4-9.

STIPA Feather grass, Needle grass
S. arundinacea. Compact clump of narrow-leaved, arching, bronze-green stems and diffuse, brownish flowers. Foliage tinged red, bronze, yellow and orange in winter. H45cm/18in, W60cm/2ft. F7-9. Z7-9.
S. calamagrostis. Clump-forming species which flowers freely with dense, buff-white, gracefully arching plumes. H1.2m/4ft, W60cm/2ft.

F7-9. Z5-10.
S. gigantea. Imposing specimen clumps. Narrow green leaves above which tall, erect stems carry oat-like flowers for months which are still attractive in winter. H1.8-2m/6-8ft, W60-75cm/2ft-2ft 6in. F6-10. Z5-10.
S. tenuissima. Beautiful ornamental grass forming a dense, grassy, deep green clump, topped in mid-summer by fluffy plumes which turn from beige to white. H60cm/2ft, W45cm/18in. F6-9. Z7-10.

Stipa gigantea

ALPINES DIRECTORY

Campanula carpatica var. *turbinata* 'Karl Foerster'

USUALLY REFERRED TO AS ALPINES OR SOMETIMES AS ROCK PLANTS, this group of plants is a diverse one that can be confusing to beginner and expert alike. Many of the plants offered by garden centres in this category are not necessarily native to mountainous regions, but are usually of dwarf or compact stature and are in fact simply dwarf perennials. Late spring and early summer is the peak flowering time for most plants classed as alpines but many flower later too. They lend themselves to associating with other dwarf and slow-growing plants such as conifers or shrubs, or can be used as frontal groups to perennial borders. The smaller ones can be used on scree gardens, raised beds, sinks and troughs, and spreading types among paving or gravel. A gravel mulch makes a good surface, retaining moisture but allowing good surface drainage. The range described here is limited to a few major groups of generally easy cultivation and to those with a flowering period or foliage attraction in late spring to late summer.

H:	Approximate height after 2 years
W:	Approximate width after 2 years
F:	Months in flower
Z:	Relevant hardiness zone(s)

A collection of alpines on the scree garden

ACHILLEA

The alpine dwarf yarrows make modestly spreading mats of soft filigree or divided foliage. All are easy to grow in poor soil. ☼ ■
A. × lewisii 'King Edward'. A form with primrose-yellow flowers and grey-green mats of foliage. H10cm/4in, W20cm/8in. F5-8. Z4-8.
A. tomentosa. Woolly yarrow has grey-green, filigree mats and dense golden-yellow heads. H15cm/6in, W30cm/1ft. F5-7. Z3-7.

AJUGA Bugle

Creeping, semi-evergreen, flowering plants and colourful ground cover.
A. reptans. Carpet or common bugle is mat-forming. Its many colourful varieties do best in some sun. All H15cm/6in, W30-45cm/12-18in. F5-6. 'Braunherz', shiny purple-bronze leaves and blue flowers. 'Burgundy Glow', light blue flowers and wine-red, bronze and cream leaves. 'Pink Surprise', lilac-pink, purplish leaves. 'Variegata' grey-green and cream leaves.

ARABIS Rock cress

This genus flowers for several weeks in spring. All prefer light soil. ☼
A. ferdinandi-coburgii. The green-leaved species has dainty sprays of flowers. 'All Gold', which shows up boldly on its evergreen mat, and the slightly less variegated, green and cream evergreen 'Variegata' (syn. *A. procurrens* 'Variegata'), both have white flowers. Remove any reversion to green. All H10cm/4in, W20cm/8in. F4-6. Z5-7.

CAMPANULA Bellflower

Among the dwarf campanulas are some choice as well as more vigorous and spreading types, several of which are suitable for use among other dwarf perennials. ☼ ❋ ■
C. carpatica. Carpathian bellflower. Long-lived, and makes shapely summer growth, with wide open, cup-and-saucer shaped, upturned flowers on thin stems. All W20cm/8in. F6-8. Z4-7. 'Blue Moonlight' has large, china-blue blooms. H10cm/4in. 'Bressingham White' is one of several whites. H20cm/8in. 'Chewton Joy' has small, smoky blue bells later than most. H13cm/5in. 'Maureen Haddon', masses of pale lavender-blue flowers. H8-10cm/3-4in. *C. carpatica* var. *turbinata.* 'Isabel' has rich blue, saucer flowers. H23cm/9in. 'Karl Foerster' has deep cobalt-blue prolific blooms. H23cm/9in. 'Snowsprite' is the purest white and very free-flowering. H20cm/8in. 'Wheatley Violet' is a charming miniature. H10cm/4in.
C. garganica. Adriatic bellflower. Forms compact, leafy tufts and lax sprays of starry flowers, good in

crevices and walls. H8cm/3in, W15-30cm/6-12in. F6-8. Z6-8.
'Dickson's Gold' has golden-green, almost evergreen leaves and sprays of mid-blue flowers. H13cm/5in, W15-30cm/6-12in. F6-8. Z6-8.
C. portenschlagiana (syn. *C. muralis*). An adaptable plant with its long display of violet, bell-shaped flowers. **'Resholt's Variety'** is the best form. Both H15cm/6in, W60cm/2ft. F6-9. Z4-8.
C. poscharskyana. Sprays of pale lavender, starry flowers make a fine show. A good wall plant. H30cm/1ft, W60-90cm/2-3ft. F6-9. Z4-7.

DIANTHUS Rock pink
Most have mats or tufts of silvery- or bluish-green, evergreen foliage. ✿ ■ ⊙
D. deltoides. Maiden pinks are distinctive trailing types with green or purplish foliage and masses of flowers in summer. Named varieties include **'Albus'**, white, **'Brilliant'**, carmine, **'Leuchtfunk'**, crimson. Good for walls. H15-23cm/6-9in, W40cm/16in. F5-7. Z3-7.
Hybrids. The following are just a few well-tried selections. All F6-8. Z4-8.

'Bombardier', red. H13cm/5in, W30cm/1ft. **'Dubarry'**, double pink, crimson-centred. H10cm/4in, W20cm/8in. **'Garland'**, pure pink. H10cm/4in, W20cm/8in. **'La Bourboule'**, pink and white. H8cm/3in, W15cm/6in. **'Nyewood's Cream'**, dwarf, cream flowers. H8cm/3in, W15cm/6in. **'Oakington'**, a soft double pink. H10cm/4in, W25cm/10in. **'Pike's Pink'**, double, showy pink. H10cm/4in, W20cm/8in.

GENTIANA Gentian
These classic alpine plants fall into three fairly distinct groups of spring, summer and autumn flowering species. The first prefer some lime, the second are lime-tolerant and the third need an acid soil. Only late spring and summer types are covered.
G. acaulis. The trumpet, or stemless, gentian has large, upstanding, blue trumpets from low, slow-spreading mats. H10cm/4in, W30-45cm/12-18in. F4-5. Z4-7. ✿ ◢ ■
G. septemfida. A popular and easy-to-grow gentian, forming clumps whose many leafy stems produce a

mass of deep blue flowers for most of the summer. H15-20cm/6-8in, W30cm/1ft. F6-9. Z4-8.

GERANIUM Cranesbill
The ever popular hardy geraniums have several dwarf varieties which make good alpines. ✿ ■
G. cinereum **'Ballerina'**. Popular for its adaptability and long display of lilac-pink flowers, charmingly flecked and veined with crimson. H13cm/5in, W25cm/10in. F5-9. Z5-8.
'Laurence Flatman' has sprays of larger flowers with heavy crimson markings, deeper than 'Ballerina'. H15cm/6in, W30cm/1ft. F5-9. Z5-8.
G. cinereum subcaulescens (syn. *G. subcaulescens*). Mounds of green leaves set off bright magenta-red flowers. **'Guiseppii'** is a vigorous selection with similarly strong but magenta-purple blooms. **'Splendens'**, less vigorous but arguably one of the most striking of all geraniums with magenta-rose flowers. All 15cm/6in, W30cm/1ft. F6-8. Z5-8.
G. × *lindavicum* **'Apple Blossom'**. Pretty hybrid, close to *G. cinereum* with grey-green leaves and soft, pale pink flowers. H15cm/6in, W23cm/9in. F5-8. Z5-8.
G. **'Sea Spray'**. An outstanding hybrid making low-spreading hummocks of soft purplish-green leaves and masses of small pink flowers fading to white. H10cm/4in, W30cm/1ft. F6-10. Z-9.

HELIANTHEMUM Sun rose
Indispensable for a bright summer display, though strictly speaking deciduous shrubs. Trim with shears after flowering to keep them neat and tidy. All are sun lovers and can withstand dry and even starved soil.
Hybrids. The following are some of the best: **'Annabel'**, soft pink, double. **'Cerise Queen'**, cherry-red, double. **'Fireball'**, deep red, double. **'Firedragon'** (syn. 'Miss Clay'), silvery grey leaves, orange-flame

Geranium × *lindavicum* 'Apple Blossom'

flowers, single. **'Henfield Brilliant'**, deep orange, single. **'Jubilee'**, clear yellow, double. **'Raspberry Ripple'**, crimson centre, petals edged white, single. **'Red Orient'**, deep crimson, yellow stamens, single. **'Wisley Pink'**, pale pink, grey foliage, single. **'Wisley Primrose'**, pale yellow, single. **'Wisley White'**, white, single. All H15-30cm/6-12in, W60-90cm/2-3ft. F5-7. Z5-7.

HYPERICUM St John's wort
A reliable source of summer colour, some are excellent in hot, dry walls. A few are tender. ✿ ■
H. olympicum (syn. *H. polyphyllum*). This and its forms are especially good in sunny crevices or on walls. Foliage is blue-grey and yellow flowers have prominent stamens. Variations include the larger-flowered *uniflorum* (syn. *H. olympicum* 'Grandiflorum') and **'Citrinum'**, with pale yellow flowers. All H15-20cm/6-8in, W30cm/1ft. F6-8. Z6-8.

LYSIMACHIA Loosestrife
L. nummularia 'Aurea'. The golden-leaved creeping Jenny is useful as ground cover or crevice planting in shade, or sun where not dry. Excellent for a container or hanging basket. Yellow, buttercup flowers. H5cm/2in, W60cm/2ft. F6-7. Z3-8.

Dianthus 'Pike's Pink'

PHLOX
The dwarf species make a fine show to follow early spring subjects. Most are easy in light soil and sun.
P. procumbens (syn. *P. amoena*). Mat-forming species with small heads of purplish-pink flowers. The vigorous '**Millstream**' has round leaves and lilac-pink flowers. '**Variegata**', leaves margined white and at times pink. All H15cm/6in, W30cm/1ft. F5-6. Z7-8.
P. douglasii. Popular for its fine spring display, this creeping evergreen is covered with almost stemless flowers. Good forms include the blue-mauve '**Eva**' and '**Kelly's Eye**', pink with a red eye, '**Lilac Cloud**' and '**Lilac Queen**', '**Red Admiral**' and '**Waterloo**', an intense crimson-red. All H2.5cm/1in, W15-45cm/6-18in. F4-6. Z5-8.
P. subulata. Like *P. douglasii* but a little less compact, moss phlox, or moss pink, carries its flowers well above the mat. '**Alexander's Surprise**' is salmon-pink. '**Benita**' is lavender-blue with a purple eye. '**MacDaniel's Cushion**' is rose pink. '**May Snow**' is white. '**Nettleton**', an attractive variegated-leaf form with pink-flushed flowers. '**Oakington Blue Eyes**' is an excellent light blue; '**Red Wings**' is crimson. '**Scarlet Flame**' is

scarlet. '**Tamaongalei**' has white flowers splashed pink. '**Temiskaming**' is rosy red. '**White Delight**' is self-descriptive. All H8-13cm/3-5in, W45cm/18in. F4-6. Z2-9.

POTENTILLA Cinquefoil
See also Perennials and Shrubs. ☼ ■
P. aurea '**Aurantiaca**'. Unusual, orange-buff flowers. H2.5cm/1in, W15cm/6in. F4-7. Z4-8. The form '**Chrysocraspeda**' (syn. *P. ternata)* has bright yellow flowers. '**Plena**' is a double, yellow form. Both H5cm/2in, W13cm/5in. Z5-8.
P. × tonguei. A striking, quite vigorous hybrid, it forms a bronzy-green clump, sending out branching, prostrate sprays of apricot-yellow flowers, suffused crimson, for weeks on end. H10cm/4in, W45cm/18in. F6-10. Z5-7.

SEDUM Stonecrop
This vast genus includes good, late-flowering alpines. ☼ ■
S. cauticolum. This has arching stems of profuse, rosy crimson flowers above bluish, deciduous foliage. '**Lidakense**' is a selection with rose-red heads. Both H10cm/4in, W30cm/1ft. F6-7. Z3-8.
S. kamtschaticum. A trouble-free deciduous species, this has dark green, spatula-shaped leaves and golden flowers. '**Variegatum**' is equally attractive. Both H15cm/6in, W20cm/8in. F6-8. Z3-8.
S. spathulifolium. Powdery, bluish, fleshy leaves and yellow flowers. '**Cape Blanco**' is more compact, with low mounds of near-white leaves, and '**Purpureum**' has larger, purplish leaves. All H5cm/2in, W25cm/10in. F6-7. Z4-7.
S. spurium. A rapid-growing nearly evergreen mat-former, this has red leaves and pale pink flowers on red stems. '**Erdblut**' has bright carmine-red flowers. '**Purple Carpet**' has reddish leaves and flowers. All H8cm/3in, W40cm/16in. F6-7. Z3-8.

SEMPERVIVUM Houseleek
Rosette-forming succulents offering a wide range of size and colour. Flowers curious and sometimes spectacular. Gritty soil. Hundreds of species and cultivars exist; the following are a few outstanding choices. Plants may vary in size but all F6-7. Z5-9. ☼ ■
S. arachnoideum '**Laggeri**'. One of the best silvered, 'cobwebby' types. H3-8cm/1-3in, W20-30cm/8-12in.
S. '**Blood Tip**', compact rosettes with upturned red tips. *S.* '**Engle's Rubrum**', soft grey-green rosettes, edged with red. *S.* '**Jubilee**', compact and free-flowering, with green and maroon foliage. *S.* '**Lavender and Old Lace**', pinkish-lavender rosettes, covered in silvery hairs. *S.* '**Othello**', large rosettes of deep crimson, tall spikes topped by pink flowers. *S.* '**Patrician**', green, bronze-tipped rosettes, red-centred in winter. *S.* '**Royal Ruby**', rich ruby-red. *S.* '**Snowberger**', jade-green rosettes have a silvery sheen. *S.* '**Wollcott's Variety**', greenish-grey foliage with silvery overtones.

THYMUS Thyme
Sun-loving aromatic plants.
T. × citriodorus. Makes lemon-scented little bushes, showier in the variegated form such as '**Archer's**

Gold' and golden-leaved '**Bertram Anderson**' (syn. '**Anderson's Gold**'), a bushy evergreen, good golden ground cover though seldom flowers. '**Silver Queen**' with creamy-white margins is colourful but may revert in parts to green. All H15cm/6in, W30cm/1ft. F5-6. Z4-8.
T. doefleri '**Bressingham Pink**'. Forms grey-green mats and gives a bright display of clear pink flowers. H2.5cm/1in, W15cm/6in. F5-6. Z4-7.
T. '**Doone Valley**'. Deep green foliage, speckled with gold. Lavender flowers are sparse. H15cm/6in, W30cm/1ft. F5-6. Z4-8.

VERONICA Speedwell
A large genus, generally hardy and easy to grow in mainly sunny positions. Their saucer-shaped flowers are carried in spikes.
V. prostrata (syn. *V. rupestris)*. Sturdy mat-former with little, upright spikes of rich blue. '**Blauspiegel**' ('Blue Mirror') is a brilliant blue. '**Blue Sheen**' is a very profuse pale blue. '**Mrs Holt**' is a deep pink, '**Rosea**' lighter pink. '**Spode Blue**' is china-blue. The golden-leaved '**Trehane**' prefers some shade. All H8-10cm/3-4in, W30-40cm/12-16in. F5-7. Z5-8.
V. teucrium. See under Perennials (p.250).

Sempervivum arachnoideum '*Laggeri*'

BIBLIOGRAPHY

The books listed below have been helpful in expanding my knowledge about plants, in particular those that have interest in autumn, winter and early spring, and as general reference. Although some may be out of print, no doubt they can be found in libraries and specialist secondhand bookshops.

Bloom, Adrian, *Conifers for your Garden.* Burrall/Floraprint, 1972.

Bloom, Adrian, *Making the Most of Conifers and Heathers.* Burrall/Floraprint, 1986. (Previously published as *A Year Round Garden*, 1979.)

Bloom, Alan and Adrian, *Blooms of Bressingham Garden Plants.* HarperCollins Publishers, 1992.

Davis, Brian, *The Gardener's Encyclopedia of Trees and Shrubs.* Viking, 1987.

Foster, Raymond, *The Garden in Autumn and Winter.* David and Charles, 1983.

Hillier Manual of Trees and Shrubs, The. Hillier/David and Charles, 1991.

Lacey, Stephen, *Scent in the Garden.* Frances Lincoln, 1991.

Thomas, Graham Stuart, *Colour in the Winter Garden.* JM Dent, 1957, 1984.

Thomas, Graham Stuart, *Perennial Garden Plants, or the Modern Florilegium.* JM Dent, 1990.

Verey, Rosemary, *The Garden in Winter.* Windward/Frances Lincoln, 1988.

INDEX